Evaluating the Obama Presidency

De Gruyter Series in Presidential Politics, Leadership, and Policy Making

---

Edited by
Meena Bose and Daniel E. Ponder

Volume 1

Evaluating the Obama Presidency

From Transformational Goals to Governing Realities

Edited by
Meena Bose and Paul Fritz

DE GRUYTER

ISBN (Hardcover) 978-3-11-138454-2
ISBN (Paperback) 978-3-11-138224-1
e-ISBN (PDF) 978-3-11-138410-8
e-ISBN (EPUB) 978-3-11-138425-2

Library of Congress Control Number: 2024935925

Bibliographic information published by the Deutsche Nationalbibliothek
The Deutsche Nationalbibliothek lists this publication in the Deutsche Nationalbibliografie;
detailed bibliographic data are available on the internet at http://dnb.dnb.de.

© 2024 Walter de Gruyter GmbH, Berlin/Boston
Cover image: President Barack Obama talks on the phone with pastors who offer a birthday prayer during a call in the Oval Office, August 4, 2015, Courtesy Barack Obama Presidential Library.
Typesetting: Integra Software Services Pvt.

www.degruyter.com

Contents

List of Figures —— IX

Meena Bose and Paul Fritz
Chapter 1
Introduction: Evaluating the Obama Presidency —— 1

Part I: Winning Elections and Building Political Coalitions

Brendan J. Doherty
Chapter 2
The Transformation of Presidential Fundraising During the Obama Years —— 13

Jeff Bloodworth
Chapter 3
The Obama Coalition's Kryptonite: Ralph Stanley, Bruce Springsteen, and the White Working Class —— 33

Part II: Planning, Governance, and Policy Making

Jack B. Greenberg
Chapter 4
Why Health Care Came First, and Other Observations on Barack Obama's Early Domestic Policy Agenda —— 55

Mark Kelso
Chapter 5
A Green Presidency? Barack Obama and the Environment —— 71

Andrew Rudalevige
Chapter 6
Obama's Domestic Policy Making and the Administrative Presidency —— 91

Nicholas O. Howard and Mark Owens
Chapter 7
Developing a Bench: President Obama's Judicial Appointment Legacy —— 109

Barbara A. Perry and Sheila M. Blackford
Chapter 8
Women and the Obama Administration: Gender Policy at Home and Abroad —— 131

Paul Fritz
Chapter 9
The US and Russia during the Obama Administration: An Inevitable Return of Great Power Politics? —— 151

David W. Kearn Jr.
Chapter 10
The Obama Legacy on Nuclear Weapons: Transformative Vision, Pragmatic Results —— 167

Daniel E. Ponder and Jeffrey VanDenBerg
Chapter 11
Why Ask? Presidential Leverage and Obama's Decision to Seek Congressional Authorization for the Use of Force against Syria —— 187

Part III: **Communication, Executive Power, and Leadership**

Donna R. Hoffman and Alison D. Howard
Chapter 12
Obama, the Pen, and the Phone: Promises to Policies —— 205

Ann E. Burnette and Wayne L. Kraemer
Chapter 13
The Genius of America and the Model Immigrant: Barack Obama's Rhetorical Characterization of DACA Recipients —— 227

Daryl A. Carter
Chapter 14
Race, Representation, and Reaction in the Obama Presidency —— 243

Stanley A. Renshon
Chapter 15
Obama's Presidency: Redemption and the Misdirected Search for Presidential Greatness —— 259

Contributors —— 275

Acknowledgments —— 279

Index —— 283

List of Figures

The Transformation of Presidential Fundraising During the Obama Years

Figure 1 Presidential Fundraisers for their Reelection Committee, and for their National Committee in Years Three and Four of their First Term, 1979–2020 —— **21**

Developing a Bench: President Obama's Judicial Appointment Legacy

Figure 1 Racial Makeup of Judicial Nominees. (a) Nominees Identified as White. (b) Race and Minority Nominees —— **116**
Figure 2 Gender Makeup of Judicial Nominees. (a) Female Nominees by President. (b) Race of Female Nominees —— **118**
Figure 3 Senatorial Partisanship and Nominee Selection. (a) Race and Opposite-Partisan States. (b) Race and Co-Partisan States. (c) Gender and Opposite-Partisan States. (d) Gender and Co-Partisan States —— **120**
Figure 4 Divided Government and Nominee Selection. (a) Race and Unified Government. (b) Race and Divided Government. (c) Gender and Unified Government. (d) Gender and Divided Government —— **122**
Figure 5 Duration of Nominees in Committee, by President and year. (a) Active Consideration in Committee. (b) Total Consideration in Committee —— **125**
Figure 6 Duration of Nominees by Race for Presidential Administrations. (a) Committee Duration. (b) Total Duration —— **126**
Figure 7 Education and Confirmed Judges —— **127**

Why Ask? Presidential Leverage and Obama's Decision to Seek Congressional Authorization for the Use of Force against Syria

Figure 1 Quarterly Presidential Approval and Government Trust, by Year (a) and Quarter (b) 1961–2020 —— **197**
Figure 2 Index of Presidential Leverage by Year (a) and Quarter (b), 1961–2020 (Obama's administration delineated by vertical lines) —— **198**

Meena Bose and Paul Fritz
Chapter 1
Introduction: Evaluating the Obama Presidency

> There is not a liberal America and a conservative America – there is the United States of America. There is not a Black America and a White America and Latino America and Asian America – there's the United States of America.
> – Illinois State Senator, and US Senate Democratic Nominee Barack Obama, Keynote Address to the Democratic National Convention, Boston, MA, July 27, 2004.

> We are in a defining moment in our history. Our nation is at war. The planet is in peril. The dream that so many generations fought for feels as if it's slowly slipping away. We are working harder for less. We've never paid more for health care or for college. It's harder to save and it's harder to retire. And most of all we've lost faith that our leaders can or will do anything about it . . . . I am running in this race because of what Dr. King called "the fierce urgency of now." Because I believe that there's such a thing as being too late. And that hour is almost upon us.
> – US Senator Barack Obama, Speech at the Jefferson-Jackson Dinner, Veterans Memorial Auditorium, Des Moines, IA, November 10, 2007.

> On this day, we gather because we have chosen hope over fear, unity of purpose over conflict and discord. On this day, we come to proclaim an end to the petty grievances and false promises, the recriminations and worn-out dogmas that for far too long have strangled our politics
> – President Barack Obama, Inaugural Address, Washington, DC, January 20, 2009.

The presidency of Barack Hussein Obama represented a significant milestone in American politics. Obama's election to the White House in 2008 showed that the United States could move forward from its ignominious past in race relations to select the country's first Black American president. The drawn-out battle and surprise victory in the 2008 Democratic nominating contests followed by Obama's election to the White House sparked excitement about the promise of progress in the United States.[1] Obama promised to change politics and policy making in

---

[1] The title of Obama's pre-presidential campaign book, taken from his 2004 Democratic National Convention keynote address, and originally the title of a sermon by his former pastor, Reverend Jeremiah Wright, represents the excitement and expectations for Obama's election in 2008 well: *The Audacity of Hope: Thoughts on Reclaiming the American Dream* (New York: Crown, 2006).

Meena Bose, Paul Fritz, Hofstra University

Washington, declaring that the United States could move past partisan divisions to work toward common goals and address pressing needs in American politics.

In practice, Obama's eight years as president witnessed significant achievements as well as deep disappointments. Obama's successes included leading the United States out of the worst economic recession since the Great Depression, passage of historic health care reform with the Affordable Care Act (ACA), successfully planning the killing of Osama bin Laden, who had planned the September 11, 2001, terrorist attacks on the United States, and ending the US war in Iraq. Disappointments included failure to enact lasting immigration reform, the rise of terrorist militants in Iraq and Syria, inability to end the war in Afghanistan, loss of Democratic control of Congress in 2010 and 2014, and, perhaps most significantly, having the Democratic presidential nominee in 2016 lose the election to a candidate who campaigned on undermining American norms of civility, weakening political institutions, and overturning the Obama administration's policy achievements and priorities.

This volume assesses Obama's leadership and legacy through the conceptual lens of adapting transformational goals, promises, and expectations to political and policy-making constraints in office. The 14 chapters examine Obama's 2008 presidential campaign, major priorities and actions in domestic and foreign policy, and achievements and challenges in communications and governance. They focus on institutional and leadership obstacles to translating campaign promises into specific policies, particularly when presidential candidates seek to change the policy-making process to achieve their pledges.

The chapters were originally a subset of a larger group of 39 conference papers that were presented at Hofstra University's Thirteenth Presidential Conference: The Barack Obama Presidency – Hope and Change, April 19 to 21, 2023. Hofstra's presidential conferences started in 1982 with a commemoration of the centennial of President Franklin Delano Roosevelt's birth. Since then, they have continued chronologically to evaluate each of the modern presidents up through the Obama administration. The conferences are unique in bringing together scholars, journalists, and policy makers to discuss the historic and institutional significance of a president's campaign for the White House, executive leadership, policy agenda, and legacy. They typically are scheduled after at least one presidential election has passed since the conclusion of the presidency under study.

Each chapter addresses the recurring challenge in the Obama presidency of developing transformational campaign promises into actual policies. Contributors build upon the unique resources of the Obama Conference to bridge scholarly analysis with practitioner perspectives from administration officials as well as journalists who covered the Obama presidency. Scholars in political science, history, and communication present a multi-faceted evaluation of the Obama presidency's ambitions and accomplishments in a pivotal period in early twenty-first century American politics. The original analysis, grounded in extensive secondary and primary research (including available archival and other primary-source data as well as commentary from administration officials in scholarly venues), makes an important contribution to understanding the Obama presidency's importance for American politics and policies.

As noted above, the unifying theme of the volume is the challenges and opportunities that the Obama administration faced in translating campaign promises into policy governance. When he launched his 2008 presidential campaign, Obama had represented Illinois in the US Senate for just over two years, after previously serving as a state senator in Illinois for eight years. He had received national attention for an inspirational keynote address that he delivered at the 2004 Democratic National Convention, in which he famously spoke of a common purpose uniting all Americans, regardless of ideological, racial, or ethnic differences (see first chapter epigraph).

This theme propelled Obama's victory in the Democratic nominating contests and the general election, and heightened expectations for a new approach to national governance that transcended partisan divisions. Obama had promised to change the culture of US policy making through increased political participation, engagement with developing policy priorities, and coalition building to achieve results. But enacting these transformational policy-making goals proved to be far more difficult than anticipated. While the Obama presidency achieved some notable and enduring policy successes, it also confronted seemingly intractable obstacles to major challenges for which Obama had promised action in his presidential campaign.

The following 14 chapters examine selected case studies on elections, domestic policy, foreign policy, communication, executive power, and presidential leadership – where Obama achieved promised transformational policy change and where his executive actions fell short of expectations, and why. The chapters are organized into three sections: Winning Elections and Building Political Coalitions (Chapters 2–3); Planning, Governance, and Policy Making (Chapters 4–11); and Communication, Executive Power, and Leadership (Chapters 12–15).

These three topics are particularly important for addressing the continuing challenge in the Obama presidency of adapting far-reaching goals for policies and process to a national institutional structure that was purposely designed for incremental decision making. In his presidential campaigns, decision making for both domestic and foreign policy priorities, and executive communication, power, and leadership, Obama demonstrated keen interest in transforming the American political landscape by moving past traditional partisan divisions and encouraging unified governance grounded in public engagement. In practice, however, party polarization, contentious policy debates, and other variables hindered these far-reaching goals, requiring traditional presidential governing strategies to achieve more limited policy results.

Chapters two and three examine Obama's unique accomplishments and longer-term challenges in campaign fundraising and development of an enduring electoral coalition. Chapters four through eight assess Obama's promises, achievements, and shortcomings in selected domestic policy areas, including the 2009 financial crisis, health care reform, environmental policy, administrative policy making, diversity in judicial appointments, and gender policy at home and abroad. Chapters nine through 11 evaluate Obama's promises and policies for the foreign policy priorities of US policy toward Russia; nuclear weapons, arms control, and nonproliferation; and the decision to seek congressional authorization for the use of force against Syria in 2013. Chapters 12 through 15 analyze Obama's use of unilateral executive actions following unsuccessful efforts to enact major legislation; presidential public communications about immigration, particularly rhetorical characterization of Deferred Action for Childhood Arrival (DACA) Program participants as "model immigrants"; race relations, representation, and reaction for the White House and American public; and Obama's efforts to achieve presidential greatness.

This volume makes a significant and original contribution to the growing scholarly literature on the Obama presidency through its conceptual focus on the challenge of meeting highly ambitious campaign promises of major policy changes in a political system that is designed for incremental governance. Several administration officials, including the former President and First Lady, have published memoirs about their time in the White House that inform scholarly understanding of the presidency.[2] Additionally, scholars have published studies of Obama's electoral victories, policies, and governance,[3] and journalists have published analyses of Ob-

---

[2] Selected examples of memoirs of the Obama presidency include: Barack Obama, *A Promised Land* (New York: Crown, 2020); Michelle Obama, *Becoming* (New York: Crown, 2018); David Axelrod, *Believer: My Forty Years in Politics* (New York: Penguin Books, 2016); David Plouffe, *The Audacity to Win: How Obama Won and How We Can Beat the Party of Limbaugh, Beck and Palin* (New York: Penguin Books, 2010); Valerie Jarrett, *Finding My Voice: My Journey to the West Wing and the Path Forward* (New York: Viking, 2019; reprint ed. Penguin Books, 2020); Susan Rice, *Tough Love: My Story of the Things Worth Fighting For* (New York: Simon & Schuster, 2019); Ben Rhodes, *The World As It Is: A Memoir of the Obama White House* (New York: Random House, 2018; paperback 2019).

[3] Selected examples of books and edited volumes by scholars include: Burton I. Kaufman, *Barack Obama: Conservative, Pragmatist, Progressive* (Ithaca: Cornell University Press, 2022); Michael Nelson, ed., *The Elections of 2008* (Washington, DC: CQ Press, 2009); Nelson, ed., *The Elections of 2012* (Washington, DC: CQ Press, 2014); Claude A. Clegg, *The Black President: Hope and Fury in the Age of Obama* (Baltimore: Johns Hopkins University Press, 2021); Colin Dueck, *The Obama Doctrine: American Grand Strategy Today* (New York: Oxford University Press, 2015); George

ama's election and presidency.⁴ None of the analyses to date, however, have systematically addressed how the Obama White House wrestled with the challenge of following through on transformational policy goals in a highly divided political environment.

By incorporating this common theme of the tensions between transformational campaign promises and incremental policy governance, this edited volume makes a unique, important, and enduring contribution to the scholarly literature on the Obama presidency. It presents a multi-faceted assessment of Obama's presidential goals, promises, accomplishments, and shortcomings, with selected case studies of political campaigns and coalitions, domestic policy, foreign policy, political communication, executive power, and presidential leadership.

Part I of this volume, *Winning Elections and Building Political Coalitions*, provides a lens through which to view Obama's road to the White House and 2012 reelection. Chapter 2, "The Transformation of Presidential Fundraising During the Obama Years," by Brendan J. Doherty, examines Obama's transformational fundraising strategies as candidate and president. Through his own actions, such as opting out of public funding and raising unprecedented amounts of campaign funds, and in responding to institutional changes, such as the rise of SuperPACs and increased fundraising opportunities for political parties from individuals, Obama fundamentally changed how presidents approach individual and party campaign donations.

Chapter 3, "The Obama Coalition's Kryptonite: Ralph Stanley, Bruce Springsteen, and the White Working Class," by Jeff Bloodworth, analyzes the challenges that Obama faced in building a lasting Democratic coalition of voters. It finds that despite Obama's significant success in winning public support in his elections and two-term presidency, Democrats could not make lasting gains with rural populists and working-class white voters. Intra-party Democratic debates about 'entitlement'

C. Edwards III, *Predicting the Presidency: The Potential of Persuasive Leadership* (Princeton, NJ: Princeton University Press, 2016); Wilbur C. Rich, ed., *Looking Back on President Barack Obama's Legacy: Hope and Change* (New York: Palgrave Macmillan, 2019); Bert A. Rockman and Andrew Rudalevige, eds., *The Obama Legacy* (Lawrence: University Press of Kansas, 2019); Steven E. Schier, ed., *Debating the Obama Presidency* (New York: Rowman & Littlefield, 2016); Julian E. Zelizer, ed., *The Presidency of Barack Obama: A First Historical Assessment* (Princeton: Princeton University Press, 2018).
4 Selected examples of books by journalists include: Peter A. Baker, *Obama: The Call of History: Updated With Expanded Text* (New York: Callaway Arts & Entertainment, 2019); Dan Balz and Haynes Johnson, *The Battle for America 2008: The Story of an Extraordinary Election* (New York: Viking, 2009); John Heilemann and Mark Halperin, *Game Change: Obama and the Clintons, McCain and Palin, and the Race of a Lifetime* (New York: Harper, 2010).

versus 'opportunity' liberalism created tensions too great for Obama's individual political achievements to translate into enduring institutional party support.

Part II, *Planning, Governance, and Policy Making*, examines critical aspects of Obama's domestic and foreign policy agenda in light of his transformational goals. Chapter 4, "Why Health Care Came First and Other Observations on Barack Obama's Early Domestic Policy Agenda," by Jack B. Greenberg, examines Obama's prioritization of health care reform with a framework that highlights presidential agency rather than institutional or other external factors. Considering the burdens of the Great Recession and traditional Democratic party concerns, Obama saw healthcare reform Obama as a critical economic and political goal. Beyond that, however, choosing to tackle health care reform first was central to Obama's effort to transform the American political economy and create a "New Foundation" that better served the people. Combined with his popularity upon taking office and strong Democratic majorities in Congress, Obama's leadership allowed him to advance transformational politics and policy making, even though results fell short of his aims.

Chapter 5, "A Green Presidency? Barack Obama and the Environment," by Mark Kelso, evaluates Obama's record in environmental policy. As one of the president's top priorities, environmental policy provides multiple examples of executive leadership. In particular, Obama had notable achievements in appointments, use of the Antiquities Act, exercise of veto power, and in his role as opinion leader. But in legislation and budgeting, Obama was less successful, relying more on executive than legislative action for policy making. The political environment and party polarization restricted Obama's ability to enact transformational goals in environmental policy.

Chapter 6, "Obama's Domestic Policymaking and the Administrative Presidency," by Andrew Rudalevige, examines Obama's use of the administrative presidency to advance domestic policy initiatives. It addresses Obama's assertion of executive authority when major legislation stalled in four policy areas: health care, labor, the environment, and immigration. Given the difficulty of institutionalizing policy through administrative action, the Obama administration made progress when embedding policy initiatives in formal regulations, rather than implementing decisions by presidential decree. Obama's use of the administrative action illustrates the limits of transformational policy making when legislation is not possible.

Chapter 7, "Developing a Bench: President Obama's Judicial Appointment Legacy," by Nicholas O. Howard and Mark Owens, examines President Obama's approach to filling the federal judiciary. Guided by a novel philosophical approach that centered empathy for judicial nominations, Obama diversified the federal bench by nominating more women than any previous president and presented the most racially diverse set of nominees the Senate has seen. Even in the face of some high-profile opposition to his judicial nominees, President Obama was thus able to transform the federal judiciary with his approach focused on empathy.

Chapter 8, "Women and the Obama Administration: Gender Policy at Home and Abroad," by Barbara A. Perry and Sheila M. Blackford, assesses the Obama administration's achievements in gender policy. In domestic policy, it evaluates executive appointments, employment policy, health care, education, and military service in combat roles. In international policy, it examines diplomacy, defense, and development. The argument presents a contrasting view of transformational promises versus governing realities: unlike other policy areas, with gender policy, the Obama administration delivered far more than anticipated, particularly with executive appointments and domestic policy, and also with commitments to policy changes to support the advancement of women and girls abroad.

Chapter 9, "The US and Russia During the Obama Administration: An Inevitable Return of Great Power Politics?" by Paul Fritz, evaluates Obama's efforts to transform US relations with Russia after famously calling for a "reset" in 2009. Despite this effort, relations between the two countries had deteriorated significantly by the end of Obama's second term and set the stage for later more significant confrontation. The combination of Obama's grand strategy ideas and Russia's determination to reestablish its role in the international system meant that a fundamental transformation of the relationship was unlikely. These same factors, however, led to opportunities for transactional cooperation that served US foreign policy interests well, especially in the areas of weapons of mass destruction proliferation and arms control.

Chapter 10, "The Obama Legacy on Nuclear Weapons, Arms Control, and Nonproliferation" by David W. Kearn, assesses President Obama's legacy in nonproliferation, strategic arms control, and nuclear weapons policy. The first US president in the nuclear age to enter office with nonproliferation as a primary foreign-policy objective, Obama's achievements in this area included a nuclear security summit process and an agreement with Iran to prevent its development of nuclear weapons, along with a US-Russian strategic arms control treaty. Although critics say the Obama administration did not meet its transformational goal of reducing the role of nuclear weapons in US national security and global politics, the most significant obstacle was not weakness in presidential leadership but geopolitical trends and shifts in the international political system that impeded further action.

Chapter 11, "Why Ask? Presidential Leverage and Obama's Decision to Seek Congressional Authorization for the Use of Force Against Syria" by Daniel E. Ponder and Jeffrey VanDenBerg, examines why Obama decided to seek congressional authorization to use military force in response to the Syrian regime's use of chemical weapons in 2013. One year earlier, Obama had declared that Syrian use of its chemical or biological weapons stockpile would cross a "red line" that would prompt US military action, but the White House did not follow through on this promise. In this episode, Obama's "presidential leverage," a measure that shows the president's place and power in the political system, was weak compared to earlier periods of his presidency. President Obama, who campaigned on transformational goals in foreign policy, was thus constrained by institutional and political dynamics.

Part III, *Communication, Executive Power, and Leadership*, examines how Obama employed communication, executive actions, and other leadership tools to advance his policy goals, and assesses ambition versus results in his presidency. Chapter 12, "Obama, the Pen, and the Phone," by Donna R. Hoffman and Alison D. Howard, analyzes Obama's rhetoric in support of unilateral executive actions in his second term. Facing obstacles accomplishing transformative change on many policy issues, Obama announced in early 2014 that he would employ a "pen and phone" strategy to take executive action and build public support for doing so. In his public communications, Obama justified his actions through the symbolism of the American Dream, saying governmental action was needed to enable people to pursue their goals and for national prosperity. Although Obama had criticized his predecessor's use of unilateral executive power, as president he declared that limited action was needed in specific policy areas where legislation was not politically feasible.

Chapter 13, "The Genius of America and the Model Immigrant: Barack Obama's Rhetorical Characterization of DACA Recipients," by Ann E. Burnette and Wayne L. Kraemer, assesses Obama's rhetoric on immigration, particularly for the Deferred Action for Childhood Arrivals (DACA) program that he created by executive action. By describing DACA recipients as representing the genius of America, Obama attempted to transform public images of immigrants to highlight their many contributions to the United States focusing on three core concepts: citizenship, opportunity, and diversity. But Obama's characterization of the model immigrant created categories for "desirable" immigrants that excluded many others. Furthermore, Obama's DACA program and related executive actions fell far short of his pledge to establish a path to citizenship for undocumented immigrants.

Chapter 14, "Race, Representation, and Reaction in the Obama Presidency" by Daryl A. Carter, examines race, representation, and reaction in the Obama presidency. As a biracial man born to a white mother and African father in Hawaii in 1961, Obama represented, in part, the culmination of the long civil rights movement of the mid-twentieth century with his transformational election as the first Black American President of the United States. Throughout his presidency, Obama contended with often highly contentious issues in race relations, and faced both praise and criticism for his representation of race in the White House. A more troubling and dangerous development during the Obama presidency was the resurgence of extremist politics, often grounded in racial politics, that continued long after Obama concluded his two-term presidency.

Chapter 15, "Obama's Presidency: Redemption and the Misdirected Search for Greatness," by Stanley A. Renshon, provides an assessment of the transformational political leadership that Obama promised as president and the constraints of public opinion in seeking to achieve those goals through a lens of personal and political redemption. Obama was a president with unusually strong ambitions, even among presidents. Most wanted to be successful, while a few, including Obama, wanted to be "great." Obama defined greatness in terms of fundamentally transforming the basic nature and politics of the United States by anchoring it in a more politically and policy liberal foundation, based on his views of fairness. However, he faced a significant mismatch between his transformational ambitions and the public's willingness and readiness to support them. Consequently, Obama will be remembered as a very smart, experienced, and competent president who missed an important opportunity to reinforce the country's political center and perhaps reduce its political divisions.

Covering a broad range of issues from a diverse set of perspectives, taken together these chapters provide an important lens through which to view President Obama's transformational goals. But just as importantly, they point to the governing realities that limit any single president's ability to transform American politics and society.

Part I: **Winning Elections and Building Political Coalitions**

Brendan J. Doherty
Chapter 2
The Transformation of Presidential Fundraising During the Obama Years

Presidential fundraising underwent fundamental transformations during the eight years of Barack Obama's presidency. After his unprecedented fundraising during the 2008 campaign when he became the first major party nominee to forgo public funding for both the nominating contest and the general election, President Obama set records with the number of reelection fundraising events he headlined and the money he raised during his bid for a second term. As he did so, he became the first sitting president to integrate all of his reelection campaign committee fundraising with his national party committee through a joint fundraising committee, the Obama Victory Fund, which enabled him to raise funds in larger amounts than would have been otherwise possible.

Obama also responded to the emergence of Super PACs and other similar groups that were not subject to contribution limits. After initially condemning their role in electoral politics, he signaled his support for a supportive Super PAC's efforts during his reelection bid but declined to personally participate in any of their events. In his second term, Obama reluctantly embraced a limited personal role in Super PAC fundraising, yielding to the incentives established by this critical change to the campaign finance landscape.

By the time of the 2016 election cycle, the Supreme Court's 2014 decision in *McCutcheon v. FEC* combined with a change in the law that allowed for larger donations to national party committees to lead to the creation of increasingly complicated joint fundraising committees. These involved state parties across the country working in concert with a presidential campaign and the national party to raise campaign funds in even larger increments. Obama was the biggest Democratic draw for these high-dollar fundraising events in 2016, which would further reshape the relationship between political parties and presidential campaigns.

While Obama promised on the campaign trail that he would fix a broken Washington and work to transform the American political system, his fundraising practices represented a pragmatic response to a campaign finance system that he was unable to reform. When lofty promises of change collided with the realities of the campaign finance landscape, he made choices that were shaped by the incentives established by the rules governing campaign cash. Obama's prodigious

---
Brendan J. Doherty, United States Naval Academy

fundraising was a means to an end as he sought to achieve his policy-making goals. Like other modern presidents, he allocated his scarce time to fundraising in order to move the country closer to his vision of a more perfect union. The money he raised for himself and for his fellow party members provided them with the resources needed to mount effective campaigns, win elections, and pursue their policy priorities.

This chapter examines the extent to which presidential fundraising practices were transformed during the Obama years. Shedding light on Obama's consequential evolving fundraising strategies illuminates a critical but understudied element of his leadership as president. He both drove changes in campaign finance practice and responded to changes that were beyond his control when he opted out of public funding, set fundraising records, and reacted to the advent of Super PACs. The ten years between the launch of Obama's bid for the White House in 2007 and the conclusion of his second term as president in 2017 witnessed dramatic and consequential shifts in presidential fundraising incentives and dynamics.

A Record-breaking Initial Campaign and the Obsolescence of Public Funding

After then-Senator Obama launched his campaign for the White House on February 10, 2007, his remarkable fundraising success drew a great deal of attention and signaled to the media that his campaign should be taken seriously. When his campaign reported its first quarter fundraising totals for 2007, a CNN headline declared, "Obama raises $25 million, challenges Clinton's front-runner status." The *New York Times* sounded a similar note with an article titled, "Obama Shows His Strength in a Fund-Raising Feat on Par With Clinton."[1] When the $32.5 million he raised in the second quarter of that year exceeded Clinton's total, another headline asserted, "Obama's money puts Clinton's 'inevitable' nomination in doubt."[2] By the end of 2007, his campaign had raised more than $100 million, and was on its way

---

1 "Obama Raises $25 Million, Challenges Clinton's Front-Runner Status," April 9, 2007, https://www.cnn.com/2007/POLITICS/04/04/obama.fundraising/index.html; Jeff Zeleny and Patrick Healy, "Obama Shows His Strength in a Fund-Raising Feat on Par With Clinton," *The New York Times*, April 5, 2007, https://www.nytimes.com/2007/04/05/us/politics/05obama.html.
2 Bill Schneider, "Obama's Money Puts Clinton's 'inevitable' Nomination in Doubt," July 2, 2007, https://www.cnn.com/2007/POLITICS/07/02/campaign.money.schneider/index.html.

to raising close to $750 million in total by the conclusion of his successful bid for the presidency.[3]

Obama's campaign raised far more than any previous presidential campaign, in large part because he was the first major party presidential nominee to opt out of the presidential public funding program for both the nominating contest and the general election. The public funding program consisted of two separate phases: matching funds during the nominating stage and a block grant of campaign funds for the general election. The condition for participating in each phase of the program was spending limits. Candidates who took the public funding agreed to caps on the amounts their campaign could spend.[4]

George W. Bush had become the first major party nominee to opt out of public funding for the nominating process during the 2000 election cycle, and he ended up raising more than $100 million during the nominating contest, far more than the approximately $40 million that would have been allowed if he had accepted the public financing program's matching funds.[5] In 2004, Bush again opted out of public funding for the nominating process, and Democratic nominee John Kerry followed suit. But in both 2000 and 2004, the nominees of both major parties accepted public funding for their campaigns during the general election, and thus agreed to limit the amount of money their campaigns could spend in the period following their party's nominating convention.

In the 2008 presidential cycle, Obama and other leading candidates from both parties, including eventual Republican nominee John McCain, followed the example of Bush and Kerry and declined to participate in the public funding program for the nominating process. On June 19, 2008, Obama announced that he had made the unprecedented decision to forgo public funds for the general election as well. It was the first such decision by any major party nominee since the public funding program had been established in the 1970s. He declared:

---

[3] "Clinton, Obama Both Raised $100M In 2007," January 1, 2008, https://www.cbsnews.com/news/clinton-obama-both-raised-100m-in-2007/; Tahman Bradley, "Final Fundraising Figure: Obama's $750M," December 4, 2008, https://abcnews.go.com/Politics/Vote2008/story?id=6397572&page=1.
[4] Brendan J. Doherty, *Fundraiser in Chief: Presidents and the Politics of Campaign Cash* (Lawrence: University Press of Kansas, 2023), 33.
[5] Don Van Natta, "Bush Forgoes Federal Funds And Has No Spending Limit," *The New York Times*, July 15, 1999, https://www.nytimes.com/1999/07/16/us/bush-forgoes-federal-funds-and-has-no-spending-limit.html; "Bush, Gore Both Reach Fundraising Records," *Tampa Bay Times*, August 21, 2000, https://www.tampabay.com/archive/2000/08/21/bush-gore-both-reach-fundraising-records/.

> It's not an easy decision, and especially because I support a robust system of public financing of elections. But the public financing of presidential elections as it exists today is broken and we face opponents who've become masters at gaming this broken system . . . . And we've already seen that he's not going to stop the smears and attacks from his allies running so-called 527 groups, who will spend millions and millions of dollars in unlimited donations.[6]

At the time of his announcement, Obama's campaign had more funds available than did McCain's, but the Republican National Committee had outraised the Democratic National Committee. Obama and his allies were also aware of the damage that had been done to John Kerry's campaign four years earlier by attacks from non-party groups, organized under section 527 of the tax code, that were not subject to contribution limits. Like Bush before him, Obama opted out of the public funding system so that he could raise sufficient funds that would put him in a position to respond to such attacks.[7]

Obama's decision to forgo the public funding program for the general election gave him a massive financial advantage over McCain in the closing months of the 2008 campaign. In total, the Obama campaign raised close to $750 million, including approximately $300 million for the general election. McCain's campaign, which accepted post-convention public funding, was limited to $84.1 million for the general election. Both campaigns were also aided by spending by their respective party's national committees and supportive interest groups. In September alone, Obama's campaign raised more than $153 million, and in the final months of the contest his campaign spent about $100 million more on television ads than McCain.[8]

After the campaign, Republican strategist Karl Rove declared that "[n]o presidential candidate will ever take public financing in the general election again and risk being outspent as badly as Mr. McCain was this year."[9] Rove's prediction was correct. In 2012, Obama again opted out of public funding at both the nominating and general election stages, and Republican nominee Mitt Romney followed suit. In both 2016 and 2020, neither major party nominee took part in the public funding system. This program, which was a post-Watergate reform that had been at the core of successful presidential campaign strategies for decades, has faded into obsolescence as candidates have concluded that it no longer offers sufficient resources to run a competitive campaign.

---

6 Fredreka Schouten, "Obama Opts out of Campaign Finance System," *ABC News*, June 19, 2008, https://abcnews.go.com/Politics/story?id=5206643&page=1.
7 Schouten, "Obama Opts out of Campaign Finance System."
8 Bradley, "Final Fundraising Figure"; Michael Luo, "Obama Hauls in Record $750 Million for Campaign," *The New York Times*, December 5, 2008, https://www.nytimes.com/2008/12/05/us/politics/05donate.html.
9 Bradley, "Final Fundraising Figure."

Responding to Super PACs and Unprecedented Reelection Fundraising

Obama took part in a total of 321 fundraisers during his first term in office, including 223 that benefited his reelection campaign, the Democratic National Committee, or both during his third and fourth years in office – totals that surpassed the efforts of any of his presidential predecessors. Obama would have to respond to the arrival of Super PACs on the political scene, and did so by becoming the first president to integrate his reelection fundraising with his national party committee from the inception of his reelection bid. In so doing, he would set records and change the ways that incumbent presidents fundraise for their bid for another term in the White House.

I have tracked the time that presidents have devoted to political fundraising dating back to the presidency of Jimmy Carter, who was the first president to be elected under the modern campaign finance regime, which was created in the 1970s. To do so, I systematically examined the *Public Papers of the Presidents of the United States* at the American Presidency Project, Digests of Other White House Announcements, presidential schedules, the White House websites of recent presidents, White House press briefings, and Associated Press and other news articles to create a detailed record of presidential fundraising events.

Time is a president's scarcest resource. Dick Cheney, the only person to have served as both Vice President and White House chief of staff, explained: "You have to have somebody disciplined running the calendar because the president's time is the most valuable thing there is."[10] How presidents allocate their scarce time can reveal a great deal about their priorities, and recent presidents have frequently prioritized spending substantial amounts of time raising campaign funds for themselves and their fellow party members.

The Emergence of Super PACs

Obama's record first-term fundraising was in part a response to the emergence of Super PACs. In January 2010, Obama made news in his State of the Union address when he criticized the Supreme Court's recent decision in the case of *Citizens United v. Federal Election Commission*. Obama declared that the ruling would,

---

10 David Bauder, "Documentary Brings Together 20 Presidential Chiefs," *The Associated Press*, September 10, 2013.

"open the floodgates for special interests – including foreign corporations – to spend without limit in our elections. I don't think American elections should be bankrolled by America's most powerful interests, or worse, by foreign entities. They should be decided by the American people."[11]

In *Citizens United*, the Supreme Court had ruled unconstitutional a federal ban on corporations funding political speech by groups not formally tied to campaigns or parties. Justice Kennedy, writing for the court's majority, asserted, "[w]e now conclude that independent expenditures, including those made by corporations, do not give rise to corruption or the appearance of corruption."[12] Kennedy's contention that expenditures that were made independently of campaigns and parties would not lead to corruption or the perception of corruption would lead to a much greater role for these groups in US elections.

A federal appeals court's decision in *Speechnow.org v. Federal Election Commission*, which was also decided in 2010, would draw on the *Citizens United* ruling to empower groups that wanted to make independent expenditures in campaigns. In *Speechnow*, the DC Circuit Court of Appeals held that individuals can make unlimited contributions to political groups that only make independent expenditures and do not give contributions to campaigns or parties. These two court decisions led to the creation of Super PACs, the informal name for non-party groups that do not contribute to campaigns or parties and thus are allowed to accept unlimited contributions that they then use to make independent expenditures.

The Federal Election Commission (FEC) requires that these committees, which are formally called Independent Expenditure-Only Committees, must disclose their donors, but other non-party groups that can raise unregulated money and are created under other portions of section 501(c) of the tax code are not required to reveal the names of their contributors. These groups, which are permitted to spend money on electoral politics as long as that is not their primary purpose, include social welfare groups organized under section 501(c)(4) of the tax code, labor unions organized under section 501(c)(5), and business groups like the Chamber of Commerce organized under section 501(c)(6). The electoral efforts by these 501(c) groups that are not required to disclose many of their donors has contributed to an increase of what is called dark money in elections – funds whose source is unknown.[13]

---

11 Alan Silverleib, "Gloves Come off after Obama Rips Supreme Court Ruling," January 28, 2010, http://www.cnn.com/2010/POLITICS/01/28/alito.obama.sotu/index.html.
12 "Citizens United v. Federal Election Commission," January 21, 2010, https://www.law.cornell.edu/supct/html/08-205.ZO.html.
13 "Types of Nonconnected PACs," FEC.gov, accessed February 7, 2023, https://www.fec.gov/help-candidates-and-committees/registering-pac/types-nonconnected-pacs/; Robert E. Mutch, *Campaign Finance: What Everyone Needs to Know* (New York: Oxford University Press, 2016), 75–88, 112–117.

It is important to note that Super PACs and the assorted 501(c) groups that proliferated after key court decisions in 2010 were not the first non-party groups that could receive unlimited contributions to play roles in federal elections. In the wake of the banning in 2002 of unregulated soft money contributions to national party committees, so-called 527 groups, named after the section of the tax code under which they were organized, raised unregulated contributions and spent substantial amounts of money in the 2004 presidential election. One study found that spending by 527 groups that election cycle aiming to help Democratic candidates was more than three times the amount spent to help Republicans, but the single most prominent such organization that year was the anti-John Kerry group called Swift Boat Veterans for Truth. They spent more than $22 million, and their ads that attacked Kerry's record of military service attracted substantial media attention.[14]

The role of non-party groups in US elections would become even greater in the wake of the *Citizens United* and *Speechnow* decisions in 2010. According to analysis of FEC records by the group Open Secrets, 83 Super PACs collectively spent more than $62 million during the 2010 midterm election cycle. In the 2012 cycle, 1,275 Super PACs combined to spend more than $609 million. In the 2016 election cycle, 2,393 Super PACS collectively spent more than $1 billion.[15] Candidates for office, including Obama, would both benefit from the activities of supportive Super PACs and, facing the prospect of attacks from opposing Super PACs, feel pressured to raise more money for their own campaigns that they would be able to direct and control. They wanted to be, as George W. Bush had said when he opted out of the public funding program during his first run for president, "in a position to respond."[16]

---

14 Michael Janofsky, "Advocacy Groups Spent Record Amount on 2004 Election," *The New York Times*, December 17, 2004, https://www.nytimes.com/2004/12/17/politics/advocacy-groups-spent-record-amount-on-2004-election.html.
15 "2010 Outside Spending, by Super PAC," OpenSecrets, accessed February 16, 2023, https://www.opensecrets.org/outside-spending/super_pacs/2010?chrt=2016&disp=O&type=S; "2012 Outside Spending, by Super PAC," OpenSecrets, accessed February 16, 2023, https://www.opensecrets.org/outside-spending/super_pacs/2012?chrt=2010&disp=O&type=S; "2016 Outside Spending, by Super PAC," OpenSecrets, accessed February 16, 2023, https://www.opensecrets.org/outside-spending/super_pacs/2016?chrt=2012&disp=O&type=S.
16 Van Natta, "Bush Forgoes Federal Funds."

The Obama Victory Fund: Raising Money in Larger Amounts

The Obama reelection campaign responded to adversarial Super PACs raising money in increments in the millions and tens of millions of dollars in two primary ways. First, they formed a joint fundraising committee, the Obama Victory Fund (OVF), which integrated the Obama campaign committee's reelection fundraising with party fundraising from the beginning of the reelection bid. This legal entity would allow them to raise money in larger amounts than otherwise would have been possible. Second, they eventually encouraged Democratic donors to contribute to a Super PAC that would aid Obama's bid for a second term.

Federal law limits contributions to federal candidates for office to amounts in the low thousands of dollars in order to prevent corruption or the appearance of corruption. When Obama ran for reelection in 2012, the limit for donations from an individual was $2,500. A person could give that amount during the nominating contest and again during the general election, for a total maximum contribution of $5,000 to Obama's reelection campaign committee.[17] When the Obama Victory Fund was established in April 2011, its proceeds jointly benefitted the Obama-Biden reelection campaign and the Democratic National Committee. Donors could give a maximum of $35,800. Of that amount, $5,000 went to Obama's campaign committee, and the DNC received the remaining $30,800, which at the time was the maximum annual individual donation to a national party committee. The OVF was later expanded to include multiple state party committees, which enabled donors to write checks of up to $75,800, the largest contribution allowed under federal law at the time.[18]

As Figure 1 depicts, Obama would go on to headline a record 220 fundraisers for the Obama Victory Fund in 2011 and 2012, as well as an additional three fundraisers solely for the DNC. The time he spent fundraising eclipsed the efforts of prior presidents to raise campaign cash for their reelection campaign committee, their national party committee, or both in their third and fourth years in office. Obama's total was more than double that of the president who held the next greatest number of such fundraisers – Bill Clinton, with 110 – and far greater than George W. Bush's 91 such events, Donald Trump's total of 81, Jimmy Carter's

---

[17] "Archive of Contribution Limits," accessed February 16, 2021, https://www.fec.gov/help-candidates-and-committees/candidate-taking-receipts/archived-contribution-limits/.
[18] "FEC Form 1, Statement of Organization for Obama Victory Fund," April 4, 2011, https://docquery.fec.gov/pdf/890/11030584890/11030584890.pdf; "Archive of Contribution Limits."

Chapter 2 The Transformation of Presidential Fundraising During the Obama Years — 21

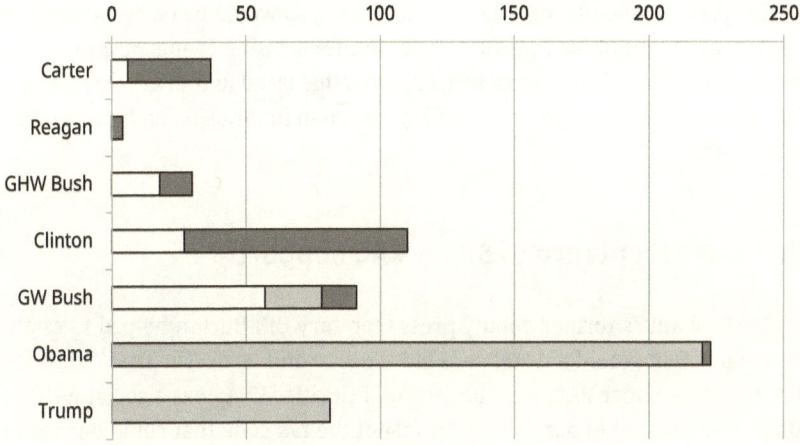

☐ Fundraisers just for reelection campaign committee
☐ First-term fundraisers jointly benefiting reelection campaign and DNC or RNC
■ Other fundraisers for DNC or RNC in years 3 and 4 of first term

Figure 1: Presidential Fundraisers for their Reelection Committee, and for their National Committee in Years Three and Four of their First Term, 1979–2020.
Sources: Data compiled from the *Public Papers of the Presidents*, Digests of Other White House Announcements, White House daily diaries, schedules, and press briefings, and Associated Press and other news articles.

37, George H.W. Bush's total of 30, and Ronald Reagan's four. The time that Obama devoted to reelection fundraising far exceeded that of his predecessors.

With Obama's record number of reelection fundraisers came an unprecedented early start to raising campaign funds, as well as a record amount of money raised. The Obama campaign and the DNC together would raise more than $1 billion in the 2012 election cycle.[19] This fundraising total was aided by an early beginning to Obama's reelection fundraising. As campaign costs rose in recent decades, presidents who sought reelection began their fundraising efforts progressively earlier. It takes a great deal of time to raise millions upon millions of dollars in the amounts prescribed by federal contribution limits. George H.W. Bush held his first reelection fundraiser on October 31 of his third year in office. Bill Clinton did so on June 22 of his third year, and George W. Bush kicked off his reelection fundraising on June 17

---

[19] Kenneth P. Vogel, Dave Levinthal, and Tarini Parti, "Barack Obama, Mitt Romney Both Topped $1 Billion in 2012," Politico, December 7, 2012, http://www.politico.com/story/2012/12/barack-obama-mitt-romney-both-topped-1-billion-in-2012-84737.html#ixzz2ENPPvAKu.

of this third year as well. Obama, whose fundraising goal would be higher than those of his predecessors, headlined his first reelection fundraising events on April 14 of his third year in office. Trump would supercharge this trend and break Obama's record for an early start when he kicked off his reelection fundraising on June 28 of his first year in office.

A Reluctant Acceptance of Super PAC Support

In April 2011, Obama's former deputy press secretary Bill Burton helped to establish two groups that would aid Obama's bid for a second term. The first, Priorities USA Action, was a Super PAC, and the second, Priorities USA, was a social welfare organization organized under Section 501(c)4 of the tax code that could engage in electoral politics as long as that was not its primary purpose. While Priorities USA Action would be required to disclose its contributors, Priorities USA would not have to do so. Both could accept unlimited contributions.[20]

After close to a year of keeping these groups at arm's length, in February 2012 Obama approved a plan in which some of his campaign and administration officials would speak at Priorities USA Action events, though he, Vice President Biden, and their spouses would not have any direct involvement. The move was seen as a sign to Democratic donors that they should feel free to support the group. One Democratic fundraiser discussed how difficult it had been to raise funds for the Super PAC without the president's blessing. "It's hard to pass the plate for [S]uper PAC money while Democratic leaders have been preaching about the sins of it. But the reality is, it is essential in 2012."[21]

Obama campaign manager Jim Messina defended the decision. "Over the last few months, Super PACs affiliated with Republican presidential candidates have spent more than $40 million on television and radio, almost all of it for negative ads. With so much at stake, we can't allow for two sets of rules in this election whereby the Republican nominee is the beneficiary of unlimited spending and Democrats unilaterally disarm." In June 2012, Burton made the case that Obama's signal of approval of his Super PAC had made a difference in his fundraising success. He attested that donors "are getting engaged at a much brisker pace than

---

[20] Jim Rutenberg, "Groups Form to Aid Democrats With Anonymous Money," *The New York Times*, April 29, 2011, sec. US, https://www.nytimes.com/2011/04/30/us/politics/30donate.html.
[21] Jeff Zeleny and Jim Rutenberg, "Obama Yields in Marshaling of 'Super PAC,'" *The New York Times*, February 6, 2012, https://www.nytimes.com/2012/02/07/us/politics/with-a-signal-to-donors-obama-yields-on-super-pacs.html.

they were previously because if they don't, there will never be reform. We go into this campaign season with the rules we have, not the rules we wish we had."[22]

By the time Obama won a second term in November 2012, the campaign finance landscape looked far different than it had for previous presidents seeking reelection. Public funding had been rendered obsolete by rising campaign costs and was no longer seen as a viable option for a winning campaign. The emergence of Super PACs had placed even more pressure on presidents to devote substantial amounts of their scarce time to raising campaign funds, and the integration of campaign and party fundraising through a joint fundraising committee allowed them to do so in larger amounts. The 2012 election cycle also highlighted the key roles that Super PACs would come to play. Although campaigns had to observe prohibitions on certain kinds of communication with a Super PAC, it would become standard practice for major party presidential nominees to have a supportive Super PAC working to increase their odds of victory, and introducing ever greater amounts of money into the campaign landscape. And while Obama did not appear at any Super PAC events himself on his way to a reelection victory, that practice would shift during his second term.

Second-term Engagement with Super PACs and Even Bigger-money Party Fundraising

Obama, like other recent two-term presidents, continued to fundraise regularly in his second term in office. His 177 fundraising events during his final four years as president ranked second among the modern two-term presidents, trailing only Bill Clinton's total. Obama's second-term fundraising would be noteworthy not for its volume, but for its beneficiaries. In his final four years in office, Obama would yield to the incentives of the Super PAC era and appear at multiple Super PAC fundraising events. He would also work with his party to raise money in even larger increments via expanded joint fundraising committees made possible by a key court decision and a piece of legislation passed in 2014. By the time Obama left office in early 2017, the campaign finance landscape had transformed dramatically.

---

22 Jeff Mason, "In Shift, Obama Campaign to Support Super PAC Fundraiser," *Reuters*, February 7, 2012, https://www.reuters.com/article/us-usa-campaign-obama-superpac-idUSTRE81617U20120207; Alina Selyukh, "Democrats Can't Afford Moral Stand on Campaign Spending," *Reuters*, June 28, 2012, https://www.reuters.com/article/us-washington-summit-money-idINBRE85Q1SR20120628.

Taking Part in Super PAC Events

In 2014, with the midterm elections approaching, Obama reversed his earlier decision not to appear at Super PAC events. He headlined two fundraisers for the Senate Majority PAC, the first on June 17 in New York City and the second on July 22 in Bellevue, Washington. The Federal Election Commission has held that candidates for federal office can take part in Super PAC fundraisers as long as they do not ask attendees to make any donation greater than the amount that individuals are allowed to contribute by law to a political committee that is bound by contribution limits.[23] This restriction does not do much to limit presidents' activities, as presidents are not the ones who ask invited guests at fundraisers to contribute a certain amount of money. Instead, that request is made by aides in advance of the fundraising event. A letter that accompanied the invitation to the July 2014 Senate Majority PAC event included a disclaimer that Obama would not be, "soliciting funds for this event or acknowledging your contribution at any point."[24]

Obama also attended three events in 2014 that were organized by a Super PAC named House Majority PAC but were not official fundraisers. Presidents sometimes meet with groups of donors at gatherings that are described as donor courting, donor reward, or donor maintenance events. As there is no price of admission for these events, they are not actual fundraisers. But House Majority PAC likely hoped that the opportunity to spend time with the president might lead prior donors to contribute more in the future. Obama's decision to attend events for Super PACs focused on elections to the Senate and the House led *Time* to run a story with the headline, "Obama Completes His Slow About-Face on Super PACs."[25]

---

[23] "Fundraising for Super PACs by Federal Candidates," FEC.gov, accessed April 13, 2021, https://www.fec.gov/help-candidates-and-committees/making-disbursements-pac/fundraising-super-pacs-federal-candidates-nonconnected-pac/.
[24] Jim Brunner, "Obama Fundraising Visit to Enrich Democratic Super PAC," *The Seattle Times*, July 21, 2014, https://www.seattletimes.com/seattle-news/obama-fundraising-visit-to-enrich-democratic-super-pac/.
[25] Zeke J. Miller, "Obama Completes His Slow About-Face on Super PACs," *Time*, February 28, 2014, https://swampland.time.com/2014/02/28/barack-obama-super-pacs-citizens-united/.

Legal Changes Led to Even Higher-dollar Joint Fundraising Committee Events

Two consequential legal developments in 2014 enabled presidents to help their parties raise money in much larger amounts. First, the Supreme Court in the case *McCutcheon v. Federal Election Commission* struck down the aggregate cap on the amount of money an individual could give to campaigns, parties, and traditional political action committees in a two-year election cycle. During the 2012 election cycle, the aggregate contribution limit was $117,000. Of that total, only $46,200 could be given to various candidates for federal office, while $70,800 was the aggregate cap for donations to all party committees and political action committees.[26] Republican donor Shaun McCutcheon challenged the constitutionality of the aggregate donation cap in court. He contended that he should be allowed to make contributions to as many individual candidates and political committees as he chose, as long as each donation did not exceed the maximum amount allowed.[27]

Chief Justice Roberts agreed with McCutcheon and wrote the opinion that struck down the aggregate caps on contributions. Roberts declared, "[t]he Government may no more restrict how many candidates or causes a donor may support than it may tell a newspaper how many candidates it may endorse." Justice Stephen Breyer wrote in dissent that, "[i]n the absence of limits on aggregate political contributions, donors can and likely will find ways to channel millions of dollars to parties and to individual candidates, producing precisely the kind of 'corruption' or 'appearance of corruption' that previously led the Court to hold aggregate limits constitutional." Breyer described the potential for establishing joint fundraising committees that could accept checks in very large amounts and then distribute those funds to various candidates and party committees.[28] The *McCutcheon* decision, in conjunction with a law passed by Congress that same year, would indeed enable campaigns and parties to create complicated joint fundraising committees that raised money in much larger amounts than had been previously possible.

In December 2014, Congress passed a $1.1 trillion appropriations bill that included a provision allowing national party committees to accept donations that were seven times larger than the previous limit. In 2014, an individual was allowed to give $32,400 each calendar year to each party's three national committee organizations – the national party committee, and the two party committees fo-

---

26 "Contribution Limits for 2011–2012," FEC.gov, March 1, 2011, https://www.fec.gov/updates/contribution-limits-for-2011–2012/.
27 "McCutcheon et al. v. Federal Election Commission," April 2, 2014, https://www.supremecourt.gov/opinions/13pdf/12-536_e1pf.pdf.
28 "McCutcheon et al. v. Federal Election Commission."

cused on electing candidates to each chamber of Congress. The new law permitted each party to receive additional donations of $97,200 for each of seven new committee funds: one to support the party's national convention; another three to fund the building or improvement of party headquarters – the national committee and the two committees focused on House and Senate elections could each set up such a fund; and an additional three funds to pay for each committee's legal expenses. If a party established all these committees, an individual donor could potentially contribute up to $777,600 a year to the national party under the fundraising limits in place in 2014. This amount would increase every two years since it was indexed to rise with inflation. A *Washington Post* headline about the new law asserted, "Fundraising Expansion Slipped into Spending Deal Could Power Financial Bonanza for Parties."[29]

The ruling in the *McCutcheon* case and the change in campaign finance law in 2014 led both parties to set up complicated joint fundraising committees with many beneficiaries that could raise money in even larger amounts. In 2016, Obama took part in seven fundraisers for the Hillary Victory Fund, which benefited the campaign of Democratic presidential nominee Hillary Clinton, the DNC, and 38 state-party committees.[30] The cost of admission to one such Obama fundraiser was $100,000 per person.[31] The next president would attend even higher-dollar fundraising events. When Donald Trump sought a second term, complicated joint fundraising committees enabled him to attend multiple fundraisers where the cost of admission was $293,300 per person.[32] Obama's second term witnessed a marked shift further in the direction of high-dollar fundraising as candidates and parties sought ways to work around contribution limits to keep up with Super PACs.

---

[29] Kenneth P. Vogel, "Budget Rider Would Expand Party Cash," Politico, December 10, 2014, http://www.politico.com/story/2014/12/budget-rider-would-expand-party-cash-113459.html; Matea Gold, "Fundraising Expansion Slipped into Spending Deal Could Power Financial Bonanza for Parties," *The Washington Post*, December 10, 2014, https://www.washingtonpost.com/news/post-politics/wp/2014/12/10/fundraising-expansion-slipped-into-spending-deal-could-power-financial-bonanza-for-parties/.
[30] "FEC Form 1, Statement of Organization for Hillary Victory Fund," June 23, 2016, https://docquery.fec.gov/cgi-bin/forms/C00586537/1080677/.
[31] Ted Johnson, "Jeffrey Katzenberg to Host President Obama for Hillary Clinton Fundraiser (EXCLUSIVE)," *Variety*, October 14, 2016, https://variety.com/2016/biz/news/jeffrey-katzenberg-president-obama-hillary-clinton-1201889609/.
[32] Josh Dawsey and Michelle Ye Hee Lee, "Trump to Headline a $580,600-per-Couple Fundraiser, the Most Expensive of His Reelection Bid," *Washington Post*, February 13, 2020, https://www.washingtonpost.com/politics/trump-to-headline-a-580600-per-couple-fundraiser-the-most-expensive-of-his-reelection-bid/2020/02/13/144b75b2-4e7a-11ea-a4ab-9f389ce8ad30_story.html.

Conclusion

The Obama era was a time of transformational change in presidential fundraising. The campaign finance landscape when he launched his bid for the presidency in 2007 had evolved dramatically by the time Obama's second term ended in 2017. His decision to forgo the public funding program, which had once been at the core of a candidate's strategy for winning the White House, contributed to its lapse into irrelevance, as it no longer offered sufficient resources for candidates to mount a competitive campaign. Freed from the voluntary spending limits that came with public funding, Obama's 2008 campaign raised record amounts of money, and every subsequent major party nominee would also decline public funding and instead raise much more money on their own.

Super PACs and other similar groups played a substantial role in the 2012 presidential election and beyond. Their ability to raise funds in unlimited amounts would put increased pressure on Obama and other candidates to spend substantial amounts of time raising funds for their campaign committees in the increments in the low thousands dictated by campaign finance law. In 2011, Obama would set a record for the earliest start to his reelection fundraising efforts, and would headline far more reelection fundraisers than any other president in the modern campaign finance era. As he did so, he integrated his campaign's fundraising with party fundraising through a joint fundraising committee that allowed him to raise funds in larger amounts than would otherwise have been possible. Additionally, in spite of his initial criticism of Super PACs, he approved a plan for aides to appear at Super PAC events, while declining to do so himself.

In his second term, Obama participated in multiple events to aid Super PACs focused on helping House and Senate candidates across the country. He also participated in high-dollar fundraising events for the Hillary Victory Fund joint fundraising committee, thanks to two key changes to the legal landscape in 2014. First, a Supreme Court decision struck down the aggregate limits on donations to candidates and political committees in a two-year election cycle. Then Congress passed a law that increased the amount of money that political parties could raise from individuals. These two developments led to the expanded use of complicated joint fundraising committees, which ushered in a return to party fundraising events where the price of admission was in the six figures.

Obama's campaign finance decisions illustrate what can happen when soaring campaign rhetoric collides with the institutional realities of the American political system. While Obama promised on the campaign trail that he would transform the workings of American politics and fix a broken Washington, his fundraising practices reflected a pragmatic response to the evolving rules and incentives of the campaign finance system. Although the system he confronted was not one that he would have designed, his fundraising strategies indicated a practical acknowledgment that his and his party's best chance of winning elections relied on working within the existing rules of the system to raise the funds needed to run competitive campaigns. Obama's fundraising efforts were a means to an end in hopes of winning elections so that he and his fellow party members could achieve their public policy goals.

Frequent, high-dollar fundraising leads to criticism that presidents are distracted from their demanding day job, and large amounts of money in politics raise concerns about corruption or the appearance of corruption. Then-Senator Obama wrote about some of the consequences of such fundraising efforts in his 2006 book, *The Audacity of Hope*:

> I can't assume that the money chase didn't alter me in some ways.... Increasingly I found myself spending time with people of means – law firm partners and investment bankers, hedge fund managers and venture capitalists. As a rule, they were smart, interesting people, knowledgeable about public policy, liberal in their politics, expecting nothing more than a hearing of their opinions in exchange for their checks. But they reflected, almost uniformly, the perspectives of their class: the top 1 percent or so of the income scale that can afford to write a $2,000 check to a political candidate.... I know that as a consequence of my fundraising I became more like the wealthy donors I met, in the very particular sense that I spent more and more of my time above the fray, outside the world of immediate hunger, disappointment, fear, irrationality, and frequent hardship of the other 99 percent of the population – that is, the people that I'd entered public life to serve.[33]

In some instances, such as when Obama opted out of the public funding program and raised unprecedented amounts of money, he drove changes in campaign finance dynamics. At other times, Obama responded to an evolving campaign finance landscape, including the Supreme Court rulings in the *Citizens United* and *McCutcheon* cases. But whether Obama was sparking change himself or taking actions shaped by the shifting institutional incentives of the campaign finance system, the ways in which presidents and presidential candidates raise campaign cash was fundamentally transformed during the Obama years.

---

[33] Barack Obama, *The Audacity of Hope: Thoughts on Reclaiming the American Dream* (New York: Crown Publishers, 2006), 113–115.

References

Bauder, Bauder. "Documentary Brings Together 20 Presidential Chiefs." *The Associated Press*, September 10, 2013.

Bradley, Tahman. "Final Fundraising Figure: Obama's $750M." *ABC News*, December 4, 2008, https://abcnews.go.com/Politics/Vote2008/story?id=6397572&page=1.

Brunner, Jim. "Obama Fundraising Visit to Enrich Democratic Super PAC." *The Seattle Times*, July 21, 2014, https://www.seattletimes.com/seattle-news/obama-fundraising-visit-to-enrich-democratic-super-pac/.

CBS News. "Clinton, Obama Both Raised $100M In 2007." January 1, 2008, https://www.cbsnews.com/news/clinton-obama-both-raised-100m-in-2007/

CNN. "Obama Raises $25 Million, Challenges Clinton's Front-Runner Status." April 9, 2007, https://www.cnn.com/2007/POLITICS/04/04/obama.fundraising/index.html.

Cornell University. "Citizens United v. Federal Election Commission." January 21, 2010, https://www.law.cornell.edu/supct/html/08-205.ZO.html.

Dawsey, Josh, and Michelle Ye Hee Lee. "Trump to Headline a $580,600-per-Couple Fundraiser, the Most Expensive of His Reelection Bid." *Washington Post*, February 13, 2020, https://www.washingtonpost.com/politics/trump-to-headline-a-580600-per-couple-fundraiser-the-most-expensive-of-his-reelection-bid/2020/02/13/144b75b2-4e7a-11ea-a4ab-9f389ce8ad30_story.html.

Digests of Other White House Announcements. Available as appendices to the Public Papers of the Presidents of the United States, https://www.govinfo.gov/app/collection/PPP/.

Doherty, Brendan J. *Fundraiser in Chief: Presidents and the Politics of Campaign Cash*. Lawrence: University Press of Kansas, 2023.

FEC.gov. "Archive of Contribution Limits." Accessed February 16, 2021, https://www.fec.gov/help-candidates-and-committees/candidate-taking-receipts/archived-contribution-limits/.

FEC.gov. "Contribution Limits for 2011–2012." March 1, 2011, https://www.fec.gov/updates/contribution-limits-for-2011-2012/.

FEC.gov. "FEC Form 1, Statement of Organization for Hillary Victory Fund." June 23, 2016, https://docquery.fec.gov/cgi-bin/forms/C00586537/1080677/.

FEC.gov. "FEC Form 1, Statement of Organization for Obama Victory Fund." April 4, 2011, https://docquery.fec.gov/pdf/890/11030584890/11030584890.pdf.

FEC.gov. "Fundraising for Super PACs by Federal Candidates." Accessed April 13, 2021, https://www.fec.gov/help-candidates-and-committees/making-disbursements-pac/fundraising-super-pacs-federal-candidates-nonconnected-pac/.

FEC.gov. "Types of Nonconnected PACs." Accessed February 7, 2023, https://www.fec.gov/help-candidates-and-committees/registering-pac/types-nonconnected-pacs/.

Gold, Matea. "Fundraising Expansion Slipped into Spending Deal Could Power Financial Bonanza for Parties." *The Washington Post*, December 10, 2014, https://www.washingtonpost.com/news/post-politics/wp/2014/12/10/fundraising-expansion-slipped-into-spending-deal-could-power-financial-bonanza-for-parties/.

Janofsky, Michael. "Advocacy Groups Spent Record Amount on 2004 Election." *The New York Times*, December 17, 2004, https://www.nytimes.com/2004/12/17/politics/advocacy-groups-spent-record-amount-on-2004-election.html.

Johnson, Ted. "Jeffrey Katzenberg to Host President Obama for Hillary Clinton Fundraiser (EXCLUSIVE)." *Variety*, October 14, 2016, https://variety.com/2016/biz/news/jeffrey-katzenberg-president-obama-hillary-clinton-1201889609/.

Luo, Michael. "Obama Hauls in Record $750 Million for Campaign." *The New York Times*, December 5, 2008, https://www.nytimes.com/2008/12/05/us/politics/05donate.html.
Mason, Jeff. "In Shift, Obama Campaign to Support Super PAC Fundraiser." *Reuters*, February 7, 2012, https://www.reuters.com/article/us-usa-campaign-obama-superpac-idUSTRE81617U20120207.
Miller, Zeke J. "Obama Completes His Slow About-Face on Super PACs." *Time*, February 28, 2014, https://swampland.time.com/2014/02/28/barack-obama-super-pacs-citizens-united/.
Mutch, Robert E. *Campaign Finance: What Everyone Needs to Know*. New York: Oxford University Press, 2016.
Obama, Barack. *The Audacity of Hope: Thoughts on Reclaiming the American Dream*. New York: Crown Publishers, 2006.
OpenSecrets. "2010 Outside Spending, by Super PAC." Accessed February 16, 2023, https://www.opensecrets.org/outside-spending/super_pacs/2010?chrt=2016&disp=O&type=S.
Presidential Daily Diaries. Available via the National Archives, https://www.archives.gov/presidential-records/research/presidential-daily-diary.
Public Papers of the Presidents of the United States. Available via The American Presidency Project, https://www.presidency.ucsb.edu/documents/app-categories/presidential/spoken-addresses-and-remarks.
Rutenberg, Jim. "Groups Form to Aid Democrats With Anonymous Money." *The New York Times*, April 29, 2011, sec. US, https://www.nytimes.com/2011/04/30/us/politics/30donate.html.
Schneider, Bill. "Obama's Money Puts Clinton's 'inevitable' Nomination in Doubt." *CNN*, July 2, 2007, https://www.cnn.com/2007/POLITICS/07/02/campaign.money.schneider/index.html.
Schouten, Fredreka. "Obama Opts out of Campaign Finance System." *ABC News*, June 19, 2008, https://abcnews.go.com/Politics/story?id=5206643&page=1.
Selyukh, Alina. "Democrats Can't Afford Moral Stand on Campaign Spending." *Reuters*, June 28, 2012, https://www.reuters.com/article/us-washington-summit-money-idINBRE85Q1SR20120628.
Silverleib, Alan. "Gloves Come off after Obama Rips Supreme Court Ruling." *CNN*, January 28, 2010, http://www.cnn.com/2010/POLITICS/01/28/alito.obama.sotu/index.html.
Supremecourt.gov. "McCutcheon et al. v. Federal Election Commission." April 2, 2014, https://www.supremecourt.gov/opinions/13pdf/12-536_e1pf.pdf.
Tampa Bay Times. "Bush, Gore Both Reach Fundraising Records." August 21, 2000, https://www.tampabay.com/archive/2000/08/21/bush-gore-both-reach-fundraising-records/.
Van Natta, Don. "Bush Forgoes Federal Funds And Has No Spending Limit." *The New York Times*, July 15, 1999, https://www.nytimes.com/1999/07/16/us/bush-forgoes-federal-funds-and-has-no-spending-limit.html.
Vogel, Kenneth P. "Budget Rider Would Expand Party Cash." *Politico*, December 10, 2014, http://www.politico.com/story/2014/12/budget-rider-would-expand-party-cash-113459.html.
Vogel, Kenneth P., Dave Levinthal and Tarini Parti. "Barack Obama, Mitt Romney Both Topped $1 Billion in 2012." *Politico*, December 7, 2012, http://www.politico.com/story/2012/12/barack-obama-mitt-romney-both-topped-1-billion-in-2012-84737.html#ixzz2ENPPvAKu.
White House Press Briefings. Formerly available via The American Presidency Project, https://www.presidency.ucsb.edu/documents/app-categories/pressmedia/press-briefings.
White House Website of Bill Clinton, https://clintonwhitehouse4.archives.gov/.
White House Website of George W. Bush, https://georgewbush-whitehouse.archives.gov/.
White House Website of Barack Obama, https://obamawhitehouse.archives.gov/.
White House Website of Donald Trump, https://trumpwhitehouse.archives.gov/.
White House Website, www.whitehouse.gov.

Zeleny, Jeff and Jim Rutenberg. "Obama Yields in Marshaling of 'Super PAC.'" *The New York Times*, February 6, 2012, https://www.nytimes.com/2012/02/07/us/politics/with-a-signal-to-donors-obama-yields-on-super-pacs.html.

Zeleny, Jeff, and Patrick Healy. "Obama Shows His Strength in a Fund-Raising Feat on Par With Clinton." *The New York Times*, April 5, 2007, https://www.nytimes.com/2007/04/05/us/politics/05obama.html.

Jeff Bloodworth
Chapter 3
The Obama Coalition's Kryptonite: Ralph Stanley, Bruce Springsteen, and the White Working Class

Barack Obama was a master coalition builder. Indeed, only Obama could have united the kings and queens of Bluegrass (Ralph Stanley), Merengue (Juan Luis Guerra), Rhythm and Blues (Stevie Wonder), Jam Bands (the Grateful Dead), Rock (Bruce Springsteen), and Hip-Hop (Jay-Z and Beyoncé) into a motley rainbow coalition of sonic and electoral support.[1] This eclectic assortment of musicians is more than a political oddity. Through it one can veritably hear the 2008 Obama coalition. With an assist from a near economic apocalypse, this diverse coalition of racial minorities, educated whites, unmarried women, a dash of Northern working-class whites, and a sprinkle of rural populist voters put Obama into the White House with large congressional majorities.

In 2009, Obama was seemingly poised to become a transformational president. But this lofty aim crashed onto the shoals of governing realities. Transformational presidents build, or at the very least establish a foundation for, enduring majorities. Lasting majorities, in turn, alter the confines of debate and force opposition parties to adapt to new political realities. A study of liberalism's twentieth-century history and analysis of the elections since the Obama presidency suggests two inter-related obstacles have thus far stopped Obama from bequeathing an enduring majority and earning the "transformational" mantle: rural populists and working-class whites in the North.

Stanley-Springsteen Voters: The White Working Class

Often lumped into one category, working-class (or non-college) whites, comprise the nation's single largest voting demographic. A function of the interplay of in-

---

[1] Daniel Kreps, "We Need a Change," *Rolling Stone*, October 3, 2008, https://www.rollingstone.com/politics/politics-news/bluegrass-legend-ralph-stanley-endorses-obama-we-need-a-change-96834/.

Jeff Bloodworth, Gannon University

https://doi.org/10.1515/9783111384108-003

come, education, and occupation, "working class" voters generally possess less formal education, make less money, and hold service or manual labor jobs. A proxy for "human capital," education, more than any other of the three above categories, is determinative in shaping an individual's economic fate and social class, especially in post-industrial America.[2]

In 2022, whites comprise the majority, 56 percent, of the overall working-class demographic.[3] For a generation, the number of working class and white working-class Americans have been on the decline. In 1975, working class whites encompassed 70 percent of the entire electorate.[4] By 2020, that number fell to 40 percent. But that was not the sole area of change for this group. Between 1979 and 2005, wages for those with a bachelor's and post-graduate degrees rose by 22 and 28 percent while those with a high-school degree or high-school dropouts plummeted by two and 18 percent respectively.[5]

Population and income were not the only areas of change. Throughout the postwar era, working-class whites shifted politically. In the 1930s, FDR made the Democrats into a working-class party. In the very early postwar decades, Democrats, at the presidential level, maintained this by winning the overall working-class presidential vote by an approximate 60 to 40 margin.[6] But since the late 1960s, the party has ceded white working-class voters. In 1964, LBJ earned a majority, 55 percent, of the white working-class vote. By 1968, the combination of civil rights, urban riots, crime, and Vietnam caused a 20-point drop in this demographic's vote for Hubert Humphrey. Four years later, Richard Nixon took a whopping 70 percent of these voters.[7] This political reality was cemented in the 1970s. An era of inflation and Democratic indifference to white working-class woes enabled Ronald Reagan to take an average of 61 percent of their vote. It was the white working class's shift to the right, which undermined the New Deal coalition and fueled the Reagan era.

---

[2] William R. Emmons, Ana Hernandez Kent, and Lowell R. Ricketts, "The White Working Class: National Trends, Then and Now," *The Federal Reserve Bank St. Louis*, May 20, 2019, https://www.stlouisfed.org/on-the-economy/2019/september/white-working-class-national-trends-then-now.
[3] Valerie Wilson, "People of Color Will Be the Majority of the American Working Class by 2032," *Economic Policy Institute*, September 11, 2022, https://www.epi.org/publication/the-changing-demographics-of-americas-working-class/.
[4] Wilson, "People of Color Will Be the Majority."
[5] Alan Abramowitz, and Ruy Teixeira, "The Decline of the White Working Class and the Rise of a Mass Upper-Middle Class," *Political Science Quarterly* 124, no. 3 (Fall 2009): 392.
[6] Charles Culhane, "White House Report/Nixon Eyes Blue-Collar Workers as Potential Source of Votes in '72," *The National Journal* (January 30, 1971): 232.
[7] Abramowitz, and Teixeira, "The Decline of the White Working Class," 399.

A diversifying and more educated electorate enabled Bill Clinton and Barack Obama to capture the White House without a majority of white working-class voters. But Obama's 2008 landslide was facilitated by spikes with working-class whites in key swing states. In terms of Obama's 2008 sonic coalition, he, his predecessors, and successors lost specific pieces of the white working-class, Ralph Stanley and Bruce Springsteen voters in successive elections. For decades, Democratic strength with white working-class voters came in specific regions of Ralph Stanley's Appalachia and with Bruce Springsteen's Northern white working class. For decades after the Civil War, Appalachia had been a GOP stronghold. But the rise of organized labor and the New Deal turned pockets of Appalachia into areas of Democratic strength. These sections made West Virginia into a Democratic bastion, helped push competitive states, Ohio and Pennsylvania, into the Democratic column, and turned once stalwart states, Kentucky, West Virginia, and North Carolina, that much more Democratic.

Bruce Springsteen's Northern white working-class voters were an even more crucial piece of the Democratic working-class vote. During the New Deal and early postwar era, unionized working-class whites were a Democratic linchpin. By the late 1940s, nearly 60 percent of the North's blue-collar jobs were unionized.[8] It was these voters who provided Democrats with the margins necessary to win the overall working-class vote and key Northern industrial states. In 1952, 56 percent of all union voters cast ballots for Adlai Stevenson while 54 percent of all non-union working-class voters opted for Eisenhower. This reality held true throughout the 1950s and 1960s. Even in 1968, when Democrats saw their share of the overall white working-class vote drop by 20 points, Hubert Humphrey won the union vote 48 to 39 over Nixon.[9] But the Democrat's domination of the Springsteen vote collapsed in the post-1968 era.

By 2008, Democrats realized that their hopes for majority wins in a presidential contest relied upon winning back the Stanley and Springsteen voters. Surprising some, Obama earned the endorsement of the Bluegrass banjo-picking legend. Stanley not only endorsed the Democrat in the primaries, he slapped an Obama sticker onto his tour bus. Going one better, he plugged the Democrat in a series of AM radio ads that played throughout his native Appalachia.[10] A symbol of hardscrabble "Jacksonian" rural populists who live throughout Appalachia, the Upper South, and lower Midwest, Stanley endorsed Obama to his fellow rural populist whites. Ironically, Stanley was wooing the very Jacksonians who had once constituted the base of the Democratic Party but had turned right.

---

8 Abramowitz, and Teixeira, "The Decline of the White Working Class," 397.
9 Culhane, "White House Report/Nixon Eyes Blue-Collar Workers," 232.
10 "Bluegrass Legend Backing Obama," *Chicago Tribune*, October 5, 2008, 22; Chris Norden, "Opinions: Ralph Stanley Was Brave," *The Spokesman Review*, January 30, 2016, https://www.spokesman.com/stories/2016/jun/30/ralph-stanley-brave-endorse-obama/.

By no means the only region with rural populists, Appalachia is, nevertheless, a tidy political barometer of this misunderstood "folk community bound together by deep cultural and ethnic ties."[11] As Appalachia goes, so too do the rural populists. A region apart, the nation's 26 million Appalachians are disproportionately white, 83 percent, rural, 33 percent, and poor, 14.6 percent.[12] Politically, the wide-ranging region that stretches from southern New York to northern Mississippi, touches key swing states, Virginia, North Carolina, Ohio, and Pennsylvania. In 2008, Obama, with the aid of Ralph Stanley, targeted these swing state Appalachian regions.[13]

Despite a relatively homogeneous population Appalachia has not been politically consistent. Southern "mountain Republicans" maintained loyalties to the GOP, while other regions in Appalachia voted Democrat or GOP based upon a variety of historic allegiances. In the 1930s, Democrats established strongholds in Appalachian regions, North and South, with intensive mining and labor organizing. As recently as the 1990s, mining regions and "distressed" counties remained in the Democratic column making Appalachia competitive politically.[14] Since 1980, Appalachia has not only shifted rightward, but the region has also grown the most Republican of any section in the nation.[15] As a result of this ideological shift, Obama, or any Democrat for that matter, faced an uphill struggle with this region's voters.

Even with Stanley's support Obama scarcely won Appalachia's rural populists in 2008. McCain won 370 of 420 Appalachian counties.[16] But a deeper dive into the numbers tells a more nuanced story. Nationally, the Democrat made small, yet significant, inroads with rural voters, especially in battleground states, that proved decisive.[17]

---

11 Walter Russell Mead, "The Jacksonian Tradition: And American Foreign Policy," *The National Interest* (Winter 1999/2000): 9.
12 "Population and Age in Appalachia," The Appalachian Regional Commission, accessed November 8, 2022, https://www.arc.gov/appalachias-population/; Melissa Martin, "Appalachian Americans," *Portsmouth Daily Times*, January 4, 2018, https://www.portsmouth-dailytimes.com/opinion/22902/appalachian-americans; "Poverty Rates in Appalachia," The Appalachian Regional Commission, accessed November 8, 2022, https://www.arc.gov/map/poverty-rates-in-appalachia-2013-2017.
13 William Hayden, "Appalachian Diversity: African-American, Hispanic/Latino, and Other Populations," *Journal of Appalachian Studies* 10, no. 3 (2004): 293–306, http://www.jstor.org/stable/41446641.
14 Kevin Oshnock, "Recent Republican Dominance in Appalachia," Master's Thesis (Appalachian State University, 2019), https://libres.uncg.edu/ir/asu/f/Oshnock_Kevin_Thesis_Dec_2019.pdf, 45–48.
15 Oshnock, "Recent Republican Dominance," 45–48.
16 "The Political Geography of Virginia & Florida," Brookings Institute Blueprint for American Prosperity, accessed November 9, 2022, https://www.brookings.edu/wp-content/uploads/2016/06/maps_figures.pdf.
17 Howard Berkes, "Obama Made Inroads into the Rural Base," *All Things Considered*, November 8, 2008, https://www.npr.org/2008/11/08/96782692/obama-made-inroads-into-rural-republican-base.

This story was repeated in Appalachia. Obama not only marginally improved upon John Kerry's overall Appalachian vote from 2004 by two points, but he did so in the Appalachian regions of key swing states, North Carolina, Ohio, and Virginia.[18]

From the very start, the Obama campaign identified Virginia as a keystone to victory. To win Old Dominion, Obama had to amplify the urban and African American turnout and avoid a swamping in Virginia's Appalachian region. Demonstrating the significance of the state and this strategy, Obama's very first campaign stop after officially clinching the Democratic nomination was Bristol, Virginia.[19] A town in the heart of Ralph Stanley's southwest Virginia, the Bristol swing, and others like it, were designed to keep the losing margins in Appalachia reasonably low. Obama achieved this modest goal in southwest Virginia. In North Carolina, he cut significantly into McCain's advantage in that state's Appalachian counties, which proved the difference in a state that Obama won by 14,000 ballots.[20]

The story was much the same in Ohio. In 2004, Ohio's 29 Appalachian counties gave Bush the Buckeye State and the presidency. In a state Bush won by 118,599 votes, out of 5.6 million cast, the Republican's 90,000 vote advantage (56.5% to 43%) in Ohio's Appalachia region was decisive.[21] Four years later, Obama improved upon Kerry's margins. In taking eight of Ohio's 29 Appalachian Counties, he cut into the GOP's 2004 landslide.[22] In all three states, Obama maintained a modicum of competitiveness with rural populists in Appalachia, which enabled urban and minority votes to sweep him to victory in these three key swing states.

Like Ralph Stanley's rural populists, Obama aimed at Bruce Springsteen's Northern white working class in a smattering of keys states, Pennsylvania, Ohio, Michigan, Wisconsin, and Iowa. Largely urban, the North's working-class whites had separate ethno-cultural roots and decidedly different historical experiences

---

18 Oshnock, "Recent Republican Dominance," 45–48.
19 Peter Boyer, "The Appalachia Problem: Obama Goes to Rural Virginia," *The New Yorker*, October 6, 2008, https://www.newyorker.com/magazine/2008/10/06/the-appalachian-problem.
20 David Sutton, "The 2008 Presidential Campaign in Appalachia: Reading from the Margins," *Appalachian Journal* 36, no. 3/4 (Spring/Summer 2009): 340; Geoffrey Skelley, "The Old Dominion's Political Map," The UVA Center for Politics, accessed November 9, 2022, https://centerforpolitics.org/crystalball/articles/the-old-dominions-political-map.
21 David Sutton, "Living Poor and Voting Rich in Appalachia," *Appalachian Journal* 32, no. 3 (Spring 2005): 190.
22 Micah Cohen, "In Ohio, Poll Shows Benefit for Auto Bailout to Obama," *New York Times*, November 5, 2012, https://archive.nytimes.com/fivethirtyeight.blogs.nytimes.com/2012/11/05/in-ohio-polls-show-benefit-of-auto-rescue-to-obama/?searchResultPosition=3.

from Appalachia's rural populists.[23] Whereas rural populists were largely descended from old stock, Scots Irish Protestants, the North's white working class significantly sprang from "white ethnic" immigrants of the late nineteenth and early twentieth century. Overwhelmingly Catholic with a smattering of Lutherans and Jews in their midst, the Springsteen demographic remained a majority of voters in key Rust Belt states and had fallen just below that mark in the Democratic northeast.[24]

For Obama, reducing the GOP's advantage with Springsteen voters spelled the difference between winning and losing.[25] Populous and located in electoral rich Northern states, the Northern white working class was the Democratic key to victory. Recent history told that tale. In two winning presidential races, Bill Clinton won a plurality of working-class whites. In contrast, Al Gore and John Kerry lost this demographic by 17 and 23 points respectively, and fell just short of the White House.[26] By winning a few percentage points more of Springsteen voters, Obama could whittle his deficit with the overall white working-class down and take key swing states en route to the White House.

To avoid the fate of Kerry, Gore, and a host of post-1960s Democratic losers, Obama took direct aim at Springsteen's white working-class demographic. Like the rural populists in Appalachia, the campaign especially targeted those voters in swing state's where they comprised a majority of the electorate, namely Ohio, Michigan, Wisconsin, Pennsylvania, and Iowa. Obama had every reason to worry. In the 2008 primaries, he suffered a rare self-inflicted injury with a now infamous remark at a San Francisco fundraiser. Asked to explain his struggles with white working-class Pennsylvanians, Obama explicated, "[working class whites] cling to guns or religion or antipathy toward people who aren't like them . . . as a way to explain their frustrations."[27] The ensuing political firestorm prompted Bruce Springsteen's inter-

---

23 Max Ehrenfreund, and Jeff Guo, "If You've Ever Described People as 'White Working Class,' Read This," *Washington Post*, November 23, 2016, https://www.washingtonpost.com/news/wonk/wp/2016/11/22/who-exactly-is-the-white-working-class-and-what-do-they-believe-good-questions/.
24 Emmons, Kent, and Ricketts, "The White Working Class: State-Level Declines & Geographic Concentration."
25 Ehrenfreund, and Guo, "If You've Ever Described People."
26 William Galston, "Why Ohio Matters: President Obama Can't Win the 2012 Without It," *Brookings*, March 4, 2011, https://www.brookings.edu/articles/why-ohio-matters-president-obama-cant-win-the-2012-election-without-it/.
27 Ben Smith, "Obama on Small Town Pa.: Clinging to Religion, Guns, & Xenophobia," *Politico*, April 11, 2008, https://www.politico.com/blogs/ben-smith/2008/04/obama-on-small-town-pa-clinging-to-religion-guns-xenophobia-007737.

vention. He not only endorsed the senator, he praised Obama for, "speak[ing] to the America I've envisioned in my music for the past 35 years."[28]

Springsteen's commendation was no pedestrian celebrity endorsement. Born to a downtrodden, Catholic working-class family in New Jersey, Springsteen came to symbolize post-New Deal blue-collar sensibilities. His music depicted estranged working-class characters who struggled to make sense of a post-industrial landscape, which prompted a devoted following from blue-collar fans. Springsteen's white working-class devotees were alienated for good reason. Since the 1970s, wages for those with a high school degree had nosedived by two percent while high school dropouts saw their pay fall by 18 percent.[29] Personally, vouching for Obama to his audiences, Springsteen did one better than Ralph Stanley; he joined the campaign by playing numerous campaign events at regions and locales with heavy white-working class populations.[30]

A free Springsteen concert was no panacea to Obama's struggles with the white working class. Tapping a working-class Scranton, Pennsylvania native, Joe Biden, to be his running mate, Obama reinforced his political weakness. Stumping intensively for these voters via surrogates, rigorous canvassing, and personal campaign stops, which included a six-day bus tour of Pennsylvania, brought results. Annihilated with the Deep South's white working class, Obama did comparatively well in the North.[31] In Pennsylvania, Obama "only" lost this demographic to McCain by 15 points. Tellingly, Obama won counties with Springsteen's white working-class voters in northwestern and northeastern Pennsylvania. By comparison, McCain did his best with the state's rural populists who lived in the Keystone State's south-central Appalachia region.[32] Buoyed by Springsteen's white working-class voters and a heavy urban and minority vote, Obama won Pennsylvania easily.[33]

---

28 Suzanne Goldenberg, "Born to Run: Springsteen Throws His Weight Behind Obama," *The Guardian*, April 16, 2008; https://www.theguardian.com/world/2008/apr/17/barackobama.uselections2008; John McCormick, "Confident Obama Campaigns with Springsteen," *Chicago Tribune*, November 2, 2008, https://www.starbeacon.com/archives/confident-obama-campaigns-with-springsteen/article_fe1155f1-a357-5f82-a383-907250804a8b.html.
29 Abramowitz, and Teixeira, "The Decline of the White Working Class and the Rise of a Mass Upper-Middle Class," *Political Science Quarterly* 124, no. 3, (Fall 2009): 391–422.
30 Goldenberg, "Born to Run: Springsteen Throws His Weight Behind Obama"; McCormick, "Confident Obama Campaigns with Springsteen."
31 "The White Working Class Vote in 2008," *Working Class Perspectives*, December 15, 2008, https://workingclassstudies.wordpress.com/2008/12/15/the-white-working-class-vote-in-2008/.
32 "Pennsylvania: Election Results 2008," *New York Times*, December 9, 2008, https://www.nytimes.com/elections/2008/results/states/pennsylvania.html.
33 Carrie Budhoff Brown, "Obama and Blue Collar Voters: Take 2," *Politico*, December 1, 2011, https://www.politico.com/story/2011/12/obama-and-blue-collar-voters-take-2-069491.

Repeating this victory elsewhere, Obama won a majority of Springsteen voters in Michigan, Minnesota, New Hampshire, Ohio, and Wisconsin.[34] He could have won a narrow White House victory without these votes. But in wooing just enough rural populists and a majority of white working-class voters in key states, he earned a mandate and huge congressional majorities. In this way, the 2008 Obama possessed all the hallmarks and makings of a transformational president.

The ensuing Great Recession and sluggish economic recovery harmed the new president with already wary rural populist and white working-class voters. In Ralph Stanley's Appalachia, the small, yet meaningful inroads of 2008 collapsed almost immediately. In 2009, a Democratic statehouse seat in Stanley's southwest Virginia, which the party had held since the 1950s, went Republican.[35] This merely foreshadowed the GOP's Appalachian avalanche that was to come. By 2012, West Virginia Democrats opted for a Texas prison inmate while Kentucky and Arkansas Democrats waffled between "uncommitted" and the incumbent president in the Democratic presidential primaries.[36] Mitt Romney erased Obama's small, hard-won gains by taking 62 percent of the Appalachian vote. Four years later, in 2016, Donald Trump won 65 percent of the vote and 95 percent of all Appalachian counties. In the Congress, the results were even more stark. In 2008, Democrats controlled a majority of the region's seats. By 2018, the GOP held 96 percent of the senate and 88 percent of Appalachia's House seats.[37]

In terms of Springsteen's white working class, Obama managed a better outcome in 2012. Losing only three points from his 2008 marker with the white working-class vote, from 39 to 36 percent, Obama stymied Romney's only chance at victory, who needed to rout the president with white working-class voters.[38] By limiting his 2012 losses with this group, Obama won key states, Pennsylvania, Ohio, Michigan, Wisconsin, Minnesota, and Iowa, where these voters comprised a majority of voters or a significant piece of the electorate.

---

34 "The White Working Class Vote in 2008," *Working Class Perspectives*, December 15, 2008, https://workingclassstudies.wordpress.com/2008/12/15/the-white-working-class-vote-in-2008/.
35 Mason Adams, "In Coal Country, A Political Journey from Blue to Deep Red," *The Virginia Center for Investigative Journalism*, November 1, 2020, https://vcij.org/stories/blue-to-deep-red.
36 While not part of Appalachia, the Arkansas Ozarks was populated by the very same Scots Irish who settled Appalachia. These regions demonstrate very similar political behaviors. Alec MacGillis, "A Gift for Snickering Pundits: A Map," *The New Republic*, May 22, 2012, https://newrepublic.com/authors/alec-macgillis?page=19.
37 Oshnock, "Recent Republican Dominance," 30–37.
38 Ruy Teixeira, and John Halpin, "The Obama Coalition in the 2012 Election and Beyond," *The Center for American Progress*, December 4, 2012, https://www.americanprogress.org/article/the-obama-coalition-in-the-2012-election-and-beyond, 7.

Residual strength with the white working class won Obama Ohio. Romney hoped to improve upon McCain's 10-point margin with this demographic. Obama, however, managed to lose only four points from 2008 totals with this demographic, and lost it 56 to 42 percent to Romney. In combination with 96 percent support from black voters, who raised their turnout by four points over 2008, Obama won Ohio by one point more in 2012 than he did in 2008.[39]

Unlike Ohio, Romney halved Obama's overall 10-point 2008 margin in Pennsylvania. He did so on the backs of white voters. In 2012, Obama's share of this vote fell from 48 to 42 percent. Thus, the bulk of Obama's five-point margin of victory came from urban voters in Philadelphia and Latinos. The Latino vote share in the state not only rose by two percent, but this demographic also increased their margins for Obama by 18 percent over 2008. The story was similar throughout the white working-class Rust Belt and Midwest. Winning Iowa, Wisconsin, Minnesota, and Michigan by anywhere from six to 10 points, the president's margins came from an increase in minority voters, which offset his small declines with those state's white voters.[40]

In one respect, Obama's 2012 map looked remarkably like 2008. Losing only North Carolina and Indiana from 2008, the Obama coalition looked ascendant and possibly enduring. The president's coattails, a gain of eight House and two Senate seats, suggested otherwise. In Ohio and Wisconsin, Obama's victory was premised upon strong showings with union households. In those states, Obama took 60 and 66 percent respectively of the union vote, which helped stanch the loss of non-union white-working class votes. In those states, and elsewhere across the industrial Midwest, union leaders credited Obama's auto industry bailout, which Mitt Romney heartily opposed, as accounting for the president's strong showing with organized labor.[41] Using the auto bailout as a Rorschach test to paint Romney as a "rapacious corporate raider," Obama was able to ride economic populism to slightly higher performances with the white working class in the Rust Belt.[42]

In retrospect, Romney was the *beau ideal* of an opponent for Obama with Rust Belt voters. The combination of his "Let Detroit Go Bankrupt" rhetoric, Bain Capital resume, and technocratic sensibility rebuffed just enough white working-

---

39 Teixeira, and Halpin, "The Obama Coalition," 12–13.
40 Teixeira, and Halpin, "The Obama Coalition," 12–13.
41 "Labor Unions Claim Credit for Obama's Victory," *New York Times*, November 7, 2012, https://archive.nytimes.com/thecaucus.blogs.nytimes.com/2012/11/07/labor-unions-claim-credit-for-obamas-victory/?searchResultPosition=1.
42 Ron Brownstein, "Obama's Support in Rust Belt, Sun Belt Very Different," *The Atlantic*, November 2, 2012, https://www.theatlantic.com/politics/archive/2012/11/obamas-support-in-rust-belt-sun-belt-very-different/429300/.

class voters to deny him victory. This was the death knell of the Republican's campaign. Indeed, had Romney scored a few points more with the white working class in Ohio, Wisconsin, Pennsylvania, and Michigan, he could have squeaked to a bare 270 to 268 Electoral College win.

Mitt Romney's share of the white working class vote mirrored Reagan's strength in 1984. Unlike 1984, when this demographic comprised 60 percent of the electorate by 2012, the white working class was merely 42 percent of all voters.[43] In 2008, working-class whites comprised 24 percent of the GOP presidential vote, which set a GOP record in terms of that demographic's share of the Republican vote. Thus, observers should have been much less surprised when Donald Trump's roughhewn populism and industrial protectionism helped him win these voters. In 2016, working-class whites comprised 31 percent of Trump's overall vote, a level he maintained in 2020.[44]

Moral Capitalism

In the past, Democrats had kept Springsteen and Stanley voters in their disparate coalition through "moral economy" appeals. The "moral economy" finds its historic roots with Stanley's rural populists. An amorphous yet identifiable demographic, Stanley's rural populists are old stock Americans hailing from the rural farmlands, small towns, and downscale suburbs of the South, Appalachia, and lower Midwest. Making monikers even more confusing, rural populists generally reject labels. They do, however, share two defining characteristics: Scotch-Irishness and Jacksonian Populism.

The "Scotch-Irish" were Protestants from Northern Ireland and the Scottish Lowlands who emigrated to the Appalachian and Allegheny backcountry. In the succeeding decades and centuries, they settled large swaths of the West Virginia, Kentucky, southern Indiana and Illinois, Tennessee, Missouri, Alabama, Mississippi, and Texas. In their trek, the Scotch-Irish took with them a distinct cultural

---

[43] Emmons, Kent, and Ricketts, "The White Working Class: National Trends, Then and Now"; Nate Cohn, "How the Obama Coalition Crumbled, Leaving an Opening for Trump," *New York Times*, December 23, 2016, https://www.nytimes.com/2016/12/23/upshot/how-the-obama-coalition-crumbled-leaving-an-opening-for-trump.html.

[44] Noam Lupu, and Nicholas Carnes, "Trump Didn't Bring White Working Class Voters to the Party, He Kept Them Away," *The Vanderbilt Project on Unity & American Democracy*, April 15, 2021, https://www.vanderbilt.edu/unity/2021/04/15/trump-didnt-bring-white-working-class-voters-to-the-republican-party-he-kept-them-away/.

legacy. A "folk community" bound by prideful honor and militant Christianity, the Scotch-Irish form the ethno-cultural basis of rural populism.[45]

Rural populists came to political maturity with Andrew Jackson's presidency. The small landowners, laborers, and shopkeepers in the South, Appalachia, and lower Midwest came natural to the Jacksonian view of the world. Following a Scotch-Irish sensibility and Jacksonian view, they saw "economic disparities between the periphery and the center" as emanating from East Coast banks and other harbingers of financial and consumer modernity.[46] Starting with Jefferson and continuing through Jackson and William Jennings Bryan, rural populists, and their worldview, comprised the integral core of the nineteenth-century Democratic Party.

In the twentieth century, demographic changes made Bruce Springsteen's Northern white working class the dominant cog in the Democratic coalition and the rural populists a junior partner. An imprecise term, the white working class refers to white ethnic, blue-collar laborers who live in scattered cities across Northeast and industrial Midwest. Settling in America during the Gilded Age, foreign-born Southern and East European immigrants comprised nearly 15 percent of the overall population in 1910.[47] The progeny of these immigrants, white ethnics accounted for an estimated 20 percent of the population in 1970.[48]

Prior to the depression, white ethnic laborers voted haphazardly and possessed few party loyalties. When Roosevelt provided federal protections for white ethnics to organize unions, membership exploded.[49] Not surprisingly, labor, of whom white ethnics were the base, swung decisively for FDR and formed the largest and most loyal demographic core of the Roosevelt coalition. White ethnics may have gained the upper hand demographically. But rural populists remained integral to the FDR coalition. Providing electoral heft at the presidential level, they also lent significant power in the House and Senate.

---

[45] David Hackett Fischer, *Albion's Seed: Four British Folkways in America* (New York: Oxford University Press, 1989), 606.
[46] Nancy Beck Young, *Wright Patman: Populism, Liberalism, and the American Dream* (Dallas: Southern Methodist University Press, 2000), 5–6.
[47] George Kozmetsky, and Piyu Yue, *The Economic Transformation of the United States, 1950–2000* (West Lafayette: Purdue University Press, 2005), 163.
[48] Jeff Bloodworth, *Losing the Center: The Decline of American Liberalism, 1968–1992* (Lexington: University of Kentucky Press, 2014), 37; Martin Marger, *Race & Ethnic Relations: American and Global Perspectives* (New York: Wadsworth, 2008), 37.
[49] Ruy Teixeira, and Alan Abramowitz, "The Decline of the White Working Class and the Rise of a Mass Upper Middle Class," Brookings Working Paper, April 2008, https://www.brookings.edu/research/the-decline-of-the-white-working-class-and-the-rise-of-a-mass-upper-middle-class/, 7.

Rural populists and the North's white working class gravitated to the Democrat's historic emphasis upon "moral capitalism." This was the connective tissue that bonded disparate downscale pieces of the coalition into a relatively coherent party. To Lizabeth Cohen, moral capitalism entailed "a form of political economy . . . that promised everyone, owner or worker, a fair share." From yeoman farmers and union organizers to FDR and Obama the moral capitalist thread is found throughout the party's history.[50]

Neither European social democracy nor *laissez faire* liberalism, moral capitalism "promised everyone, owner or worker, a fair share."[51] Moral capitalism hewed to dominant cultural norms in which Americans labored in return for a "fair share." Rooted in Jacksonian populism's rugged individualism formed in their frontier experience, "moral capitalism" called for Americans to engage in "honest work."[52] Once an individual meets that test, a political economy that fails to provide material security in exchange for consistent labor loses legitimacy, at least in the eyes of Jacksonian populists and their definition of a moral capitalism. Class appeals founded upon moral capitalism offer much political potential. Working-class wages have stagnated for a generation, if not more. Income inequality is ubiquitous. The American working class has every reason to believe that moral capitalism's social contract has been violated. But Obama was unable to convince Springsteen and Stanley voters that he could return the nation to moral capitalist norms.

The 2016 and 2020 presidential election results reveal a simple reality, Bruce Springsteen and Ralph Stanley's voters joined the Obama Coalition due to an economic emergency and foreign policy crisis. Once this moment transpired, they returned to their original voting patterns. Indeed, since the 1960s, liberals have struggled mightily to woo what had heretofore been the party's base. In tough economic times or eras of tumult, 1976, 1992, 2006, 2008, and 2018, Democrats can win slices of these voters. But as Mudcat Saunders, an Appalachia Democratic operative, once warned, "Democrats go after class, Republicans go after culture." To Saunders, class wins some white working class and rural populist voters but culture "you get them from top to bottom."[53]

Mudcat Saunders gets it right and wrong. Democrats lose the white working-class because they fundamentally fail to understand the cultural component of "class." Class is both a function of the pocketbook and culture. In the minds of the

---

50 Michael Kazin, *What it Took to Win: A History of the Democratic Party* (New York: Farrar, Straus, & Giroux, 2022), x-xi.
51 Kazin, *What it Took to Win*, x-xi.
52 Mead, "The Jacksonian Tradition: And American Foreign Policy," 12.
53 Sutton, "The 2008 Presidential Campaign in Appalachia: Reading from the Margins," 190.

progressive political class, Bernie Sanders' assaults against corporate, crony capitalism are the essence of a "class" appeal. But his solutions, free college and Medicare-for-All violate "moral economy" norms. For white working-class voters, federal activism first requires hard work from beneficiaries. "Earned benefits," not "relief" or the "dole" are the twenty-first century essence of a moral capitalist system. For decades, Sanders and other American left-liberals have been shoving the square American peg into the round European social democratic hole. Class appeals, in the American context, have only been successful when they hew to cultural norms first molded by rural populists.

FDR's Moral Economy

It was Franklin Roosevelt who first brought Ralph Stanley's rural populists and Bruce Springsteen's white working-class into a New Deal coalition premised upon federal activism that promoted a "moral economy."[54] Opportunity liberalism, the New Deal promoted enhancing equality of opportunity, which called for "hard work" along with federal activism to achieve greater social justice. The 1936 landslide signaled the emergence of the New Deal coalition. At the center of this alliance were rural populists and the North's white working class. Symbolizing the Springsteen-Stanley coalition was the "Austin-Boston" alliance. For nearly five decades, 1937 to 1989, the Democratic House leadership team was comprised of a Texan and Bostonian.[55] The Austin-Boston alliance was an expression of the New Deal coalition and more. Joined together by FDR's "Forgotten Man" populism and opportunity liberalism, rural populists and the North's white working class provided Democrats with substantial electoral wallop.[56]

In the postwar era, many leftists assumed that the New Deal Coalition would inevitably ((Blockade)) toward a social democratic future, led by recent European immigrants and their progeny. But Springsteen's Northern working classes embarked upon an "inward assimilation" which involved an Americanization into Jacksonian rural populism. In words of Walter Russel Mead "the social and economic solidarity rooted in European peasant communities has been overmas-

---

54 Alonzo Hamby, *Liberalism and Its Challengers: From FDR to Bush* (New York: Oxford University Press, 1992), 33.
55 Anthony Champagne, Douglas Harris, James Riddlesperger, and Garrison Nelson, *The Austin-Boston Connection: Five Decades of House Democratic Leadership, 1937–1989* (College Station: Texas A&M University Press, 2009), 1–2.
56 Champagne, Harris, Riddlesperger, and Nelson, *The Austin-Boston Connection*, 14–15.

tered by the individualism of the (crabgrass) frontier."[57] Thus, rural populists and the North's white working class merged culturally. They also maintained a political alliance within the New Deal coalition because FDR had performed a creative act of political jujitsu by making social welfare, American style, hew to broad cultural norms. He constructed and bequeathed a New Deal state that provided a floor of economic security without violating "self-reliance" principles. Partially funded by payroll deductions from earned wages, Social Security is politically sacrosanct because recipients believe, with good reason, that this constitutes an "earned benefit." Following in these footsteps were Truman and LBJ. Their signature and enduring additions to New Deal liberalism, other than expanding Social Security to additional beneficiaries, included the GI Bill[58] and Medicare. Extraordinarily popular and stupendously effective, the GI Bill and Medicare remain politically unassailable because both, in the popular mind, are "earned benefits."

The New Politics

In the late 1960s, crime, riots, civil rights, Vietnam, and the Youth Revolt eroded working-class allegiance to the Democratic Party. But those issues and events were merely transitory. What cemented this devolution was the rise of the educated middle class.[59] It was these educated middle-class, or so-called New Politics liberals, who ousted the working class from party machinery and slowly took control of the Democratic Party. They were able to do so due to their rising numbers. In 1960, only 7.7 percent of Americans earned a bachelor's degree or higher. By 1980 that number had more than doubled to 16.2 percent. By 2020, that number had more than doubled again with 37.2 percent of Americans holding a bachelor's degree or higher.[60]

In the process of taking control of the Democratic Party, New Politics liberals also pushed "entitlement" liberalism to replace the opportunity liberalism of the working class. For the latter, equality of opportunity and earned benefits animated liberal programs. For educated middle-class liberals, they increasingly em-

---

57 Mead, "The Jacksonian Tradition: And American Foreign Policy," 11.
58 This bill was signed into law by FDR and enacted by Truman.
59 Bloodworth, *Losing the Center*, 4–5.
60 "Educational Attainment Distribution in the United States, 1960–2021," *Statista*, accessed November 9, 2022, https://www.statista.com/statistics/184260/educational-attainment-in-the-us/.

phasized "equality of result" and dispensed with "earned benefits" in favor of universal social welfare programs.[61]

Obama is no entitlement liberal. Indeed, his auto bailout was the quintessence of a moral economy. Using federal largesse, the president saved the auto industry and enabled Springsteen voters to keep their jobs. In this way, "big government" buttressed working-class norms of "earned" benefits. In 2012, Springsteen voters rewarded Obama with their votes. A savvy politician, Obama understands this political calculus. But the educated middle class who comprise the Democratic Party's policy intellectual class and primary electorate push entitlement liberalism and boutique social issues. The platforms of the 2020 Democratic presidential aspirants were littered with Medicare-for-All, free college, defund-the-police, and open borders proposals that were an anathema to working-class voters. So long as the Obama coalition pushed a liberalism that antagonized working class norms, Democrats, no matter the racial and demographic profile of who they nominate, will struggle with these voters.

Race matters. White working-class racism complicated Obama's political task. But Obama's struggles are not novel. For a generation, white Democrats have also scuffled to win the Springsteen and Stanley voters. Obama failed to reach the transformational summit because a loud and influential segment of the progressive political class embrace policies that antagonize white-working class voters. Obama's multiracial lineage was surely a significant obstacle in keeping white working-class voters in his coalition. But the more significant impediment was a progressive political class totally blind to white working-class sensibilities.

By any standard metric, Obama's political career and presidency were glowing successes. The three-term state senator took the nation by storm via an electric and unifying keynote at the 2004 Democratic National Convention. Defeating Hillary Clinton for the 2008 Democratic presidential nomination in a historic and grinding campaign, Obama earned the highest vote share, 53 percent, of any Democrat presidential candidate since LBJ in 1964. In the White House, he passed signature domestic legislation, Obamacare, the auto industry bailout, and 2009 stimulus bill, oversaw seven years of historic job growth, and presided over significant foreign policy achievements, the Libyan Intervention, Paris Climate Accords, and the Iranian Joint Comprehensive Plan of Action. Leaving office with an

---

[61] Gareth Davies, *From Opportunity to Entitlement: The Transformation and Decline of Great Society Liberalism* (Lawrence: Kansas University Press, 1996).

approval rating of 58 percent, he placed a notch just below Bill Clinton and Ronald Reagan, which was doubly impressive in an era of hyper partisanship.[62]

But Obama did not set a standard metric for himself. Long before he had even clinched the Democratic nomination, he made Ronald Reagan his measuring stick for success. Rightly sensing that the Iraq War and President Bush's unpopularity had created a unique political moment, Obama cast his candidacy and the 2008 election as a liberal reply to Reagan and 1980.[63] It was Obama who set the "transformational presidential" bar. He and his presidency should be judged by his own standards. By that metric, his presidency, despite its many markers of success, ultimately fell short of its potential. Springsteen and Stanley voters are necessary for the Obama coalition to become an enduring majority. To be competitive with these voters, Democrats can look to a past in which class politics were also culturally harmonized with these groups' norms and values.

References

Abramowitz, Alan and Ruy Teixeira. "The Decline of the White Working Class and the Rise of a Mass Upper-Middle Class." *Political Science Quarterly* 124, no. 3 (Fall 2009): 391–422.

Abramowitz, Alan and Ruy Teixeira, "The Decline of the White Working Class and the Rise of a Mass Upper Middle Class." *Brookings Working Paper*, April 2008, https://www.brookings.edu/articles/the-decline-of-the-white-working-class-and-the-rise-of-a-mass-upper-middle-class/.

Adams, Mason. "In Coal Country, A Political Journey from Blue to Deep Red." *The Virginia Center for Investigative Journalism*, November 1, 2020, https://vcij.org/stories/blue-to-deep-red.

Berkes, Howard. "Obama Made Inroads into the Rural Base." *All Things Considered*, November 8, 2008, https://www.npr.org/2008/11/08/96782692/obama-made-inroads-into-rural-republican-base.

Bloodworth, Jeff. *Losing the Center: The Decline of American Liberalism, 1968–1992*. Lexington: University of Kentucky Press, 2014.

Boyer, Peter. "The Appalachia Problem: Obama Goes to Rural Virginia." *The New Yorker*, October 6, 2008, https://www.newyorker.com/magazine/2008/10/06/the-appalachian-problem.

Brookings Institute Blueprint for American Prosperity. "The Political Geography of Virginia & Florida." Accessed November 9, 2022, https://www.brookings.edu/wp-content/uploads/2016/06/maps_figures.pdf.

---

[62] "Obama Leaves Office on High Note, But Public Has Mixed Views of Accomplishments," *Pew Research Center*, December 14, 2016, https://www.pewresearch.org/politics/2016/12/14/obama-leaves-office-on-high-note-but-public-has-mixed-views-of-accomplishments/.

[63] Michael Duffy and Michael Scherer, "The Role Model: What Obama Sees in Reagan," *Time*, January 27, 2011, http://content.time.com/time/magazine/article/0,9171,2044712-2,00.html; "In Their Own Words: Obama on Reagan," *New York Times*, https://archive.nytimes.com/www.nytimes.com/ref/us/politics/21seelye-text.html?source=post_page/, accessed November 9, 2022.

Brown, Carrie Budhoff. "Obama and Blue Collar Voters: Take 2." *Politico*, December 1, 2011, https://www.politico.com/story/2011/12/obama-and-blue-collar-voters-take-2-069491.

Brownstein, Ron. "Obama's Support in Rust Belt, Sun Belt Very Different." *The Atlantic*. November 2, 2012, https://www.theatlantic.com/politics/archive/2012/11/obamas-support-in-rust-belt-sun-belt-very-different/429300/.

Champagne, Anthony, Douglas Harris, James Riddlesperger, and Garrison Nelson. *The Austin-Boston Connection: Five Decades of House Democratic Leadership, 1937–1989*, College Station: Texas A&M University Press, 2009.

Chicago Tribune. "Bluegrass Legend Backing Obama." October 5, 2008.

Cohen, Micah. "In Ohio, Poll Shows Benefit for Auto Bailout to Obama." *New York Times*, November 5, 2012, https://archive.nytimes.com/fivethirtyeight.blogs.nytimes.com/2012/11/05/in-ohio-polls-show-benefit-of-auto-rescue-to-obama/?searchResultPosition=3.

Cohn, Nate. "How the Obama Coalition Crumbled, Leaving an Opening for Trump." *New York Times*, December 23, 2016, https://www.nytimes.com/2016/12/23/upshot/how-the-obama-coalition-crumbled-leaving-an-opening-for-trump.html.

Culhane, Charles. "White House Report/Nixon Eyes Blue-Collar Workers as Potential Source of Votes in '72." *The National Journal* (January 30, 1971): 232 ((Blockade Seitenzahlen)).

Davies, Gareth. *From Opportunity to Entitlement: The Transformation and Decline of Great Society Liberalism*. Lawrence: Kansas University Press, 1996.

Duffy, Michael, and Michael Scherer. "The Role Model: What Obama Sees in Reagan." *Time*, January 27, 2011, http://content.time.com/time/magazine/article/0,9171,2044712-2,00.html.

Ehrenfreund, Max, and Jeff Guo. "If You've Ever Described People as 'White Working Class,' Read This." *Washington Post*, November 23, 2016, https://www.washingtonpost.com/news/wonk/wp/2016/11/22/who-exactly-is-the-white-working-class-and-what-do-they-believe-good-questions/.

Emmons, William R., Ana Hernandez Kent, and Lowell R. Ricketts, "The White Working Class: National Trends, Then and Now," *The Federal Reserve Bank St. Louis*, 20 May 20, 2019, https://www.stlouisfed.org/on-the-economy/2019/september/white-working-class-national-trends-then-now.

Galston, William. "Why Ohio Matters: President Obama Can't Win the 2012 Without It." *Brookings*, March 4, 2011, https://www.brookings.edu/articles/why-ohio-matters-president-obama-cant-win-the-2012-election-without-it/.

Goldenberg, Suzanne. "Born to Run: Springsteen Throws His Weight Behind Obama." *The Guardian*, April 16, 2008; https://www.theguardian.com/world/2008/apr/17/barackobama.uselections2008.

Hackett Fischer, David. *Albion's Seed: Four British Folkways in America*. New York: Oxford University Press, 1989, 606.

Hamby, Alonzo. *Liberalism and Its Challengers: From FDR to Bush*, New York: Oxford University Press, 1992.

Hayden, William. "Appalachian Diversity: African-American, Hispanic/Latino, and Other Populations." *Journal of Appalachian Studies* 10, no. 3 (2004): 293–306. http://www.jstor.org/stable/41446641.

Kazin, Michael. *What it Took to Win: A History of the Democratic Party*, New York: Farrar, Straus, & Giroux, 2022.

Kozmetsky, George, and Piyu Yue. *The Economic Transformation of the United States, 1950–2000*. West Lafayette: Purdue University Press, 2005, 163.

Kreps, Daniel. "We Need a Change." *Rolling Stone*, October 3, 2008, https://www.rollingstone.com/politics/politics-news/bluegrass-legend-ralph-stanley-endorses-obama-we-need-a-change-96834/.

Lupu, Noam, and Nicholas Carnes. "Trump Didn't Bring White Working Class Voters to the Party, He Kept Them Away." *The Vanderbilt Project on Unity & American Democracy*, April 15, 2021, https://www.vanderbilt.edu/unity/2021/04/15/trump-didnt-bring-white-working-class-voters-to-the-republican-party-he-kept-them-away/.

MacGillis, Alec. "A Gift for Snickering Pundits: A Map." *The New Republic*, May 22, 2012, https://newrepublic.com/authors/alec-macgillis?page=19.

Marger, Martin. *Race & Ethnic Relations: American and Global Perspectives*. New York: Wadsworth, 2008, 37.

Martin, Melissa. "Appalachian Americans." *Portsmouth Daily Times*, January 4, 2018, https://www.portsmouth-dailytimes.com/opinion/22902/appalachian-americans.

McCormick, John. "Confident Obama Campaigns with Springsteen." *Chicago Tribune*, November 2, 2008, https://www.starbeacon.com/archives/confident-obama-campaigns-with-springsteen/article_fe1155f1-a357-5f82-a383-907250804a8b.html.

Mead, Walter Russell. "The Jacksonian Tradition: And American Foreign Policy." *The National Interest* (Winter 1999/2000): 5–29.

New York Times. "In Their Own Words: Obama on Reagan." https://archive.nytimes.com/www.nytimes.com/ref/us/politics/21seelye-text.html?source=post_page/, accessed November 9, 2022.

New York Times. "Labor Unions Claim Credit for Obama's Victory." November 7, 2012, https://archive.nytimes.com/thecaucus.blogs.nytimes.com/2012/11/07/labor-unions-claim-credit-for-obamas-victory/?searchResultPosition=1.

New York Times. "Pennsylvania: Election Results 2008." December 9, 2008, https://www.nytimes.com/elections/2008/results/states/pennsylvania.html.

Norden, Chris. "Opinions: Ralph Stanley Was Brave." *The Spokesman Review*, January 30, 2016, https://www.spokesman.com/stories/2016/jun/30/ralph-stanley-brave-endorse-obama/.

Oshnock, Kevin. "Recent Republican Dominance in Appalachia," Master's Thesis. Appalachian State University. 2019, https://libres.uncg.edu/ir/asu/f/Oshnock_Kevin_Thesis_Dec_2019.pdf.

Pew Research Center. "Obama Leaves Office on High Note, But Public Has Mixed Views of Accomplishments." December 14, 2016, https://www.pewresearch.org/politics/2016/12/14/obama-leaves-office-on-high-note-but-public-has-mixed-views-of-accomplishments/.

Ruy Teixeira, and Alan Abramowitz, "The Decline of the White Working Class and the Rise of a Mass Upper Middle Class." Brookings Working Paper. April 2008, https://www.brookings.edu/research/the-decline-of-thewhite-workingclass-and-therise-of-a-massupper-middleclass/, 7.

Skelley, Geoffrey. "The Old Dominion's Political Map." The UVA Center for Politics. Accessed November 9, 2022, https://centerforpolitics.org/crystalball/articles/the-old-dominions-political-map.

Smith, Ben. "Obama on Small Town Pa.: Clinging to Religion, Guns, & Xenophobia." *Politico*. April 11, 2008, https://www.politico.com/blogs/ben-smith/2008/04/obama-on-small-town-pa-clinging-to-religion-guns-xenophobia-007737.

Statista. "Educational Attainment Distribution in the United States, 1960–2021." Accessed November 9, 2022, https://www.statista.com/statistics/184260/educational-attainment-in-the-us/.

Sutton, David. "Living Poor and Voting Rich in Appalachia." *Appalachian Journal* 32, no. 3 (Spring 2005): 340–351.

Sutton, David. "The 2008 Presidential Campaign in Appalachia: Reading from the Margins." *Appalachian Journal* 36, no. 3/4 (Spring/Summer 2009): 188–198.

Teixeira, Ray, and John Halpin. "The Obama Coalition in the 2012 Election and Beyond." *The Center for American Progress*. December 4, 2012, https://www.americanprogress.org/article/the-obama-coalition-in-the-2012-election-and-beyond.

The Appalachian Regional Commission. "Population and Age in Appalachia." Accessed November 8, 2022, https://www.arc.gov/appalachias-population/.

The Appalachian Regional Commission. "Poverty Rates in Appalachia." Accessed November 8, 2022, https://www.arc.gov/map/poverty-rates-in-appalachia-2013-2017.

Wilson, Valerie. "People of Color Will Be the Majority of the American Working Class by 2032." *Economic Policy Institute*. September 11, 2022, https://www.epi.org/publication/the-changing-demographics-of-americas-working-class/.

Working Class Perspectives. "The White Working Class Vote in 2008." December 15, 2008, https://workingclassstudies.wordpress.com/2008/12/15/the-white-working-class-vote-in-2008/.

Young, Nancy Beck. *Wright Patman: Populism, Liberalism, and the American Dream*. Dallas: Southern Methodist University Press, 2000.

Part II: **Planning, Governance, and Policy Making**

Jack B. Greenberg
Chapter 4
Why Health Care Came First, and Other Observations on Barack Obama's Early Domestic Policy Agenda

"What's the first thing you're going to do as president?," Malia Obama asked her father soon after his election as the 44th President of the United States. In reply, the elder Obama reaffirmed his election night commitment that a puppy would be joining the First Family when it moved into the White House. In fact, Malia was pushing further. "I'm serious, like the first political thing?"[1]

Barack Obama's oldest daughter was pressing her president-elect father on a question that often surrounds incoming executives and even presidential candidates – what is going to be your top priority, your signature issue?[2] This consideration was, perhaps, especially salient in Obama's case. On the one hand, he was seemingly well-situated to enact considerable change. He defeated Arizona Senator John McCain (R-AZ) by a comfortable seven-point margin in the popular vote, winning the most votes of any presidential nominee heretofore and flipping nine states that George W. Bush had won in 2004 from red to blue (along with Nebraska's 2nd congressional district). He would enter office with the highest approval rating of any president at the outset of his term since John F. Kennedy and enjoyed strong Democratic majorities in both chambers of Congress, even achieving a filibuster-proof Democratic majority in the Senate from July 2009 to January 2010.

At the same time, Obama's political inexperience and associated lack of a legislative track record amplified ambiguity regarding the direction of his administration. His campaign had steered away from defining itself in explicitly ideological terms, relying on the watchwords of "hope," "change," and "yes we can" versus a catechism in the vein of his predecessor's "compassionate conservatism." This flexibility

---

[1] Jonathan Alter, *The Promise: President Obama, Year One* (New York: Simon & Schuster, 2010), p. 38.
[2] For example, Chuck Todd of NBC News, citing Obama's experience in office, admonished the 2020 Democratic presidential candidates during a debate he moderated that they may only get "one shot at doing something big" in their first term and proceeded to ask them on what issue they would thus expend their political capital. NBC News, "Democratic Presidential Debate – June 27 (Full)," YouTube, June 27, 2019.

Jack B. Greenberg, Yale University

was, in a sense, central to his appeal. He was, by his own admission, a "Rorschach test."[3] Voters were free to interpret his promise of transformation amidst political and economic crisis in a direction amenable to their aims. Where Obama's presidency would ultimately go, though, would have to be settled in due course.

In a larger project, I interrogate the premises upon which Obama and every other president from Richard Nixon onward (save Gerald Ford) developed his domestic policy agenda at the start of his tenure. I evaluate each president's top domestic priorities on the basis of their *selection*, *specification*, and *sequencing* and seek to recover the president's agency in elevating these agenda items. Specifically, I discuss the president's agenda with reference to his "political project," his evaluation of the country's challenges and how he wishes to bring about transformational change to the polity.[4] In so doing, I attempt to clarify the significance of presidential leadership across American political development.

For the purposes of this entry, I take up the most significant domestic policy prioritization decision Obama made: his elevation of health care reform as his "signature issue." I adopt an agency-centered approach to evaluating this choice, illustrating how a focus solely on the external environment Obama confronted fails to account for health care's prioritization and highlighting why this issue fit the President's political project. I argue that making health care reform a top priority afforded Obama the opportunity to reconstruct the American political economy in a manner sensitive to the burdens the Great Recession imposed on households and the state. Additionally, it would allow him to claim victory on, arguably, the proverbial policy issue for Democratic administrations past. Given his political aims, elevating health care was the right choice for the start of his tenure.

The Case for Agency

Getting comprehensive health care reform enacted, particularly achieving universal coverage, was a daunting task. Presidents ranging from Franklin D. Roosevelt to Bill Clinton attempted to get it done – and failed. The administration understood, no matter Obama's standing in Washington and nationally, how difficult passing health care reform would be. Chief-of-staff Rahm Emanuel, alongside Vice President Joe Biden and Senate Majority Leader Harry Reid (D-NV), advised

---

3 Peter Baker, "Obama Team Weighs What to Take On First," *New York Times*, November 8, 2008.
4 I take this term from Stephen Skowronek, *The Politics Presidents Make: Leadership from John Adams to Bill Clinton* (Cambridge: Belknap Press, 1997), p. 79.

against taking on this battle. It was ultimately a prioritization decision of which Obama maintained full authorship, with only Domestic Policy Council Chair Melody Barnes backing him. Emanuel had been especially vocal in attempting to persuade Obama to adopt a different path forward. "I begged him not to do this," Emanuel recalled, thinking the political risk was too great.[5] Part of the pushback had to do with the administration's reading of public opinion data, which suggested – consistent with polling Obama's presidential campaign had consulted – that energy was a higher priority for voters than health care was.[6] In fact, according to polling conducted by Pew Research Center in January 2009, both "dealing with the energy problem" and "improving the education system" (along with creating jobs and improving the economy amidst the recession) took precedence over reducing health care costs and providing coverage to the uninsured.[7] Health care was a salient issue, but other significant problems likewise registered with the public and could have taken precedence in the new administration.

Meanwhile, Congress would pull Obama in competing directions. Some on Capitol Hill were fervent about the new president pursuing health care reform, including Senate Finance Chair Max Baucus (D-MT). In a message to Obama the day after the new president was elected, Baucus immediately went to work urging his Senate colleague to elevate health care reform as an issue.[8] Baucus continued this campaign in the public eye, releasing an 89-page health care proposal a week later.[9]

Other prominent members of Congress, however, had other priorities in mind for the green Obama. A politically diverse group of senators from the President's side of the aisle, ranging from the moderate Jim Webb (D-VA) to the self-declared socialist Bernie Sanders (I-VT), convened soon after Obama's inauguration to develop an informal working group that would press the administration to adopt a more zealous tact on Wall Street.[10] All the while, prospects for an early bipartisan victory seemed to emerge with the assemblage of a new "Three Amigos" coalition comprising Senators John Kerry (D-MA), Joe Lieberman (I-CT), and

---

5 Alter, *The Promise*, p. 395.
6 Alter, *The Promise*, p. 32, 245.
7 Pew Research Center for the People & the Press, Pew Research Center: January 2009 Political Survey, Princeton Survey Research Associates International (Ithaca: Roper Center for Public Opinion Research, 2009).
8 Petra Bartosiewicz and Marissa Miley, "The Too Polite Revolution: Why the Recent Campaign to Pass Comprehensive Climate Legislation in the United States Failed," *SSRN*, http://dx.doi.org/10.2139/ssrn.2200690, January 14, 2013.
9 Drew Armstrong, "Baucus Outlines Health Care Plan," *CQ Almanac*, November 12, 2008.
10 Manu Raju, "Dorgan Emerges as Obama's Dem Foe," *Politico*, April 27, 2009; Ron Suskind, *Confidence Men: Wall Street, Washington, and the Education of a President* (New York: Harper, 2011), p. 238.

Lindsey Graham (R-SC) that was committed to developing a moderate alternative to Senator Barbara Boxer's (D-CA) "cap-and-trade" environmental legislation.[11] John McCain had even become involved in the effort early on, meeting with his erstwhile rival during the transition to discuss the prospects for such a bill.[12] On the House side, Energy and Commerce Chair Henry Waxman (D-CA) and his staff threw themselves into developing cap-and-trade legislation, which ultimately passed the House in June 2009 as "Waxman-Markey."[13] Though Waxman had a considerable role to play in the drafting of health care reform,[14] environmental reform appeared to be the powerful committee chair's "top priority."[15]

Therefore, Obama's prioritization decision on health care indicates that he was more than a passive cipher in relation to the external environment he confronted. He had room to set the course of his agenda for himself. In so doing, he likewise appeared to have agency to go beyond the confines of his campaign commitments. As late in the campaign as his second general election debate with McCain, Obama referred to health care as "priority number two." Energy was what "we have to deal with today," the top concern.[16] Moreover, Obama had merely pledged during his campaign to enact comprehensive health care reform by the end of his first *term*. He had offered no explicit indication that it would feature as a first move.[17]

Many other issues had been the subject of consistent attention throughout his campaign. Surveying Obama's campaign book (*Change We Can Believe In*) and speeches at major junctures in the campaign (his launch, becoming the presumptive nominee, accepting the Democratic nomination, and declaring victory in November), health care and energy both come up a lot. However, education, tax reform, infrastructure, research and development/innovation, Social Security, pensions, and "fiscal responsibility" (e.g., a promise to cut the deficit in half and remain mindful of America's debt obligations) likewise featured prominently.[18] For Obama, introducing

---

11 Ryan Lizza, "As the World Burns," *New Yorker*, October 3, 2010.
12 Barack Obama, *A Promised Land* (Crown: New York, 2022), p. 499.
13 Amanda Reilly and Kevin Bogardus, "7 Years Later, Failed Waxman-Markey Bill Still Makes Waves," *E&E News*, June 27, 2016.
14 Darren Samuelson and Joanne Kenen, "Obamacare Writer Turns a Page," *Politico*, January 30, 2014.
15 Jeanne Cummings, "Waxman Coup Has Loud Echo on K Street," *Politico*, November 25, 2008.
16 C-SPAN, "Second 2008 Presidential Debate," YouTube, October 8, 2008.
17 Barack Obama, "Remarks at the Iowa Jefferson-Jackson Dinner in Des Moines," American Presidency Project, November 10, 2007.
18 Barack Obama, *Change We Can Believe In: Barack Obama's Plan to Renew America's Promise* (New York: Three Rivers Press, 2008); Barack Obama, "Remarks Announcing Candidacy for President in Springfield, Illinois," American Presidency Project, February 10, 2007; Barack Obama,

an issue on the trail was necessary but not sufficient for its elevation once he was in the White House.[19] He conceded during his bid that "we'll have to set priorities" and "we'll have to make hard choices" once he was in office.[20] Understanding his particular choices thus necessitates looking beyond the campaign.

A Project in Motion

For some presidents, having agency in office means elevating issues of personal significance, as was the case with George W. Bush and his administration's early focus on education.[21] While Obama claimed at the time – and has since asserted retrospectively – that health care reform was of personal significance to him,[22] the track record that would verify the depth of this personal commitment was thin. For example, in the Senate, Obama privately commented that his main foci were energy, education, and non-proliferation. Health care did not make the cut.[23] During a March 2007 health care forum with his Democratic primary opponent, Sen. Hillary Clinton (D-NY), Clinton's expertise on the issue (which owed to her unsuccessful leadership on health care reform at the start of her husband's presidency) clearly dwarfed Obama's, who appeared out of his depth in discussing the topic.[24]

Thus, I argue less that health care reform was of intrinsic importance to Obama than of instrumental value to his political prospects: reconstructing the American political economy and securing his standing as a hero of American liberalism. On this first aspect, Obama's orientation toward politics and policy was deeply structural. Americans needed to come together to remake the American political economy into a more just order. It was a sensibility that first emerged in

---

"Remarks in St. Paul, Minnesota Claiming the Democratic Presidential Nomination Following the Montana and South Dakota Primaries," American Presidency Project, June 3, 2008; Barack Obama, "Address Accepting the Presidential Nomination at the Democratic National Convention in Denver: 'The American Promise,'" American Presidency Project, August 28, 2008; Barack Obama, "Address in Chicago Accepting Election as the 44th President of the United States," American Presidency Project, November 4, 2008.

19 Alter, *The Promise*, p. 32.
20 Obama, "Remarks Announcing Candidacy."
21 I develop this argument further in Jack B. Greenberg, "The Case for Agency: Three Dimensions of Discretion in Presidential Agenda Construction."
22 Obama, *A Promised Land*, p. 87.
23 Alter, *The Promise*, p. 33.
24 Glenn Thrush and Carrie Budoff Brown, "Obama's Health Care Conversion," *Politico*, September 23, 2013.

his co-authored tract with his law school classmate Robert Fisher, a manifesto in which he denounced the "rudderless pragmatism" of the post-Reagan era and called for "long-term, structural change, change that might break the zero-sum equation that pits powerless blacks [against] only slightly less powerless whites."[25] The critique cuts deeper, with Obama and Fisher orienting themselves against a particular pathology of Democratic politics – "a static conception of pluralism" – that calls for "buying off" interest groups, particularly the middle class, in service of electoral victories.[26] Obama lacked patience with this approach, as historian Timothy Shenk notes, seeing it as at odds with the articulation of clear principles around which a new (and "lasting") Democratic majority could form.[27]

He had a more substantive reformulation in mind, both in "Transformative Politics" and as his career progressed. As Obama ascended to the national stage, he continued to castigate the myopia and superficiality he found in Democratic thinking, lamenting in his 2006 book (*Audacity of Hope*) that "individually, Democratic legislators and candidates propose a host of sensible if incremental ideas, on energy and education, health care and homeland security, hoping that it all adds up to something resembling a governing philosophy."[28] His leadership would offer something more comprehensive. His governing approach called back to the Progressive tradition, reimagining structures to better service the common good.[29] As the Hudson Institute's William Schambra highlighted, "for [Obama], governing means not just addressing discrete challenges as they arise, but formulating comprehensive policies aimed at giving large systems – and indeed society itself – more rational and coherent forms and functions."[30] This impulse toward comprehensiveness, as Schambra notes, is evident across Obama's discussion of different policy priorities once he was president. On health care, he highlighted how "there are those who believe we should wait to solve this problem or take a more incremental approach or simply do nothing . . . It's the same kind of Washington that

---

25 Barack Obama and Robert Fisher, "Outline" in "Transformative Politics," 1991, 1; Barack Obama and Robert Fisher, "Race and Rights Rhetoric" in "Transformative Politics," 1991, p. 64. I thank David Garrow for providing me with access to this manuscript.
26 Obama and Fisher, "Outline," pp. 1.
27 Timothy Shenk, "A Lost Manuscript Shows the Fire Barack Obama Couldn't Reveal on the Campaign Trail," *New York Times*, October 7, 2022.
28 Barack Obama, *The Audacity of Hope: Thoughts on Reclaiming the American Dream* (New York: Crown, 2006), p. 39.
29 For more on the relationship between Obama and Progressivism, see James T. Kloppenberg's chapter, "Barack Obama and the Traditions of Progressive Reform," in *The Progressives' Century: Political Reform, Constitutional Government, and the Modern American State*, eds. Stephen Skowronek, Stephen M. Engel and Bruce Ackerman (New Haven: Yale University Press, 2016), pp. 431–52.
30 William Schambra, "Obama and the Policy Approach," *National Affairs* 57, Fall 2009.

has ignored big challenges and put off tough decisions for decades, and it is precisely the kind of small thinking that has led us into the current predicament."[31] With education and job training, "it's time to move beyond the idea that we need several different programs to address several different problems. We need one comprehensive policy that addresses our comprehensive challenges."[32] And in response to the unfolding economic crisis, Obama predicted that "what I think will change ... was a situation where corporate profits in the financial sector were such a heavy part of our overall profitability over the last decade."[33]

Across these issues, Obama was building toward a "New Foundation," a political program he unveiled in a speech at Georgetown in April 2009. The mantra was not invoked frequently (as George W. Bush's "compassionate conservatism" or Donald Trump's "America First" ideology were during their presidencies), but it struck at the intentionality behind Obama's program.[34] It conveyed, according to Obama adviser John Podesta, how "three big reform projects – health, energy, and education – are part of a coherent overall economic strategy for sustainable equitable growth."[35] Interrelated problems needed to be addressed comprehensively. In distilling his thinking, Obama detailed how the "house upon a rock" the country would build during his presidency would consist of five pillars:

> Number one, new rules for Wall Street that will reward drive and innovation, not reckless risk-taking; number two, new investments in education that will make our workforce more skilled and competitive; number three, new investments in renewable energy and technology that will create new jobs and new industries; number four, new investments in health care that will cut costs for families and businesses; and number five, new savings in our federal budget that will bring down the debt for future generations.[36]

Only through this comprehensive approach could the United States set itself up for prosperity in the long term, not only recovering from the recession but providing for a more equitable and prosperous society. Change on the margin was insufficient for Obama coming out of law school, and it remained so when he was in the Oval Office.

---

31 Barack Obama, "Remarks on the Nomination of Regina M. Benjamin to be Surgeon General and an Exchange with Reporters," American Presidency Project, July 13, 2009.
32 Barack Obama, "Remarks on the National Economy and Job Training," American Presidency Project, May 8, 2009.
33 David Leonhardt, "After the Great Recession," *New York Times Magazine*, April 28, 2009.
34 For more context on the phrase and its usage, see Peter Baker, "From Obama, a New Deal, or at Least a New Phrase," *New York Times*, May 15, 2009.
35 Baker, "From Obama, a New Deal, or at Least a New Phrase."
36 Barack Obama, "Remarks on the National Economy," American Presidency Project, April 14, 2009.

This tendency toward comprehensiveness appears to have been more than a public posture. Two senior White House officials attested to how Obama appreciated the depth of the crises the nation faced and their interrelated nature. Mona Sutphen, Deputy Chief-of-Staff for policy at the start of the Obama presidency, emphasized that the administration did not consider these issues in isolation:

> . . . the President-elect was very clear at the time that he didn't want his entire affirmative agenda to disappear just because we were dealing with crises. So during the transition and after, we had policy teams do what Rahm would call "racking and stacking" priorities and policy fixes. Teams would come in and say "this is what this problem is. This is the path to solving it" – legislative, administrative, combination of both . . . so whether it was education or the energy transition for example, we'd find a range of opportunities both legislatively and policy-wise to respond to a crisis but do it in a way that also had some affirmative agenda bits in it. The Recovery Act and associated policy became a very clear opportunity zone, I would say, for the administration.[37]

Another White House official offered comments in kind, emphasizing the depth of the challenges the administration confronted and the need Obama felt to address them all over the length of his tenure:

> I always think of it as four separate once-in-a-generation challenges. The very first one was the imploding economy, losing 600,000 jobs a month. So that was an enormous challenge, and economists were saying the same. Our country ran the very real risk of falling into a second Great Depression. So there's that issue. The second is the President inherited two wars, so he had to deal with those. Third, we had a broken health care system. It was affecting all parts of the economy and was terrible for the American families. And the [fourth] was climate change, which is an existential threat. So instead of the President saying "I am only going to deal with one of these," his approach was we have to deal with all four, and we're going to deal with all four, and we're going to try to get legislation passed on all four.[38]

There were more isolated items on the agenda early on, like passage of the Lily Ledbetter Fair Pay Act and the attempted closure of the Guantanamo Bay detention camp.[39] Yet what guided Obama and his team from the start was a keen recognition of the interconnected nature of the American political economy. Building the "new foundation" the President envisioned would require untangling these knots in a manner that made the most of the opportunities embedded in the political and economic circumstances the administration encountered.

---

37 Author's interview with Mona Sutphen, January 13, 2023.
38 Author's interview with senior White House official, May 22, 2023.
39 Carol E. Lee, "Obama Legacy Defense Gets Early Start," *Politico*, October 28, 2009.

Of course, health care reform was not the only way that Obama could have made his mark as a comprehensive reformer. Prospects for the administration's energy policy – the "close second" priority behind health care, according to one senior White House official – were likewise understood in comprehensive terms.[40] As Obama relayed in his "New Foundation" speech at Georgetown, "Transitioning to a clean energy economy will not be easy. But we can no longer delay putting a framework for a clean energy economy in place. That needs to be done now."[41] The cap-and-trade legislation that advanced through the House under the purview of Energy and Commerce Chair Henry Waxman fulfilled that criteria, which Obama referred to as "a major step forward in building the kind of clean energy economy that will reduce America's dependence on foreign oil."[42] And yet, at the critical moment of decision, a call Obama compared to "choosing between two of your children," he directed Waxman to prioritize comprehensive health care legislation over the energy bill.[43]

Among this set of opportunities for comprehensive change consistent with Obama's project, putting health care first made particular sense in the context of the financial crisis, both at the micro- and macrolevels of the economy. As Ron Suskind reported, "Obama thought this reform was the ideal match for the stimulus: a temporary boost coupled with a long-term restructuring *of every kitchen table's budget, and that of the federal government.*" On the one hand, he thought it was the best way "to restore the underlying confidence of a people who lived with too little security and too much fear in their lives,"[44] furnishing a more sustainable future for a people in dire need of relief. At the same time, getting health care costs down was urgent for the fiscal state of the country more broadly. ". . . the President felt very passionately that you cannot spend 20% of GDP on health care – a single sector – and think you're going to have a healthy and growing economy," Sutphen said. "It's just not feasible, particularly as the country gets grayer. So he was really passionate about trying to take it on."[45] Another senior White House official backed up this claim, saying that "there was no way to be financially responsible without dealing with health care reform" and that there

---

40 Author's interview with senior White House official, May 22, 2023.
41 Obama, "National Economy," April 14, 2009.
42 Barack Obama, "Remarks Following a Meeting with Democratic Congressional Leadership," American Presidency Project, May 13, 2009.
43 Alter, *The Promise*, 255.
44 Suskind, *Confidence Men*, 178. Emphasis added.
45 Author's interview with Mona Sutphen, January 13, 2023.

was "a personal commitment" from Obama on the issue in part because "he knew ... how damaging it was to our overall economic health."[46]

The White House very much believed that the climate crisis was an existential threat.[47] However, there was no doubt within the administration that economic recovery, specifically averting another Great Depression, was the overriding (though not the singular) priority for this presidency.[48] Health care reform was deemed part and parcel of that effort.[49] Climate change failed to inspire the same recognition, and it was thus placed on the back burner – and, with the Senate's ultimate refusal to take on the cap-and-trade legislation that had cleared the House, a priority deferred became a policy proposal unrealized.[50]

Echoes of Camelot

Even absent the financial crisis, though, there was a particular partisan and ideological legacy to health care reform that made tackling it an attractive prospect for Obama in defining his legacy. Massachusetts Senator Ted Kennedy (D-MA), in a final consequential act of his nearly half-century-long career in public office, had offered to endorse Obama before the "Super Tuesday" primaries with the proviso that the Illinois senator would make health care reform his "top priority," a condition to which Obama acceded.[51]

Kennedy would have limited opportunity to enforce this bargain; he was diagnosed with brain cancer in May 2008, making only limited appearances in the Senate during the 111th Congress before succumbing to his illness in August 2009.[52] Yet what this deal signified was less a practical political transaction than a shared sense between Kennedy and Obama of where they stood in the history of the Democratic Party and American liberalism. Kennedy cemented that mutual recognition in his primetime address during the Democratic National Convention, where the

---

[46] Author's interview with senior White House official, May 22, 2023.
[47] Author's interview with senior White House official, May 22, 2023.
[48] Timothy F. Geithner, *Stress Test: Reflections on Financial Crises* (New York: Crown, 2014), p. 258.
[49] Michael D'Antonio, *A Consequential President: The Legacy of Barack Obama* (New York: Thomas Dunne Books, 2017), 126.
[50] Alan Greenblatt, "How Cap and Trade Was 'Trashed,'" *NPR*, April 26, 2010.
[51] Dan Balz and Haynes Johnson, "How Obama Snared the Lion of the Senate," *Washington Post*, August 3, 2009.
[52] Emily Pierce, "Kennedy's Death Starts to Hit Home in the Capitol," *Roll Call*, September 4, 2009.

ailing liberal icon cast Obama as the agent who would "begin anew" the work he had undertaken: "And this is the cause of my life – new hope that we will break the old gridlock and guarantee that every American – north, south, east, west, young, old – will have decent, quality health care as a fundamental right and not a privilege. We can meet these challenges with Barack Obama. Yes, we can, and finally, yes, we will." With Obama at the helm, "the torch will be passed again to a new generation of Americans" and the "country will be committed to *his* cause" – albeit one that Kennedy was defining around a particular policy priority of his choosing.[53] As Kennedy had in his speech endorsing Obama earlier in the year, he availed himself of the opportunity at the twilight of his career to name the heir to Camelot.[54] Obama would supply the leadership that Kennedy had offered to his party for decades and rise to the liberal pantheon his slain brothers inhabited.

For Obama, whose ambition was as profound as it was documented,[55] picking the proverbial fight of enacting comprehensive health care reform was a noble and fitting challenge, and he took his commitment to Kennedy seriously. As Tom Daschle (D-SD), former Senate majority leader and Obama's initial choice to lead the Department of Health and Human Services, reflected, the candidate "felt an obligation" to pick up the defining effort of Kennedy's career.[56] Obama reinforced this idea in his post-presidential memoir, *A Promised Land*. In discussing Kennedy's endorsement of his campaign, he lent credence to how his administration was meant to deliver on the promise of Camelot. "[Senior adviser David Axelrod] would call it a symbolic passing of the torch, and I could see what it meant to him," Obama wrote. "It was as if, in our campaign, Teddy recognized a familiar chord, and was reaching back to a time before his brothers' assassinations, Vietnam, white backlash, riots, Watergate, plant closings, Altamont, and AIDS, back to when liberalism brimmed with optimism and a can-do spirit – the same spirit that had shaped my mother's sensibilities as a young woman and that she had funneled into me."[57] Later in the memoir, Obama offered further reference to Kennedy when discussing the day he signed the Affordable Care Act into law, tes-

---

53 Ted Kennedy, "2008 Democratic National Convention Speech," *American Rhetoric*, August 25, 2008. Emphasis added.
54 Ted Kennedy, "Kennedy Endorses Barack Obama," *CNN*, January 28, 2008.
55 Allison J. Pugh, "Harvard Law Review's New Leader Aims for Change," *The Ithaca Journal*, April 23, 1990; Liza Mundy, "A Series of Fortunate Events; Barack Obama Needed More than Talent and Ambition to Rocket from Obscure State Senator to Presidential Contender in Three Years. He Needed Serious Luck.," *Washington Post*, August 12, 2007.
56 Thrush and Brown, "Obama's Health Care"; Controversy surrounding Daschle's taxes ultimately led him to withdraw his nomination. Jeff Zeleny, "Daschle Ends Bid for Post; Obama Concedes Mistake," *New York Times*, February 3, 2009.
57 Obama, *Promised Land*, p. 129.

tifying to the late senator's influence on this policy push: "After everyone had left, well past midnight, I walked down the hallway to the Treaty Room . . . I thought about Ted Kennedy, and I thought about my mom. It was a good day."[58]

The claim that Obama picked health care because it was a singular Democratic priority is a common refrain.[59] Certainly, there have been numerous cases where a presidential administration appears to move forward on an issue for little reason beyond the fact that it is a standard partisan priority.[60] In the Obama case, though, health care allowed him to do more than simply make his copartisans happy. In an ode to the era of political possibilities that characterized Camelot, getting health care reform enacted would exemplify "how government can still get things done,"[61] fulfilling a Crohlian ambition of the state as a tool of "social and economic amelioration" familiar to Obama's Progressive sensibilities.[62] He would recover the unfulfilled promise of the presidency of John F. Kennedy. He would make his play for icon status in the history of American liberalism.

Reflections on 44

As scholars and citizens alike continue to contemplate the Obama presidency, an effort that, no doubt, will be aided immensely by the increased availability of archival materials from the administration and oral histories conducted by both the Columbia Center for Oral History Research and the University of Virginia's Miller Center, debates will endure as to whether Obama made the right prioritization

---

58 Obama, *Promised Land*, p. 426.
59 See, for example, Jamelle Bouie, "Why Did Obama Choose Health Care?," *American Prospect*, September 8, 2010 and Gabriel Debenedetti, *The Long Alliance: The Imperfect Union of Joe Biden and Barack Obama* (New York: Henry Holt and Company, 2022), p. 126.
60 One example of this dynamic is George W. Bush's elevation of tax cuts, which Joshua Bolten (who served as Bush's campaign policy director and deputy chief-of-staff for policy before ultimately becoming chief-of-staff) referred to as reflective of Bush's "relatively traditional Republican catechism" in an interview with me on October 27, 2021.
61 Robert Kuttner, *A Presidency in Peril: The Inside Story of Obama's Promise, Wall Street's Power, and the Struggle to Control Our Economic Future* (Chelsea Green: White River Junction, 2010), p. 238.
62 For more on the influence of Herbert Crohly on Obama's thinking, see James T. Kloppenberg, *Reading Obama: Dreams, Hopes, and the American Political Tradition* (Princeton: Princeton University Press, 2011).

decisions and picked the optimal strategies for pursuing his agenda.[63] These discussions will certainly extend beyond the bounds of what I am able to cover here,[64] but I hope they are nevertheless mindful of a few salient considerations on which this essay touched. Namely, that for whatever Obama's faults, there was genuine intentionality, cognizance, and risk associated with his decisionmaking.

Some of the very same sensibilities that informed the construction of Obama's agenda harken back to the earliest indications of his political thought at the beginning of his career. He had long been predisposed to "target" the American political economy as a site of comprehensive reform, deeply skeptical of change at the margins.[65] So too did his sensibilities and the events he confronted interact to configure his policy program. His agency to act was not boundless, but he evaluated the circumstances he inherited and set a course to maximize the political possibilities before him. In the language of his chief-of-staff, he would not let "a good crisis go to waste."[66]

As internal White House debate highlighted, Obama got to exercise much discretion in setting the trajectory for his administration. Reckoning with the economic crisis, and the other problems that beset the country at the time Obama took over, was a contest of interpretation – a contest in which Obama, by virtue of his standing as president, was well positioned to engage. Finally, though much ink has been spilled on where the administration's record of accomplishment fell short, especially against the early prognostications that Obama would usher in a "New New Deal" or harbored "reconstructive" potential,[67] observers of American politics ought not lose sight of the consequentiality of what Obama managed to get done: averting a Great Depression, reconfiguring the regulatory landscape of

---

[63] For an example of the former, see David Bookbinder, "Obama Had a Chance to Really Fight Climate Change. He Blew It," *Vox*, April 29, 2017. On the latter, see Steven M. Chu, Interview by the Columbia Center for Oral History Research, October 14, 2020.

[64] Among other considerations, this account did not tackle race and racism in the context of Obama's decisionmaking directly. For insight into both, see Claude A. Gregg III, *The Black President: Hope and Fury in the Age of Obama* (Baltimore: Johns Hopkins University, 2021) and Ta-Nehisi Coates, "Fear of a Black President," *The Atlantic*, September 2012 (along with much other work).

[65] I take this language from Lawrence R. Jacobs and Desmond S. King, "Varieties of Obamaism: Structure, Agency, and the Obama Presidency," *Perspectives on Politics* 8, no. 3 (2010): pp. 793–802.

[66] Wall Street Journal, "Rahm Emanuel on the Opportunities of Crisis," YouTube, November 19, 2008.

[67] Peter Beinart, "The New New Deal," *TIME*, November 24, 2008; Steven E. Schier, "Introduction: A Controversial Presidency," in *Debating the Obama Presidency*, ed. Steven E. Schier (Lanham: Rowman & Littlefield, 2016).

finance, and transforming American health care – to say nothing of foreign policy, nominations and confirmations, or his latter six years in office.

What we thus get out of the Obama administration is an indication of how presidential leadership matters. Obama, like other executives before (and after) him, leveraged agency embedded in the presidential office to stamp his brand on the polity. He set up political arrangements that friends and foes alike would have to navigate in his wake, even if he failed to realize the depth of his ambitions. His "first things" as president were reflective of that effort and set the trajectory for his tenure. Malia Obama was thus wise to press him on what they would be.

References

Alter, Jonathan. *The Promise: President Obama, Year One*. New York: Simon & Schuster, 2010.
Armstrong, Drew. "Baucus Outlines Health Care Plan." *CQ Almanac*, November 12, 2008.
Baker, Peter. "From Obama, a New Deal, or at Least a New Phrase." *New York Times*, May 15, 2009.
Baker, Peter. "Obama Team Weighs What to Take On First." *New York Times*, November 8, 2008.
Balz, Dan, and Haynes Johnson. "How Obama Snared the Lion of the Senate." *Washington Post*, August 3, 2009.
Bartosiewicz, Petra, and Marissa Miley. "The Too Polite Revolution: Why the Recent Campaign to Pass Comprehensive Climate Legislation in the United States Failed." *SSRN*. January 14, 2013. https://dx.doi.org/10.2139/ssrn.2200690.
Beinart, Peter. "The New New Deal." *TIME*, November 24, 2008.
Bookbinder, David. "Obama Had a Chance to Really Fight Climate Change. He Blew It." *Vox*, April 29, 2017.
Bouie, Jamelle. "Why Did Obama Choose Health Care?" *American Prospect*, September 8, 2010.
Chu, Steven M. Interview by the Columbia Center for Oral History Research, October 14, 2020.
Coates, Ta-Nehisi. "Fear of a Black President." *The Atlantic*, September 2012.
C-SPAN. "Second 2008 Presidential Debate." YouTube, October 8, 2008. https://www.youtube.com/playlist?list=PL38EC6F667EFC8BA2.
Cummings, Jeanne. "Waxman Coup Has Loud Echo on K Street." *Politico*, November 25, 2008.
D'Antonio, Michael. *A Consequential President: The Legacy of Barack Obama*. New York: Thomas Dunne Books, 2017.
Debenedetti, Gabriel. *The Long Alliance: The Imperfect Union of Joe Biden and Barack Obama*. New York: Henry Holt and Company, 2022.
Geithner, Timothy F. *Stress Test: Reflections on Financial Crises*. New York: Crown, 2014.
Greenberg, Jack B. "The Case for Agency: Three Dimensions of Discretion in Presidential Agenda Construction."
Greenblatt, Alan. "How Cap and Trade Was 'Trashed.'" *NPR*, April 26, 2010.
Gregg III, Claude A. *The Black President: Hope and Fury in the Age of Obama*. Baltimore: Johns Hopkins University, 2021.
Jacobs, Lawrence R., and Desmond S. King. "Varieties of Obamaism: Structure, Agency, and the Obama Presidency." *Perspectives on Politics* 8, no. 3 (2010): 793–802.

Kennedy, Ted. "2008 Democratic National Convention Speech." *American Rhetoric*. August 25, 2008. https://www.americanrhetoric.com/speeches/convention2008/tedkennedy2008dnc.htm.

Kennedy, Ted. "Kennedy Endorses Barack Obama." *CNN*. January 28, 2008. https://www.youtube.com/watch?v=0Eawu8pQxRI.

Kloppenberg, James T. *Reading Obama: Dreams, Hopes, and the American Political Tradition*. Princeton: Princeton University Press, 2011.

Kloppenberg, James T. *"Barack Obama and the Traditions of Progressive Reform,"* in The Progressives' Century: Political Reform, Constitutional Government, and the Modern American State, eds. Stephen Skowronek, Stephen M. Engel and Bruce Ackerman. New Haven: Yale University Press, 2016.

Kuttner, Robert. *A Presidency in Peril: The Inside Story of Obama's Promise, Wall Street's Power, and the Struggle to Control Our Economic Future*. Chelsea Green: White River Junction, 2010.

Lee, Carol E. "Obama Legacy Defense Gets Early Start." *Politico*, October 28, 2009.

Leonhardt, David. "After the Great Recession." *New York Times Magazine*, April 28, 2009.

Lizza, Ryan. "As the World Burns." *New Yorker*, October 3, 2010.

Mundy, Liza. "A Series of Fortunate Events; Barack Obama Needed More than Talent and Ambition to Rocket from Obscure State Senator to Presidential Contender in Three Years. He Needed Serious Luck." *Washington Post*, August 12, 2007.

Obama, Barack. "Address Accepting the Presidential Nomination at the Democratic National Convention in Denver: 'The American Promise.'" American Presidency Project, August 28, 2008.

Obama, Barack. "Address in Chicago Accepting Election as the 44th President of the United States." American Presidency Project, November 4, 2008.

Obama, Barack. *A Promised Land*. Crown: New York, 2022.

Obama, Barack. *Change We Can Believe In: Barack Obama's Plan to Renew America's Promise*. New York: Three Rivers Press, 2008.

Obama, Barack. *The Audacity of Hope: Thoughts on Reclaiming the American Dream*. New York: Crown, 2006.

Obama, Barack. "Remarks Announcing Candidacy for President in Springfield, Illinois." American Presidency Project, February 10, 2007.

Obama, Barack. "Remarks at the Iowa Jefferson-Jackson Dinner in Des Moines." American Presidency Project, November 10, 2007.

Obama, Barack. "Remarks Following a Meeting with Democratic Congressional Leadership," American Presidency Project, May 13, 2009.

Obama, Barack. "Remarks in St. Paul, Minnesota Claiming the Democratic Presidential Nomination Following the Montana and South Dakota Primaries." American Presidency Project, June 3, 2008.

Obama, Barack. "Remarks on the National Economy and Job Training." American Presidency Project, May 8, 2009.

Obama, Barack. "Remarks on the National Economy," American Presidency Project, April 14, 2009.

Obama, Barack. "Remarks on the Nomination of Regina M. Benjamin to be Surgeon General and an Exchange with Reporters." American Presidency Project, July 13, 2009.

Obama, Barack, and Robert Fisher. "Outline" in "Transformative Politics," 1991, 1.

Obama, Barack, and Robert Fisher. "Race and Rights Rhetoric" in "Transformative Politics," 1991.

Pew Research Center for the People & the Press, Pew Research Center. January 2009. Political Survey. Princeton Survey Research Associates International. Ithaca: Roper Center for Public Opinion Research, 2009.

Pierce, Emily. "Kennedy's Death Starts to Hit Home in the Capitol." *Roll Call*, September 4, 2009.

Pugh, Allison J. "Harvard Law Review's New Leader Aims for Change." *The Ithaca Journal*, April 23, 1990.

Raju, Manu. "Dorgan Emerges as Obama's Dem Foe." *Politico*, April 27, 2009.

Reilly, Amanda, and Kevin Bogardus. "7 Years Later, Failed Waxman-Markey Bill Still Makes Waves." *E&E News*, June 27, 2016.

Samuelson, Darren, and Joanne Kenen. "Obamacare Writer Turns a Page." *Politico*, January 30, 2014.

Schambra, William. "Obama and the Policy Approach." *National Affairs* 57 (Fall 2009).

Schier, Steven E. "Introduction: A Controversial Presidency." In *Debating the Obama Presidency*, edited by Steven E. Schier. Lanham: Rowman & Littlefield, 2016.

Shenk, Timothy. "A Lost Manuscript Shows the Fire Barack Obama Couldn't Reveal on the Campaign Trail." *New York Times*, October 7, 2022.

Skowronek, Stephen. *The Politics Presidents Make: Leadership from John Adams to Bill Clinton*. Cambridge: Belknap Press, 1997.

Suskind, Ron. *Confidence Men: Wall Street, Washington, and the Education of a President*. New York: Harper, 2011.

Thrush, Glenn, and Carrie Budoff Brown. "Obama's Health Care Conversion." *Politico*, September 23, 2013.

Todd, Chuck. "Democratic Presidential Debate – June 27 (Full)," *NBC News*, YouTube, June 27, 2019. https://www.youtube.com/watch?v=cX7hni-zGD8.

Wall Street Journal. "Rahm Emanuel on the Opportunities of Crisis." YouTube, November 19, 2008. https://www.youtube.com/watch?v=_mzcbXi1Tkk.

Zeleny, Jeff. "Daschle Ends Bid for Post; Obama Concedes Mistake." *New York Times*, February 3, 2009.

Mark Kelso
Chapter 5
A Green Presidency? Barack Obama and the Environment

The Obama presidency faced numerous challenges, from a global recession to extreme political polarization, to health care reform. One particular challenge was environmental policy. The administration had significant victories here, such as the millions of acres protected through the Antiquities Act. The administration had losses too, such as the failure of the legislation to address climate change. Additionally, there were numerous controversies over environmental protection in the Obama years, such the Keystone XL pipeline dispute. The Obama presidency was rich in examples of attempts to influence environmental policy, and this chapter will examine that legacy, by comparing the Obama environmental record to its predecessors. Was Obama a traditional Democratic president when it came to the environment? Did he go beyond expectations and do something more?

Barack Obama had a new vision for environmental politics in the US, and transformative goals. Gone would be climate change skepticism, challenges to longstanding environmental laws, and lack of leadership by the United States in global politics. The transformational dimension of Obama's vision is demonstrated in many ways. First, the 2008 Democratic Party platform contained criticisms of the Bush administration, as well as promises of change. These promises included promotion of green energy, increases in fuel efficiency, and a cap-and-trade system to address climate change.[1] Second, while campaigning for president, as well while in office, President Obama made specific promises to address environmental concerns. In fact, about 1/6 of all promises made by Obama during his presidency addressed environmental issues.[2] Many of these promises reflected the goals laid out in the party platform. Third, there was a sense, among political observers, that major policy changes would occur during the Obama Administration.[3] Fourth,

---

[1] American Presidency Project, "Democratic Party Platform 2008," August 25, 2008, https://www.presidency.ucsb.edu/documents/2008-democratic-party-platform.
[2] Politifact, "Obameter," November 26, 2023, https://www.politifact.com/truth-o-meter/promises/obameter/?ruling=true.
[3] Theda Skocpol, and Lawrence R. Jacobs, "Accomplished and Embattled: Understanding Obama's Presidency," *Political Science Quarterly* 127 (Spring 2012): 4–6.

Mark Kelso, Queens University of Charlotte

https://doi.org/10.1515/9783111384108-005

Obama had a strong pro-environment voting record as a senator, although he had many missed votes in 2008.[4] There is considerable evidence that Obama sought an environmental transformation in the United States. The question is: Did he succeed in this endeavor?

This chapter has two arguments. The first is that Obama was a traditional Democratic president in the area of environment, pursuing policies that were supportive of environmental protection. The second is that Obama, because of the political realities of his time in office, was better in the executive rather than the legislative realm. On the latter point, this study will examine Obama's environmental presidency through three lenses or roles: chief executive, chief legislator, and opinion/party leader. Chief executive refers to efforts to make policy through executive branch decisions. Chief legislator consists of efforts to work with Congress to pass environmental legislation. Opinion/party leader focuses on efforts to win over public opinion and/or use the power of the political party to achieve environmental policy goals. These three roles are identified by Soden as the most important roles of the environmental president.[5]

Scholarly Foundations

Soden's work on the environmental presidency is the starting point for this analysis. Daynes and Sussman also address the environmental presidency. The authors use a chronological approach, examining presidents from Franklin Roosevelt to George W. Bush,[6] and categorize presidents based on support for environmental protection. Some, like FDR and Clinton, created mostly pro-environmental policies, while others, like Eisenhower and George HW Bush, took a moderate approach. A third category of president did not focus on environmental protection, such as Ronald Reagan and George W. Bush.[7] Partisanship plays a key role here. Other than Nixon, the most pro-environmental presidents have been Democrats, while all of the moderate and weak environmental presidents have been Republicans.[8]

---

4 League of Conservation Voters, "National Environmental Scorecard: Barack Obama," November 26, 2023, https://scorecard.lcv.org/moc/barack-obama.
5 Dennis L. Soden, "Presidential Roles and Environmental Policy," in *The Environmental Presidency*, ed. Dennis L. Soden (Albany: State University of New York Press, 1999), 3–4.
6 Byron Daynes, and Glen Sussman, *White House Politics and the Environment: Franklin D. Roosevelt to George W. Bush* (College Station: Texas A&M University Press, 2010), 4–5.
7 Daynes, and Sussman, *White House Politics and the Environment*, 215–235.
8 Daynes, and Sussman, *White House Politics and the Environment*, 216, 235.

Skocpol and Jacobs examine the context of the Obama presidency, and note the extreme polarization of this time, which had affected the ability of President Obama to implement his agenda. Obama faced a partisan Congress when he took office in 2009 and an energized opposition.[9] These challenges applied to many areas and environmental policy was no exception. While environmental policy was a bipartisan concern in the 1970s, the issue had become increasingly polarized over time, due to the anti-government views prominent in the Republican Party since Reagan.[10] The opposition of Republicans in Congress was the biggest challenge the Obama administration had to face. As Skocpol and Jacobs state, on almost every issue, "Obama was almost totally rebuffed by the GOP."[11] This created a situation where legislative solutions to environmental problems were not tenable and Obama was forced to go in the direction of executive action.[12]

Klyza and Sousa identify the advantages of legislative action on environmental policy,[13] and note that the environmental framework of earlier decades has endured. They argue that earlier laws have become "embedded" and "institutionalized" and efforts to weaken these laws have met with failure over the last three decades.[14] An example of this were the "politically disastrous" efforts of Newt Gingrich and his allies to remake the environmental state in the 1990s. As the authors state, "[b]y the end of the 104th Congress, the forces protecting those laws had routed the so-called 'Republican revolution'"[15] Klyza and Sousa believe that the "death of environmentalism" has been exaggerated, and "contend that environmental policy in the United States is characterized by the resilience of the basic policy commitment of the golden age of environmentalism."[16] Those seeking to change this structure are confronted by structural barriers that keep the policy commitments in place.

The main arguments in this chapter are derived from the sources above. The first is that the Obama administration's environmental policies were equal to, or stronger than, most other presidencies since World War Two. In line with the analysis of his predecessors by Daynes and Sussman, he was a pro-environmental

---

9 Skocpol, and Jacobs, "Accomplished and Embattled: Understanding Obama's Presidency," 3–4, 13–15.
10 James Norton Turner, and Andrew C. Isenberg, *Republican Reversal, Conservatives and the Environment from Nixon to Trump* (Cambridge: Harvard University Press, 2018), 16–17, 27–28
11 Skocpol, and Jacobs, "Accomplished and Embattled: Understanding Obama's Presidency," 13.
12 Skocpol, and Jacobs, "Accomplished and Embattled: Understanding Obama's Presidency," 24.
13 Christopher McGrory Klyza, and David Sousa, "Beyond Gridlock: Green Drift in American Environmental Policymaking," *Political Science Quarterly* 125 (Fall 2010): 443–463.
14 Klyza, and Sousa, "Beyond Gridlock," 444, 463.
15 Klyza, and Sousa, "Beyond Gridlock," 445.
16 Klyza, and Sousa, "Beyond Gridlock," 444.

president, who had significant achievements to his credit. The second is that the Obama administration did not accomplish as much as it wanted in the area of legislation, due to the fierce partisanship of the era, but it did score significant wins in areas related to executive power. To use the terminology of Soden, in environmental policy Obama was a better chief executive than a legislative leader.

A Successful Environmental Chief Executive

Three factors are addressed here: appointments to environmental agencies, protection of public lands, and the Paris Climate Agreement. These factors reflect key executive powers used by presidents in environmental policy. Beginning with nominations, Soden and Steel note that, "[a]ll presidents since Nixon have proven capable of setting the tone through their appointments and control over the federal bureaucracy."[17] The policy goals of presidents are often reflected in appointments to key agencies. Landy, Roberts and Thomas note that high-level appointments to EPA have had a great impact on the agency's ability to perform its functions.[18] Appointments also set the tone of an administration's approach. Jimmy Carter's appointment of Cecil Andrus as Interior Secretary stands in sharp contrast to Reagan's appointment of James Watt.[19] Obama's key goals in environmental policy, which included clean energy, addressing climate change, and aggressive enforcement of environmental laws, were an important guide to his picks to head key agencies.[20]

Table 1 shows the key differences between Democratic and Republican nominees for these positions. Republican nominees receive more negative votes on confirmation, and are more likely to be opposed by key environmental groups.

---

[17] Dennis L. Soden, and Brent S. Steele, "Evaluating the Environmental Presidency," in *The Environmental Presidency*, ed. Dennis L. Soden. (Albany: State University of New York Press, 1999), 346.

[18] Marc K. Landy, Marc J. Roberts, and Stephen R. Thomas, *The Environmental Protection Agency: Asking the Wrong Questions—From Nixon to Clinton*, Expanded Edition (New York: Oxford University Press, 1994), 317.

[19] Jonathan Lash, Katherine Gillman, and David Sheridan, *A Season of Spoils: The Reagan Administration's Attack on the Environment* (New York: Pantheon Books, 1984), 231–235; Samuel P. Hays, *Beauty, Health, and Permanence: Environmental Politics in the US, 1955–1985* (New York: Cambridge University Press, 1987), 495.

[20] John M. Broder, and Matthew L. Wald, "Cabinet Picks Could Take On Climate Policy," *New York Times*, March 4, 2013; Frances Beinecke, "Five Reasons to Support Gina McCarthy's Nomination to Lead EPA," *National Resources Defense Council*, April 11, 2013, https://www.nrdc.org/experts/frances-beinecke/five-reasons-support-gina-mccarthys-nomination-lead-epa.

Table 1: Nominees, Secretary of Interior, EPA Administrator: Presidents Nixon through Obama.

Interior Secretary	10 or more negative votes	9 or fewer negative votes
Democratic Nominees	1 (25%)	3 (75%)
Republican Nominees	5 (50%)	5 (50%)
EPA Administrator	Any negative votes	No negative votes
Democratic Nominees	1 (25%)	3 (75%)
Republican Nominees	2 (22%)	7 (78%)
Interior Secretary	Support from Environmental Groups	Opposition from Environmental Groups
Democratic Nominees	4 (100%)	0 (0%)
Republican Nominees	2 (20%)	8 (80%)
EPA Administrator	Support from Environmental Groups	Opposition from Environmental Groups
Democratic Nominees	4 (100%)	0 (0%)
Republican Nominees	6 (67%)	3 (33%)

Sources: Congressional Quarterly Press, 1995, Section 5, 3–29; Congressional Quarterly Almanac. Washington: Congressional Quarterly Press, 1999, Section 4, 3–32; Congressional Quarterly Almanac. Washington: Congressional Quarterly Press, 2000, Section 10, 3–24; Congressional Quarterly Almanac. Washington: Congressional Quarterly Press, 2001, Section 10, 4; Juliet Eilperin, Philip Rucker and Michael Branigin, "Obama Names Salazar as Secretary of Interior," *Washington Post.* December 17, 2008. Retrieved from: http://www.washingtonpost.com/wp- dyn/content/ article/2008/12/17AR2008121701589.html; Environmental Protection Agency, "Chronology of EPA Administrators," January 12, 2023. Retrieved from: http://www2.epa.gov/aboutepa/chronology-epa-administrators; *Facts on File Yearbook*. New York: Facts on File New Services, 1941–1999; Sierra Club, "It's Past Time to Confirm EPA Chief Nominee Gina McCarthy," July 55, 2013. Retrieved from: http://blogs.sierraclub.org/compass/2013/07/senate-epa-chief-nominee-gina-mccarthy.html; Brian Turnbaugh, "Transparency Concerns Raised about EPA Nominee". *Center for Effective Government.* January 13, 2009. Retrieved from http://www.foreffectivegov.org/node/3875; United States Senate. "Presidential Cabinet Nominations: Presidents Jimmy Carter through George W. Bush," January 24, 2023. Retrieved from: http://www.senate.gov/reference/resources/pdf/cabinettable.pdf; United States Senate, "Barack H. Obama: Cabinet Nominations."; United States Senate. "Nomination of Regina McCarthy"; United States Senate, "Committee on Energy and Natural Resources," January 16, 2023. Retrieved from: www.energy.senate.gov; United States Senate, "On the Nomination (Confirmation: Michael O. Leavitt, of Utah to be Administrator of the E.P.A.)," *Roll Call Vote 412, 108th Congress, 1st Session*. Retrieved from: https://www.senate.gov/legislative/LIS/roll_call_votes/.vote1081/vote_108_1_00412.htm; United States Senate, "Committee on Environment and Public Works," January 166, 2023, www.epw.senate.gov; Brian Walsh, "Can An Outdoorsy CEO Manage the Interior Department's Split Personality?" *Time*. February 17, 2013, http://science.time.com/2013/02/07/can-an-outdoorsy-ceo-manage-the-interior-departments-split-personality; Center for Biological Diversity, "Wildlife Advocates Oppose Kempthorne for Interior Secretary," May 9, 2006, https://www.biologicaldiversity.org/news/press_releases/kempthorne-05-09-2006.html.

How did Obama's appointees compare to this record? He had two appointments as EPA Administrator, Lisa Jackson and Gina McCarthy. Jackson was confirmed by voice vote. McCarthy was confirmed 59 to 40, but only after Republicans used procedural moves to block the nomination.[21] Obama's two appointees as Secretary of Interior were Ken Salazar and Sally Jewell. Salazar was confirmed by voice vote, while Jewell was confirmed by a vote of 87 to 11.[22] Obama's appointees generally received support from environmental organizations, although there was some criticism directed at early picks such as Salazar.[23]

Nomination votes for these positions vary considerably. Many votes for both positions were either voice or unanimous consent (42.9% for Interior and 84.6% for EPA). The recorded votes for each position are in Table 2. Several points are related to this information. First, almost all the negative confirmation votes have come from the opposition party. Second, 75 percent of the confirmations in which no votes were cast came when the president's party controlled the Senate. Third, opposition from environmental groups for Republicans likely drives some of the no votes on their confirmations. For example, the Clark confirmation vote in 1983 was a "scorecard vote" for the League of Conservation Voters, a key component of how they rated senators that year.[24]

Turning to land protection, the Antiquities Act dates from 1906, during the presidency of Theodore Roosevelt, and allows presidents to declare national monuments without congressional approval.[25] Roosevelt used this power extensively, and it has been used frequently by recent Democratic presidents seeking

---

21 United States Senate, "Nomination of Regina McCarthy," *Roll Call Votes, 113th Congress, 1st Session*, accessed January 23, 2023, https://www.senate.gov/legislative/LIS/roll_call_votes/vote1131/vote_113_1_00180.htm; Valerie Volcovici, and Roberta Rampton, "Obama's EPA Nominee Stalled as Republicans Boycott Vote," *Reuters*, May 9, 2013, https://www.reuters.com/article/us-usa-energy-mccarthy/obamas-epa-nominee-stalled-as-republicans-boycott-vote-idUSBRE9480LE20130509.
22 United States Senate, "Barack H. Obama: Cabinet Nominations," January 23, 2023. https://www.senate.gov/legislative/nominations/Obama_cabinet.htm.
23 Beinecke, "Five Reasons"; David Biello, "Obama Names Energy Secretary, EPA Chief," *Scientific American*, December 15, 2008, https://www.scientificamerican.com/article/obama-names-energy-and-environment-team; *HuffPost*, "Sally Jewell's Interior Department Nomination Draws Praise From Range of Groups," February 7, 2013, https://www.huffpost.com/entry/sally-jewell-interior-department_n_2632775; Jen Quraishi, "What Environmentalists Really Think of Ken Salazar," *Mother Jones*, December 17, 2008, https://www.motherjones.com/politics/2008/12/what-environmentalists-really-think-ken-salazar.
24 League of Conservation Voters, "1983 Scorecard Vote."
25 Mark Kelso, "The Contemporary Presidency: A Lasting Legacy? Presidents, National Monuments and the Antiquities Act," *Presidential Studies Quarterly* 47 (2017): 803–805; Barbara Mantel, "Managing Western Lands," *CQ Researcher* 26, no. 16 (2016): 373.

Table 2: Nominees, Secretary of Interior, EPA Administrator: Recorded Votes, Presidents Nixon through Obama.

Department of Interior				
Nominee	President	Vote	No Votes by Opposition	Opposition in Control of Senate
*Hickel	Nixon	73–16	16	Yes
*Hathaway	Ford	60–36	32	Yes
*Watt	Reagan	83–12	12	No
*Clark	Reagan	71–18	18	No
*Norton	G.W. Bush	75–24	24	No
Jewell	Obama	87–11	11	No
Environmental Protection Agency				
Nominee	President	Vote	No Votes by Opposition	Opposition in Control of Senate
*Leavitt	G.W. Bush	88–8	8	No
McCarthy	Obama	59–40	39	No

*—opposed by environmental organizations

Sources: United States Senate, "State Timelines: Alaska," November 29, 2023, https://www.senate.gov/states/AK/timeline.shtml; United States Senate, "Senate Proceedings for September 10, 1973," Congressional Record. September 10, 1973, 28985; GovTrack, "To Confirm the Nomination of James G. Watt, of Colorado, to be the Secretary of the Interior (Motion Passed)," January 22, 1981, https://www.govtrack.us/congress/votes/97-1981/s13?q; League of Conservation Voters, "1983 Scorecard Vote: Clark Nomination for Secretary of the Interior," Senate Roll Call Vote 369, https://scorecard.lcv.org/roll-call-vote/1983-369-clark-nomination-secretary-interior; United States Senate, "George W. Bush: Cabinet Nominations," November 29, 2023; United States Senate, "Barack H. Obama: Cabinet Nominations."; United States Senate, "On the Nomination"; United States Senate. "Nomination of Regina McCarthy."

to expand land protection.[26] Overall, use of this act has varied over time. From Roosevelt to Roosevelt (Theodore to Franklin), the act was used 111 times (a mean of 15.9 per president), with little distinction between Democrats and Republicans. Presidents Truman through Ford used the act sparingly (a mean of 5.2), with Democrats more likely to use it than Republicans. The partisan gap on the use of this act grew under President Carter. Democrats from 1977 onward used the act 70 times, while Republicans only used it six times, all by George W. Bush.[27] In this area, Obama outdid all his predecessors, using the act 31 times.[28] In addition, Obama "[p]rotected more land and water than any administration in history –

---

26 Brinkley, 642–649; Kelso, "Contemporary Presidency," 805, 808.
27 National Parks and Conservation Association, "Monuments Protected Under the Antiquities Act," January 22, 2023, https://www.npca.org/resources/2658-monuments-protected-under-the-antiquities-act.
28 National Parks and Conservation Association, "Monuments Protected Under the Antiquities Act."

more than 548 million acres – and designated more national monuments than any other president."[29]

A third example of Obama's use of executive action is the Paris Climate Agreement. Enacted in 2015, this agreement was approved by almost every country in the world, and it contained real commitments to greenhouse reductions.[30] However, it was not a treaty. In the 1980s, increasing political polarization made environmental treaty ratification in the Senate very difficult with treaties ranging from the Convention on Biodiversity to the Kyoto Protocol not adopted by the Senate, leaving the US on the sidelines globally.[31]

The Obama Administration worked around these difficulties with the Paris Agreement.[32] First, the agreement would have voluntary reductions with no firm commitments.[33] Second, the administration argued that the agreement was a continuation of US commitments under the original UN climate change treaty, signed by President George H.W. Bush and ratified by the Senate.[34] Third, the administration sought to use Section 115 of the Clean Air Act as the legislative foundation, as the act makes reference to obligations to "duly constituted international agencies."[35] While the Clean Air Act does not mention climate change, the Supreme Court's ruling in *Massachusetts v EPA* (2007) said that regulating climate change was covered by the legislation.[36]

---

[29] League of Conservation Voters, "Protecting Public Lands and Waters," January 15, 2023, https://www.lcv.org/obama-legacy/protecting-public-lands-waters/.

[30] United Nations Climate Change, "The Paris Agreement: What is the Paris Agreement?," November 27, 2023, https://unfccc.int/process-and-meetings/the-paris-agreement.

[31] Jessica Durney, "Defining the Paris Agreement: Study of Executive Power and Policy Commitments," *Climate and Carbon Law Review* 11 (2010): 239; Andrea Kienast, "Consensus Behind Action: The Fate of the Paris Agreement in the United States of America," *Climate and Carbon Law Review* 9 (2015): 315, 319.

[32] Inside Washington Publishers, "Obama Administration Will Seek Climate Accord in Place of Treaty," *Inside EPA's Clean Air Report* 25 (September 11, 2014): 42; Kienast, "Consensus Behind Action," 314.

[33] Durney, 238; David F. Gordon, Divya P. Reddy, and Elizabeth Rosenberg, "After Paris: A Climate Agenda That Serves US Interests," *Center for a New American Security*, 2017, http://www.jstor.com/stable/resrep20412; Raymond Clemencon, "The Two Sides of the Paris Climate Agreement," *The Journal of Environment and Development* 25 (March 2016): 3–5.

[34] Kienast, "Consensus Behind Action," 321, 325; Adam D. Orford, "Clean Air Act Section 115: Is the IPCC a 'Duly Constituted International Agency?'" *Georgia Environmental Law Review* 34 (2022): 215–273.

[35] Inside Washington Publishers, "Obama Administration"; Kienast, "Consensus Behind Action," 321; Orford, "Clean Air Action Section 115," 217.

[36] Kienast, "Consensus Behind Action," 316; Orford, "Clean Air Action Section 115," 266.

The administration avoided court challenges and the Paris Agreement was safe while Obama was president.[37] This was a double-edged sword, however.[38] Once Obama was replaced in office by a Republican, things fell apart as President Trump very quickly ended US participation in the agreement.[39] Worse, the US commitments to the agreement were based on Obama executive orders in areas such as clean power plants, and the US under Trump did not move forward with the agreement's goals.[40] The Biden Administration immediately rejoined the Paris Agreement and through its policy decisions is trying to live up to US commitments.[41] Even so, the inconsistent nature of US participation in this agreement is not positive for American global leadership on environmental policy.

In his role as chief executive, Obama's record is strong. His picks to lead key agencies won approval. They were largely supported by the environmental community, and they carried out their duties in ways consistent with their role.[42] With the Antiquities Act, Obama earns high marks, as both the use of this law and the overall effects put him above other presidents. The Paris Climate Agreement was a successful use of executive power, at least while Obama was president. As a chief executive on the environment, Obama's record is excellent.

---

37 Kienast, "Consensus Behind Action," 323, 327.
38 Durney, "Defining the Paris Agreement," 240.
39 Rebecca Hersher, "US Officially Leaving Paris Climate Agreement," *National Public Radio*, November 3, 2020, https://www.npr.org/2020/11/03/930312701/u-s-officially-leaving-paris-climate-agreement.
40 Clemencon, "The Two Sides of the Paris Climate Agreement," 15.
41 Antony J. Blinken, "The United States Officially Rejoins Paris Agreement," *US Department of State*, February 19, 2021, https://www.state.gov/the-united-states-officially-rejoins-the-paris-agreement/; Juliet Eilperin, Brady Dennis, and John Muyskens, "Tracking Biden's Environmental Actions," *Washington Post*, November 24, 2023, https://www.washingtonpost.com/graphics/2021/climate-environment/biden-climate-environment-actions/.
42 Environmental Integrity Project, "EPA Enforcement Totals in Fiscal 2022 were Lowest in Decades in Key Areas," December 16, 2022, https://environmentalintegrity.org/news/epa-enforcement-plummets-to-new-low-under-biden-in-key-areas; Alex Guillen, "Ken Salazar's Legacy," *Politico*, January 16, 2013, https://www.politico.com/story/2013/01/salazars-legacy-includes-push-for-wind-solar-086267; Brian Calvert, "Sally Jewell Defends Interior Department Legacy," *High Country News*, September 12, 2017, https://www.hcn.org/issues/49.17/department-of-the-interior-an-exit-interview-with-sally-jewell.

Legislative Disappointment

The first variable is legislation. Both approval and disapproval are considered. Table 3 shows environmental legislation passed during each president's term since Nixon. The Obama record is relatively sparse, with only the two Bushes below him. Additionally, the main legislative initiative of the Obama's first two years, when the Democrats held both houses of Congress, was climate change legislation. Although this did pass the House, it languished in the Senate.[43] Once the Republicans took over the House after the 2010 elections, there was little Obama could do on the legislative front.

Obama did promote his environmental priorities with vetoes. Obama vetoed 12 bills and four of those were related to environmental policy.[44] His first two environmental vetoes, in 2015, dealt with standards of performances for greenhouse gas emissions (S.J. Res. 23) and carbon pollution emission guidelines (S.J.Res. 24). He also vetoed S.J.Res. 22 in 2016, which was a rule clarifying the boundaries of the Clean Water Act. His most famous veto occurred in February 2015, when he vetoed the Keystone XL Pipeline Approval Act (S.1).[45] He did so because it infringed upon the discretion of executive agencies to make decisions on the project.[46] Obama later decided against the project, which thrilled the environmental community.[47]

The second variable is budgeting. Two key areas for environmental policy are the EPA and the Department of Interior. The Obama administration started strong here, as the EPA budget for FY 2010 increased 36.4 percent over the previous year. There were also substantial increases in FY 2012 (+18.8%) and FY 2016 (+24.5%).

There were also significant years of decline in this budget: FY 2013 (−25.9%) and FY 2015 (−25.4%). The EPA budget was only slightly higher at the end of the

---

43 Center for Climate and Energy Solutions, "Congress Climate History," January 20, 2023, https://www.c2es.org/content/congress-clmate-history.
44 United States Senate, "Vetoes by President Barack Obama," January 24, 2023, https://www.senate.gov/legislative/vetoes/ObamaBH.htm; Kelso, "Contemporary Presidency," 140.
45 United States Senate, "Vetoes."
46 White House, Office of the Press Secretary, "Statement by the President on the Keystone XL Pipeline," November 6, 2015, https://obamawhitehouse.archives.gov/the-press-office/2015/11/06/statement-president-keystone-xl-pipeline; Rebecca Leber, "Four Reasons Obama Rejected the Keystone XL Pipeline," *New Republic* November 6, 2015, https://newrepublic.com/article/123369/four-reaons-obama-rejected-keystone-xl-pipeline.
47 Kelly McEvers, "Environmentalists Cheer Keystone XL Pipeline Decision as 'Decisive Moment,'" *National Public Radio: All Things Considered*, November 66, 2015, https://www.npr.org/2015/11/06/455049068/environmentalists-cheer-keystone-xl-pipeline-decision-as-decisive-moment.

Table 3: Environmental Legislation by Presidential Administration.

President	Years in Office	Environ Laws Passed	Enviro Laws Per Year of Admin	Enviro Laws Supported*	Enviro Laws Supported Per Year of Admin
Nixon	5.55	14	2.52	13	2.34
Ford	2.45	5	2.04	3	1.22
Carter	4.00	5	1.25	5	1.25
Reagan	8.00	8	1.00	5	0.63
Bush 1	4.00	2	0.50	2	0.50
Clinton	8.00	6	0.75	6	0.75
Bush 2	8.00	2	0.25	2	0.25
Obama	8.00	5	0.63	5	0.63
Totals	48.00	47	0.98	41	0.85
Democrats	20.00	16	0.80	16	0.80
Republicans	28.00	31	1.11	25	0.89

*—or at least did not actively oppose

Sources: *Congressional Quarterly Almanac*, 1995, 1999, 2000, 2001; Michael E. Kraft, *Environmental Policy and Politics* (New York: Harper Collins Publishers, 1996), 72; Natural Resources Defense Council, "The Obama Record," January 2010, http://www.nrdc.org/legislation/obamarecord/files/obamarecord.pdf; Jacqueline Vaughn Switzer, *Environmental Politics: Domestic and Global Dimensions*, 4th Edition (Belmont: Wadsworth/Thompson, 2002), 311–314; Norman J. Vig, and Michael E. Kraft, eds., *Environmental Policy in the 1980s: Reagan's New Agenda* (Washington: Congressional Quarterly Press, 1984), 10–13; Keith Gaby, "Ready to Defend Obama's Environmental Legacy: Top Ten Accomplishments to Focus On," *Environmental Defense Fund*, January 12, 2017, https://www.edf.org/blog/2017/01/12/ready-defend-obamas-environmental-legacy-top-10-accomplishments-focus; National Oceanic and Atmospheric Administration, "President Signs a National Microbeads Ban," December 30, 2015, https://blog.marinedebris.noaa.gov/president-signs-national-microbead-ban; Angela Nelson, "15 Things Obama Has Done for the Environment," *Treehugger*, June 5, 2017, https://www.treehugger.com/things-obama-has-done-environment-4863938.

Obama Administration than the beginning.[48] Also troubling was the decrease in the EPA workforce, with a 9.6 percent decline over the course of the Obama Administration.[49] At Interior, the story is similar. A healthy increase in year one of the administration, significant cutbacks in other years. In the end, Interior spending was a little over three percent higher than the beginning of the administration.[50] Previous research has found that the key variable in environmental

---

[48] White House. Office of Management and Budget. "Historical Tables. Outlays by Agency, 1962–2027," January 14, 2023, https://www.whitehouse.gov/omb/budget/historical-tables/.
[49] Environmental Protection Agency, "EPA's Budget and Spending," January 23, 2023, https://www.epa.gov/planandbudget/budget.
[50] White House, Office of Management and Budget, "Historical Tables."

spending is the partisan breakdown in Congress, not the party of the president, and that seems to be the case here.[51]

Why did Obama fall short in legislative achievements in environmental policy? There were several reasons. First, the Administration's environmental policy faced competition from several other issues, including the Great Recession and health care reform.[52] Second, there was unwavering opposition from Republicans on every issue, including the environment.[53] Third, Obama tended to lead from behind, and let Congress take the initiative, which worked in health care reform, but it did not work with environmental policy.[54] Fourth, public opinion was split on environmental issues, such as climate change, and Obama did not enjoy a clear public consensus as President Bush did during the effort to enact the 1990 Clean Air Act.[55] The public did support climate change action, but this support was undermine by the doubts and fears created by the opposition party.[56] As Sheppard states, "ultimately, the threat of global warming did not galvanize the public to the point where they would demand change."[57] Fifth, the Democratic party was split, with some members in the House and Senate less enthusiastic about major environmental initiatives than the administration or the party leadership in Congress.[58] Sixth, Obama faced the daunting challenge of a weak economy, a situation that often diminishes support for environmental protection.[59] Ultimately, climate change legislation, as Foreman notes, was a "casualty of Republican and independent opposition, the sheer scope of the overall legislative agenda, a weak economy

---

51 Leonard G. Ritt, and John M. Ostheimer, "Congressional Voting and Ecological Issues," *Boston College Environmental Affairs Law Review* 3, no. 3 (1974): 1–15; Glen Sussman, and Mark Kelso, "Environmental Priorities and the President as Legislative Leader," in *The Environmental Presidency*, ed. Dennis L. Soden (Albany: State University of New York Press), 113–146.
52 Skocpol, and Jacobs, "Accomplished and Embattled: Understanding Obama's Presidency," 6–7.
53 Skocpol, and Jacobs, "Accomplished and Embattled: Understanding Obama's Presidency," 13.
54 Christopher H. Foreman, Jr., "Ambition, Necessity, and Polarization in the Obama Domestic Agenda," in *The Obama Presidency: Appraisals and Prospects*, eds. Andrew Rudalevige, Bert A Rockman, and Colin Campbell (Washington: CQ Press, 2011), 254.
55 Richard E. Cohen, *Washington at Work: Back Rooms and Clean Air*. (Needham Heights: Allyn and Bacon, 1995), 47; Gallup Organization, "Americans Not Likely to Be Upset if No Climate Change Bill Is Passed This Year," October 5, 2009, https://news.gallup.com/opinion/polling-matters/170342/americans-not-likely-upset-no-climate-change-bill-passed-year.aspx.
56 Gallup, "Americans Not Likely."
57 Kate Sheppard, "Was Waxman-Market a Waste of Energy?"
58 Skocpol, and Jacobs, "Accomplished and Embattled: Understanding Obama's Presidency," 17.
59 Charles R. Shipan, and William R. Lowry, "Environmental Policy and Party Divergence in Congress," *Political Research Quarterly* 54 (June 2001): 260.

and a lack of time before the fall elections."[60] This is true for most of Obama's legislative initiatives on the environment.

The Battle for Public Opinion

There are two aspects to the public perception of Obama as president: overall approval, and approval on the environment. On overall approval, Obama's rating fluctuated over time, starting at a very high rate and ending high. There were some low spots in between.[61] Of 12 presidents from Truman to Obama, Obama ranked ninth, with an average over his terms of 47.9 percent.[62]

On the environment, Obama's approval was steadier, as Table 4 shows. Like his overall approval, he was high in year one, but afterward, held steady in the 50s, with the range between 51 and 56. He ended with an overall rating of 56.8.[63] This is significantly higher than his immediate predecessor (GW Bush), and much higher than that of his successor, Trump (and also, higher than Biden's early ratings). The average rating is also almost nine points higher than his overall approval rating. Obama's ratings in this area varied by party, as Democrats were much more likely to approve of Obama on the environment than Republicans, with Independents somewhere in the middle.[64] Based on these numbers, we can conclude that the public saw Obama as a characteristic Democrat in environmental policy.

The second variable is President Obama's efforts to mold public opinion on environmental issues. There are several ways to evaluate this. The first is party platforms. In 2008 and 2012, the Democratic Party platform each year devoted

---

60 Foreman, "Ambition, Necessity, and Polarization in the Obama Domestic Agenda," 259.
61 Gallup Organization, "Presidential Approval Ratings—Barack Obama," January 17, 2023, https://news.gallup.com/poll/116479/barack-obama-presidential-job-approval.aspx.
62 Gallup Organization, "Presidential Approval Ratings—Gallup Historical Statistics and Trends," January 17, 2023, https://news.gallup.com/poll/116677/presidential-approval-ratings-gallup-historical-statistics-trends.aspx.
63 Gallup Organization, "Environmental Job Approval," January 17, 2023, https://news.gallup.com/poll/1615/environment.aspx.
64 Some representative numbers to illustrate this point: In 2009, on Obama's job approval on the environment, Democrats had 95 percent approval, Independents 75 percent and Republicans 65 percent. See Frank Newport, "High Expectations for Obama on the Environment," Gallup Organization, April 22, 2009, https://news.gallup.com/poll/117775/high-expectations-obama-environment.aspx. In 2015, the numbers were Democrats 75, Independents 52 and Republicans 29. See Justin McCarthy, "In US, About Half Say Obama Doing Good Job on Environment," Gallup Organization, March 19, 2015, https://news.gallup.com/poll/182048/half-say-obama-doing-good-job-environment.aspx.

over 1,100 words to the environment. This compares to an average of 721 words in 1992 and 1996, and 825 words for the Republicans in 2000 and 2004. Furthermore, for Obama, 46 specific pledges on the environment were made in his two platforms, compared to 42 for Clinton and 24 for GW Bush.[65]

Obama's overall rhetoric on the environment also differed. He mentioned the environment or energy 122 times in major speeches, 8.1 percent of his total quotes. This compares to 28 for Bill Clinton (4.6%), and 72 for George W. Bush (5.8%).[66] In terms of public speeches, Obama had 13 public speeches over his term that focused on environmental issues, while George W. Bush had only one.[67] Based on this, we can say that Obama's attempts to guide public opinion on the environment were higher than his immediate predecessors.

Table 4: Public Approval of Presidents on Environmental Policy, GW Bush through Trump (Annual).

Year	Bush	Obama	Trump	Biden
1	51	79	36	65
2	50	52	31	45
3	44	55	37	43
4	41	56	39	
5	39	55		
6	33	51		
7	30	52		
8	31	54		
MEAN	39.9	56.8	35.75	51.0

Percentage saying the current president is doing a "Good Job" on the environment
Source: Gallup Organization, "Environmental Job Approval," January 17, 2023, https://news.gallup.com/poll/1615/environment.aspx; Megan Brenan, "Biden Overall Approval at 40%, Key Issue Ratings Lackluster," Gallup Organization. March 28, 2023, https://news.gallup.com/poll/472895/biden-overall-approval-key-issue-ratings-lackluster.aspx.

As opinion/party leader, Obama's record is positive. The public perceived him positively on the environment, and he had better numbers here than his overall approval numbers. In terms of leading his party and the public on the environ-

---

[65] American Presidency Project, "Party Platforms." January 17, 2023, https://www.presidency.ucsb.edu/documents/app-categories/elections-and-transitions/party-platforms.
[66] *On the Issues*, "Past Presidents," January 16, 2023, https://www.ontheissues.org/Presidents.htm.
[67] *American Rhetoric*, "Barack Obama Speeches," January 20, 2023, https://www.americanrhetoric.com/barackobamaspeeches.htm; *American Rhetoric*, "George W. Bush Speeches," January 20, 2023, https://www.americanrhetoric.com/gwbushspeeches.htm.

ment, there were more words devoted to the environment in the party platforms, more specific pledges made, more mentions of environment and energy in major speeches than his immediate predecessors, and more public speeches on the environment than George W. Bush. Obama's ability to move public opinion in this area was challenging due to the political environment, but his efforts were considerable.

What We Have Learned

This chapter has three major conclusions. First, in environmental policy, Obama was a typical Democratic president as his policies were generally pro-environmental. This includes his various roles as an environmental president, especially in terms of executive, legislative, and public opinion efforts. His record is particularly notable in terms of his appointments, his use of the Antiquities Act, his use of veto power, and his role as opinion leader. The record is weaker in legislation and budgeting.

Second, much of Obama's legacy was based on executive actions. This is due to the challenging political environment he faced, with Republican opposition in Congress being particularly strong and bitter, making bipartisanship difficult. However, Obama's legislative legacy in the area of the environment also was limited even in his first two years, when Democrats controlled both houses of Congress. His top environmental priority, climate change legislation, was not passed even with substantial majorities of Democrats in each house. Because there were barriers on the legislative front, Obama had to go the executive route in many areas, most notably on climate change.

Third, the reliance on executive action, which is common in polarized times, is problematic. First, executive actions can be challenged in court, and this happened often in the Obama administration.[68] Second, executive actions can be undone by the next administration, in contrast to legislation, which requires a long and arduous process. An environmental legacy built on executive actions is thus very fragile, and much of the Obama environmental legacy was undone by his successor, Donald Trump. After winning the presidency in 2020, President Biden restored some of that legacy, but this pattern of inconsistency may continue in the future as the parties swap presidencies.[69] Legislation does not suffer this fate, as Klyza and Sousa point out. Despite many shifts in power at both the presiden-

---

68 Josh Gerstein, "Obama v. Supreme Court," *Politico*, February 10, 2016, https://www.politico.com/story/2016/02/courts-action-on-climate-threatens-obamas-legacy-219088.
69 Eilperin, Dennis, and Muyskens, "Tracking Biden's Environmental Actions."

tial and legislative levels, the main contours of the green state remains intact.[70] Third, executive actions are often incomplete, and while Obama's executive actions on climate change were important, the passage of the cap-and-trade legislation could have been more comprehensive.[71]

Future Relevance

The first implication of these findings is that the political environment does limit presidents. Richard Neustadt famously said that the power of the president is the "power to persuade."[72] That may be, but the power to persuade is helped considerably by the political environment. Political capital is a precious commodity, and when President Obama had it he chose to use it on other things rather than environmental policy. Certainly, those choices can be justified, but there was not enough capital left over for a major legislative breakthrough on the environment.

The second implication is that, given the level of polarization today, legislative wins on the environment are difficult. This is true for presidents of both parties and may be true for the near future. That means that future presidents are likely to follow the same path as Obama did, making policy through executive action. The limitations of such action were noted above, and while this does move things forward, and has some short-term effects, it is not the most desirable course of action. In addition to fragile legacies, executive action often leads to policy instability which has effects beyond the realm of US politics. Environmental issues are increasingly global, and because the US is a key international player on the environment, inconsistency in US policy can create problems worldwide. Trump's dismissal of the US participation in the Paris Climate Agreement is a good example. While Biden was quick to rejoin the agreement and re-assert American leadership, a legitimate question from the rest of the world is how long will this last?[73] Will another change in administration lead the US back out the door? These are important questions that need to be addressed, both in the US and globally.

---

70 Klyza, and Sousa, "Beyond Gridlock," 444–448.
71 Michael D. Shear, "An Unfinished Presidency," *New York Times*, November 7, 2016.
72 Richard E. Neustadt, *Presidential Power and Modern Presidents: The Politics of Leadership from Roosevelt to Reagan* (New York: Free Press, 1991).
73 Rachel Myrick, "America is Back—But for How Long?," *Foreign Affairs*, June 14, 2021, https://www.foreignaffairs.com/articles/world/2021-06-14/america-back-how-long.

References

American Presidency Project. "Democratic Party Platform 2008." August 25, 2008. https://www.presidency.ucsb.edu/documents/2008-democratic-party-platform.

American Presidency Project. "Party Platforms." January 17, 2023, https://www.presidency.ucsb.edu/documents/app-categories/elections-and-transitions/party-platforms.

American Rhetoric. "Barack Obama Speeches." January 20, 2023, https://www.americanrhetoric.com/barackobamaspeeches.htm.

American Rhetoric. "George W. Bush Speeches." January 20, 2023, https://www.americanrhetoric.com/gwbushspeeches.htm.

Beinecke, Frances. "Five Reasons to Support Gina McCarthy's Nomination to Lead EPA." National Resources Defense Council. April 11, 2013. https://www.nrdc.org/experts/frances-beinecke/five-reasons-support-gina-mccarthys-nomination-lead-epa.

Biello, David. "Obama Names Energy Secretary, EPA Chief." *Scientific American*. December 15, 2008, https://www.scientificamerican.com/article/obama-names-energy-and-environment-team.

Blinken, Antony J. "The United States Officially Rejoins Paris Agreement." *US Department of State*. February 19, 2021, https://www.state.gov/the-united-states-officially-rejoins-the-paris-agreement/.

Broder, John M., and Matthew L. Wald. "Cabinet Picks Could Take On Climate Policy." *New York Times*. March 4, 2013

Calvert, Brian. "Sally Jewell Defends Interior Department Legacy." *High Country News*. September 12, 2017, https://www.hcn.org/issues/49.17/department-of-the-interior-an-exit-interview-with-sally-jewell.

Center for Climate and Energy Solutions. "Congress Climate History." January 20, 2023, https://www.c2es.org/content/congress-clmate-history.

Clemencon, Raymond. "The Two Sides of the Paris Climate Agreement." *The Journal of Environment and Development* 25 (March 2016).

Cohen, Richard E. *Washington at Work: Back Rooms and Clean Air*. Needham Heights: Allyn and Bacon, 1995.

Daynes, Byron, and Glen Sussman. *White House Politics and the Environment: Franklin D. Roosevelt to George W. Bush*. College Station: Texas A&M University Press, 2010.

Durney, Jessica. "Defining the Paris Agreement: Study of Executive Power and Policy Commitments." *Climate and Carbon Law Review* 11 (2010).

Environmental Integrity Project. "EPA Enforcement Totals in Fiscal 2022 were Lowest in Decades in Key Areas." December 16, 2022, https://environmentalintegrity.org/news/epa-enforcement-plummets-to-new-low-under-biden-in-key-areas.

Environmental Protection Agency. "EPA's Budget and Spending." January 23, 2023, https://www.epa.gov/planandbudget/budget.

Eilperin, Juliet, Brady Dennis, and John Muyskens. "Tracking Biden's Environmental Actions." *Washington Post*. November 24, 2023, https://www.washingtonpost.com/graphics/2021/climate-environment/biden-climate-environment-actions/.

Foreman, Jr., Christopher H. "Ambition, Necessity, and Polarization in the Obama Domestic Agenda." In *The Obama Presidency: Appraisals and Prospects*, edited by Andrew Rudalevige, Bert A Rockman, and Colin Campbell. Washington: CQ Press, 2011.

Gallup Organization. "Americans Not Likely to Be Upset if No Climate Change Bill Is Passed This Year." October 5, 2009, https://news.gallup.com/opinion/polling-matters/170342/americans-not-likely-upset-no-climate-change-bill-passed-year.aspx.

Gallup Organization, "Environmental Job Approval." January 17, 2023, https://news.gallup.com/poll/1615/environment.aspx.

Gallup Organization. "Presidential Approval Ratings – Barack Obama." January 17, 2023, https://news.gallup.com/poll/116479/barack-obama-presidential-job-approval.aspx.

Gallup Organization. "Presidential Approval Ratings – Gallup Historical Statistics and Trends." January 17, 2023, https://news.gallup.com/poll/116677/presidential-approval-ratings-gallup-historical-statistics-trends.aspx.

Gerstein, Josh. "Obama v. Supreme Court." *Politico*. February 10, 2016, https://www.politico.com/story/2016/02/courts-action-on-climate-threatens-obamas-legacy-219088.

Gordon, David F., Divya P. Reddy, and Elizabeth Rosenberg. "After Paris: A Climate Agenda That Serves US Interests." Center for a New American Security. 2017, http://www.jstor.com/stable/resrep20412.

Guillen, Alex. "Ken Salazar's Legacy." *Politico*. January 16, 2013, https://www.politico.com/story/2013/01/salazars-legacy-includes-push-for-wind-solar-086267.

Hays, Samuel P. *Beauty, Health, and Permanence: Environmental Politics in the US, 1955–1985*. New York: Cambridge University Press, 1987.

Hersher, Rebecca. "US Officially Leaving Paris Climate Agreement." *National Public Radio*. November 3, 2020, https://www.npr.org/2020/11/03/930312701/u-s-officially-leaving-paris-climate-agreement.

HuffPost. "Sally Jewell's Interior Department Nomination Draws Praise From Range of Groups." February 7, 2013, https://www.huffpost.com/entry/sally-jewell-interior-department_n_2632775.

Inside Washington Publishers. "Obama Administration Will Seek Climate Accord in Place of Treaty." *Inside EPA's Clean Air Report* 25. September 11, 2014.

Klyza, Christopher McGrory and David Sousa. "Beyond Gridlock: Green Drift in American Environmental Policymaking." Political Science Quarterly 125 (Fall 2010).

Kelso, Mark. "The Contemporary Presidency: A Lasting Legacy? Presidents, National Monuments and the Antiquities Act." *Presidential Studies Quarterly* 47 (2017): 803–805.

Kienast, Andrea. "Consensus Behind Action: The Fate of the Paris Agreement in the United States of America." *Climate and Carbon Law Review* 9 (2015).

Landy, Marc K., Marc J. Roberts, and Stephen R. Thomas. *The Environmental Protection Agency: Asking the Wrong Questions – From Nixon to Clinton, Expanded Edition*. New York: Oxford University Press, 1994.

Lash, Jonathan, Katherine Gillman, and David Sheridan. *A Season of Spoils: The Reagan Administration's Attack on the Environment*. New York: Pantheon Books, 1984.

League of Conservation Voters. "National Environmental Scorecard: Barack Obama." November 26, 2023. https://scorecard.lcv.org/moc/barack-obama.

League of Conservation Voters. "Protecting Public Lands and Waters." January 15, 2023, https://www.lcv.org/obama-legacy/protecting-public-lands-waters/.

Leber, Rebecca. "Four Reasons Obama Rejected the Keystone XL Pipeline." *New Republic*. November 6, 2015, https://newrepublic.com/article/123369/four-reaons-obama-rejected-keystone-xl-pipeline.

Mantel, Barbara. "Managing Western Lands," *CQ Researcher* 26, no. 16 (2016).

McCarthy, Justin. "In US, About Half Say Obama Doing Good Job on Environment." Gallup Organization. March 19, 2015, https://news.gallup.com/poll/182048/half-say-obama-doing-good-job-environment.aspx.
McEvers, Kelly. "Environmentalists Cheer Keystone XL Pipeline Decision as 'Decisive Moment.'" *National Public Radio: All Things Considered*. November 66, 2015, https://www.npr.org/2015/11/06/455049068/environmentalists-cheer-keystone-xl-pipeline-decision-as-decisive-moment.
Myrick, Rachel. "America is Back – But for How Long?" *Foreign Affairs*. June 14, 2021, https://www.foreignaffairs.com/articles/world/2021-06-14/america-back-how-long.
National Parks and Conservation Association. "Monuments Protected Under the Antiquities Act." January 22, 2023, https://www.npca.org/resources/2658-monuments-protected-under-the-antiquities-act.
Neustadt, Richard E. *Presidential Power and Modern Presidents: The Politics of Leadership from Roosevelt to Reagan*. New York: Free Press, 1991.
Newport, Frank. "High Expectations for Obama on the Environment." Gallup Organization. April 22, 2009, https://news.gallup.com/poll/117775/high-expectations-obama-environment.aspx.
On the Issues. "Past Presidents." January 16, 2023, https://www.ontheissues.org/Presidents.htm.
Orford, Adam D. "Clean Air Act Section 115: Is the IPCC a 'Duly Constituted International Agency?'" *Georgia Environmental Law Review* 34 (2022): 215–273.
Politifact. "Obameter." November 26, 2023. https://www.politifact.com/truth-o-meter/promises/obameter/?ruling=true.
Quraishi, Jen. "What Environmentalists Really Think of Ken Salazar." *Mother Jones*. December 17, 2008, https://www.motherjones.com/politics/2008/12/what-environmentalists-really-think-ken-salazar.
Ritt, Leonard G., and John M. Ostheimer. "Congressional Voting and Ecological Issues." *Boston College Environmental Affairs Law Review* 3, no. 3 (1974): 1–15.
Shear, Michael D. "An Unfinished Presidency." *New York Times*. November 7, 2016.
Shipan, Charles R., and William R. Lowry. "Environmental Policy and Party Divergence in Congress." *Political Research Quarterly* 54 (June 2001).
Skocpol, Theda, and Lawrence R. Jacobs. "Accomplished and Embattled: Understanding Obama's Presidency." *Political Science Quarterly* 127 (Spring 2012): 1–24
Soden, Dennis L. "Presidential Roles and Environmental Policy." In *The Environmental Presidency*, edited by Dennis L. Soden. Albany: State University of New York Press, 1999.
Soden, Dennis L., and Brent S. Steele. "Evaluating the Environmental Presidency." In The Environmental Presidency, edited by Dennis L. Soden. Albany: State University of New York Press, 313–354.
Sussman, Glen, and Mark Kelso. "Environmental Priorities and the President as Legislative Leader." In *The Environmental Presidency*, edited by Dennis L. Soden. Albany: State University of New York Press, 113–146.
Turner, James Norton, and Andrew C. Isenberg. *Republican Reversal, Conservatives and the Environment from Nixon to Trump*. Cambridge: Harvard University Press, 2018.
United Nations Framework Convention on Climate Change. "The Paris Agreement: What is the Paris Agreement?" November 27, 2023, https://unfccc.int/process-and-meetings/the-paris-agreement.
United States Senate. "Barack H. Obama: Cabinet Nominations." January 23, 2023, https://www.senate.gov/legislative/nominations/Obama_cabinet.htm.
United States Senate. "Nomination of Regina McCarthy." Roll Call Votes. 113th Congress, 1st Session. Accessed January 23, 2023, https://www.senate.gov/legislative/LIS/roll_call_votes/vote1131/vote_113_1_00180.htm

United States Senate. "Vetoes by President Barack Obama." January 24, 2023, https://www.senate.gov/legislative/vetoes/ObamaBH.htm.

Volcovici, Valerie, and Roberta Rampton. "Obama's EPA Nominee Stalled as Republicans Boycott Vote." *Reuters*. May 9, 2013, https://www.reuters.com/article/us-usa-energy-mccarthy/obamas-epa-nominee-stalled-as-republicans-boycott-vote-idUSBRE9480LE20130509.

White House. Office of the Press Secretary. "Statement by the President on the Keystone XL Pipeline." November 6, 2015, https://obamawhitehouse.archives.gov/the-press-office/2015/11/06/statement-president-keystone-xl-pipeline.

White House. Office of Management and Budget. "Historical Tables. Outlays by Agency, 1962–2027," January 14, 2023, https://www.whitehouse.gov/omb/budget/historical-tables/.

Andrew Rudalevige
Chapter 6
Obama's Domestic Policy Making and the Administrative Presidency

"I've got a pen and I've got a phone," President Barack Obama announced at his first Cabinet meeting of 2014. "I can use that pen to sign executive orders and take executive actions and administrative actions that move the ball forward . . . "; his phone, patched through the presidency's bully pulpit, would rally public support for those initiatives.[1] The result, according to the president, would be "a year of action," centered on the executive branch rather than the legislative process. Even before his reelection, after all, Obama had declared that "we can't wait" for "an increasingly dysfunctional Congress to do its job."[2]

History was repeating itself here, or at least rhyming. Presidents have long sought to use their administrative authority as a substitute for congressional action, for purposes both good and ill. That trend accelerated as the size and scope of government did. Indeed, by the 1980s, Richard Nathan posited that "in a complex, technologically advanced society in which the role of government is pervasive, much of what we would define as policymaking is done through the execution of laws in the management process."[3] By 2001, Elena Kagan had transmuted Nathan's "administrative presidency" into a strategy of "presidential administration" that used executive management tools to enhance presidential control of the bureaucracy.[4] Bill Clinton, she stated, was aggressive in that arena because he was "faced for most of his time in office with a hostile Congress but eager to show progress on domestic issues."[5]

Obama found himself in a parallel situation. While his presidency began with large Democratic majorities in Congress and an ambitious legislative program, it ended with Republicans in charge of both chambers, increased partisan polariza-

---

1 Barack Obama, "Remarks Prior to a Cabinet Meeting," January 14, 2014, via the online American Presidency Project, https://www.presidency.ucsb.edu/node/305044.
2 Barack Obama, "Remarks in Las Vegas," October 24, 2011, https://www.presidency.ucsb.edu/node/297388.
3 Richard Nathan, *The Administrative Presidency* (New York: Macmillan, 1983), 82.
4 Elena Kagan, "Presidential Administration," *Harvard Law Review* 114 (June 2001): 2385.
5 Kagan, "Presidential Administration," 2248.

Andrew Rudalevige, Bowdoin College

tion, and a firmly cemented gridlock. In early 2011, Senate Republican leader Mitch McConnell had presented his version of bipartisanship as Obama "work[ing] with us to accomplish things that we're already for."[6] Mostly, Obama did not. Instead, he turned to a new iteration of the administrative presidency.[7]

Doing so meant toning down his aspirations. To be sure, the taxonomy of the administrative "orders and actions" Obama utilized was quite extensive. A range of executive actions shaped policies in key areas such as health care, environmental protection, and immigration. But their crucial commonality was a reliance on aggressive statutory interpretation, guiding the implementation of policy to suit presidential preferences. Public administration scholar Martha Derthick could have been speaking of the Obama years when she observed that "[m]uch of the activity of American policymaking consists of attempts not to pass new laws but to invest old ones with new meanings."[8] That strategy, nearly by definition, led to incremental rather than transformational change. Though his opponents charged him with overreach and even dictatorship, the changes that endured through inevi-table court challenges were within the constraints of existing law. Even then, in the wake of the 2016 election, Obama's policy legacy proved unexpectedly vulnerable from a new angle: While some of his directives proved resilient to his successor's fervent efforts to overturn them, others were easily reversed.

After all, statutory interpretation, by its nature, can be changed by future interpreters. Thus, as Obama told an NPR interviewer in December 2016, "[m]y suggestion to the president-elect is, you know, going through the legislative process is always better, in part because it's harder to undo."[9]

Means, Motive, and Opportunity

Presidents have long used "the executive power" vested in them through the first sentence of Article II in creative ways. The Constitution does not mention a presidential power to issue unilateral directives, yet every president has done so.[10]

---

6 Jeff Winkler, "McConnell Skeptical of Obama's Centrist Rhetoric Ahead of State of the Union," *Daily Caller*, January 25, 2011, http://dailycaller.com/2011/01/25/mcconnell-skeptical-about-obamas-centrist-rhetoric-ahead-of-state-of-the-union/.
7 See Andrew Rudalevige, "The Obama Administrative Presidency: Some Late-Term Patterns," *Presidential Studies Quarterly* 46 (December 2016): 868–890.
8 Martha Derthick, *Up in Smoke*, 3rd rev. ed. (Washington, DC: CQ Press, 2011), 56.
9 "NPR's Exit Interview with President Obama," December 19, 2016, http://www.npr.org/2016/12/19/504998487/transcript-and-video-nprs-exit-interview-with-president-obama.
10 See Graham Dodds, *Take Up Your Pen* (Philadelphia: University of Pennsylvania Press, 2013).

However, the growth of the "administrative state" markedly increased the reach of presidential administration. Since the 1930s, the American national state has expanded dramatically in size and responsibility. As Obama prepared to take office, the Office of Management and Budget (OMB) counted 1,003 programs carrying out separate projects across 15 cabinet departments containing some 220 subunits (along with close to a 100 stand-alone agencies of different types), with more than 3.5 million federal employees and a budget of just under three trillion dollars.[11] Even that dramatically undercounts the total number of jobs associated with federal government programs, including contract employees and grant-funded workers.[12]

Providing leadership and direction to such a far-flung empire is difficult. It would be so even if the president commanded prompt and unquestioning obedience. Instead, bureaucratic recalcitrance is a presidential birthright. Long before Donald Trump railed against the "deep state," Richard Nixon groused that the "bureaucracy [was] crawling with at best unloyal people and at worst treasonable people." For that matter Franklin Roosevelt complained that trying to prompt organizational change was like "punching a feather bed ... and then you find the damn bed is just as it was before you started punching."[13]

Yet presidential lamentations about bureaucracy should often be love songs instead. As the administrative state bequeathed an administrative presidency, presidents developed executive tools to impose their preferences on the wider (deeper?) bureaucracy. Studies identify more than two dozen types of unilateral directives. Some are well-known, like executive orders and presidential proclamations, but many others are less salient, including memoranda (that might prod the production of regulations by departments and agencies), guidance documents, designations and findings, and a wide range of national security orders.[14] Over time, presidents have both enhanced opportunity and motive to utilize administrative strategies that aim to control the executive branch and shape policy implementation, and – as in any good "whodunnit" – they also have the means.

---

11 See OMB, "Assessing Program Performance," 2008 archive of documents available at https://georgewbush-whitehouse.archives.gov/omb/performance/index.html, and the fiscal 2009 budget documents at https://www.govinfo.gov/app/collection/budget.
12 Paul Light estimates the "true" total at close to 10 million in 2019, in *The Government-Industrial Complex: The True Size of Government, 1984–2017* (New York: Oxford University Press, 2019), Table 2.1.
13 Peter Dombrowski, and Andrew Ross, "Transforming the Navy," *Naval College War Review* 56 (Summer 2003): 107; Garrett Graff, *Watergate: A New History* (New York: Simon & Schuster, 2022), 320.
14 See Harold C. Relyea, *Presidential Directives: Background and Overview* (Washington, DC: Congressional Research Service, 2008); Dodds, *Take Up Your Pen*, 6. Many actions that are not executive orders are often wrongly identified as such, even by elected officials; see Rudalevige, "Late Term Patterns" for numerous examples.

Obama's array of directives thus fit comfortably into a broader presidential goal of executing the law according to the administration's preferences regarding that execution. This is possible because a "faithful" following of the law is hardly black and white. We usually think of "statutory interpretation" as a judicial function, and certainly courts proffer the *Marbury v. Madison* decision as a sacred relic, sol-emnly incanting their job to say "what the law is."[15] But Congress and the executive branch have a role to play here as well. Questions over a president's interpretations of the Constitution date back to the Washington administration.[16] If nothing else, presidents have many laws to choose between – some of them contradicting others, and still more sitting in the statute books awaiting rediscovery. Such authority ag-gregates with the *US Code* itself. Given the difficulty of passing laws and the multi-plicity of circumstances to which they must apply, it rarely makes sense to try to anticipate every possible outcome in legislative language. Thus, executive departments and agencies are routinely delegated power to promulgate regulations specifying how a given law will work in practice.

Further, complex substantive debates tend to generate complex statutes: The 2010 Affordable Care Act ran to more than 900 pages, containing vague provisions, multiple drafting errors, and any number of unintended consequences. But even in the best circumstances, maneuvering a bill through Congress requires ambiguous statutory language, the better to allow all sides to point to the same wording as supportive of their own specific ideals. Statutes also frequently grant waiver authority, allowing presidents or departmental secretaries to suspend provisions of the law under certain conditions.

In contrast with the George W. Bush administration – and in large part to make that contrast clear – Obama did not want to justify his directives by making broad claims of presidential prerogative. Rather, he wanted to ground each action in written law: "[A]cting like Bush meant a president overriding statutory constraints," as the *New York Times*' Charlie Savage puts it, while "lawyerliness suffused the Obama administration."[17] Obama himself promised that he would act "with an abiding confidence in the rule of law and due process; in checks and balances and accountability."[18]

---

15 R. Shep Melnick, *Between the Lines* (Washington, DC: Brookings Institution, 1994).
16 Harold Bruff, *Untrodden Ground: How Presidents Interpret the Constitution* (Chicago: University of Chicago Press, 2015); Keith Whittington, *Constitutional Construction* (Cambridge, MA: Harvard University Press, 2001).
17 Charlie Savage, *Power Wars: Inside Obama's Post-9/11 Presidency* (Boston: Little Brown, 2015), 52, 65.
18 Barack Obama, "Remarks by the President," May 21, 2009, https://www.presidency.ucsb.edu/node/286247.

But the rule of law depends on what the law says. "Creative lawyers can find lots of lawful ways for a determined president to advance a decision," Bush official John Graham once noted; more cynically, law professor Bruce Ackerman argues that a "steady stream of authoritative-looking opinions is produced under conditions that allow short-term presidential imperatives to overwhelm sober legal judgments."[19] The president's lawyers, of course, work for the president.

Better yet, that "authoritative-looking" advice serves to undergird future claims – a self-justifying process much like the reflexive citation of *Marbury*. Savage traces a 2011 Justice Department memo effectively nullifying a law that constrained certain presidential staff from dealing with Chinese officials in which Justice's Office of Legal Counsel (OLC) held that "ample precedent" existed to show that the Constitution intended the president to have "absolute discretion" over the people chosen for diplomatic tasks. The original source of that claim, however, was a 1990 opinion by George H.W. Bush's legal team. Repeated frequently enough over the years, that single memo became "ample precedent."[20]

Obama's Statutory Implementation in Practice: Four Cases

Thus, the specifics of policy implementation are often up for grabs. As the Obama administration progressed, interpretations of the law that justified presidential preferences arose in many policy areas. As White House aide David Axelrod noted in late 2010, "[t]he next phase is . . . less about legislative action than it is about managing the change that we've brought about" – implementing enormous, complex statutes passed in 2009 to 2010, including the Affordable Care Act and the Dodd-Frank financial sector reforms.[21] By the summer of 2012, the "We Can't Wait" section of the White House website included 40-plus unilateral initiatives, ranging from cutting lending fees on government-backed mortgages to the creation of a new national park in Virginia. Later came exercises of prosecutorial dis-

---

19 Graham quoted in Rebecca Adams, "Lame Duck or Leapfrog?" *CQ Weekly*, February 12, 2007, 450; Bruce Ackerman, *The Decline and Fall of the American Republic* (Cambridge, MA: Harvard University Press, 2010), 88. See also Chris Edelson, "In Service to Power: Legal Scholars as Executive Branch Lawyers in the Obama Administration," *Presidential Studies Quarterly* 43 (September 2013): 618–640.
20 Savage, *Power Wars*, 677–681.
21 Peter Nicholas and Christi Parsons, "Rebuilding Staff, Obama Charts New Course," *Philadelphia Inquirer*, October 10, 2010.

cretion that ranged from the administration's decision not to defend the Defense of Marriage Act (DOMA) against legal challenges in advance of the *Obergefell* decision regarding same-sex marriage, to the wide use of his commutation power to shorten jail terms for those convicted of non-violent drug crimes. We could include the war powers as well.[22]

The remainder of this chapter will focus on several domestic policy areas where the idea of "managing change" developed to include longer-standing laws, especially when newer ones could not be passed – for example, when large-scale legislation stalled. The examples explored here include Obama's aggressive claims about his abilities under statutory authority in the arenas of health care, labor, the environment, and immigration. Obama sought important and even transformational change, but that proved difficult to achieve in the long term. Those initiatives the administration was able to embed in formal regulation found much firmer purchase than those imposed simply by presidential decree.

Health Care

"This Administration's lawlessness has been most widely noticed with President Obama's implementation of Obamacare," complained Representative Diane Black (R-TN) in 2014.[23] Much of that implementation involved Treasury's issuance of tax regulations (since the individual mandate was enforced via the tax code) or interpretations of the law's text within the department's broader statutory authority under the Internal Revenue code – as "an exercise of [the Treasury's] longstanding administrative authority to grant transition relief when implementing new legislation," as assistant secretary Mark Mazur put it in July 2013. Other specific rule changes in March 2014 were announced by an administrative bulletin from the Centers for Medicaid and Medicare Services.

Black's direct reference was to a series of delays to Affordable Care Act requirements beginning in February 2013. The administration put off the employer mandate portion of the law for 12 months in July 2013, and in February 2014 extended the deadline again for medium-sized companies. Other administrative amendments to the law shifts included changing the deadline for implementation

---

22 Savage, *Power Wars*; Andrew Rudalevige, "Barack Obama and the Administrative Presidency," in *Obama's Fractured Legacy*, ed., François de Chantal (Edinburgh: Edinburgh University Press, 2020).
23 Hearing of the Committee on the Judiciary, US House of Representatives, "Enforcing the President's Constitutional Duty to Faithfully Execute the Laws," February 26, 2014.

of the individual mandate, adjustments to the online marketplace for small businesses and, with the website HealthCare.gov still in tatters, extension of the general deadline for enrollment online. When insurance companies (quite properly) began to cancel plans that did not meet the ACA's minimum requirements, contradicting the president's famous pledge that "if you like your plan, you can keep it," Obama gave insurers the discretion to extend such plans for an additional year. He did so again in early 2014, to push any such cancelations safely past the 2016 elections. It was not clear whether these changes were lawful; Black obviously thought not. But since those affected could hardly claim to have suffered "harm" in a legal sense (indeed, they welcomed the delays) they did not sue to reverse the relief Obama had granted.

The courts did get involved, though, when the IRS announced that it would read the ACA to give policy-subsidizing tax credits to individuals enrolled via the federal insurance "exchange" as well as in state-run exchanges. What became the Supreme Court case *King v. Burwell* centered on this question, since one section of the law seemed to say that subsidies could be given only to those purchasing coverage from an exchange run by one of the states, while others seemed to treat all exchanges equally. It didn't help that the ACA, thanks in part to its tortuous legislative history, suffered from (as the *Burwell* majority opinion gently put it) "inartful drafting." Arguably the key section in question was simply an elaborate typographical error.[24] But it became a crucial issue when two dozen or so states refused to set up their own exchanges, forcing the federal government to do the work.

Thus, unlike its first judicial audition in *NFIB v. Sebelius* (2010), where a split Court upheld the ACA's individual mandate as within Congress's power to tax, *King v. Burwell* dealt not with interpreting the Constitution but with interpreting the ACA's text.

In the 1984 *Chevron* case, the Supreme Court had preached judicial deference to an executive branch agency's reading of a vague law. Following this logic, in *Burwell* the Fourth Circuit Court of Appeals ruled in favor of the government. That is, the court decided that the section was ambiguous, that the agency (here, the IRS) had come up with a reasonable interpretation, and thus that the tax credits for users of federal exchanges were acceptable. But following the same process, the DC Circuit Court of Appeals came up with the opposite result. It decided instead that the law was unambiguous – that the IRS could therefore not have reached the conclusion it did – and that the tax credits were therefore invalid.

---

24 Robert Pear, "Four Words Imperil Health Law; All a Mistake, Its Writers Say," *New York Times*, May 26, 2015, A1.

To the surprise of most observers, the Supreme Court reacted by discarding the *Chevron* framework and interpreting the law itself. The IRS could not be expected to be expert in health insurance and its workings, undercutting the usual reason for deference. "This is not a case for the IRS," Chief Justice John Roberts wrote. "It is instead our task to determine the correct reading of Section 36B." Having done so, the Court found the notion of an exchange "established by the State" could indeed include a federal exchange when taken in the context of the law as a whole. Otherwise, the law's health care marketplace – the law's key element – would collapse in a "death spiral," something Congress could not have meant to do. Thus, allowing subsidies to flow to federal exchanges "can fairly be read consistent with what we see as Congress's plan, and that is the reading we adopt."[25]

Some justices were unimpressed with this line of reasoning: Antonin Scalia's dissent accused his colleagues of judicial malpractice, plain stupidity, and even of "jiggery-pokery." But the law lived on – to battle against yet another court effort, for example, where opponents charged that Obama was spending money on provisions of the ACA without that money having been specifically appropriated by Congress. That case, which continued into the Trump administration, was made moot when the new president decided to stop making the payments in question. (Trump bragged via Twitter that "The Democrats ObamaCare is imploding. Massive subsidy payments to their pet insurance companies has stopped. Dems should call me to fix!"[26] They did not.)

Labor

Executive orders (EOs) generally constituted a relatively small proportion of Obama's executive actions.[27] However, EOs did play an important role in shaping the administration's approach towards the American workforce.

Executive orders are directed to government officials and agencies. Obama could thus not issue an order implementing his desired increase in the federal minimum wage, a proposal Congress repeatedly failed to enact.[28] He could, however, require that contracts negotiated with private sector companies seeking to

---

25 *King v. Burwell*, 576 US 473 (2015).
26 Tweet of October 13, 2017.
27 For counts of various presidents' use of different types of directives, see Rachel Potter et al., "Not by the Numbers," *Presidential Studies Quarterly* 52 (September 2022): 596–625.
28 Its increase to $7.25/hour in July 2009 was pursuant to a 2007 law.

do business with the federal government mandate that higher wage. Since the US government buys hundreds of billions of dollars of contracted products and services every year, requiring that the businesses receiving those contracts meet certain conditions can have an important impact on the wider economy. (John F. Kennedy's 1962 order barring racial discrimination in federally funded housing is an earlier example of this.)[29]

Obama's idea was to use this tool to rework a wide swathe of private workplaces. His orders required government procurement to be limited to companies who agreed to pay a higher minimum wage (February 2014), ban discrimination on the basis of sexual orientation or identity (July 2014), comply fully with laws mandating "integrity and business ethics" so as to ensure "fair pay and safe workplaces" (July 2014), and provide paid sick leave (September 2015). The Department of Labor then developed regulations to implement the law. For example, the rules governing sick leave were issued in final form in early September 2016, to take effect on January 1, 2017.

The rules gave the orders more stability than the orders by themselves could claim. An EO, after all, can be reversed by a subsequent EO by a new president. The Fair Pay and Safe Workplaces order, for example, was rescinded by President Trump in early 2017.

But even before that a federal judge in Texas had issued an injunction against that order subject to a lawsuit brought by trade associations representing builders and security guard companies.[30] Other Obama efforts to boost workers' rights were also held up in court as the administration wound to a close. In March 2014, Obama issued a presidential memorandum directing the Department of Labor to update its interpretation of the 1938 Fair Labor Standards Act so as to expand the number of workers eligible for increased overtime pay (at the time, the threshold was income of $23,660 or less per year, a figure not seriously examined since the 1960s.) The Labor Department issued a proposed regulation in July 2015, greatly expanding overtime pay. After a public comment period, the final regulation was issued in May 2016; it rolled back the requirements slightly, but the department

---

29 Daniel Gitterman, *Calling the Shots: The President, Executive Orders, and Public Policy* (Washington, DC: Brookings Institution Press, 2017).
30 Texas was the favorite site for those filing suit against Obama's EOs, since it had many federal judges unsympathetic to regulation and the 5th Circuit Court of Appeals was also dominated by Republican appointees. "Another day, another Obama administration regulation blocked nationwide by a federal court in Texas," noted *Politico*. Josh Gerstein, "Judge Blocks Obama Contracting Rules Nationwide," *Politico*, October 25, 2016, http://www.politico.com/blogs/under-the-radar/2016/10/obama-government-contractors-regulation-blocked-texas-court-230295.

still estimated the new threshold of $47,676 would benefit 4.2 million workers. Further, the new figure would rise at the rate of inflation each year.

Businesses, which had provided most of the 270,000 public comments received by the department concerning the regulation, were not happy. Nor were some state governments. In September 2016, the US Chamber of Commerce sued (in, naturally, a Texas courtroom), as did public officials in 21 states (including, naturally, Texas). The complainants argued that "once again, President Obama is trying to unilaterally rewrite the law," which in their view did not permit the department to raise the threshold so dramatically nor to index it to inflation. The latter, plaintiffs argued, could be interpreted as a new regulation in its own right, but had appeared without the advance notice and ability to comment required by federal law.[31]

Two weeks after the 2016 election, the district court issued a national stay, preventing the rule from going into effect on December 1 as planned. The judge agreed that the Department had gone beyond its statutory authority, especially in creating the "automatic updating mechanism."[32] The Labor Department quickly appealed – but when the case returned to court in 2017, the Trump administration switched sides, leaving the new rule literally defenseless.[33]

Environmental Protection

The Obama administration had more, but hardly universal, success in the environmental arena. Its administrative tactics largely arose as substitutes for the failure of the Senate to pass a carbon emissions "cap and trade" bill combatting global warming in 2009 to 2010.

In May 2010, Obama sent a memorandum to four agency heads, directing them to tighten greenhouse gas and fuel efficiency standards. One strand aimed to "produce a new generation of clean vehicles," reducing sulfur in gasoline and boosting mileage requirements.[34] After some hiccups – and some White House stalling designed to make sure controversial rules were not issued in time to become an issue

---

31 Daniel Wiessner, "States, Interest Groups Sue US Government on Overtime Pay Rule," *Reuters.com*, September 20, 2016, http://www.reuters.com/article/us-overtime-lawsuit-idUSKCN11Q2E2.
32 Melanie Trottman, "Federal Judge Issues Nationwide Injunction," *Wall Street Journal*, November 23, 2016.
33 In 2020, the threshold increased to $35,568, without adjustments for inflation.
34 Barack Obama, "Presidential Memorandum Regarding Fuel Efficiency Standards," May 22, 2010, https://obamawhitehouse.archives.gov/the-press-office/presidential-memorandum-regarding-fuel-efficiency-standards.

in the 2012 election – the rule-writing project also resulted in draft rules aiming to extend Clean Air Act (CAA) authority to existing power plants, especially those fueled by coal, and to limit greenhouse gases produced by new development. Even agency attorneys suggested that EPA's interpretation of the CAA was aggressive, even "challenging."[35] It was not surprising, then, that a series of lawsuits soon questioned that interpretation.

The first case that wound up before the Supreme Court in 2014 was *Utility Air Regulatory Group (UARG) v. EPA*. This dealt with EPA regulation of larger industrial plants emitting greenhouse gases. The Court wound up largely upholding the EPA's substantive position, noting that "Congress's profligate use of [the phrase] 'air pollutant' is not conducive to clarity."[36] Vague legal language had led to administrative discretion.

However, in its regulations, the EPA had also sought to change the threshold for regulating carbon emissions produced by new (as opposed to existing) developments. The Clean Air Act states that regulation should kick in when a facility generates more than 250 tons of a given pollutant – but while that is a lot of mercury, it is a tiny amount of greenhouse gas. The EPA's new rule thus raised the limit for carbon pollutants to 75,000 tons per year. That was better for industry, in fact, but it disregarded language in the law that was certainly not vague – and the court did not allow it to stand. In oral argument, even Justice Kagan of "presidential administration" fame mused disapprovingly that "the solution that EPA came up with actually seems to give it complete discretion to do whatever it wants, whenever it wants." As Justice Scalia later put the point in the decision, "[a]n agency may not rewrite clear statutory terms to suit its own sense of how the statute should operate."[37]

Kagan and Scalia did not agree for long about the letter of the law. In *Michigan v. Environmental Protection Agency* (2015), Scalia went back to the *Chevron* case noted above, which (as he put it) "directs courts to accept an agency's reasonable resolution of an ambiguity in a statute that the agency administers."[38] But in

---

35 Coral Davenport, "E.P.A. Staff Struggling to Create Pollution Rule," *New York Times*, February 4, 2014, https://www.nytimes.com/2014/02/05/us/epa-staff-struggling-to-create-rule-limiting-carbon-emissions.html; Coral Davenport, and Gardiner Harris, "Obama to Unveil Tougher Environmental Plan with His Legacy in Mind," *New York Times*, August 2, 2015, https://www.nytimes.com/2015/08/02/us/obama-to-unveil-tougher-climate-plan-with-his-legacy-in-mind.html.
36 UARG v. EPA, 573 US 302 (2014).
37 Kagan's remarks are from oral arguments for *Utility Air Regulatory Group v. Environmental Protection Agency*, February 24, 2014, https://www.supremecourt.gov/oral_arguments/argument_transcripts/2013/12-1146_8n6a.pdf. See more generally, the opinion of the Court: *UARG v. EPA*, 573 US 302 (2014).
38 *Michigan v. Environmental Protection Agency*, 576 US 743 (2015).

a five to four decision Scalia and Kagan disagreed entirely on what constituted a "reasonable" interpretation of the Clean Air Act when it came to regulating the specific power plants under review in the case. Scalia accused the agency of "interpretive gerrymanders" that "keep parts of statutory context it likes while throwing away parts it does not."[39] Kagan and the dissenters complained instead of judicial "micromanagement" by the Court.

As detailed below, *Michigan* was a larger loss for the administration in theory than in practice. But the next round of litigation to reach the Court was more uniformly problematic for Obama's administrative efforts to combat climate change. Just days before Justice Scalia's unexpected death in February 2016, he cast the deciding vote forcing a stay of the administration's Clean Power Plan (CPP) regulations.[40] The Supreme Court's intervention at that early stage of the proceedings was unprecedented – the appeals process had not played itself out yet – but so, some argued, was the CPP, which used a very broad reading of the Clean Air Act to impose carbon pollution emission guidelines on existing electric utility plants.[41] The administration's legal case faced several problems, beginning with yet another typographical error. This one had occurred when Congress managed to revise the same section of the CAA twice in contradictory ways when it amended the law in 1990. As legal scholar Jonathan Adler explained, the EPA had to argue that "either a) the wrong language was put in the US Code, b) the 1990 revisions, read properly, actually allow such regulation or c) the conflicting statutory language creates an ambiguity that the EPA has resolved by interpreting the language to allow for such regulation. This is an aggressive argument, and if the courts reject it, there is no CPP."[42] Opponents also held that the changes made to the regulations during the process of developing them from their original draft were so extensive as to basically create a new rule – itself requiring another round of public comment.

The case became before the DC Circuit Court of Appeals in September 2016 and, with no decision reached by the time Trump took office, the regulatory

---

39 Michigan v. Environmental Protection Agency, 576 US 743 (2015).
40 Jonathan H. Adler, "Supreme Court Puts the Brakes on the EPA's Clean Power Plan," Volokh Conspiracy blog, *Washington Post*, February 9, 2016, https://www.washingtonpost.com/news/volokh-conspiracy/wp/2016/02/09/supreme-court-puts-the-brakes-on-the-epas-clean-power-plan/?utm_term=.4a359fb75e87.
41 Jonathan H. Adler, "Placing Obama's Clean Power Plan in Context," Volokh Conspiracy blog, *Washington Post*, February 10, 2016, https://www.washingtonpost.com/news/volokh-conspiracy/wp/2016/02/10/placing-the-clean-power-plan-in-context/?utm_term=.bc1435759a3f.
42 Adler, "Placing Obama's Clean Power Plan in Context." See also Coral Davenport, "Obama Climate Plan, Now in Court, May Hinge on Error in 1990 Law," *New York Times*, September 25, 2016, https://www.nytimes.com/2016/09/26/us/politics/obama-court-clean-power-plan.html.

framework defaulted to the pre-Obama status quo.[43] This made the timing of the Supreme Court intervention in February 2016 important. In the *Michigan* case, the regulations that were ultimately overturned had already been in effect, pushing industry toward compliance by shaping business decisions about what kind of plants to build or expand. Those decisions involved high sunk costs and were unlikely to be reversed even after the Court's ruling. By contrast, the CPP was not yet embedded in private-sector decision making. It would subsequently be replaced by a far weaker Trump rule – which was itself replaced by a strong Biden rule which was then undermined by a new Court decision. Only when Congress acted to empower EPA in 2022 did lasting change occur.[44]

Immigration

In June 2012, his reelection bid approaching, Obama announced a program of Deferred Action for Childhood Arrivals (DACA). DACA aimed to protect from deportation about 1.2 million people who were in the US illegally. This was a very sympathetic group: Young people who had been brought to the United States before they were 16; they were high-school students or graduates or had served in the armed forces and had no criminal record. The Immigration and Nationality Act (INA) first passed in the 1950s gives presidents substantial discretion over who enters and remains in the country. Even so, DACA was criticized as a unilateral implementation of the so-called DREAM Act, which had failed to pass Congress in 2010.

After Obama's reelection, most observers thought there was a window for congressional action on immigration since key Republicans blamed their 2012 losses on the party's militant refusal to appeal to minority voters. But a Senate bill passed in June 2013 was never taken up by the House. The 2014 midterms, in which Democrats lost their Senate majority, put the final nail in the legislative coffin.

On November 20, 2014, then, Obama took to the national airwaves to announce a large expansion of his earlier initiative. Saying that he wanted to deport "felons, not families," the president announced that he would enlarge the DACA program,

---

[43] As they would remain. Trump's substitute rules were never finalized, and in 2022 the Supreme Court ruled against the CPP, even though the Biden administration had not actually implemented it. See *West Virginia v. Environmental Protection Agency* 597 US __ (2022).
[44] See the 2022 case, *West Virginia v. EPA*, and the subsequent authority Congress provided EPA in the Inflation Reduction Act, Public Law 117–169.

while creating a new, massive extension called Deferred Action for Parents of Americans (DAPA).[45] As with DACA, the upshot was that in certain circumstances, the government would defer the deportation of as many as four million parents of US citizens. In the meantime, they would be able to work legally in the country.

The policy was implemented not by formal presidential directive, but by the enforcement of the INA by the Department of Homeland Security. The Department of Justice memo advising the action was legal was addressed to DHS rather than to the president. The Secretary of Homeland Security, in turn, issued guidance to law enforcement officials, reshaping their "removal priorities." The Justice Department's analysis focused on the INA's emphasis on keeping families together.

Even so, did the INA allow so much discretion – in this case what is known as "prosecutorial discretion"? Obama's directives did not change the law, *per se*; rather, they set forth who was to be prosecuted (in this case deported), and in what order. The administration took solace in the 1985 Court decision *Heckler v. Chaney*: "[A]n agency's decision not to prosecute or enforce, whether through civil or criminal process, is a decision generally committed to an agency's absolute discretion." As applied to immigration cases, discretion had a strong jurisprudential pedigree – as recently as 2012, in *Arizona v. US*, the Court had stressed "the broad discretion exercised by immigration officials" in order to deal with "immediate human concerns" as well as "policy choices that bear on this Nation's international relations."[46]

Opponents of the president's agenda again turned to the judiciary, as Texas brought a suit on behalf of some two dozen states and state officials. They argued that the "brazen lawlessness" of the president's administrative actions did not make individual exceptions within the realm of prosecutorial discretion but was instead affirmatively bestowing new rights on large groups of people.[47] In February 2015, a district court judge in Texas imposed an injunction blocking the DAPA program, an injunction upheld in May by a three-judge panel of the 5th Circuit Court of Appeals. Though the Circuit Court signaled its doubts about the administration's case, neither decision directly addressed the merits of the question.

In January 2016, the Supreme Court agreed to hear Obama's appeal of the case and asked the parties to answer both the procedural questions and the substantive ones. The administration argued that it had no choice but to set priorities: Con-

---

45 Barack Obama, "Address to the Nation on Immigration Reform," November 20, 2014, https://www.presidency.ucsb.edu/node/308498.
46 *Heckler v. Chaney*, 470 US 821 (1985); *Arizona v. US* 567 US 387 (2012).
47 See the December 2014 "Complaint for Declaratory and Injunctive Relief," https://www.clearinghouse.net/detail.php?id=14308.

gress's annual appropriation for dealing with "removable aliens" amounted to 3.5 percent of the amount needed to actually remove them. But Justice Anthony Kennedy worried that "defining the limits of discretion" should be "a legislative, not an executive act." The attorney representing Texas thus argued that perhaps "[DHS] could do forbearance from removal, but what they can't do is grant authorization to be in the country" if that meant also providing positive benefits like the right to work legally.[48]

In the end, the Court – down to eight members, after Scalia's death – was deadlocked, affirming the lower courts' injunction by default, and the merits of the case remained undecided as of election day. A Clinton victory would have forced the issue back through the system again, starting in Texas; but the Trump victory ended the case, and DAPA.

Indeed, in the fall of 2017, Trump also sought to rescind the DACA program. He cited advice from Attorney General Jeff Sessions that provided a completely new reading of the INA. According to Trump's DOJ, Obama's had been wrong about DACA's legality – showing the malleability of presidential legal interpretation in rather dramatic fashion.[49]

Imperial, or Imperiled?

The cover, drenched in funereal black, hoped to evoke the darkness of tyranny. Inside, the report claimed to document a "pattern of overreach," under President Obama, amounting to a "break-down in the rule of law."[50] The title chosen by House Majority Leader Eric Cantor was practically foreordained: *The Imperial Presidency*.[51]

But that reference in itself makes clear that Obama's efforts to exercise presidential power were simply new skirmishes along an old inter-branch frontier. Whatever his trespasses across those boundary lines, in some ways his version of executive unilateralism laid open the fragility of the enterprise. Was his presidency imperial – or (to channel Gerald Ford) instead imperiled?

Clearly Obama wanted to establish a substantive legacy. That in turn required substantive achievements – and that, at least after 2010, seemed to require

---

48 OYEZ, "Oral arguments," *US v. Texas*, April 18, 2016, https://www.oyez.org/cases/2015/15-674.
49 However, in 2020 the Supreme Court kept DACA in effect, ruling Trump did not follow proper procedure in rescinding it.
50 Office of the House Majority Leader, *The Imperial Presidency*, October 2012 (updated March 2014).
51 See Arthur M. Schlesinger, Jr., *The Imperial Presidency* (Boston: Houghton Mifflin, 1973).

detours around congressional gridlock. The 2009 to 2010 session did result in extensive new laws, allowing additional regulatory action that continued in a rush to the end of the president's term.[52] But later it was hard to argue that Obama could have achieved his ends by congressional action. In the *King v. Burwell* oral arguments, the solicitor general was asked why Congress couldn't simply fix any problems with the ACA, if they stemmed from a drafting error. He replied, to knowing laughter, "*this* Congress?" Or as Obama put it in his 2014 immigration address, almost as a taunt, "to those members of Congress who question my au-thority . . ., I have one answer: Pass a bill."[53]

Congress's ability to do that was limited, as Obama well knew. Many of the actions above were substitutes for bills he had not been able to pass, mostly after 2010, but in some cases even under unified government.

This does not mean the administration did not achieve important change – the Dreamers would testify otherwise. But it did mean the changes achieved via administrative action were incremental rather than transformational: They could not rewrite the law. Thus, if the use of statutory interpretation was inevitable, it was also invitational: It attracted both political flak and, perhaps more crucially, challenges from other political institutions. In that vein courts were active – often activist – players in the administrative arena during the Obama years, sometimes affirming but also delaying or reversing executive orders, regulations, and the statutory interpretations that undergirded them.

Finally, of course, executive actions can be rescinded not just by new law or court rulings but by future executives. This is exactly what President Trump promised to accomplish. Administrative action is inherently fragile compared to legislative change – thus another part of the Obama legacy will be to highlight the brittle nature of unilateral change in a system that demands, but can rarely induce, consensus and coalition-building to achieve permanent reform.

---

52 See, e.g., Dave Boyer, "The 'Most Transparent' Administration in History Issues Record Number of 'Midnight' Regulations," *Washington Times*, January 5, 2017, http://www.washingtontimes.com/news/2017/jan/5/obama-issuing-record-number-midnight-regulations/.
53 Barack Obama, "Address to the Nation on Immigration Reform," November 20, 2014, http://www.presidency.ucsb.edu/ws/?pid=107923.

References

Ackerman, Bruce. *The Decline and Fall of the American Republic*. Cambridge, MA: Harvard University Press, 2010.
Adler, Jonathan H. "Placing Obama's Clean Power Plan in Context." Volokh Conspiracy blog, *Washington Post*. February 10, 2016, https://www.washingtonpost.com/news/volokh-conspiracy/wp/2016/02/10/placing-the-clean-power-plan-in-context/?utm_term=.bc1435759a3f.
Adler, Jonathan H. "Supreme Court Puts the Brakes on the EPA's Clean Power Plan." Volokh Conspiracy blog. *Washington Post*. February 9, 2016, https://www.washingtonpost.com/news/volokh-conspiracy/wp/2016/02/09/supreme-court-puts-the-brakes-on-the-epas-clean-power-plan/?utm_term=.4a359fb75e87.
American Presidency Project. "Remarks Prior to a Cabinet Meeting." January 14, 2014, https://www.presidency.ucsb.edu/node/305044.
Boyer, Dave. "The 'Most Transparent' Administration in History Issues Record Number of 'Midnight' Regulations." *Washington Times*. January 5, 2017, http://www.washingtontimes.com/news/2017/jan/5/obama-issuing-record-number-midnight-regulations/.
Bruff, Harold. *Untrodden Ground: How Presidents Interpret the Constitution*. Chicago: University of Chicago Press, 2015.
Davenport, Coral. "E.P.A. Staff Struggling to Create Pollution Rule." *New York Times*. February 4, 2014, https://www.nytimes.com/2014/02/05/us/epa-staff-struggling-to-create-rule-limiting-carbon-emissions.html.
Davenport, Coral. "Obama Climate Plan, Now in Court, May Hinge on Error in 1990 Law." *New York Times*. September 25, 2016, https://www.nytimes.com/2016/09/26/us/politics/obama-court-clean-power-plan.html.
Davenport, Coral, and Gardiner Harris. "Obama to Unveil Tougher Environmental Plan with His Legacy in Mind." *New York Times*. August 2, 2015, https://www.nytimes.com/2015/08/02/us/obama-to-unveil-tougher-climate-plan-with-his-legacy-in-mind.html.
Derthick, Martha. *Up in Smoke*. Third revised edition. Washington, DC: CQ Press, 2011.
Dodds, Graham. *Take Up Your Pen*. Philadelphia: University of Pennsylvania Press, 2013.
Dombrowski, Peter, and Andrew Ross. "Transforming the Navy." *Naval College War Review* 56, no. 3 (Summer 2003), https://digital-commons.usnwc.edu/nwc-review/vol56/iss3/6.
Edelson, Chris. "In Service to Power: Legal Scholars as Executive Branch Lawyers in the Obama Administration." *Presidential Studies Quarterly* 43 (September 2013): 618–640.
Gerstein, Josh. "Judge Blocks Obama Contracting Rules Nationwide." *Politico*. October 25, 2016, http://www.politico.com/blogs/under-the-radar/2016/10/obama-government-contractors-regulation-blocked-texas-court-230295.
Gitterman, Daniel. *Calling the Shots: The President, Executive Orders, and Public Policy*. Washington, DC: Brookings Institution Press, 2017.
Graff, Garrett. *Watergate: A New History*. New York: Simon & Schuster, 2022.
Hearing of the Committee on the Judiciary. US House of Representatives. "Enforcing the President's Constitutional Duty to Faithfully Execute the Laws." February 26, 2014.
Kagan, Elena. "Presidential Administration." *Harvard Law Review* 114 (June 2001).
Light, Paul. *The Government-Industrial Complex: The True Size of Government, 1984–2017*. New York: Oxford University Press, 2019.
Melnick, R. Shep. *Between the Lines*. Washington, DC: Brookings Institution, 1994.
Nathan, Richard. *The Administrative Presidency*. New York: Macmillan, 1983.

Nicholas, Peter, and Christi Parsons. "Rebuilding Staff, Obama Charts New Course." *Philadelphia Inquirer*, October 10, 2010.
NPR. "NPR's Exit Interview with President Obama." December 19, 2016, http://www.npr.org/2016/12/19/504998487/transcript-and-video-nprs-exit-interview-with-president-obama.
Obama, Barack. "Address to the Nation on Immigration Reform." November 20, 2014, https://www.presidency.ucsb.edu/node/308498.
Obama, Barack. "Address to the Nation on Immigration Reform." November 20, 2014, http://www.presidency.ucsb.edu/ws/?pid=107923.
Obama, Barack. "Presidential Memorandum Regarding Fuel Efficiency Standards." May 22, 2010, https://obamawhitehouse.archives.gov/the-press-office/presidential-memorandum-regarding-fuel-efficiency-standards.
Obama, Barack. "Remarks by the President." May 21, 2009, https://www.presidency.ucsb.edu/node/286247.
Obama, Barack. "Remarks in Las Vegas," October 24, 2011, https://www.presidency.ucsb.edu/node/297388.
OYEZ. "Oral arguments." *US v. Texas*, April 18, 2016, https://www.oyez.org/cases/2015/15-674.
Pear, Robert. "Four Words Imperil Health Law; All a Mistake, Its Writers Say." *New York Times*, May 26, 2015, A1.
Potter, Rachel, et al., "Not by the Numbers." *Presidential Studies Quarterly* 52 (September 2022): 596–625.
Relyea, Harold C. *Presidential Directives: Background and Overview*. Washington, DC: Congressional Research Service, 2008.
Rudalevige, Andrew. "Barack Obama and the Administrative Presidency." In *Obama's Fractured Legacy*, edited by François de Chantal. Edinburgh: Edinburgh University Press, 2020.
Rudalevige, Andrew. "The Obama Administrative Presidency: Some Late-Term Patterns." *Presidential Studies Quarterly* 46 (December 2016): 868–890.
Savage, Charlie. *Power Wars: Inside Obama's Post-9/11 Presidency*. Boston: Little Brown, 2015.
Schlesinger, Jr., Arthur M. *The Imperial Presidency*. Boston: Houghton Mifflin, 1973.
Trottman, Melanie. "Federal Judge Issues Nationwide Injunction." *Wall Street Journal*. November 23, 2016.
Whittington, Keith. *Constitutional Construction*. Cambridge, MA: Harvard University Press, 2001.
Wiessner, Daniel. "States, Interest Groups Sue US Government on Overtime Pay Rule." *Reuters.com*. September 20, 2016, http://www.reuters.com/article/us-overtime-lawsuit-idUSKCN11Q2E2.
Winkler, Jeff. "McConnell Skeptical of Obama's Centrist Rhetoric Ahead of State of the Union." *Daily Caller*. January 25, 2011, http://dailycaller.com/2011/01/25/mcconnell-skeptical-about-obamas-centrist-rhetoric-ahead-of-state-of-the-union/.

Nicholas O. Howard and Mark Owens
Chapter 7
Developing a Bench: President Obama's Judicial Appointment Legacy

President Obama's electoral victory in 2008 was matched with an increase of newly elected Democratic senators. The victories in the Senate increased President Obama's potential to guide nominations to the federal judiciary to confirmation. Though it took several months, the Democratic caucus' first 60-vote filibuster-proof majority since the Carter presidency (1977–1979) was reached when Senator Al Franken (D-MN) won Minnesota's Senate recount in late June and Senator Arlen Specter (D-PA) switched to join the Senate Democrats in April of 2009. The party switch was especially relevant to judicial nominations as Senator Spector was a former Republican chairman of the Senate Judiciary Committee.[1] Amidst this momentum, the filibuster-proof majority was not a reliable expectation as Senator Ted Kennedy was absent from voting for long periods to seek treatment for a brain tumor.[2] This meant the public had high expectations for President Obama, but the White House still faced hurdles to overcome any objection or delay.

The narrative that the president could usher in change quickly was often blind to the situation and to diversity within the Democratic caucus. Despite the underlying turmoil, 317 of Obama's judicial nominees were confirmed to lower federal courts. This ranks him fourth among all presidents since 1933.[3] Obama's success in appointing federal judges can be understood two ways. He nominated a higher percentage of women than prior presidents, as many Black judges as President Clinton, and as many Hispanic judges as President Bush. Also, the total number of judges confirmed under Obama (317 judges) was almost the same as his immediate predecessor George W. Bush (322 judges). Obama and Bush were

---

[1] Senator Specter was the Chair of the Judiciary Committee during the confirmation processes of Justice Roberts and Justice Alito.
[2] After Senator Ted Kennedy died on August 25, 2009, he was replaced by Senator Paul Kirk (D-MA).
[3] US Courts, "Judgeship Appointments by President," Administrative Office of the US Courts on behalf of the Federal Judiciary, Washington, DC, accessed September 19, 2023, https://www.uscourts.gov/sites/default/files/apptsbypres.pdf.

Nicholas O. Howard, Concordia College
Mark Owens, The Citadel

both able to work with Majority Leaders from their own party, except for the last Congress of their presidency.[4]

The process of confirming judges was more acrimonious for Obama than his predecessors. The use of blue slips and objecting to cloture emerged as a strategy for delay in the 1980s, and spiked during the George W. Bush presidency and continued into Obama's administration. The White House Counsel for President Obama needed to be aware of these procedural actions in the Senate, as senators became more interested in how the federal judiciary was shaped.

The reality of judicial confirmation politics is thus that presidents and the Senate are both motivated to use their power to influence the judiciary. These political motivations exist regardless of the characteristics of the individual put forward for a judicial vacancy. Additionally, with respect to lower court nominations, presidents engage with home state senators during the confirmation process – and co-partisan home state senators – before a nomination is ever made.[5] Even then, senators of the opposite party assert themselves in the advice and consent role, following examples from Carter's administration based on policy views and desires to have vacancies filled by a new president.[6] If senators are expected to champion a nominee through the Senate – communicating with the Chair of the Senate Judiciary Committee and working to resolve a filibuster on the floor – they expect their desires to be heard.

Research in political science has identified that the duration of a nomination is the most comprehensive outcome in nomination politics.[7] This is because while a nomination is on the committee's calendar it can end multiple ways (withdraw or a

---

4 Ironically, Presidents George W. Bush and Barack Obama both faced volatile first years with party switches, however the switch of Senator Jeffords (VT) from Republican to independent altered who held the majority. The later switch in 2009 of Senator Specter (PA) from Republican to Democrat helped Democrats reach a three-fifths majority that could defeat a filibuster if it held together. It is also important to recognize that these presidents who served eight years both lagged Presidents Reagan (368 judges) and Clinton (367 judges) who operated in a political context where different parties controlled the Senate and White House.
5 Nicholas O. Howard, and David A. Hughes, "Revisiting Senatorial Courtesy and the Selection of Judges to the US Courts of Appeals," *Political Research Quarterly* 75, no. 1 (2022): 61–75.
6 "Republicans Stall Late Carter Appointments," in *CQ Almanac*, 36th edition, 15-A-22-A (Washington, DC: Congressional Quarterly, 1981), accessed December 11, 2023, https://library.cqpress.com/cqalmanac/document.php?id=cqal80-860-25878-1173433.
7 Charles R. Shipan, and Megan L. Shannon, "Delaying justice(s): A Duration Analysis of Supreme Court Confirmations," *American Journal of Political Science* 47, no. 4 (2003): 654–668; Sarah A. Binder, and Forrest Maltzman, *Advice and Dissent: The Struggle to Shape the Federal Judiciary* (Lanham: Rowman & Littlefield, 2009).

vote by the committee).[8] A president must think about how quickly a nominee may make it through committee. The speed of deliberation is valuable, because it may serve as a signal that additional scrutiny of the nominee was not needed.[9] If any nominee is likely to be delayed, then a president may shift the debate to see if a certain characteristic can help a nominee break through the logjam.

How the Senate Judiciary Committee responds to a presidential nomination serves as a proxy battle for the larger chamber, because it is the first venue a judicial nominee is received. Delay in committee contributes to the length of time a nomination may be pending in the Senate.[10] The Senate often values the recommendation of the committee, because the membership of the Senate Judiciary Committee is likely to be more interested in the selection of lower federal court judges than other senators.[11]

It is into this separation of power environment that President Obama implemented a different strategy than other presidents in the modern era. Using all District and Appeals court nominations from 1989 to 2020, or the presidencies of George H.W. Bush, Bill Clinton, George W. Bush, Barack Obama, and Donald Trump, we show the effects of President Obama's new approach. While presidents all nominate individuals to the federal bench that are seen as meritorious and fitting their general outlook, Obama expanded efforts from prior Democratic administrations at diversifying the appointees within the lower federal courts. His efforts to use empathy as a philosophy for judicial selection helped diversify the courts, and the White House Counsel's Office left nominations active to pursue this philosophy. Obama's nominations did not try to make up for an absence of diversity, rather there was a gender and racial balance to Obama's nominations. The final breakdowns made it appear as if the White House was trying to meet identified targets, despite the lengthy process of each step along the way.

---

[8] Efforts could be made to circumvent this process, but to this point the committee remains a powerful venue to the confirmation process because senators on the committee have less ambiguity towards the outcome of a nomination.

[9] Lisa M. Holmes, "Presidential Strategy in the Judicial Appointment Process: 'Going Public' in Support of Nominees to the US Courts of Appeals," *American Politics Research* 35, no. 5 (2007): 567–594.

[10] Between 1868 and 1980 there was only one instance that the Senate Judiciary Committee was the venue to block a nomination. In 1951, the committee failed to report Federal Communications Commissioner Frieda Hennock to be confirmed by the Senate until she asked President Truman to withdraw her nomination.

[11] Lauren Bell, "Senatorial discourtesy: The Senate's use of delay to shape the federal judiciary," *Political Research Quarterly* 55, no. 3 (2002): 589–607; Christine C. Bird, and Zachary A. McGee, "Going Nuclear: Federalist Society Affiliated Judicial Nominees' Prospects and a New Era of Confirmation Politics," *American Politics Research* 51, no. 1 (2023): 37–56.

The associations we find identify a pattern that the extended judicial vacancies that received high-profile attention during the Obama administration were not personal. The longer delays and declining rate of success resemble an institutional trend that already existed, and reflected the institutional contexts during Obama's eight years in office. Our ability to build comparisons across time and measure when moving a nominee through the Senate quickly is difficult offers an empirical way to capture how presidents focus on working their list of nominees to achieve diversity in the courts.

As an institution with the constitutional authority to consent to the president's nominee, the Senate retains its own perspective. President Obama described his nominees as mainstream. They were also nominees who exhibited empathy in their judicial decision making and were different from past nominees. As the basis for evaluating a nominee expanded beyond merit-qualifications, we expect that senators increasingly started to look to their peers for advice. Often this advice emerges from the Senate Judiciary Committee which can filter multiple sources of information and sees time spent with a lower court nominee before making a recommendation to the broader Senate chamber.

Seeking a New Judicial Philosophy: Mainstream, plus Empathy

On the campaign trail Obama articulated that his judicial nominees would be well-intentioned people in addition to being well-qualified reflecting that he saw the critical ingredient to resolve complex legal questions "is supplied by what is in the judge's heart."[12] Obama believed it was important for judges to have "[t]he empathy to understand what it's like to be poor or African-American or gay or disabled or old. That's the criteria by which I'm going to be selecting my judges."[13] As a candidate or as president, he did not say that his nominees had to resemble any of those characteristics, but they did need to see beyond typical personal experience.

The self-described inspiration for Obama's nomination philosophy was a quote from Supreme Court Justice Oliver Wendell Holmes: "It is experience that can give a person a common touch and a sense of compassion and understanding of how

---

12 Congress.gov, "Nomination of John Roberts," *Congressional Record* 151, no. 119 (2005): S10273.
13 Debra Cassens Weiss, "Empathy Focus for Obama Justices," *ABA Journal* (July 18, 2007), accessed September 19, 2023, https://www.abajournal.com/news/article/empathy_focus_for_obama_justices.

the world works and how ordinary people live."[14] Empathy was the new umbrella term to understand Obama's rationale for selecting nominees. The challenge of bringing Justice Holmes's viewpoint to the twenty-first century was that the well-qualified individuals Obama could select had risen in a system where merit and ideology defined a nominee. This was apparent from statements given by Sonia Sotomayor and Elena Kagan, the two women confirmed to the Supreme Court following their nomination by President Obama, clarifying what this could be in the twenty-first century. In response to a question from Senator Kyl (R-AZ), Judge Sotomayor said "Judges can't rely on what's in their heart . . . . It's not the heart that compels conclusions in cases, it's the law."[15] Several years later Supreme Court Justice Elena Kagan said, "[p]eople look at an institution and they see people who are like them, who share their experiences, who they imagine share their set of values, and that's a sort of natural thing and they feel more comfortable if that occurs." This leads us to the expectation that to appoint judges who understood how ordinary people live, the Obama administration produced a set of judicial nominees that closely mirrored the gender, race, and ethic distribution of the nation. These nominations were a way for the president to stoke political discourse,[16] and appoint individuals from underrepresented groups to increase public approval.[17]

A clear challenge before Obama was to educate the Senate that his nominees were mainstream, as he embarked on a strategy to diversify the courts and make their rulings more compassionate. The strategy to nominate moderates who were empathetic is clearly articulated in Obama's first judicial nomination. The President nominated Judge David Hamilton from the US District Court of Indiana to be elevated to the US Court of Appeals for the Seventh Circuit in March 2009.[18] Judge Hamilton had the support of Senator Richard Lugar (R-IN) to satisfy senatorial courtesy. Then Judge Hamilton became the test case to define the "empathy standard" in committee. He received numerous written questions from members of

---

14 Barack Obama, "Remarks by the President in Nominating Judge Sonia Sotomayor to the United States Supreme Court," *Office of the Press Secretary, The White House*, May 26, 2009, accessed December 11, 2023, https://obamawhitehouse.archives.gov/the-press-office/remarks-president-nominating-judge-sonia-sotomayor-united-states-supreme-court.
15 Ari Shapiro, "Sotomayor Differs With Obama on 'Empathy' Issue," *NPR*, July 14, 2009, https://www.npr.org/2009/07/14/106569335/sotomayor-differs-with-obama-on-empathy-issue.
16 Lisa M. Holmes, "Why 'Go Public'? Presidential Use of Nominees to the US Courts of Appeals," *Presidential Studies Quarterly* 38, no. 1 (2008): 110–122.
17 Alex Badas, and Katelyn E. Stauffer, "Descriptive Representation, Judicial Nominations, and Perceptions of Presidential Accomplishment," *Representation* 59, no. 2 (2022): 249–270.
18 Jeffrey Toobin, "Bench Press," *New Yorker*, September 21, 2009, http://www.newyorker.com/magazine/2009/09/21/bench-press; David Fontana, "Cooperative Judicial Nominations During the Obama Administration," *Wisconsin Law Review* 2 (2017): 285–323.

the Senate Judiciary Committee that explicitly drew language from Obama's speeches to ask how empathy shaped his judicial ideology. Hamilton repeatedly clarified that empathy was important but was separate from sympathy. He would put the law first.[19]

This first nomination also hinted that empathetic mainstream moderates would not sail through confirmation faster than other nominees. The time to confirm Judge Hamilton took two months longer than the Senate's attention to confirm Justice Sotomayor to the Supreme Court of the United States. The contrast between these two confirmations reminds us that some clarity about the confirmation process is needed. The Senate does not consider nominations in the order they are received, but rather has a standard process to consider nominees that it will depart from under situations such as a Supreme Court vacancy.[20] To really understand if a nominee is being delayed as a means of political opposition, we should recognize the circumstances that contributed to the delay.

During President Obama's two terms in office, the expedience that each nominee was able to receive a vote in the Senate was a function of politics and procedural context. Between 2009 and 2013, nominees to the lower federal bench were frequently delayed in committee as was the case with each succeeding administration. However, from 2013 to 2017, if the Democratic Party controlled the Senate the time to confirmation was significantly shorter. This was because Senate Majority Leader Harry Reid (D-NV) invoked the nuclear option to overcome filibusters by nominations with a majority vote. What is genuinely interesting is that when nominees could fly through to a floor vote – the time a nominee was reviewed by the Senate Judiciary Committee did not change.

In this chapter, we compare the judicial nominations of President Barack Obama to his predecessors and successor to establish a theoretical framework of how Obama's new philosophy about what makes a great judge set a new trajectory for diversity across the federal courts. The stories we have discussed about the confirmation processes of Judge Hamilton, Justice Kagen, and Justice Sotomayor show that statements from the nominees about empathy sometimes match the President's own words and sometimes they do not. Since we cannot solely rely on the descriptions of the President, nominees, or senators we gathered all

---

19 David F. Hamilton, "Responses of David F. Hamilton: Nominee to the US Court of Appeals for the Seventh Circuit to the Written Questions of Senator Jeff Sessions, Senator John Cornyn, and Senator Tom Coburn, M.D," Senate Judiciary Committee (April 29, 2009).
20 Anthony J. Madonna, James E. Monogan III, and Richard Vining, Jr., "Confirmation Wars, Legislative Time, and Collateral Damage: The Impact of Supreme Court Nominations on Presidential Success in the US Senate," *Political Research Quarterly* 69, no. 4 (2016): 746–759.

nominations made from 1989 to 2020 to analyze empirical trends that reveal the fingerprints of the successful implementation of a new standard.

Empathy, Nominee Selection Patterns, and Senate Evaluations

The statements of candidate Obama when paired with a scholarly understanding of court nominations produces a focus on nominee perception and situation. As with previous studies, we expect that presidents prioritize a judge's legal philosophy (or ideology) when making a nomination over the individual characteristics of a nominee. Likewise, senators are expected to see a nominee as holding the president's philosophy regardless of the individual nominee's characteristics.[21] We also assume the attention by senators and the public waxes and wanes across nominations.

Candidate – and then President – Obama's focus on empathy as a means of evaluating judicial nominees offered a novel approach for selection. As discussed above, this standard was discussed by the administration as the jurist's ability to see themselves in the shoes of a party before the court, no matter their circumstance. Observers such as Joel Goldstein stated, "[l]et's hope that senators of both parties include this bipartisan criterion as a desirable trait in a justice" when looking at nominations, a hope mirrored by the administration.[22] Given President Obama's desire for empathy specifically related to less frequently included classes of individuals, we begin with an exploration of nominees' demographic features to see how this translated into nominee selection.

The inclusion of race in President Obama's definition of empathy leads us to begin with an exploration of racial makeup. Figure 1a shows that Obama pre-

---

[21] Ashlyn Kuersten, and Donald R. Songer, "Presidential success through appointments to the United States Courts of Appeals," *American Politics Research* 31, no. 2 (2003): 107–137. Donald R. Songer, Susan W. Johnson, and Ronald Stidham, "Presidential success through appointments to the United States District Courts," *Justice System Journal* 24, no. 3 (2003): 283–300. How presidential preferences shape judicial decision making is complicated by the role of the Senate, both statically and dynamically. For discussion of this, see Howard, and Hughes, "Revisiting Senatorial Courtesy," as well as Michael W. Giles, Virginia A. Hettinger, and Todd Peppers, "Picking Federal Judges: A Note on Policy and Partisan Selection Agendas," *Political Research Quarterly* 54, no. 3 (2001): 623–641.
[22] Joel K. Goldstein, "How Empathy Makes Superior Judges – and Justice," *Origins: Current Events in Historical* Perspective, August 2010, https://origins.osu.edu/history-news/how-empathy-makes-superior-judges-and-justice.

sented the most racially diverse set of nominees for consideration by the Senate. For him, only slightly more than six of every 10 nominees are identified as white, whereas the next closest is President Clinton with 7.5 out of every 10 nominees similarly identified. This is even more stark compared with Republican presidents over the last 30 years. In short, it appears that President Obama's administration carried out the broad strokes of increasing the potential empathy toward minority groups through increasing racial diversity.

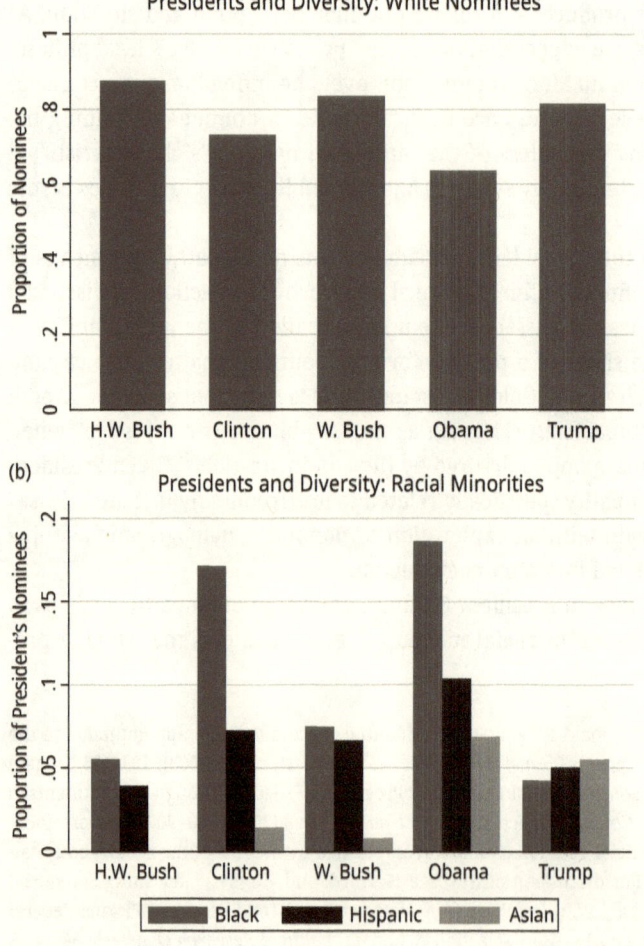

Figure 1: Racial Makeup of Judicial Nominees. (a) Nominees Identified as White. (b) Race and Minority Nominees.

The racial breakdown of minority nominees is also intriguing for Obama's pursuit of empathy. Figure 1b shows the racial makeup of non-white nominees across the last five presidents. President Obama again stands out, with almost two out of every 10 nominees being Black and one of every 10 Hispanic. Each of these figures is the highest for all administrations in our sample, though President Clinton's proportion of Black nominees is close to President Obama's. Interestingly, we also see that Obama nominated the highest proportion of Asian nominees – much higher than his predecessors and a pattern continued by President Trump. Obama's desire to increase the diversity – and potential empathy – on the federal bench is consistent through his nominees, along with the rise of Asian Americans as a solid block on the federal bench. Interest groups often highlight when nominations are historic in terms of representation, such as race and gender together and separately, further pushing the importance of this change.

We next turn to gender on the bench to understand how Obama's pursuit of empathy as a defining feature may have shaped his administration's behavior. We see in Figure 2a that Obama indeed presented the highest proportion of female nominees for Senate consideration. More than four of every 10 nominees put forward by Obama was female, over 25 percent more than his predecessors or successor.

The pattern for race in for all nominees in Figure 1b is less apparent when only looking at the racial breakdown of female nominees. Figure 2b shows that while Obama did nominate female jurists at a record pace, those nominations were largely concentrated on African Americans. Obama nominated twice as many African American judges for appointment than any other non-white racial category, mirroring again a pattern from President Clinton. This is the opposite of all Republican presidents, who nominated either Hispanic (Presidents H.W. and W. Bush) or Asian (President Trump) female jurists at a higher rate than African Americans. Thus, we see interesting nuance in what empathy could mean when applied to observable characteristics for Obama, with the least white and most female pool of nominees of any administration.

This effort to increase empathy through diversity exists in the cold reality of Senate politics. Senators desire that courts carry out their will, and frequently try to shape the nomination process at nearly every step.[23] Presidents and their nominees risk failure if they presume the Senate will always support a nominee. Each nomination is an independent evaluation and often requires presidents to be selective in the application of tools and rationales for a nominee. Indeed, Elena Kagan – Obama's own nominee to the US Supreme Court, and former Solicitor General – rejected the empathy philosophy as a basis for jurisprudence in her

---

23 See Binder, and Maltzman, *Advice and Dissent*, among others for an overview.

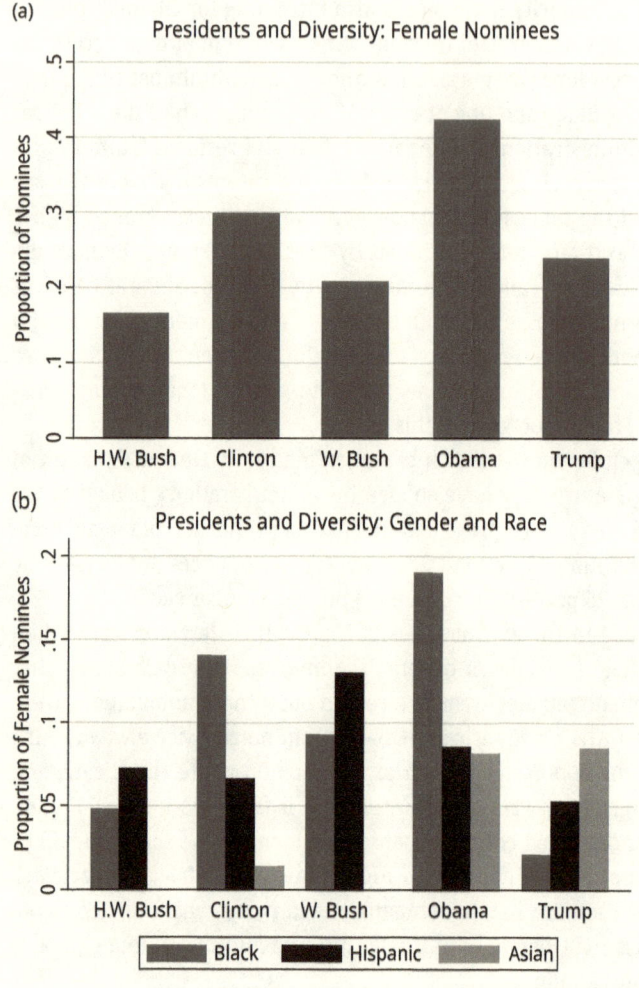

Figure 2: Gender Makeup of Judicial Nominees. (a) Female Nominees by President. (b) Race of Female Nominees.

Senate Judiciary Committee hearing.[24] Thus, we next turn to the intersection of an effort for increasing empathy and the political realities facing nominees.

---

[24] This was part of an exchange with Senator John Kyl (R-AZ) over how the law should be carried out in practice. See committee hearing transcript, page 103: "Committee on the Judiciary, Hearing on the Nomination of Elena Kagan to be an Associate Justice of the Supreme Court of the United States," 111–1044, June 18–20 and July 1, 2010, accessed December 11, 2023, CHRG-111shrg67622.pdf (govinfo.gov).

One element facing judicial selection and the desire for empathy in jurisprudence is the ability for the Senate to alter the nomination process. We first look at this from the perspective of individual senators in Figures 3a and 3b, which consider racial breakdowns and the partisanship of a state's senators relative to the president. We see in directly comparing Figures 3a to 3b that presidents generally nominate a lower proportion of racial minorities in states which feature opposite partisans. This is true for almost every president, with limited exceptions mostly tied to specific racial makeups.[25] Obama generally fits this pattern, with nominees to vacancies in states with co-partisan senators (Figure 3b) having higher proportions of African American and Hispanic jurists. However, opposite-partisan states (Figure 3a) featured a higher proportion of Asian-American nominees relative to co-partisan states. We thus see some evidence of governing realities meeting Obama's aspirations, but the pattern is generally similar.

Similarly, the presence of female nominees may be affected by the presence of home-state co-partisan senators. Figures 3c and 3d reflect this, with the former depicting the nomination of female jurists in states with opposite-partisan senators, and the latter with co-partisan senators. We observe generally similar patterns across the formations of state partisanship, with Presidents H.W. Bush, Clinton, and G.W. Bush nominating nearly identical proportions of female jurists for Senate consideration regardless of co-partisan senators. Obama broke with this balance in an unexpected fashion. Unlike his predecessors, who nominated female jurists at equal or slightly elevated proportions to vacancies with co-partisan home-state senators, he nominated a lower proportion of female jurists in states with co-partisans. This difference, representing a nearly six-point drop, represents a departure from previous patterns and a new practice under the Obama administration. This break with tradition is consistent with the idea that Obama may have prioritized the empathy standard while balancing senatorial courtesy with Senate Republicans.

We next consider the whole Senate using divided government in Figures 4a and 4b. One element first stands out here, that President Donald Trump only had a unified government – thus appearing in only Figures 4a and 4c – while President George H.W. Bush only had a divided government – thus appearing only in Figures 4b and 4d. Apart from these differences, we also observe that Presidents Clinton, G.W. Bush, and Obama responded to divided and unified governments differently. Presidents Clinton and G.W Bush nominated a higher proportion of racial minority nominees under a unified government (4a) than under a divided government (4b). Obama's was perhaps the most consistent administration of those facing

---

[25] Alex Badas and Katelyn E. Stauffer, "Descriptive Representation, Judicial Nominations, and Perceptions of Presidential Accomplishment." *Representation* 59, no. 2 (2022), 249–270.

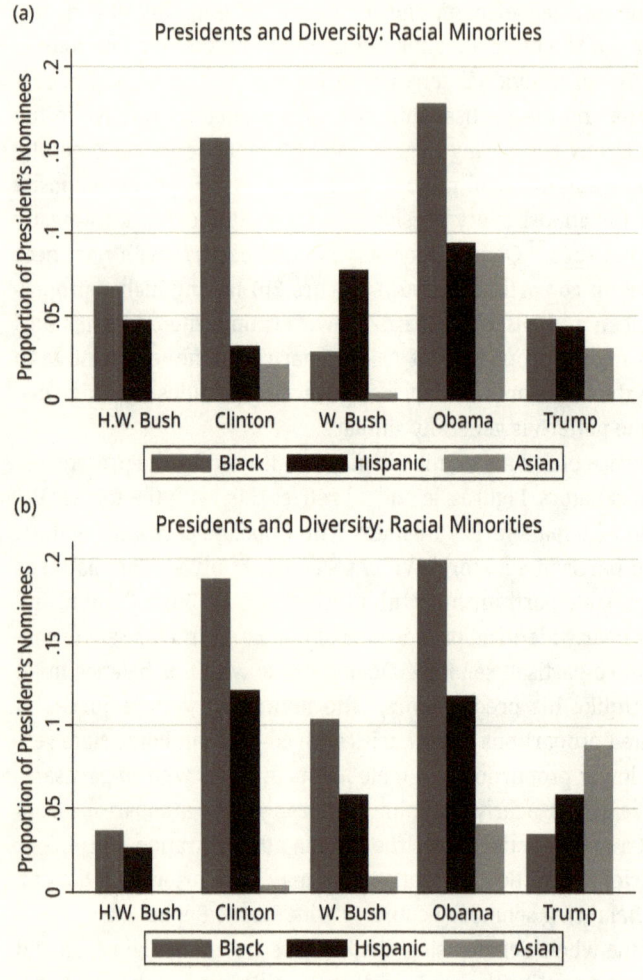

Figure 3: Senatorial Partisanship and Nominee Selection. (a) Race and Opposite-Partisan States. (b) Race and Co-Partisan States. (c) Gender and Opposite-Partisan States. (d) Gender and Co-Partisan States.

both divided and unified governments, with nearly identical proportions of nominees being African American and Asian, and only a slight decrease in Hispanic nominees. Thus, we see that presidents generally respond to divided government in their nominee selection, but Obama's emphasis on empathy may have kept nominee selection more constant with respect to race across unified and divided governments.

Presidents may also respond to a divided government with respect to the gender dynamics of their nominees. Figures 4c and 4d consider this, showing some interest-

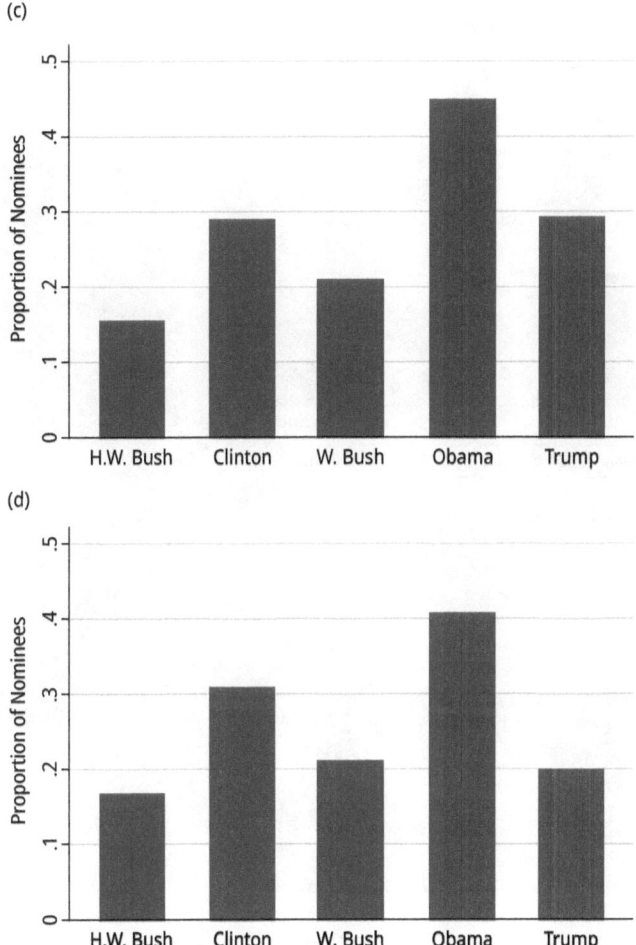

Figure 3 (continued)

ing patterns. While President Clinton nominated almost identical proportions of female jurists under divided and unified governments, President G.W. Bush nominated slightly more women under a divided government. Obama continued this practice, increasing the gap between unified and divided governments to five points. This is the largest gap of the three presidents operating under divided and unified governments, presenting partisan nuance into the desire for empathy in nominees.

Together, these patterns for the partisanship of the state to which a president makes a judicial nomination and the general partisan agreement of the Senate provide an interesting picture of Obama's nomination practices. While the administration

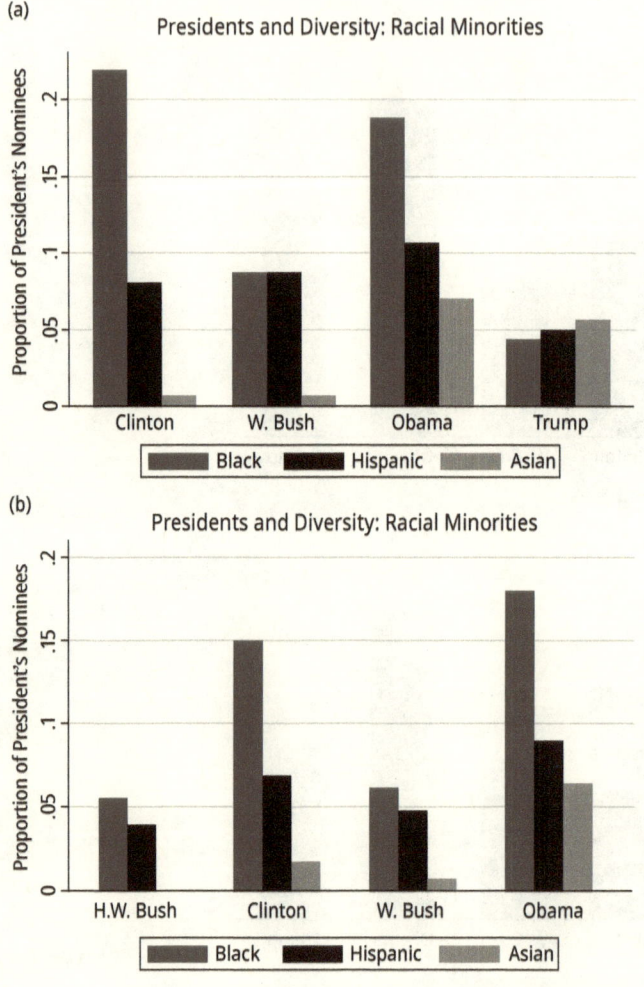

Figure 4: Divided Government and Nominee Selection. (a) Race and Unified Government. (b) Race and Divided Government. (c) Gender and Unified Government. (d) Gender and Divided Government.

espoused a desire for empathetic decision making and carried this out through their broad patterns of nominee selection, the applications of partisan dynamics show the structures encountered due to Senate partisan politics. Obama appears to have shaped his selection of nominees to offer Senates that were controlled – and individual vacancies overseen – by Republicans more diverse nominees. This may be in line with the expressed desire for empathy, but also fits a pattern to pressure Republican senators. Providing more diverse nominees, both in terms of race and gender, appears likely designed in response to the governing realities of judicial nominations.

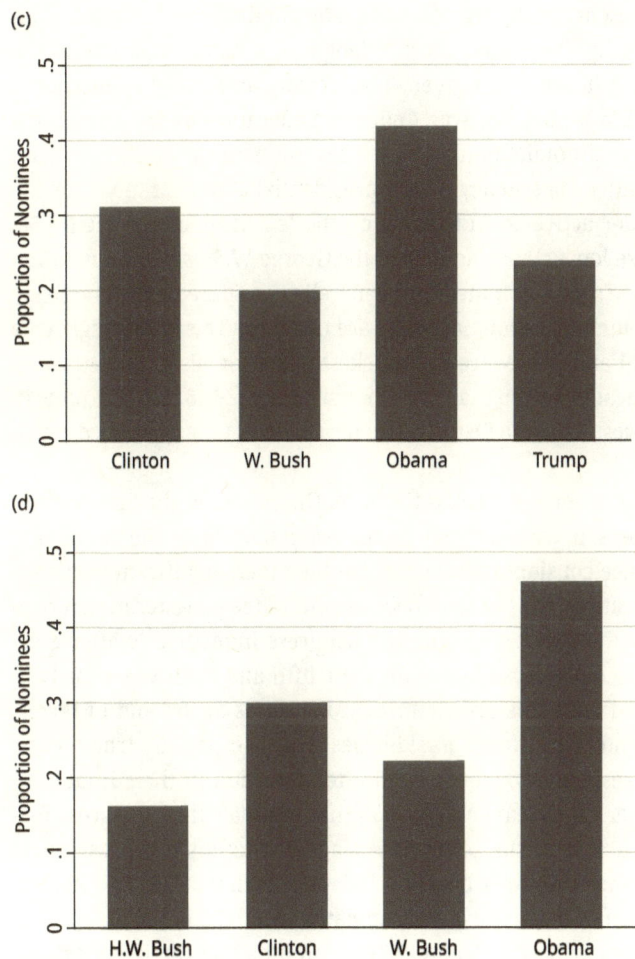

Figure 4 (continued)

Given these governing realities and the patterns observed for nominations, we consider the ultimate interaction of aspiration and governing realities for nominations – the duration of nominations themselves. We focus on the committee stage for duration across nominees, as much of the effect of home-state senators and co-partisan control of the chamber is borne out in pre-floor action. We later move to full consideration when discussing different iterations of duration.

The Senate Judiciary Committee generally functions in two ways regarding the pace of nominee consideration. The committee chooses both how long it will wait to take up a nomination, and how long active debate is required for the nominee in committee. Figure 5 presents these two ways of understanding consideration, with the left-hand side showing the annual average length of a nomination before the committee once the first hearing was given. The plotting on the right reflects the total committee duration a nominee was under consideration by the committee once the Senate received a nomination.[26] We see several patterns of interest here, beginning with the relative consistency within presidential administrations for the time a nominee is under active consideration on the left-hand side in Figure 5a. While certain years take longer, such as 2003 in the George W. Bush administration and 2020 under Donald Trump, nominees are generally considered equally quickly at all points across an administration once they are taken up. This is strikingly true for Obama. While 2009 and 2015 were the quickest years for his administration, they were not dramatically slower than his slowest year of 2016. Indeed, only 10 days separates the slowest from the fastest years for Obama's nominees once active consideration began.

The two plot patterns show a stark difference. On one hand the Senate Judiciary committee dispensed with judicial nominees generally at the same rate within a presidency once consideration began. On the other, significant variation exists within administrations for the total pace of committee consideration. Presidents are generally at their fastest during the Congress immediately after election – their first and second years along with their fifth and sixth years for two-term presidents. Paired with this are significant increases at the end of terms, and especially at the end of two-term presidencies. This is especially true for the Clinton and Obama presidencies, where committee duration in their final Congresses are much higher. It is clear in Figure 5b that Obama's final Congress featured unprecedented delays at the committee stage during his last presidency, with the average nominee spending nearly a full year at that stage. This clearly demonstrates that Obama's desire for a new empathy standard in judicial philosophy met with resistance from the Senate. The committee had the longest duration of active consideration for his nominees, and the end of his presidency saw an unprecedented committee delay in rendering decisions.

The connection between nominee duration and race is central to Obama's ability to implement an empathy standard in judicial nominations. Figure 6 provides an overview of this, with the left-hand Figure 6a considering time in committee by race in an administration, and the right-hand Figure 6b presenting total time by race in an administration. Apart from President Clinton, there are mini-

---

[26] Disposition of nominees includes reporting to the chamber, returning to the president due to failure, returning to the president *sine die*, and presidential withdrawal of a nominee. Figures 5a and 5b do not differentiate between these outcomes.

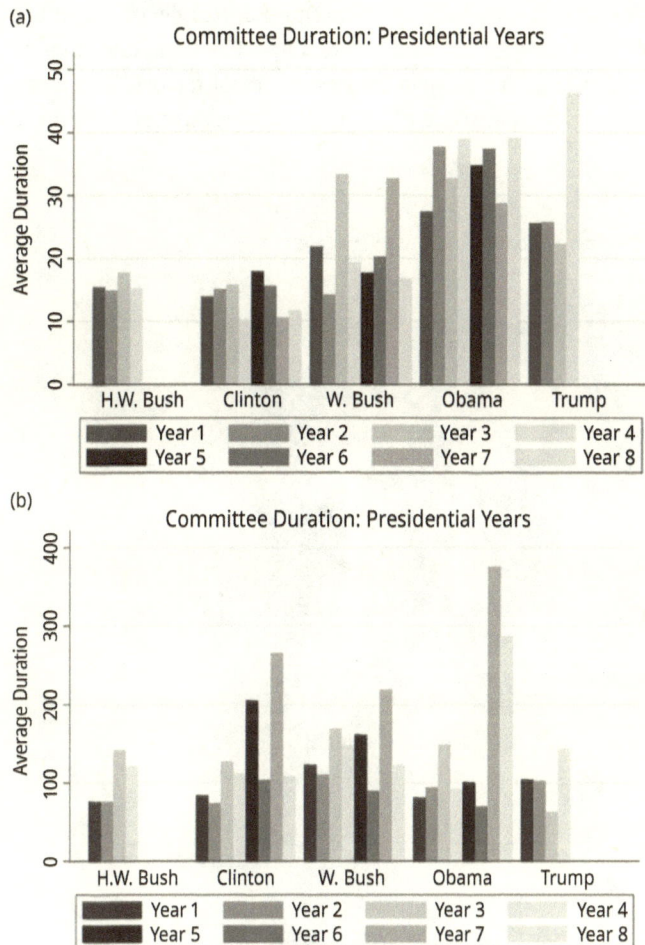

Figure 5: Duration of Nominees in Committee, by President and year. (a) Active Consideration in Committee. (b) Total Consideration in Committee.

mal differences in terms of duration for each race and ethnicity. Obama's administration fits this pattern almost perfectly, with some variation across races but remarkable similarity. African Americans have the highest average duration for President Obama, but this is only slightly higher than the average duration for white nominees. Additionally, Hispanic and Asian nominees have lower average durations than white nominees, illustrating the relatively limited connection between nominee race and duration under this new judicial philosophy. In short, it appears that Obama was able to diversify the court with relatively limited pushback or unexpected delay. This may be due in part to political decisions within the administration, as the patterns for home-state co-partisanship and divided government suggest that attention was paid to these political factors. This, however, leaves a question of potential trade-offs for the administration to achieve these goals.

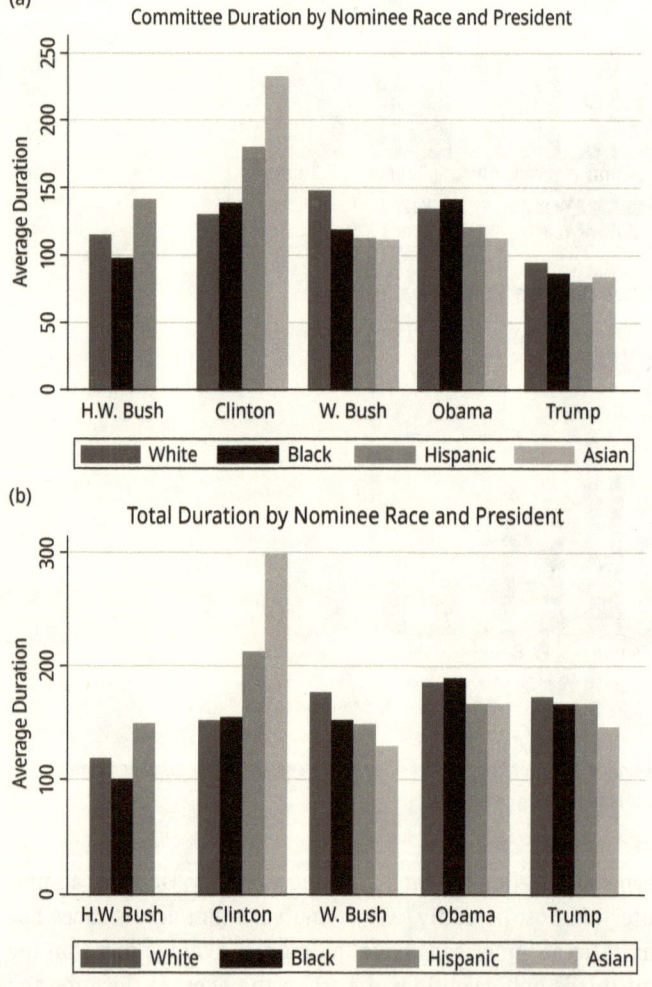

Figure 6: Duration of Nominees by Race for Presidential Administrations. (a) Committee Duration. (b) Total Duration.

One area of attention during public debates over judges as well as confirmation hearings is the qualifications of nominees. While ABA scores measure part of this, they come with some questions about the process underlying the scores.[27] Senators and public commentators also frequently mention the training and pedigree of judicial nominees, so we turn to this in Figure 7. In this figure we show the percentage of confirmed nominees for total administrations, as well as for each level of federal court, which attended Ivy League law schools. It is clear in this figure that presidents generally nominate a much higher proportion of judges who attended Ivy League law schools for seats on the Courts of Appeals than for District courts. This difference is most stark for President George H.W. Bush whose proportion of Ivy League attendees for Courts of Appeals was more than double that of District Courts.

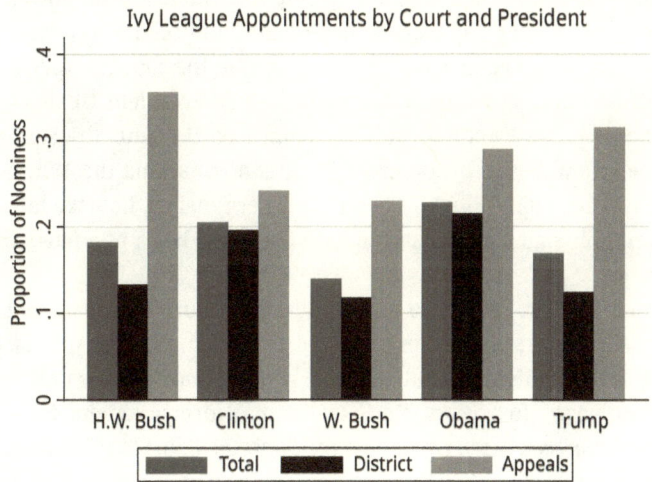

Figure 7: Education and Confirmed Judges.

Obama presents two different pictures of nominee education. His administration does not appear unique in the difference between District and Appeals court nominees, as the difference is the second lowest after President Clinton. Where President Obama stands out is in the District courts, where his administration is the only one to have more than two of every 10 nominees attend an Ivy League

---

27 Susan Navarro Smelcer, Amy Steigerwalt, and Richard L. Vining, Jr., "Bias and the Bar: Evaluating the ABA Ratings of Federal Judicial Nominees," *Political Research Quarterly* 65, no. 4 (2012): 827–840.

law school. This is higher than all other administrations, and significantly higher than all contemporary Republican administrations. This may be an effort by the Obama administration to use prestige to help ensure the success of nominees selected under the new empathy standard, as senators are likely to understand the quality of a nominee's pedigree even if they do not understand the selection criteria for empathy.

Recognizing the Legacy

President Obama's desire to implement a new criterion for judicial selection presented a new method of understanding why nominees are selected and is a significant part of his administration's legacy of appointing individuals to the lower federal courts. The Obama strategy appears to have been mindful and opportunistic in how race, ethnicity, and gender would be changed in the court. Despite a decline in the rate of nominating white males to the bench, President Obama's male appointees such as Judge Hamilton publicly embraced the empathy standard more than other nominees. The totality of the confirmations the White House waited to see succeed changed who sits on the federal bench, how we talk about them, and potentially had a causal shift in what is in the heart of a federal judge.

We find substantial historical evidence to conclude that future presidents are increasingly likely to select diverse nominees to the federal bench. Obama's judicial appointments reinvigorated a discussion about race, gender, and representation. This was followed by a pledge – four years later – by Obama's former running-mate Joe Biden to "make sure there's a Black woman on the Supreme Court to make sure we in fact get everyone represented."[28] The ability of President Biden to nominate someone with the race and gender perspective built on the previous confirmations of lower federal court judges. We must recognize that while Justice Ketanji Brown Jackson is the first female African American Justice, she was nominated to the US Sentencing Commission by Obama in 2009 and to the US District Court in 2012. Justice Brown Jackson joined other females appointed to the Supreme Court of the United States – including Justices Sotomayor, Kagen, and Coney Barrett. One way to see the full effect of Obama's vision is to reflect on the questions and new perspectives these women add regardless of differences concerning which president nominated them or the judicial philosophies under which they interpret the law.

---

28 Michael D. Shear, "Biden Made a Campaign Pledge to Put a Black Woman on the Supreme Court," *New York Times*, January 26, 2022.

Almost a decade after the Obama presidency ended, the details of the empathy standard are not defined or discussed on a regular basis. However, the appeals made to senators as to why a nominee should be confirmed more closely reflect the quote from Justice Oliver Wendell Holmes than they did before. We also still believe it is important for students, as well as those who counsel the President of the United States, to remember that the US Senate may be skeptical of any new standard to evaluate a nominee. A new narrative will not stop senators from expecting a president will use individual characteristics of a nominee to further the president's own policy goals and legal ideology. If a nominee has a shorter judicial record than their peers or their biography is a bit more unique, the senators may become even more skeptical. Another reason senators may become skeptical is if the focus of a nomination drifts from merit and judicial decision making. This can occur if the salience of an appointment rises as advocacy groups and the media recognize a nominee has the potential to increase the representativeness of the court.[29]

President Obama said this in his own words, his interest was what was in the heart of the nominee. Obama was often silent about the goals of diversifying the demographics of the court. One drawback of analyses that rely on counts is that demographic diversity is something that is easier to discuss and recognize than the balance of judicial ideology among judges who serve in one circuit. In this chapter, we used the goals that a president repeatedly stated to contextualize our analysis of where the patterns of his nominations stand out from those of other presidents.

References

"Republicans Stall Late Carter Appointments." In *CQ Almanac*, 36th edition, 15-A-22-A. Washington, DC: Congressional Quarterly, 1981. Accessed December 11, 2023, https://library.cqpress.com/cqalmanac/document.php?id=cqal80-860-25878-1173433.

Badas, Alex, and Katelyn E. Stauffer. "Descriptive Representation, Judicial Nominations, and Perceptions of Presidential Accomplishment." *Representation* 59, no. 2 (2022): 249–270.

Bell, Lauren. "Senatorial discourtesy: The Senate's use of delay to shape the federal judiciary." *Political Research Quarterly* 55, no. 3 (2002): 589–607.

Binder, Sarah A., and Forrest Maltzman. *Advice and Dissent: The Struggle to Shape the Federal Judiciary*. Lanham: Rowman & Littlefield, 2009.

Bird, Christine C., and Zachary A. McGee. "Going Nuclear: Federalist Society Affiliated Judicial Nominees' Prospects and a New Era of Confirmation Politics." *American Politics Research* 51, no. 1 (2023): 37–56.

---

[29] We do not assume that the public prioritizes descriptive representation over substantive agreement on policy but, understanding that advocacy organizations seek to shape the narrative of a nomination, we think the pressure can be elevated enough to alter the committee's activities.

Congress.gov. "Nomination of John Roberts." *Congressional Record* 151, no. 119 (2005): S10273. https://www.congress.gov/congressional-record/volume-151/issue-119/senate-section/article/S10273-2?q=%7B%22search%22%3A%22Housing%2C%5C%5C%22%7D&s=1&r=75.

Fontana, David. "Cooperative Judicial Nominations During the Obama Administration." *Wisconsin Law Review* 2 (2017): 285–323.

Giles, Michael W., Virginia A. Hettinger, and Todd Peppers. "Picking Federal Judges: A Note on Policy and Partisan Selection Agendas." *Political Research Quarterly* 54, no. 3 (2001): 623–641.

Goldstein, Joel K. "How Empathy Makes Superior Judges – and Justice." *Origins: Current Events in Historical Perspective*. August 2010, https://origins.osu.edu/history-news/how-empathy-makes-superior-judges-and-justice.

Hamilton, David F. "Responses of David F. Hamilton: Nominee to the US Court of Appeals for the Seventh Circuit to the Written Questions of Senator Jeff Sessions, Senator John Cornyn, and Senator Tom Coburn, M.D." Senate Judiciary Committee. April 29, 2009.

Holmes, Lisa M. "Presidential Strategy in the Judicial Appointment Process: 'Going Public' in Support of Nominees to the US Courts of Appeals." *American Politics Research* 35, no. 5 (2007): 567–594.

Holmes, Lisa M. "Why 'Go Public'? Presidential Use of Nominees to the US Courts of Appeals." *Presidential Studies Quarterly* 38, no. 1 (2008): 110–122.

Howard, Nicholas O., and David A. Hughes. "Revisiting Senatorial Courtesy and the Selection of Judges to the US Courts of Appeals." *Political Research Quarterly* 75, no. 1 (2022): 61–75.

Kuersten, Ashlyn, and Donald R. Songer. "Presidential success through appointments to the United States Courts of Appeals." *American Politics Research* 31, no. 2 (2003): 107–137.

Madonna, Anthony J., James E. Monogan III, and Richard Vining, Jr. "Confirmation Wars, Legislative Time, and Collateral Damage: The Impact of Supreme Court Nominations on Presidential Success in the US Senate." *Political Research Quarterly* 69, no. 4 (2016): 746–759.

Obama, Barack. "Remarks by the President in Nominating Judge Sonia Sotomayor to the United States Supreme Court." *Office of the Press Secretary, The White House*. May 26, 2009. https://obamawhitehouse.archives.gov/the-press-office/remarks-president-nominating-judge-sonia-sotomayor-united-states-supreme-court.

Shapiro, Ari. "Sotomayor Differs With Obama on 'Empathy' Issue." *NPR*. July 14, 2009. https://www.npr.org/2009/07/14/106569335/sotomayor-differs-with-obama-on-empathy-issue.

Shear, Michael D. "Biden Made a Campaign Pledge to Put a Black Woman on the Supreme Court." *New York Times*. January 26, 2002. https://www.nytimes.com/2022/01/26/us/politics/biden-supreme-court-black-woman.html#:~:text=At%20the%20time%2C%20his%20campaign,Biden%20said%20that%20night.

Shipan, Charles R., and Megan L. Shannon. "Delaying justice(s): A Duration Analysis of Supreme Court Confirmations." *American Journal of Political Science* 47, no. 4 (2003): 654–668.

Smelcer, Susan Navarro, Amy Steigerwalt, and Richard L. Vining Jr. "Bias and the Bar: Evaluating the ABA Ratings of Federal Judicial Nominees." *Political Research Quarterly* 65, no. 4 (2012): 827–840.

Songer, Donald R., Susan W. Johnson, and Ronald Stidham. "Presidential success through appointments to the United States District Courts." *Justice System Journal* 24, no. 3 (2003): 283–300.

Toobin, Jeffrey. "Bench Press," *New Yorker*, September 21, 2009, http://www.newyorker.com/magazine/2009/09/21/bench-press.

US Courts. "Judgeship Appointments by President." Administrative Office of the US Courts on behalf of the Federal Judiciary, Washington, DC. Accessed September 19, 2023, https://www.uscourts.gov/sites/default/files/apptsbypres.pdf.

Weiss, Debra Cassens. "Empathy Focus for Obama Justices." *ABA Journal* (July 18, 2007). https://www.abajournal.com/news/article/empathy_focus_for_obama_justices.

Barbara A. Perry and Sheila M. Blackford
Chapter 8
Women and the Obama Administration: Gender Policy at Home and Abroad

Introduction

Nine days into his presidency, President Barack Obama strode into the White House's East Room for his first bill-signing ceremony. He and First Lady Michelle Obama were pleased that the Lilly Ledbetter Fair Pay Restoration Act had arrived. Walking to the podium with the president was Mrs. Ledbetter, gratified that the act was intended to protect against wage discrimination on the basis of gender, race, or age.[1]

She had brought her quest to remedy the salary inequities she had suffered as a Goodyear employee all the way to the US Supreme Court – and lost. Despite the cost to her of more than $200,000 in salary, and even more in pension and Social Security benefits, her case, which clearly demonstrated disparity in pay between men and women, failed to convince a majority of justices that the 1964 Civil Rights Act provided her a vehicle for righting the wrong. She had missed the statute's time limit. Claimants had only six months from the first instance of discrimination to file their suits. How could she have brought a claim against her employer when she didn't even know Goodyear had discriminated against her until well into her career when she discovered vast differences in her pay compared to male counterparts? Justice Ruth Bader Ginsburg issued a blistering dissent, calling on Congress to revise the law. The House and Senate passed the Lilly Ledbetter Fair Pay Restoration Act on January 22, 2009.[2]

---

1 Michelle Obama, *Becoming* (New York: Crown, 2018), 306–307; "President Obama signs the Lilly Ledbetter Fair Pay Act," January 29, 2009, https://www.youtube.com/watch?v=UtKAKlurRAY.
2 Barack Obama, *A Promised Land* (New York: Crown, 2020), 234; *Ledbetter v. Goodyear Tire & Rubber Co.*, 550 US 618 (2007). Justice Samuel Alito, named by President George W. Bush in 2006 to replace the first woman justice, Sandra Day O'Connor, wrote the majority opinion. Barbara A. Perry, *"The Supremes": An Introduction to the US Supreme Court Justices*, 2nd edition (New York: Peter Lang, 2009), 138. Linda Hirshman, *Sisters in Law: How Sandra Day O'Connor and Ruth Bader Ginsburg Went to the Supreme Court and Changed the World* (New York: Harper, 2015), 274–276.

Barbara A. Perry, Sheila M. Blackford, University of Virginia's Miller Center

https://doi.org/10.1515/9783111384108-008

New White House staffers scrambled to invite women's rights and employee advocacy groups to the event.[3] The president handed a signing pen to Ledbetter, whom he and Michelle got to know during the campaign and who spoke at the 2008 Democratic National Convention about her plight, indicating Senator Obama's commitment to women's rights. During the 2008 campaign, Michelle embraced the role of speaking about work-life balance and listening to military wives about their special challenges.[4]

Signing the law, President Obama "thought not just about Lilly but also about my mother and [his grandmother] and all the other working women across the country who had ever been passed over for promotions or been paid less than they were worth."[5] He invoked his young daughters and hoped that they would experience equitable workplaces.[6]

From this ceremony to his closing months as president, when he campaigned for Hillary Clinton's historic presidential run, Obama's leadership and the effective females he placed in powerful positions promoted the interests of women in both domestic and foreign policy. Domestically, the Obama administration focused on women's rights, especially in employment, health care, and education; established a White House Council for Women and Girls; added women to the Cabinet, White House staff, and federal judiciary; and opened military service in combat roles to females.

Internationally, the 44th presidency elevated women, girls, and gender issues in diplomacy, defense, and development. The administration sought opportunities to codify and institutionalize innovative approaches to improve the lives of females around the world. These efforts included the State Department's Office of Global Women's Issues and the Quadrennial Diplomacy and Development Review (QDDR); the National Action Plan on Women, Peace, and Security; and the Executive Order preventing and responding to violence against women.

Facing the realities of rising polarization, Obama relied on executive orders for implementing many gender policies. His most enduring impact on women, through enhanced health care, came in the Affordable Care Act, before his party lost the House of Representatives in 2008's midterms.

---

[3] Sheryl Gay Stolberg, "Obama Signs Equal-Pay Legislation," *New York Times*, January 29, 2009, https://www.nytimes.com/2009/01/30/us/politics/30ledbetter-web.html.
[4] Michelle Obama, *Becoming*, 269–270.
[5] Barack Obama, *A Promised Land*, 234.
[6] "Remarks of President Barack Obama at the Lilly Ledbetter Fair Pay Restoration Act Bill Signing, January 29, 2009," Obama Library, https://www.obamalibrary.gov/sites/default/files/uploads/documents/Lilly%20Ledbetter%20Fair%20Pay%20Restoration%20Act%20Bill%20Signing%202009%20(TRANSCRIPT).pdf.

Domestic Policy

Prime West Wing real estate in the Obama White House initially housed three powerful women staffers (Valerie Jarrett, Tina Tchen, and Cecilia Muñoz), indicating symbolically and substantively the new president's vision of gender. His and the First Lady's long-time colleagues and friends from Chicago, Jarrett and Tchen, were senior advisor and deputy assistant to the president, respectively, and served with Muñoz, also a deputy assistant to the president, in leading the White House Office of Public Engagement and Intergovernmental Affairs. This trio's role was to liaise with key constituencies, including women's groups, as well as with state and local governments.

Jarrett, who had served as Michelle Obama's mentor when they worked in the Chicago mayor's office, circled in the closest personal and professional orbit to the president and First Lady. Staffers could rely on Mrs. Obama to speak to women about medical insurance, educational opportunities, breast cancer awareness, healthful nutrition, and mentorship. Eventually, Tchen also served as Mrs. Obama's Chief of Staff, while being promoted to assistant to the president. Just six weeks into the presidency, Obama established the White House Council on Women and Girls, with Jarrett and Tchen as leaders. Its mission was to ensure that policies, programs, and events throughout the federal government considered women's interests.[7] Soon, Nancy-Ann DeParle, director of the Office of Health Reform, moved into the West Wing as well, where she would subsequently serve as Deputy Chief of Staff for policy.

Obama named Melody Barnes, Senator Edward Kennedy's Judiciary Committee chief counsel, as an assistant to the president and director of his Domestic Policy Council. Other high-ranking staffers included Susan Rice (National Security Advisor), Sylvia Matthews Burwell (Director of the Office of Management and Budget), Mona Sutphen (Deputy Chief of Staff for Policy), Kathryn Ruemmler (White House Counsel), Cassandra Butts (Deputy White House counsel), Carol Browner (Assistant to the President and Director of the White House Office of Energy and Climate Change Policy), Stephanie Cutter (Assistant to the President for Special Projects; Deputy Senior Advisor to the President), Susan Sher (Deputy General Counsel and First Lady's Chief of Staff), Anita Dunn (acting Communications Director), and Jen Psaki (Deputy Press Secretary, Deputy Communications Director, Communications Director).

---

7 "The White House Council on Women and Girls," accessed January 23, 2023, https://obamawhitehouse.archives.gov/administration/eop/cwg.

Yet two-thirds of the staff were men, and Jarrett had to alert the president that female advisors felt stymied by the patriarchal White House. Embarrassed that he had overlooked this problem, Obama hosted a dinner where a dozen women staffers explained their workplace issues. The president corrected offending males,[8] and women developed a coordinated strategy so that men wouldn't poach their ideas at meetings. One female aide gave Obama credit for calling on women more frequently. They eventually felt that they were participating as equals with male advisors.[9]

Throughout his two terms, Obama appointed nearly a dozen women to prominent Cabinet posts, including his opponent for the 2008 Democratic nomination, Hillary Clinton (Secretary of State), Susan Rice (UN Ambassador), Samantha Power (UN Ambassador), Janet Napolitano (Secretary of Homeland Security), Kathleen Sebelius (Secretary of Health and Human Services), Sylvia Burwell (Secretary of Health and Human Services), Loretta Lynch (Attorney General), Penny Pritzker (Secretary of Commerce), Sally Jewell (Secretary of the Interior), Hilda Solis (Secretary of Labor), and Christina Romer (Chair of the Council of Economic Advisors).[10]

For the more than 80 federal government positions requiring Senate confirmation, 35 percent of Obama's appointees were women, surpassing all previous five presidents:

Obama	35.3%
Bush II	16.4%
Clinton	23.3%
Bush I	18.7%
Reagan	7.4%
Carter	9.9%[11]

---

8 Barack Obama, *A Promised Land*, 535–537.
9 Juliet Eilperin, "Obama Has Vastly Changed the Fact of the Federal Bureaucracy," *Washington Post*, September 20, 2015, https://www.washingtonpost.com/politics/obama-has-vastly-changed-the-face-of-the-federal-bureaucracy/2015/09/20/73ef803a-5631-11e5-abe9-27d53f250b11_story.html; Emily Crockett, "The Amazing Tool That Women in the White House Used to Fight Gender Bias," *Vox*, September 14, 2016, https://www.vox.com/2016/9/14/12914370/white-house-obama-women-gender-bias-amplification.
10 "Women Appointed to Presidential Cabinets," Center for American Women and Politics, Eagleton Institute of Politics, Rutgers University, March 16, 2022, https://cawp.rutgers.edu/sites/default/files/resources/womenapptdtoprescabinets.pdf.
11 Anne Joseph O'Connell, *Washington Post*, September 20, 2015, https://www.washingtonpost.com/politics/obama-ups-diversity-in-appointees/2015/09/20/5b042aac-5ffb-11e5-8e9e-dce8a2a2a679_graphic.html.

Chapter 8 Women and the Obama Administration: Gender Policy at Home and Abroad

Upon the 2009 retirement of Justice David Souter, the president produced a shortlist of three women – Judges Diane Wood, Sonia Sotomayor, and Solicitor General Elena Kagan. As a constitutional law professor, Obama knew all three were qualified by education and experience, but he was intrigued by Sotomayor's up-from-poverty story as the daughter of Puerto Rican immigrants. He ignored comments from those who questioned her qualifications (despite her Princeton and Harvard Law degrees), finding such sniping consistent with how elites view women and people of color. Moreover, Sotomayor had served as both a US District Court judge and as a jurist on the Second US Circuit Court of Appeals, to which she had been nominated by Presidents H.W. Bush and Clinton, respectively.[12] To join Justice Ginsburg on the highest court, President Obama made the historic appointment of the first Latina and only third woman to reach the Supreme Court. Gender was the primary factor in Sotomayor's nomination.

With Justice John Paul Stevens's 2010 retirement, Obama could have reverted to the tradition of appointing men. Since its establishment in 1789, 113 males had served on the Supreme Court.[13] But Obama became the first president to name two female justices, when he chose former Harvard Law School Dean Elena Kagan. Now one-third of the tribunal's membership was women.

On the lower federal courts, Obama set records in the numbers and percentages of women he placed on the appellate tribunals. His 24 female appointments to the US Courts of Appeals surpassed G.W. Bush (17) and Clinton (20).[14] Obama's percentage of women appellate judges is even more impressive in comparison with predecessors going back to the early twentieth century:

Obama	42%
Bush II	22%
Clinton	28%
Bush I	19%
Reagan	8%
Carter	16%

---

12 Barack Obama, *A Promised Land*, 389–391.
13 Henry J. Abraham, *Justices, Presidents, and Senators: A History of US Supreme Court Appointments from Washington to Clinton* (Lanham: Rowman & Littlefield), 353.
14 Laura Moyer, "Assessing President Obama President Obama's Appointment of Women to the Federal Appellate Courts," *British Journal of American Legislative Studies* 3, no. 10 (2021): 1.

Prior to President Jimmy Carter, who established selection commissions to promote diversity in judicial nominations, no president's federal judicial appointments of women (as far back as Coolidge) had topped two percent.[15]

Do diverse officials actively pursue the interests of the groups whence they originate, or do they merely "stand for" them in a symbolic way? Are they appointed simply to make their institution "look like America"?[16] In judicial appointments, presidents focus on the different life experiences that women or people of color bring to the bench. The symbolism of a diverse appointee is not lost on presidents, however. As Obama's White House Counsel Ruemmler explained the president's rationale, "[d]iversity in and of itself is a thing that is strengthening the judicial system. It enhances the bench and the performance of the bench and the quality of discussion . . . to have different perspectives, different life experiences, different professional experiences, coming from a different station in life." She added, "the president wants the federal courts to look like America. He wants people who are coming to court to feel like it's their court as well."[17] Most presidents also consider the electoral advantages of appealing to gender, racial, and ethnic groups by placing their members in office.

Obama's 2012 reelection campaign emphasized his gender policies, especially the fair pay and health care laws as promises kept from his first presidential run. Support for workplace fairness, contraceptive coverage, and abortion access served as centerpieces for women's speeches at that year's Democratic Convention and in video ads, celebrity testimonials, and interest group messages to voters.[18] Women made the difference in the president's victory over Mitt Romney. Fifty-five percent of 2012 voters were female, and 53 percent of them voted for Obama.[19]

What were the lasting effects of Obama's gender policies at home? When the president signed the Lilly Ledbetter Act, women were earning 78 cents to every

---

15 John Gramlich, "Trump Has Appointed a Larger Share of Female Judges Than Other GOP Presidents, But Lags Obama," Pew Research Center, October 2, 2018, https://www.pewresearch.org/fact-tank/2018/10/02/trump-has-appointed-a-larger-share-of-female-judges-than-other-gop-presidents-but-lags-obama/.
16 Barbara A. Perry, A "Representative" Supreme Court: Religion, Race, and Gender in Appointments (Westport: Greenwood, 1999), 10–11.
17 Moyer, "Assessing President Obama President Obama's Appointment of Women to the Federal Appellate Courts," 4–5.
18 Patricia Zengerle, "Women Voters Helped Make Obama; Could They Break Him?" Reuters, November 3, 2012, https://jp.reuters.com/article/usa-campaign-women-obama-idINDEE8A300U20121104.
19 Margie Omero, and Tara McGuinness, "How Women Changed the Outcome of the Election," Center for American Progress, December 12, 2012, https://www.americanprogress.org/article/how-women-changed-the-outcome-of-the-election/.

dollar earned by men. Today that figure is 84 cents.[20] The Obama administration fought hard to pass the Paycheck Equity Act, but each of the three times Congress considered it, the bill died in committee or fell short of the 60 votes needed to overcome the Senate filibuster.[21] The president took unilateral action in issuing executive orders to require pay equity in the federal government and wage transparency by federal contractors.[22]

The Obama administration's crowning legislative achievement was the 2011 Affordable Care Act, which increased insurance coverage for women at all income levels. For those in the lower economic strata, the impact was remarkable. The percentage of uninsured plummeted from 40 to 18 percent, and those women now have access to affordable flu shots, mammograms, and cholesterol and blood pressure screenings.[23]

When conservative evangelical businesses and Catholic institutions challenged the ACA's requirement of contraceptive coverage, however, Obama judicial appointments couldn't save this key component of reproductive health.[24] Justices Sotomayor and Kagan joined a narrow majority in the 2016 abortion case that invalidated Texas's restriction on the procedure, but they couldn't hold the line against the new conservative majority on the Court when it struck down a federal right to abortion.[25] If Republicans hadn't blocked Obama's 2016 nomination of Merrick Garland to replace Antonin Scalia, it is conceivable that Justices Sotomayor, Kagan, Garland, and Breyer could have persuaded Chief Justice Roberts to uphold at least a portion of *Roe* and its progeny.

President and Mrs. Obama took a keen interest in education, knowing how it had made possible their spectacular rise to the White House. Michelle often accompanied Secretary of Education Arne Duncan on his visits to schools, where they encouraged low-income students to pursue college opportunities and even

---

20 Amanda Barroso, and Anna Brown, "Gender Pay Gap in US Held Steady in 2020," Pew Research Center, May 25, 2021, https://www.pewresearch.org/fact-tank/2021/05/25/gender-pay-gap-facts/.
21 "Paycheck Fairness Act," https://en.wikipedia.org/wiki/Paycheck_Fairness_Act.
22 Tom Risen, "Obama Seeks Wage Transparency With Executive Orders," *US News*, April 7, 2014, https://www.usnews.com/news/articles/2014/04/07/obama-seeks-wage-transparency-with-executive-orders.
23 Carol Potera, "Women Benefit from the Affordable Care Act," *American Journal of Nursing* 7, no. 119 (July 2019): 15, https://journals.lww.com/ajnonline/Fulltext/2019/07000/Women_Benefit_from_the_Affordable_Care_Act.14.aspx.
24 *Burwell v. Hobby Lobby Stores, Inc.*, 573 US 682 (2014); *Little Sisters of the Poor Saints Peter and Paul Home v. Pennsylvania*, et al., 591 US __ (2020).
25 *Whole Woman's Health v. Hellerstedt*, 579 US 582 (2016); *Dobbs v. Jackson Women's Health Organization*, 597 US __ (2022).

provided workshops on completing convoluted financial aid forms.[26] The president and First Lady also initiated a program, Let Girls Learn, for educating females around the globe.[27]

One of the administration's most focused education initiatives was the president's 2014 creation of the White House Task Force to Protect Students from Sexual Assault, especially on college campuses. An estimated one out of five women experienced such a crime. The president asked the Office of the Vice President and the White House Council on Women and Girls to coordinate the effort, with Jarrett and Tchen leading this interagency endeavor.[28] One of their most public achievements was the creation of It's on Us, a peer-to-peer organization to teach students about the epidemic of sexual assault and how to prevent it. To date, more than 500 campuses have established chapters and nearly a half-million students have pledged to be a part of the solution.[29]

The Task Force issued a preliminary report in 2014 to guide their efforts and published a final report just prior to the administration's end, which offered detailed protocols and policies for education institutions.[30] Universities now require training for all students, faculty, and staff on how to define and counter sexual assault and harassment. It is too early to discern the full impact of the anti-sexual assault initiatives, especially with the COVID pandemic shutdown of universities disrupting data collection, but one telling statistic evinces hope. More students now report that they understand the meaning of nonconsensual sex and how to combat it.[31]

Ironically, one progressive gender policy put females in harm's way. Defense Secretary Ash Carter made the decision in 2015 with the president's full support.

---

26 Arne Duncan Briefing Materials, President Barack Obama Oral History Project, Timeline, prepared by Bryan Craig, University of Virginia Miller Center, March 2022, 17.
27 Let Girls Learn, https://obamawhitehouse.archives.gov/letgirlslearn.
28 "Memorandum—Establishing a White House Task Force to Protect Students from Sexual Assault," The White House, Office of the Press Secretary, January 22, 2014, https://obamawhitehouse.archives.gov/the-press-office/2014/01/22/memorandum-establishing-white-house-task-force-protect-students-sexual-a.
29 It's on Us, accessed January 23, 2023, https://www.itsonus.org/about-us/our-story/.
30 "Fact Sheet: Final It's On Us Summit and Report of the White House Task Force to Protect Students from Sexual Assault," The White House, Office of the Press Secretary, January 5, 2017, https://obamawhitehouse.archives.gov/the-press-office/2014/01/22/memorandum-establishing-white-house-task-force-protect-students-sexual-a.
31 "Report on the AAU Campus Climate Survey on Sexual Assault and Misconduct," American Association of Universities, January 17, 2020, https://www.aau.edu/sites/default/files/AAU-Files/Key-Issues/Campus-Safety/Revised%20Aggregate%20report%20%20and%20appendices%201-7_(01–16-2020_FINAL).pdf.

Women had served in combat zones for decades, particularly as nurses and pilots, but positions that prepared service members for war remained closed to females, along with the promotions that result from such experience. As Carter explained, "I concluded that the data confirmed that opening all positions to women, without exceptions, was the right decision to assemble the strongest possible military force today and tomorrow."[32]

A few months before leaving office, President Obama was the warm-up act for his wife and Oprah Winfrey at the United States of Women Summit. The audience cheered when he announced that he is a feminist, becoming the first incumbent president to do so. He also asserted that policies and programs can only change the lives of women when society stops limiting them with stereotypes.[33]

He and Mrs. Obama campaigned hard in 2016 to eliminate presidential stereotypes and make his former Secretary of State Hillary Clinton the first woman chief executive, but it was not to be.[34] And because women are not a monolith, there is no guarantee that the first female chief executive will be a progressive, devoted to federal government policies that improve women's lives. Thus, both the symbolism and substance of Barack Obama's gendered appointments and domestic policies may either represent a transformational landmark on the way to even higher goals or a highpoint from which the country recedes.

International Policy

One of President Obama's earliest and most high-profile efforts to promote the interests of women was his appointment of Hillary Clinton as Secretary of State. Following Lincoln's "team of rivals" model, Obama sought to heal the Democratic Party rift prompted by his fraught race with Senator Clinton for the presidential nomination. The former First Lady brought extensive experience to the role, and Obama wanted "Hillary's star power, relationships, and comfort on the world

---

[32] Ash Carter, *Inside the Five-Sided Box: Lessons from a Lifetime of Leadership in the Pentagon* (New York: Dutton, 2019), 400.

[33] "Remarks by the President at United States of Women Summit," The White House, Office of the Press Secretary, June 14, 2016, https://obamawhitehouse.archives.gov/the-press-office/2016/06/14/remarks-president-united-states-women-summit; Emily Crockett, "Read President Obama on Why Men Need to be Feminists Too," *Vox*, January 19, 2017, https://www.vox.com/2016/8/4/12375558/obama-first-feminist-president-legacy-malia-sasha-glamour-essay.

[34] Hillary Clinton, *Hard Choices* (New York: Simon & Schuster, 2014); Ali Vitali, *Electable: Why America Hasn't Put a Woman in the White House . . . Yet* (New York: Day Street Books, 2022).

stage" to help rebuild US diplomatic relationships around the world.[35] Out of more than 70 secretaries of state in US history, Clinton was only the third woman to serve in that position, after Madeleine Albright (1997–2001) and Condoleezza Rice (2005–2009).[36] Clinton had spent much of her career – as an attorney, Arkansas's First Lady, First Lady of the US, and US senator – working to improve the lives of women and girls throughout the world and to promote gender equality. She first gained attention on the international stage for these issues at the 1995 United Nations Fourth World Conference on Women in Beijing, China, when she proclaimed, "human rights are women's rights . . . . And women's rights are human rights."[37]

Secretary Clinton came to the State Department with the belief that US national security was intrinsically linked to gender equality because the world would be a safer, more stable place if half of its population had better access to education, employment, and health care. As Professors Valerie M. Hudson and Patricia Leidl have observed, she was "the world's most influential and eloquent exponent of the proposition that the situation of women and the destiny of nations are integrally linked."[38] Clinton often quoted her good friend Albright by noting that "advancing the cause of women is not just the right thing to do. It is the smart thing to do for any society."[39] As Secretary Clinton asserted in 2010, "the United States has made empowering women and girls a cornerstone of our foreign policy, because women's equality is not just a moral issue, it's not just a humanitarian issue, it is not just a fairness issue; it is a security issue. It is a prosperity issue, and it is a peace issue."[40]

President Obama largely supported Clinton's worldview on the importance of improving women's and girls' opportunities across the globe. The administration's first National Security Strategy of 2010 included a subsection that specifically advocated female rights. The administration pledged to prevent violence against women and girls, provide equal access to justice, promote maternal and

---

35 Barack Obama, *A Promised Land*, 218.
36 National Museum of American Diplomacy, "A High Honor: Women Secretaries of State," accessed January 23, 2023, https://diplomacy.state.gov/exhibits/explore-online-exhibits/herdiplomacy/a-high-honor-secretaries-of-state/.
37 Hillary Clinton, "Remarks for the United Nations Fourth World Conference on Women," September 5, 1995, https://www.un.org/esa/gopher-data/conf/fwcw/conf/gov/950905175653.txt.
38 Valerie M. Hudson, and Patricia Leidl, *The Hillary Doctrine* (New York: Columbia University Press, 2015), xiii.
39 Hillary Clinton, "Remarks at Vital Voices Conference," September 2, 1998. https://clintonwhitehouse4.archives.gov/WH/EOP/First_Lady/html/generalspeeches/1998/19980908.html.
40 Hillary Clinton, "Remarks at the TEDWomen Conference," December 8, 2010, https://2009-2017.state.gov/secretary/20092013clinton/rm/2010/12/152670.htm.

child health, and support education and employment.[41] In a 2012 executive order, President Obama reaffirmed his commitment: "Under the leadership of my administration, the United States has made gender equality and women's empowerment a core focus of our foreign policy."[42]

Early in Secretary Clinton's tenure, the Office of Global Women's Issues (GWI) – previously known as the Office of International Women's Issues – was elevated and placed in the Office of the Secretary, and its head was designated as an ambassador-at-large, reporting directly to the Secretary of State.[43] This move, while seemingly bureaucratic, was significant, sending a signal about the importance of women's issues in the administration. Obama named Melanne Verveer the first ambassador-at-large for Global Women's Issues just six weeks after his inauguration.[44] She had served as Clinton's Chief of Staff when she was First Lady, and their long and close relationship indicated the secretary's commitment to women's issues. Ambassador Verveer traveled throughout the world making the case for gender equality, and the GWI office collected data as evidence to make the case that creating opportunities for women and girls increased security and prosperity for all.[45]

On one of Secretary Clinton's last days at the State Department in 2013, President Obama signed the Presidential Memorandum on Coordination of Policies and Programs to Promote Gender Equality and Empower Women and Girls Globally. The document noted that advancing gender equality required a commitment from senior leadership, dedicated resources, and personnel with relevant expertise. It also made the position of ambassador-at-large for Global Women's Issues permanent and ensured that it would continue to report directly to the Secretary of State. Similarly, it stated that the senior coordinator for Gender Equality and Women's Empowerment at the United States Agency for International Development (USAID) would provide

---

[41] The White House, "National Security Strategy," May 2010, https://obamawhitehouse.archives.gov/sites/default/files/rss_viewer/national_security_strategy.pdf.

[42] The White House, "Executive Order–Preventing and Responding to Violence Against Women and Girls Globally," August 10, 2012, https://obamawhitehouse.archives.gov/the-press-office/2012/08/10/executive-order-preventing-and-responding-violence-against-women-and-gir.

[43] Jacquelyn Ingrassia, "Women's Rights and the US State Department Under and After Hillary Clinton: An Interview with Jennifer Klein," *Brown Journal of World Affairs* 23, no. 1 (Fall/Winter 2016): 271.

[44] Julia M. Santucci, "Gender Equality as a National Security Priority," *Center for a New American Security*, September 15, 2017.

[45] Clinton, *Hard Choices*, 569.

guidance to the head of USAID. Solidifying these positions in diplomacy and development offered proof of the administration's dedication to gender equality.[46]

Early in her tenure, Secretary Clinton also created the State Department's first Quadrennial Diplomacy and Development Review (QDDR) in 2009, following the example of the Defense Department's Quadrennial Defense Review.[47] The State Department released the initial QDDR in 2010, encompassing both the State Department and USAID. While the QDDR focused on four broad areas – diplomacy for the twenty-first century, transforming development to deliver results, preventing and responding to conflict and crisis, and "working smarter" – it integrated issues related to women and girls throughout the review.[48] According to Jennifer Klein, senior advisor on Women's and Girl's Issues in the Office of Global Women's Issues, "there were 130 references to gender throughout the QDDR."[49]

The QDDR worked to institutionalize efforts around gender equality, putting women at the center of diplomacy and development as not only beneficiaries but also as agents.[50] It incorporated support for women and girls in the areas of policy development, budget planning, and personnel training.[51] For example, foreign service officers' training now included updates on gender, and a new three-day course on gender integration became part of the Foreign Service Institute's curriculum.[52]

The QDDR also made USAID the lead agency for the Feed the Future program, which recognized that "most of the world's food is grown, harvested, stored, and prepared by women, who have specific needs for training and access to financial services and markets."[53] In partnership with two other organizations, USAID developed the Women's Empowerment in Agriculture Index (WEAI) in 2011 to 2012 as part of the Feed the Future program.[54] The WEAI was an innovative tool designed to evaluate projects and gauge their effectiveness. It measured women's empowerment in agriculture through five domains: women's household decision-

---

[46] The White House, "Presidential Memorandum—Coordination of Policies and Programs to Promote Gender Equality and Empower Women and Girls Globally," January 30, 2013, https://obamawhitehouse.archives.gov/the-press-office/2013/01/30/presidential-memorandum-coordination-policies-and-programs-promote-gende.
[47] Clinton, *Hard Choices*, 551.
[48] The State Department, "The QDDR: Leading Through Civilian Power," 2010, https://2009-2017.state.gov/documents/organization/153142.pdf.
[49] Ingrassia, "Women's Rights and the US State Department Under and After Hillary Clinton," 272.
[50] The State Department, "The QDDR: Leading Through Civilian Power," 23.
[51] Hudson, and Leidl, *The Hillary Doctrine*, 192.
[52] Hudson, and Leidl, *The Hillary* Doctrine, p. 56, and Ingrassia, "Women's Rights and the US State Department Under and After Hillary Clinton," 273.
[53] The State Department, "The QDDR: Leading Through Civilian Power," 92.
[54] International Food Policy Research Institute, "About WEIA," https://weai.ifpri.info/about-weai/.

making, access to credit and land, adequacy of women's income in relation to food access, community leadership roles, and women's labor time allocations.[55] It also helped to provide a better understanding of gender dynamics in communities through measurement of women's empowerment relative to men within their households.[56]

The international community had long recognized that women suffer disproportionately from the violence that accompanies warfare. The majority of refugees fleeing violence are usually women and children, and rape as a weapon of war is most often waged against women and girls. On October 31, 2000, the United Nations Security Council adopted Resolution 1325 on Women, Peace, and Security, expressing concern that combatants often target women and children who are particularly affected by armed conflict and that women play crucial roles in peace negotiations. It urged member states to increase the women's representation at all levels of decision making.[57] As former Assistant Secretary of State Donald Steinberg has explained, "[e]mpirical and anecdotal evidence has long shown that women's leadership and participation in peace processes, political structures, and democratic transitions lead to more stable and resilient societies."[58]

In December 2011, President Obama announced the US National Action Plan on Women, Peace, and Security, along with Executive Order 13595 instituting the NAP.[59] "The hub of the action for this undertaking was in the White House," former Ambassador Verveer has noted, but it involved efforts across the entire federal government.[60] The NAP resulted from collaboration among various executive departments and civil society organizations and included commitments from the Departments of Defense, State, Justice, Treasury, and Homeland Security; the US Mission to the United Nations; USAID; the Centers for Disease Control and Preven-

---

55 Melanne Verveer, "The Vital Role of Women in Agriculture and Rural Development," June 27, 2011, https://2009-2017.state.gov/s/gwi/rls/rem/2011/167899.htm.
56 Feed the Future, "The Women's Empowerment in Agriculture Index," accessed January 23, 2023, https://www.feedthefuture.gov/the-womens-empowerment-in-agriculture-index/.
57 Office of the Special Adviser on Gender Issues and Advancement of Women (OSAGI), United Nations, "Landmark Resolution on Women, Peace, and Security," accessed January 23, 2023, https://www.un.org/womenwatch/osagi/wps/.
58 Donald Steinberg, "Seizing the Moment? The US Strategy for Women, Peace and Security," *Our Secure Future*, June 2019.
59 Office of the Press Secretary, "Executive Order—Instituting a National Action Plan on Women, Peace, and Security," December 19, 2011, https://obamawhitehouse.archives.gov/the-press-office/2011/12/19/executive-order-instituting-national-action-plan-women-peace-and-securit.
60 Melanne Verveer, "An Interview with Melanne Verveer," *Georgetown Journal of International Affairs* 20 (Fall 2019): 79.

tion; and the Office of the US Trade Representative.[61] In June 2016, the Obama administration released an updated plan, and the next year, "the United States became the first country in the world with a comprehensive law on Women, Peace, and Security (WPS)" – the Women, Peace, and Security Act of 2017.[62]

The NAP constituted a consequential step in advancing women's equality in US foreign policy by outlining specific outcomes associated with each objective and assigning accountability to specific executive branch agencies to achieve them.[63] Government departments integrated the goals of the NAP into their structures. The Defense Department's Joint Professional Military Education system incorporated WPS as a special area of emphasis so that it would be covered in professional military education.[64] The DOD also worked to integrate WPS "through peacekeeping training, seminars at regional centers and the Combatant Commands, and the National Guard State Partnership Program."[65] The military also partnered with allies to create organizational innovations such as Team Lioness, Female Engagement Teams, Cultural Support Teams, Gender Field Advisors, and Gender Focal Points to improve situational awareness and engage local women.[66] Similarly, USAID trained more than 9,000 technical and program staff to integrate gender in strategies and programs.[67] The 2016 updated NAP noted that through its efforts, more than 60,000 women globally participated in peacebuilding processes and that the United States reached more than four million survivors of gender-based violence.[68]

The Obama administration also addressed the global scourge of violence against women. On August 10, 2012, President Obama signed Executive Order 13623 – Preventing and Responding to Violence Against Women and Girls Glob-

---

[61] Hudson, and Leidl, *The Hillary Doctrine*, 191; Jamille Bigio, and Rachel Vogelstein, *How Women's Participation in Conflict Prevention and Resolution Advances US Interests* (New York: Council on Foreign Relations, 2016).

[62] The State Department, "Women, Peace, and Security," https://www.state.gov/women-peace-and-security/. US Congress, "Women, Peace, and Security Act of 2017," Public Law 115–168, October 6, 2017, https://www.congress.gov/115/plaws/publ68/PLAW-115publ68.pdf.

[63] Hudson, and Leidl, *The Hillary Doctrine*, 191.

[64] Anne A. Witkowsky, "Integrating Gender Perspectives within the Department of Defense," *Prism* 6, no. 1 (2016): 36.

[65] Witkowsky, "Integrating Gender Perspectives within the Department of Defense," 39.

[66] Robert Egnell, "Gender Perspectives and Military Effectiveness," *Prism* 6, no. 1 (2016): 74.

[67] The White House, "The United States National Action Plan on Women, Peace, and Security," June 5, 2016, https://obamawhitehouse.archives.gov/sites/whitehouse.gov/files/documents/women-national-action-plan.pdf.

[68] "The United States National Action Plan on Women, Peace, and Security," 1.

ally,[69] promulgating the Strategy to Prevent and Respond to Gender-Based Violence Globally, which had four objectives – increased coordination, enhanced integration within the US government, improved collection, analysis and use of data and research, and more programming within the US government around gender-based violence – with specific actions under each category.[70] It also established an interagency working group to implement the strategy, headed by co-chairs Secretary Clinton and USAID Administrator Rajiv Shah.

Four years later, the administration updated the strategy to address challenges such as insufficient resources and expertise, insecure environments that made it difficult to implement efforts to decrease gender-based violence, and cultural norms that protected perpetrators. Recommendations focused on continuing efforts to coordinate government agencies and external partners, grow new partnerships, and expand educational programming about gender-based violence.[71]

Evaluations of the Obama administration's efforts to promote the interests of women and girls in foreign policy are mixed. One of the barriers to effective elevation of gender issues internationally is that the foreign policy establishment remains heavily male-dominated. In 2017, *The Washington Post* surveyed nearly 500 US foreign policy leaders, 80 percent of whom were male, and only 13 percent of respondents thought that gender inequality was a threat to US national security.[72]

Foreign policy expert Julia M. Santucci has observed that the infrastructure of the foreign policy apparatus limited some of the Obama administration's efforts. For instance, the National Security Council staff is organized by both functional and regional directorates, and the NAP implementation was placed within one of the functional directorates, which meant that when a regional crisis erupted, the issues around women and girls were not at the forefront. In addition, the Obama administration did not include the intelligence community in its gender integration

---

[69] The White House, "Executive Order 13623–Preventing and Responding to Violence Against Women and Girls Globally," August 10, 2012, https://www.govinfo.gov/content/pkg/DCPD-201200631/pdf/DCPD-201200631.pdf.

[70] USAID, "United States Strategy to Prevent and Respond to Gender-Based Violence Globally," 2012, https://2009-2017.state.gov/documents/organization/196468.pdf.

[71] The State Department, "Evaluations of Implementation," August 2015, https://2009-2017.state.gov/documents/organization/251034.pdf. USAID, "Evaluations of Implementation," July 2015, https://www.usaid.gov/sites/default/files/documents/1865/GBV-Exec-Summary-Nov-2015.pdf.

[72] Joshua Busby and Heather Hurlburt, "Do Women Matter to National Security?" *The Washington Post*, February 2, 2017, https://www.washingtonpost.com/news/monkey-cage/wp/2017/02/02/do-women-matter-to-national-security-the-men-who-lead-u-s-foreign-policy-dont-think-so/.

efforts.[73] Finally, Hudson and Leidl argue that although the Obama administration institutionalized some change in Washington's legal and regulatory framework, the administration faced tougher challenges in trying to implement reforms in other countries.[74]

Nevertheless, President Obama and his administration did not simply talk about gender equality and the importance of women and girls; they endeavored to create lasting change. They understood that the United States needed to institutionalize the administration's goals into the governmental structure to integrate gender equality in foreign policy. A shining example of their efforts that lasted until the next administration was the bipartisan 2017 Women, Peace, and Security Act, signed by President Donald Trump, which required government agencies such as the Departments of State, Defense, and Homeland Security, and USAID, to submit a Women, Peace, and Security Strategy to congressional committees for review.[75] These strategic plans must include specific and measurable goals, benchmarks, timetables, and monitoring and evaluation schemes to "ensure the accountability and effectiveness of all policies and initiatives carried out under the strategy."[76] The WPS legislation created accountability for government agencies with congressional oversight – a landmark for moving toward gender equity abroad that matched the Obama administration's parallel efforts to reach similar goals for women and girls at home.

Conclusion

On Election Night 2008, when Barack Obama took the stage in Chicago's Grant Park to thunderous applause from 200,000 supporters, his unprecedented victory forever secured his place in American history as the first Black president. Many of his fellow African Americans shed tears of joy at the sight of the new president-elect and his family on their way to the White House built by their enslaved ancestors. Yet the 44th president's eight years in the Oval Office also enshrined his legacy as the most consequential American president in supporting women's

---

73 Julia Santucci, "Gender Equality as a National Security Priority," *Center for a New American Security*, September 15, 2017, https://www.cnas.org/publications/reports/gender-equality-as-a-national-security-priority.
74 Hudson, and Leidl, *The Hillary Doctrine*, 183.
75 US Congress, "Women, Peace, and Security Act of 2017."
76 Department of Homeland Security, "Department and Agency Implementation Plans for the US Strategy on Women, Peace, and Security," 2019, https://www.dhs.gov/sites/default/files/publications/wps-dhs-implementation-plan.pdf.

rights at home and abroad. Whether history will solidify those rights, and deem Obama's leadership transformational, remains unanswered.

References

Abraham, Henry J. *Justices, Presidents, and Senators: A History of US Supreme Court Appointments from Washington to Clinton*. Lanham: Rowman & Littlefield, 353.

American Association of Universities. "Report on the AAU Campus Climate Survey on Sexual Assault and Misconduct." January 17, 2020, https://www.aau.edu/sites/default/files/AAU-Files/Key-Issues/Campus-Safety/Revised%20Aggregate%20report%20%20and%20appendices%201-7_(01-16-2020_FINAL).pdf.

Arne Duncan Briefing Materials. President Barack Obama Oral History Project, Timeline, prepared by Bryan Craig, University of Virginia Miller Center, March 2022, 17.

Barroso, Amanda, and Anna Brown. "Gender Pay Gap in US Held Steady in 2020." Pew Research Center. May 25, 2021, https://www.pewresearch.org/fact-tank/2021/05/25/gender-pay-gap-facts/.

Bigio, Jamille, and Rachel Vogelstein. *How Women's Participation in Conflict Prevention and Resolution Advances US Interests*. New York: Council on Foreign Relations, 2016.

Busby, Joshua, and Heather Hurlburt. "Do Women Matter to National Security?" *The Washington Post*. February 2, 2017, https://www.washingtonpost.com/news/monkey-cage/wp/2017/02/02/do-women-matter-to-national-security-the-men-who-lead-u-s-foreign-policy-dont-think-so/.

Carter, Ash. *Inside the Five-Sided Box: Lessons from a Lifetime of Leadership in the Pentagon*. New York: Dutton, 2019.

Clinton, Hillary. *Hard Choices*. New York: Simon & Schuster, 2014.

Clinton, Hillary. "Remarks at the TEDWomen Conference." December 8, 2010, https://2009-2017.state.gov/secretary/20092013clinton/rm/2010/12/152670.htm.

Clinton, Hillary. "Remarks at Vital Voices Conference." September 2, 1998. https://clintonwhitehouse4.archives.gov/WH/EOP/First_Lady/html/generalspeeches/1998/19980908.html.

Clinton, Hillary. "Remarks for the United Nations Fourth World Conference on Women." September 5, 1995, https://www.un.org/esa/gopher-data/conf/fwcw/conf/gov/950905175653.txt.

Crockett, Emily. "Read President Obama on Why Men Need to be Feminists Too." *Vox*. January 19, 2017, https://www.vox.com/2016/8/4/12375558/obama-first-feminist-president-legacy-malia-sasha-glamour-essay.

Crockett, Emily. "The Amazing Tool That Women in the White House Used to Fight Gender Bias." *Vox*. September 14, 2016, https://www.vox.com/2016/9/14/12914370/white-house-obama-women-gender-bias-amplification.

Department of Homeland Security. "Department and Agency Implementation Plans for the US Strategy on Women, Peace, and Security," 2019, https://www.dhs.gov/sites/default/files/publications/wps-dhs-implementation-plan.pdf.

Egnell, Robert. "Gender Perspectives and Military Effectiveness." *Prism* 6, no. 1 (2016): 72–89.

Eilperin, Juliet. "Obama Has Vastly Changed the Fact of the Federal Bureaucracy." *Washington Post*. September 20, 2015, https://www.washingtonpost.com/politics/obama-has-vastly-changed-the-face-of-the-federal-bureaucracy/2015/09/20/73ef803a-5631-11e5-abe9-27d53f250b11_story.html.

Feed the Future. "The Women's Empowerment in Agriculture Index." Accessed January 23, 2023, https://www.feedthefuture.gov/the-womens-empowerment-in-agriculture-index/.

Gramlich, John. "Trump Has Appointed a Larger Share of Female Judges Than Other GOP Presidents, But Lags Obama." Pew Research Center. October 2, 2018, https://www.pewresearch.org/fact-tank/2018/10/02/trump-has-appointed-a-larger-share-of-female-judges-than-other-gop-presidents-but-lags-obama/.

Hirshman, Linda. *Sisters in Law: How Sandra Day O'Connor and Ruth Bader Ginsburg Went to the Supreme Court and Changed the World*. New York: Harper, 2015.

Hudson, Valerie M., and Patricia Leidl, *The Hillary Doctrine*. New York: Columbia University Press, 2015.

Ingrassia, Jacquelyn. "Women's Rights and the US State Department Under and After Hillary Clinton: An Interview with Jennifer Klein." *Brown Journal of World Affairs* 23, no. 1 (Fall/Winter 2016).

It's on Us. Accessed January 23, 2023. https://www.itsonus.org/about-us/our-story/.

Joseph O'Connell, Anne. *Washington Post*. September 20, 2015, https://www.washingtonpost.com/politics/obama-ups-diversity-in-appointees/2015/09/20/5b042aac-5ffb-11e5-8e9e-dce8a2a2a679_graphic.html.

Let Girls Learn, https://obamawhitehouse.archives.gov/letgirlslearn.

Moyer, Laura. "Assessing President Obama's Appointment of Women to the Federal Appellate Courts." *British Journal of American Legislative Studies* 3, no. 10 (2021). https://doi.org/10.2478/bjals-2021-0008.

National Museum of American Diplomacy. "A High Honor: Women Secretaries of State." Accessed January 23, 2023, https://diplomacy.state.gov/exhibits/explore-online-exhibits/herdiplomacy/a-high-honor-secretaries-of-state/.

Obama, Barack. *A Promised Land*. New York: Crown, 2020.

Obama, Barack. "Remarks by the President at United States of Women Summit." The White House, Office of the Press Secretary. June 14, 2016, https://obamawhitehouse.archives.gov/the-press-office/2016/06/14/remarks-president-united-states-women-summit.

Obama, Barack. "Remarks of President Barack Obama at the Lilly Ledbetter Fair Pay Restoration Act Bill Signing, January 29, 2009." Obama Library. https://www.obamalibrary.gov/sites/default/files/uploads/documents/Lilly%20Ledbetter%20Fair%20Pay%20Restoration%20Act%20Bill%20Signing%202009%20(TRANSCRIPT).pdf.

Obama, Michelle. *Becoming*. New York: Crown, 2018.

Office of the Press Secretary. "Executive Order – Instituting a National Action Plan on Women, Peace, and Security." December 19, 2011, https://obamawhitehouse.archives.gov/the-press-office/2011/12/19/executive-order-instituting-national-action-plan-women-peace-and-securit.

Office of the Special Adviser on Gender Issues and Advancement of Women (OSAGI). United Nations, "Landmark Resolution on Women, Peace, and Security." Accessed January 23, 2023, https://www.un.org/womenwatch/osagi/wps/.

Omero, Margie, and Tara McGuinness. "How Women Changed the Outcome of the Election." Center for American Progress. December 12, 2012, https://www.americanprogress.org/article/how-women-changed-the-outcome-of-the-election/.

Perry, Barbara A. *A "Representative" Supreme Court: Religion, Race, and Gender in Appointments*. Westport: Greenwood, 1999.

Perry, Barbara A. *"The Supremes": An Introduction to the US Supreme Court Justices*. Second edition. New York: Peter Lang, 2009.

Potera, Carol. "Women Benefit from the Affordable Care Act." *American Journal of Nursing* 7, no. 119 (July 2019), https://journals.lww.com/ajnonline/Fulltext/2019/07000/Women_Benefit_from_the_Affordable_Care_Act.14.aspx.

Risen, Tom. "Obama Seeks Wage Transparency With Executive Orders." *US News*. April 7, 2014, https://www.usnews.com/news/articles/2014/04/07/obama-seeks-wage-transparency-with-executive-orders.
Santucci, Julia M. "Gender Equality as a National Security Priority." *Center for a New American Security*, September 15, 2017.
Steinberg, Donald. "Seizing the Moment? The US Strategy for Women, Peace and Security." *Our Secure Future*, June 2019. https://oursecurefuture.org/sites/default/files/seizing-the-moment-us-strategy-wps.pdf.
Stolberg, Sheryl Gay. "Obama Signs Equal-Pay Legislation." *New York Times*. January 29, 2009, https://www.nytimes.com/2009/01/30/us/politics/30ledbetter-web.html.
The State Department. "Evaluations of Implementation." August 2015, https://2009-2017.state.gov/documents/organization/251034.pdf.
The State Department. "The QDDR: Leading Through Civilian Power." 2010, https://2009-2017.state.gov/documents/organization/153142.pdf.
"The White House Council on Women and Girls." Accessed January 23, 2023, https://obamawhitehouse.archives.gov/administration/eop/cwg.
The White House. "Executive Order 13623–Preventing and Responding to Violence Against Women and Girls Globally." August 10, 2012, https://www.govinfo.gov/content/pkg/DCPD-201200631/pdf/DCPD-201200631.pdf.
The White House. "Executive Order–Preventing and Responding to Violence Against Women and Girls Globally." August 10, 2012, https://obamawhitehouse.archives.gov/the-press-office/2012/08/10/executive-order-preventing-and-responding-violence-against-women-and-gir.
The White House. "National Security Strategy." May 2010, https://obamawhitehouse.archives.gov/sites/default/files/rss_viewer/national_security_strategy.pdf.
The White House. Office of the Press Secretary. "Fact Sheet: Final It's On Us Summit and Report of the White House Task Force to Protect Students from Sexual Assault." January 5, 2017, https://obamawhitehouse.archives.gov/the-press-office/2014/01/22/memorandum-establishing-white-house-task-force-protect-students-sexual-a.
The White House. Office of the Press Secretary. "Memorandum – Establishing a White House Task Force to Protect Students from Sexual Assault." January 22, 2014, https://obamawhitehouse.archives.gov/the-press-office/2014/01/22/memorandum-establishing-white-house-task-force-protect-students-sexual-a.
The White House. "The United States National Action Plan on Women, Peace, and Security," June 5, 2016, https://obamawhitehouse.archives.gov/sites/whitehouse.gov/files/documents/women-national-action-plan.pdf.
The White House. "Presidential Memorandum – Coordination of Policies and Programs to Promote Gender Equality and Empower Women and Girls Globally." January 30, 2013, https://obamawhitehouse.archives.gov/the-press-office/2013/01/30/presidential-memorandum-coordination-policies-and-programs-promote-gende.
US Congress. "Women, Peace, and Security Act of 2017." Public Law 115–168, October 6, 2017, https://www.congress.gov/115/plaws/publ68/PLAW-115publ68.pdf.
USAID. "Evaluations of Implementation." July 2015, https://www.usaid.gov/sites/default/files/documents/1865/GBV-Exec-Summary-Nov-2015.pdf.
USAID. "United States Strategy to Prevent and Respond to Gender-Based Violence Globally." 2012, https://2009-2017.state.gov/documents/organization/196468.pdf.
Verveer, Melanne. "An Interview with Melanne Verveer." *Georgetown Journal of International Affairs* 20 (2019): 77–80. https://www.jstor.org/stable/26794944.

Verveer, Melanne. "The Vital Role of Women in Agriculture and Rural Development." June 27, 2011. https://2009-2017.state.gov/s/gwi/rls/rem/2011/167899.htm.

Vitali, Ali. *Electable: Why America Hasn't Put a Woman in the White House . . . Yet*. New York: Day Street Books, 2022.

Witkowsky, Anne A. "Integrating Gender Perspectives within the Department of Defense," *Prism* 6, no. 1 (2016): 34–45.

"Women Appointed to Presidential Cabinets," Center for American Women and Politics, Eagleton Institute of Politics, Rutgers University, March 16, 2022, https://cawp.rutgers.edu/sites/default/files/resources/womenapptdtoprescabinets.pdf.

Youtube. "President Obama signs the Lilly Ledbetter Fair Pay Act," January 29, 2009, https://www.youtube.com/watch?v=UtKAKIurRAY.

Zengerle, Patricia. "Women Voters Helped Make Obama; Could They Break Him?" *Reuters*. November 3, 2012, https://jp.reuters.com/article/usa-campaign-women-obama-idINDEE8A300U20121104.

Paul Fritz
Chapter 9
The US and Russia during the Obama Administration: An Inevitable Return of Great Power Politics?

President Obama courted better relations with Russia from the outset of his administration, famously calling for a "reset" in 2009. Welcomed at first by Russian President Dmitry Medvedev, the initial fanfare of the reset would lead to some limited warming and hope for better US-Russian relations. Yet by 2017, Russo-American relations had spiraled downward to a new post-Cold War nadir and set the stage for later more serious confrontations between the two powers.

Why did US.-Russian relations deteriorate so markedly during Obama's presidency? This is a critical question for President Obama's foreign policy legacy. Although not an ascendant state like China, Russia was and remains an important and potentially powerful, nuclear-armed state. More directly, Russian actions both during and after the Obama presidency presented serious challenges to the US and American-led international liberal order, including Russia's interference in the 2016 US election and its invasion of Ukraine in 2022. Was another direction in US-Russian relations possible during the Obama presidency?

I argue the general deterioration of US-Russian relations during Obama's time in office was nearly inevitable. The Obama reset was unlikely to fundamentally transform relations because post-Cold War Russian foreign policy has been driven largely by the desire to reestablish the status and position in the international system that it lost following the collapse of the Soviet Union. As Russia increasingly attempted to exert its status, instances of cooperation between the US and Russia were possible only when that cooperation conferred a type of equality between the two states. In the absence of a perception of equality – something generally withheld by all post-Cold War American Presidents – Russia was bound to resist American-defined terms of cooperation and push against American interests. The desire to reclaim great power status also led to a much more confrontational Russia, with the state more willing to take risks to exert its status in international politics. As such, Obama's early effort to reset relations was an attempt to seize a window of opportunity to transform relations with Russia but may have been too hopeful in terms of what could realistically be achieved.

Paul Fritz, Hofstra University

But at the same time, Obama's grand strategy – which stressed great power cooperation, engaging rivals, and reemphasizing diplomacy – set the stage for some important instances of transactional US-Russian cooperation, especially in areas related to weapons of mass destruction and nuclear arms control. While cooperation in these areas did not fundamentally transform Russo-American relations nor prevent serious confrontations, President Obama's shift toward a pragmatic management strategy of Russia over his time in office produced results that served important US foreign policy goals.

In this chapter, I first lay out some of the critical aspects of Obama's grand strategy that informed his foreign policy choices, with an emphasis on great power politics, Obama's view of America's role in the world, and how this relates to Russia. In a similar way to all post-Cold War presidents, Obama saw US primacy as the lynchpin of world politics. But given what he perceived as overextension under the previous administration, eliciting cooperation from great powers was key to husbanding American power and thus sustaining US primacy. In the following section, I show how Russia's actions in the post-Cold War era have generally been driven by status concerns vis-à-vis the US, but Obama generally relegated Russia to a secondary role. The next section demonstrates how some significant episodes of cooperation between the US and Russia during the Obama administration such as the New START arms control treaty and the Iran Nuclear Deal were, at least in some important ways, a product of President Obama's desire to use great power engagement to deal with global problems that simultaneously fulfilled Russia's desire for equality. This did not, however, prevent Russia from acting in ways contrary to US foreign policy interests in its effort to exert status and power. The conclusion provides an assessment of Obama's approach to Russia given the limited possibilities of transforming the relationship.

Obama's Grand Strategy

Like most newly elected American presidents, Barack Obama entered office believing he had to correct the mistakes of the previous administration. This was likely most clear in foreign policy. The George W. Bush administration was perceived to have alienated much of the international community, including American allies, by choosing a unilateral and militarized foreign policy and squandering American power with a costly war of choice in Iraq. But Obama's own view seems to have been that it was more than just specific policy mistakes like the invasion of Iraq or alienating allies that needed to be corrected. International politics had changed, with globalization dispersing power and bringing about new threats that could not be adequately addressed through military might or by the US alone. All of this was coupled with Obama's clear need to address problems at home stemming from the Great Recession and other domestic issues that required significant resources. Thus, the need to conserve American power combined with the changing nature of international politics meant that the US needed to expand the number of partners it had to be able to effectively tackle the biggest foreign policy challenges and do so not through intimidation but by diplomacy.[1]

While sometimes portrayed as a significant departure from US grand strategic thought, President Obama's approach was consistent with traditional American grand strategy in many ways. Hal Brands notes that the first and most broad feature of Obama's grand strategy was maintaining US primacy through the spread of liberal institutions, democracy promotion, maintenance of a vast alliance system, and significant defense spending.[2] As the 2015 National Security Strategy notes:

> Any successful strategy to ensure the safety of the American people and advance our national security interests must begin with an undeniable truth – America must lead. Strong and sustained American leadership is essential to a rules-based international order that promotes global security and prosperity as well as the dignity and human rights of all peoples. The question is never whether America should lead, but how we lead.[3]

At least in framing, this consistency with post-World War Two grand strategy is notable, especially given the criticisms of President Obama's approach. For example, Robert Kaufman argues that Obama's leadership weakened the United States in foreign affairs with a dangerous assumption that the US could prevent hostile powers from expanding by strengthening multilateral institutions based on shared responsibility for global stability rather than a unique role for America and its military might.[4] Similarly, Colin Dueck argues Obama abdicated American leadership with

---

[1] James M. Lindsay, "George W. Bush, Barack Obama and the Future of US Global Leadership," *International Affairs* 87, no. 4 (July 2011): 765–779. Obama made this view clear in his writing before entering the White House. See Barack Obama, "Renewing American Leadership," *Foreign Affairs* 86, no. 4 (Jul/Aug 2007): 2–16. For a general examination of Obama's approach, see Hal Brands, "Barack Obama and the Dilemmas of American Grand Strategy," *The Washington Quarterly* 39, no. 4 (Winter 2017): 101–125. For a more critical view of Obama's approach, see Colin Dueck, *The Obama Doctrine: American Grand Strategy Today* (New York: Oxford University Press, 2015).
[2] Brands, "Barack Obama and the Dilemmas of American Grand Strategy," 104.
[3] *National Security Strategy, 2015*, https://obamawhitehouse.archives.gov/sites/default/files/docs/2015_national_security_strategy_2.pdf. Previous national security strategy documents under the Obama administration all share this same view.
[4] Robert Kaufman, *Dangerous Doctrine: How Obama's Grand Strategy Weakened America* (Lexington: University of Kentucky Press, 2016).

retrenchment and accommodation of rivals, in large part because he was so focused on domestic issues.[5]

The disconnect between Obama's declared strategy and his critics' charges may be partly explained by how Obama viewed leadership and his focus on the changing nature of international politics. Globalization had fundamentally shifted the center of power in international politics, and Obama saw a clear need to encourage other states to act in ways that could support the US-led liberal international order. According to Obama, this would preserve American leadership and its ability to shape a fluid strategic environment and reduce reliance on military action abroad to protect American interests.[6]

To his critics, this may appear to be abdication when it comes to American military dominance. To much of the rest of the world, however, the use of American military power in Obama's ramped-up drone wars, the 2009 surge in Afghanistan, the decision to use of force in Libya in 2011, and redeployment of US military forces to Iraq to take on the Islamic State, among other instances, may not have looked like American retrenchment or abdication. Nor did American defense expenditures under Obama change that greatly from previous presidents.[7] In short, this leg of the Obama grand strategy was indeed about America maintaining primacy and military dominance, but with a different outward appearance and a continuation of US military advantages by using them in a "more disciplined, limited-liability approach."[8]

This different outward appearance and approach to sustaining American primacy did represent some real shifts in American grand strategy. The search for partners noted earlier opened opportunities for other states to take the lead on certain issues. The military intervention in Libya possibly typifies this, with the notion that the US would "lead from behind" in a way that could limit direct costs

---

5 Dueck, *The Obama Doctrine*.
6 The latter is a focus of many retrenchment criticisms, with some charging that Obama gutted the US military and was unwilling to use it abroad. See, for example, Mark Moyar, "How Obama Shrank the Military," *The Wall Street Journal*, August 2, 2015.
7 To be clear, there was a reduction in military spending under President Obama. However, despite cuts after 2010 driven by so-called sequestration and the historically consistent pattern of contracting military spending after major wars, in 2015, US military spending was still nearly three times as much as any other state. See Brands, "Barack Obama and the Dilemmas of American Strategy," 104–106. The *Stockholm International Peace Research Institute* data show that defense spending in terms of percentage of GDP under the Obama administration was generally consistent with the previous Bush administration. In fact, defense spending as a percentage of GPD never dropped below 3.5 percent under Obama, which was higher than the lowest level of spending in the post-9/11 era of the Bush administration. See https://milex.sipri.org/sipri.
8 Brands, "Barack Obama and the Dilemmas of American Strategy," 106.

to the US yet still protect interests and ideals abroad.[9] This was coupled with reemphasizing diplomacy, both with friends as well as adversaries. Other states, including great powers, could thus be seen as potential partners to tackle the most pressing international problems and serve to enhance the liberal international order with the US in the lead.

This approach was consistent with Obama's view as a candidate for president that great power competition no longer existed.[10] Instead, great powers should and, with some effort, could unite to tackle common, transnational challenges. Much of Obama's focus was on a rising China, which needed to be engaged where possible to nudge it into being a "responsible" rising power to elicit cooperation and manage competition.[11] Russia, a declining great power, would also need to be engaged but seemingly on different terms. While Obama acknowledged competition with China as a state that would soon rival the US in terms of economic power and maybe one day in military capabilities, Russia did not fundamentally compete with America. As Obama would say later in his presidency, Russia was a "regional power," implying it was not a global power on equal footing with the US.[12]

This perspective was not dissimilar to other post-Cold War American presidents. Since the collapse of the Soviet Union, Russia has experienced a fairly dramatic drop in power and influence in the world.[13] While previous post-Cold War administrations had attempted to cultivate good relations with Russia, the Obama administration's efforts – guided by President Obama's notion that there really could be no more great power competition if the world was to tackle the most serious global problems – were initially more robust. The so-called "Russia reset" was an initiative with wide-ranging goals of promoting US-Russian cooperation on arms control, Afghanistan, Iran, and North Korea. In addition, the reset was designed to take advantage of Russian President Medvedev's perceived Western

---

9 Ivo Daadler, and James Stavridis, "NATO's Victory in Libya: The Right Way to Run and Intervention," *Foreign Affairs* 91, no. 2 (March/April 2012): 2–7. For a critical view of the Libya intervention that focuses on the aftermath of the conflict, see Alan Kuperman, "Obama's Libya Debacle: How a Well-Meaning Intervention Ended in Failure," *Foreign Affairs* 94, no. 2 (March/April 2015): 66–77.
10 Barack Obama, *The Audacity of Hope* (New York: Crown Publishing, 2006).
11 Obama, "Renewing American Leadership."
12 "Obama Dismisses Russia as 'Regional Power' Acting Out of Weakness," *Washington Post*, March 25, 2014.
13 Persistently high oil prices led to some rebounding of Russian power after its low point in the 1990s, and fueled a new assertiveness in Russia foreign policy beginning in the mid-2000s. See Jeffrey Mankoff, *Russian Foreign Policy: The Return of Great Power Politics* (New York: Rowman & Littlefield, 2009), 3–6.

liberal leanings.[14] This was consistent with Obama's grand strategy, where primacy remained at the forefront but there was a type of transformation of the tools with which the US would seek to maintain it.

The Limits of Cooperation with a Status-Seeking, Declining State

The Russia reset failed to alter the trajectory of US-Russian relations and, despite some significant examples of cooperation, relations with Russia markedly declined during the Obama presidency. One of the largest obstacles to bettering US-Russia relations can be found in the nature of the Russian state itself. This is not to say that specific policies and interests or the nature of the Russian regime and leadership did not present obstacles to Russo-American relations during the Obama administration.[15] They certainly did. But at a different level, the Russian state was a defeated great power driven by desires to regain status and autonomy equal to that of its former great power foe, and thus cooperation was likely only on certain terms.

With the collapse of the Soviet Union, Russia emerged as a weakened state struggling to come to terms with its role in the post-Cold War international system. Suffering a deep crisis in identity as a result, Russia has attempted to increase its status in world politics ever since.[16] Larson and Shevchenko show Russia's initial attempts to gain acceptance as a peer or equal of the United States in the early post-Cold War period through various, largely nonconfrontational means in the early post-Cold War period. After being rebuffed by the West and the US in particular, Russia turned to more competitive strategies to attempt to regain a sense of equal status. Most of these efforts by Russia, however, were met with indifference by the Clinton and Bush administrations, effectively denying Russia the equal status it was seeking.[17] By the time President Obama entered of-

---

14 Brands, "Barak Obama and the Dilemmas of American Grand Strategy," 107.
15 Dueck, *The Obama Doctrine*, and Kaufman, *Dangerous Doctrine*, both criticize the Obama administration for minimizing problems that emerge from cooperating with nondemocracies.
16 See Anne L. Clunan, *The Social Construction of Russia's Resurgence: Aspiration, Identity, and Security Interests* (PLACE: Johns Hopkins University Press, 2009), Mankoff, *Russian Foreign Policy: The Return of Great Power Politics*, and Angela E. Stent, *The Limits of Partnership: US-Russian Relations in the Twenty-First Century, Updated Edition* (Princeton: Princeton University Press, 2015).
17 Deborah Welch Larson, and Alexei Shevchenko, "Status Seekers: Chinese and Russian Responses to US Primacy," *International Security* 34, no. 4 (2010): 90.

fice, Moscow's main purpose in foreign affairs had already become to assert Russian great power status and have an equal partnership with the West.[18]

Combining this perspective with President Obama's grand strategy provides a window into US-Russian relations. Given the Russian need for equality with the US, any proposal or policy with a level structure for both were opportunities for cooperation. Moreover, in places where the US decided to focus on allowing others to operate in ways that were consistent with husbanding American power and allowing partners do the heavy lifting provided Moscow with an opportunity to demonstrate its equal status. The former is a type of conferring of status through cooperation, while the latter is Russia claiming that equal status through its own actions.

This combination drove much of the American-Russian relationship under the Obama administration. On initiatives where Russia was seen as important to help achieve the desired end – things related to nuclear weapons and weapons of mass destruction proliferation, for example – the Obama administration actively engaged Russia, thereby conferring equal status and making cooperation more likely.[19] Instances such as this, though, were relatively few. In addition, they were transactional and limited in scope rather than anything that could transform the overall relationship.

In other areas of concern for the Obama administration, Moscow was simply not a key player. The Obama administration's desire to rebalance toward Asia, for example, relegated Russia to a secondary role at best. Much of this had to do with the weakness of Russia, both economically and militarily.[20] Even though clearly objectively not on a par with the US on these terms, Russia – and Russian President Vladimir Putin in particular – still desired the sense of equality. By the

---

[18] Mankoff, *Russian Foreign Policy*, 30. There is some variation on the intensity of anti-Western views expressed as part of the Russian desire to reclaim status and equality given leadership changes. Russian President Dmitry Medvedev (2008–2012) was, at least early in his tenure, relatively more open to the West than Vladimir Putin who, starting at least as early as 2007 often couched his arguments for Russian status in anti-Western terms. See Mikhail Zygar, "The Russian Reset that Never Was," *Foreign Policy*, December 9, 2016.
[19] Angela E. Stent, "Putin's Power Play in Syria," *Foreign Affairs* 95, no. 1 (January/February 2016): 106–113.
[20] US GPD was between 11 and 14 times the size of Russia's economy between 2009 and 2016, according to the World Bank (https://data.worldbank.org/indicator/NY.GDP.MKTP.CD?locations=RU-US). Military spending similarly diverged, where even with some defense spending cuts under the Obama administration, the US spent nine-times more than Russia (https://data.worldbank.org/indicator/MS.MIL.XPND.CD?locations=RU-US).

end of his presidency, Obama's view on this became quite clear. In an interview with Jeffrey Goldberg, Obama noted this about Putin:

> He's constantly interested in being seen as our peer and as working with us, because he's not completely stupid. He understands that Russia's overall position in the world is significantly diminished. And the fact that he invades Crimea or is trying to prop up Assad doesn't suddenly make him a player. You don't see him in any of these meetings out here helping to shape the agenda. For that matter, there's not a G20 meeting where the Russians set the agenda around any of the issues that are important.[21]

Obama's assessment of Russia and Putin, like the "regional power" comment noted earlier in the chapter, is probably objectively correct in terms of Moscow's position in the international politics. Yet the dismissiveness reinforced the notion that Russia was not equal and would only be treated as though it was in areas the US defined as appropriate.

More than just a dig at Putin or relegating Russia to a lower status, this stance is consistent with the first pillar of grand strategy under the Obama administration: The US was the key player in world politics. With primacy at its forefront, by definition the Obama grand strategy was clearly intended to prevent Russia (or other states) from being an actual equal player. Under Obama as well as previous administrations, other pillars of American grand strategy such as democracy promotion were perceived to threaten Russian interests at home, in the former Soviet space, and beyond. In these areas, then, there was little possibility but for confrontation. Russia's former Soviet sphere of influence in particular was an area that it could attempt to exert status rather than be given equal status to the US in terms of the "right" of a great power to exert influence over its neighbors.

Given Obama's grand strategy and Russia's position in the post-Cold War order, there was room for relatively straightforward transactional cooperation between Washington and Moscow which filled Russian status desires while also addressing pressing concerns of the Obama administration. But the very same factors prevented any type of transformation of US-Russian relations for the better, and indeed set the stage for growing confrontation.

---

21 Jeffrey Goldberg, "The Obama Doctrine," *The Atlantic* April 2016.

Limited Transactional Successes in the Context of Overall Deterioration of Relations

Some of the most pressing foreign policy concerns for the Obama administration revolved around weapons of mass destruction (WMD). The first Obama National Security Strategy document laid out the President's concern for the spread of nuclear, chemical, and biological weapons in stark terms, focusing on partnerships to limit the dangers these weapons posed to the US and to the world.[22] At a speech in Prague in 2009, President Obama famously called for the eventual elimination of nuclear weapons, saying, "[w]e [the US] cannot succeed in this endeavor alone, but we can lead it, we can start it. So today, I state clearly and with conviction America's commitment to seek the peace and security of a world without nuclear weapons."[23] Both preventing the proliferation of WMDs and reducing, possibly even eliminating, existing nuclear weapons stockpiles required working with Russia and doing so in a way that provided Moscow equal status with the US.

The New START Treaty is the first instance of this. One of the few tangible successes stemming from the early effort to "reset" relations with Russia, New START (2011) was a bilateral arms control treaty that significantly reduced the number of deployed strategic nuclear weapons in both states' arsenals.[24] One view of New START is that it was simply a continuation of arms control designed to stabilize nuclear deterrence that began in the Cold War. But this in itself is critical. Bilateral arms control treaties present structural equality between both sides. Even with Moscow unhappy that the US had pushed ahead with ballistic missile defense – something it feared could reduce its nuclear deterrent – the deal was struck to limit both sides to 1,550 deployed strategic nuclear weapons, achieving an important goal for the Obama administration.[25]

The Iranian Nuclear Deal is likely one of the most consequential foreign policy achievements of the Obama administration. But in the context of US-Russian relations, it was another example of the type of transactional cooperation possi-

---

22 United States National Security Strategy, 23, 2010, https://obamawhitehouse.archives.gov/sites/default/files/rss_viewer/national_security_strategy.pdf.
23 Remarks by President Barack Obama in Prague, April 5, 2009, https://obamawhitehouse.archives.gov/the-press-office/remarks-president-barack-obama-prague-delivered.
24 New START Treaty, https://www.state.gov/new-start/.
25 President Obama provided some concessions to President Medvedev on US missile defense plans in Europe as part of the negotiation, something his domestic political opponents decried. But given US advantages in nuclear weapons delivery systems, even a scaled-back missile defense system in Europe could be seen as a threat to Russia. See Keir Leiber, and Daryl Press, "The Rise of US Nuclear Primacy," *Foreign Affairs* 85, no. 2 (March/April 2006): 42–54.

ble between Washington and Moscow during the Obama administration. The US and Russia have long shared a mutual interest in preventing nuclear weapons proliferation to additional states, dating back to the Cold War.[26] Thus, there is a convergence of interests between the US and Russia on the issue of the Iranian nuclear program in a general sense. However, Iran could be an important market for Russian nuclear technology and military equipment. There were also some fears in Moscow that the Iran Deal could sideline Russia as an interlocuter with Iran should Iranian-American relations improve as a result of the deal.[27] The overarching interest in preventing nuclear proliferation was present, but clearly Moscow had multiple motives.[28]

Russia's key role in the process of bringing about negotiations through the application of sanctions against Iran also placed it at the center of world politics. Moreover, the mechanisms by which Iran's nuclear program would be limited cemented Russia's status as indispensable in this instance. The deal itself was also routed through the United Nations Security Council, where Russia is equal to the US in every way. This, combined with the potential that Russia could benefit with the normalization of Iran, provided the context for Russian cooperation on an important Obama foreign policy initiative.

Other opportunities for limited transactional cooperation presented themselves. The most prominent example of this is the deal reached to address Syria's stockpiling and use of chemical weapons in the context of the country's ongoing civil war. Asked about Syrian chemical weapons in August 2012, President Obama said, "[w]e have been very clear to the Assad regime ... that a red line for us is we start seeing a whole bunch of chemical weapons moving around or being utilized. That would change my calculus. That would change my equation."[29] This statement clearly implied some sort of military punishment if Syrian President Assad used chemical weapons on his opponents. But when this occurred in 2013, President Obama had started to question the efficacy of retaliatory military strikes and ultimately decided against it.[30]

---

26 See Francis Gavin, "Strategies of Inhibition: US Grand Strategy, the Nuclear Revolution, and Nonproliferation," *International Security* 40, no. 1 (July 2015): 9–46.
27 On Russia's fears, see Mark Katz, "Russia Secretly Feared the Iran Nuclear Deal. Here's Why," The Atlantic Council, April 28, 2021, https://www.atlanticcouncil.org/blogs/iransource/russia-secretly-feared-the-iran-nuclear-deal-heres-why/.
28 The negotiations to reach the Iran Deal were extremely complex. Because of space constraints, this account is necessarily limited.
29 Remarks by the President to the White House Press Corps, August 20, 2012, https://obamawhitehouse.archives.gov/the-press-office/2012/08/20/remarks-president-white-house-press-corps.
30 Jeffrey Goldberg, "The Obama Doctrine." This episode led to bitter criticism for harming the credibility of the US by both Republicans and some Democrats. Even Obama's former Defense

Russia, a long-time key player in Syria, had an opportunity to demonstrate its weight as a great power. President Obama opened this possibility with a suggestion to Russian President Putin that "if he forced Assad to get rid of chemical weapons, that would eliminate the need for us taking a military strike."[31] Shortly after the chemical weapons attacks and through intense diplomacy, a deal was struck that would lead to Syria – which had never previously acknowledged its chemical weapons program, stockpiles, or use – to submit to international oversight of the destruction of its chemical weapons.

While the merits of the Syrian chemical weapons deal can be debated, this episode is consistent with Obama's ideas about US grand strategy as well as the need for a sense of equality to elicit significant Russian cooperation to achieve goals consistent with the president's view of American foreign policy interests. Given all the other foreign and domestic policy challenges facing the US, it would be a waste of American resources to strike if, as Obama believed, the use of force in Syria would be ineffective as a punishment and was driven solely by a perceived need to follow through on the red line. This decision demonstrates the "more disciplined, limited liability approach to military action" that was a hallmark of Obama grand strategy.[32] Having a partner to achieve the desired end of getting rid of chemical weapons thus also contributed to the goal of husbanding American power. For Russia, this was an opportunity to demonstrate its indispensability as a key world player.[33]

Involving weapons of mass destruction in one form or another, the New START Treaty, the Iranian nuclear deal, and the Syrian chemical weapons deal all demonstrate how limited but successful cooperation emerged based on Obama administration foreign policy priorities that fit squarely with Russia's need to be seen and treated as an equal of the US. Each of the episodes discussed above have multiple causes, and the interests of both the US and Russia are complex. There can also be various judgments made for each regarding the results for the Obama administration in terms of US foreign policy. But the common factor is the basic structural equality between the US and Russia, suggesting the importance of this

---

Secretary Leon Panetta claimed the episode was damaging for the US. But according to Goldberg, the day he decided against enforcing the red line was Obama's "liberation day" from the normal Washington playbook.

31 Quoted in Jeffrey Goldberg, "The Obama Doctrine."
32 Brands, "Barak Obama and the Dilemmas of American Grand Strategy," 106.
33 See, for example, "Russia's Syria Plan Gains Momentum," *The Moscow Times*, September 10, 2013.

factor in US-Russian relations.[34] Moreover, the outcome of each was consistent with Obama's stated foreign policy goals, and hailed by the administration as examples of successful Russo-American cooperation where Russian assistance was noted as critical.[35]

In other ways, though, Obama's grand strategy ideas – especially the first pillar of maintaining American primacy and preserving the American-led liberal international order – created significant obstacles for US-Russian relations and set the stage for confrontation. Much of the deterioration of relations can be thought of as Moscow's determination to demonstrate equality when that sense of equality was not forthcoming from the Obama administration. With the perception that the US had long dismissed Russian interests in the region, the military intervention in Syria in 2015 was a way for President Putin to demonstrate Russian military prowess as well as support a secular strong-man in the Middle East that had run afoul of the US and liberal international norms with his brutal tactics in the Syrian civil war.[36] The Russian annexation of Crimea and support for separatists in Eastern Ukraine in 2014 came as a reaction to the Maidan protests that eventually ousted a Kremlin-supported Ukrainian president, something the US was seen to support at the expense of Russia's interests in its former Soviet holdings. Along with alleging US meddling leading to the democratic uprisings in Russia's region, President Putin directly blamed the US for protests against his government in late 2011 and early 2012.[37] In this light, Russia's actions in Ukraine and its meddling in the 2016 American presidential election can be seen as attempts to claim equal power and influence.

Much of Putin's ire toward the US pre-dates the Obama administration, of course. But the key issue is that the focus on equality, and the perception that the US under multiple presidents did not see or treat Moscow as an equal, is one of the structural features of the Russian regime that contributed to the marked decline in US-Russian relations during the Obama administration. This is perhaps best demonstrated with the Iran Nuclear Deal. The final negotiations for the deal

---

34 One could also argue that Russian not blocking the United Nations Security Council resolution authorizing the use of force in Libya demonstrates elements of this, because Russia's veto power as a P5 member gave it equal authority to legitimize the US-supported military intervention. Russian President Medvedev played a key role in this episode, agreeing with Obama during consultations that something needed to be done about the Libyan leader before the Security Council vote. See Zygar, "The Russian Reset that Never Was."

35 "Obama Thanks Putin for 'Important Role' in Iran Nuclear Deal," *Radio Free Europe/Radio Liberty*, July 16, 2015.

36 Stent, "Putin's Power Play in Syria."

37 Michael McFaul, "Russia as it Is: A Grand Strategy for Confronting Putin," *Foreign Affairs* 97, no. 4 (July/August 2018): 82–91.

took place after the Russian annexation of Crimea and the subsequent application of significant US economic sanctions. Shortly after the signing of the deal, President Obama said "Russia was a help on this. I'll be honest with you. I was not sure – given the strong difference we are having with Russia right now around Ukraine – whether this would sustain itself."[38] Even in this context of significant confrontation, cooperation emerged at least in part because Russia was an undeniably an indispensable and equal player.

Conclusion

Russia's interreference in the 2016 US presidential election was a fitting, albeit unsettling, encapsulation of how far Russo-American relations deteriorated under the Obama administration. Even before this brazen act by Russia, it was clear that relations between the two states had spiraled downward in multiple ways. By the end of Obama's first term in office, the president seemed to settle on a pragmatic management approach toward Russia rather than hoping to reshape the relationship.[39] Yet the areas of cooperation between the US and Russia during the Obama administration are significant. Especially in the area of weapons of mass destruction, President Obama's grand strategy opened up the possibility of meaningful cooperation with Russia to address an important foreign policy concern in a way that was consistent with his view of US grand strategy in a globalized world where partners and preserving American power were paramount concerns.

Because it could not address Russia's overriding concern for equal status with the US without giving up key tenants of American foreign policy interests, however, the Obama administration was fundamentally limited in how much it could better relations with Russia. In this way, despite efforts to reset the relationship, a return to rivalry and confrontation was all but inevitable. Instead of a fundamental transformation of this important bilateral relationship, transactional deals with Moscow were probably the best that could be achieved. Clearly, some of these deals served US foreign policy interests well. But given the strong Russian desire to reemerge as an equal to the United States, it was likely beyond the ability of any president or strategy to avoid growing discord in US-Russian relations.

---

38 "Obama Thanks Putin for "Important Role" in Iran Nuclear Deal," *Radio Free Europe/Radio Liberty*, July 16, 2015.
39 Ruth Deyermond, "Assessing the Reset: Successes and Failures in the Obama Administration's Russia Policy, 2009–2012," *European Security* 22, no. 4 (2013): 500–523.

By the end of his presidency, Obama seemed resigned to this fact. Ultimately his view was that Moscow's growing number of actions that ran counter to US interests displayed Russian weakness. In Obama's words:

> Putin acted in Ukraine in response to a client state that was about to slip out of his grasp. And he improvised in a way to hang on to his control there . . . . He's done the exact same thing in Syria, at enormous cost to the well-being of his own country. And the notion that somehow Russia is in a stronger position now, in Syria or in Ukraine, than they were before they invaded Ukraine or before he had to deploy military forces to Syria is to fundamentally misunderstand the nature of power in foreign affairs or in the world generally. Real power means you can get what you want without having to exert violence. Russia was much more powerful when Ukraine looked like an independent country but was a kleptocracy that he could pull the strings on.[40]

In the areas where Russia was attempting to claim power and status through the use of force, Obama is clearly saying that Moscow is not equal to the United States. This, as much as anything, probably defined the limits of US-Russian relations during the Obama presidency.

Coming to a full assessment of the Obama administration's approach to Russia is challenging given the scale and complexity of US-Russian relations. Moreover, the argument presented here – that the combination of Obama's grand strategy ideas and Russia's need for status and equality with the United States constrained prospects for transformational policy making – cannot capture all the dynamics in the Russo-American relationship during the Obama presidency. But this framework does provide an insight into what drove important instances of cooperation and also the sources of discord between the US and Russia during President Obama's time in office.

References

Brands, Hal. "Barack Obama and the Dilemmas of American Grand Strategy." *The Washington Quarterly* 39, no. 4 (Winter 2017): 101–125.

Clunan, Anne L. *The Social Construction of Russia's Resurgence: Aspiration, Identity, and Security Interests*. Baltimore: Johns Hopkins University Press, 2009.

Daadler, Ivo, and James Stavridis. "NATO's Victory in Libya: The Right Way to Run and Intervention." *Foreign Affairs* 91, no. 2 (March/April 2012): 2–7.

Deyermond, Ruth. "Assessing the Reset: Successes and Failures in the Obama Administration's Russia Policy, 2009-2012." *European Security* 22, no. 4 (2013): 500–523.

Dueck, Colin. *The Obama Doctrine: American Grand Strategy Today*. New York: Oxford University Press, 2015.

---

40 Quoted in Goldberg, "The Obama Doctrine."

Gavin, Francis. "Strategies of Inhibition: US Grand Strategy, the Nuclear Revolution, and Nonproliferation." *International Security* 40, no. 1 (July 2015): 9–46.

Goldberg, Jeffrey. "The Obama Doctrine." *The Atlantic*. April 2016. https://www.theatlantic.com/magazine/archive/2016/04/the-obama-doctrine/471525/.

Katz, Mark. "Russia Secretly Feared the Iran Nuclear Deal. Here's Why." The Atlantic Council. April 28, 2021, https://www.atlanticcouncil.org/blogs/iransource/russia-secretly-feared-the-iran-nuclear-deal-heres-why/.

Kaufman, Robert. *Dangerous Doctrine: How Obama's Grand Strategy Weakened America*. Lexington: University of Kentucky Press, 2016.

Kuperman, Alan. "Obama's Libya Debacle: How a Well-Meaning Intervention Ended in Failure." *Foreign Affairs* 94, no. 2 (March/April 2015): 66–77.

Larson, Deborah Welch and Alexei Shevchenko. "Status Seekers: Chinese and Russian Responses to US Primacy." *International Security* 34, no. 4 (2010).

Leiber, Keir, and Daryl Press. "The Rise of US Nuclear Primacy." *Foreign Affairs* 85, no. 2 (March/April 2006): 42–54.

Lindsay, James M. "George W. Bush, Barack Obama and the Future of US Global Leadership." *International Affairs* 87, no. 4 (July 2011): 765–779.

Mankoff, Jeffrey. *Russian Foreign Policy: The Return of Great Power Politics*. New York: Rowman & Littlefield, 2009.

McFaul, Michael. "Russia as it Is: A Grand Strategy for Confronting Putin." *Foreign Affairs* 97, no. 4 (July/August 2018): 82–91.

Moyar, Mark. "How Obama Shrank the Military." *The Wall Street Journal*. August 2, 2015.

Obama, Barack. Remarks by President Barack Obama in Prague, April 5, 2009, https://obamawhitehouse.archives.gov/the-press-office/remarks-president-barack-obama-prague-delivered.

Obama, Barack. Remarks by the President to the White House Press Corps. August 20, 2012, https://obamawhitehouse.archives.gov/the-press-office/2012/08/20/remarks-president-white-house-press-corps.

Obama, Barack. "Renewing American Leadership." *Foreign Affairs* 86, no. 4 (Jul/Aug 2007): 2–16.

Obama, Barack. *The Audacity of Hope*. New York: Crown Publishing, 2006.

"Obama Dismisses Russia as 'Regional Power' Acting Out of Weakness." *Washington Post*. March 25, 2014. https://www.washingtonpost.com/world/national-security/obama-dismisses-russia-as-regional-power-acting-out-of-weakness/2014/03/25/1e5a678e-b439-11e3-b899-20667de76985_story.html.

Radio Free Europe/Radio Liberty. "Obama Thanks Putin for 'Important Role' in Iran Nuclear Deal." July 16, 2015.

Stent, Angela E. "Putin's Power Play in Syria." *Foreign Affairs* 95, no. 1 (January/February 2016): 106–113.

Stent, Angela E. *The Limits of Partnership: US-Russian Relations in the Twenty-First Century*, Updated Edition. Princeton: Princeton University Press, 2015.

The Moscow Times. "Russia's Syria Plan Gains Momentum." September 10, 2013.

Zygar, Mikhail. "The Russian Reset that Never Was." *Foreign Policy*. December 9, 2016. https://foreignpolicy.com/2016/12/09/the-russian-reset-that-never-was-putin-obama-medvedev-libya-mikhail-zygar-all-the-kremlin-men/.

David W. Kearn Jr.
Chapter 10
The Obama Legacy on Nuclear Weapons: Transformative Vision, Pragmatic Results

Barack Obama was the first American president in the nuclear era to enter office with nonproliferation as a primary foreign policy objective.[1] Outlined in his heralded April 2009 speech in Prague, what became known as the "Prague Agenda" shaped US foreign policy with important results.[2] Starting with a "reset" of relations with Moscow that produced a strategic arms control treaty, through the diplomatic innovation of the Nuclear Security Summit process, to the conclusion of a multilateral agreement to prevent Iran's development of nuclear weapons, the Obama presidency delivered several important achievements in the nuclear realm.

Yet for advocates of nuclear abolition energized by Obama's transformational rhetoric at Prague, the administration did not go far enough to reduce the role of nuclear weapons in US national security and global politics.[3] This criticism is misplaced. The greatest impediment to further progress toward achieving the Prague Agenda was not Obama's "reluctance," but a fundamental shift in geopolitics that accelerated during his time in office.[4] At home, Republican intransigence also presented challenges, but the Obama administration pragmatically devised and implemented nonproliferation policies to the extent possible, given external and internal constraints.[5] The Obama administration's accomplishments in nonproliferation, nuclear security, and strategic arms control are laudable by any objective measure.[6]

---

[1] Barack Obama, *A Promised Land* (New York: Random House, 2020); Ben Rhodes, *The World As It Is: A Memoir of the Obama White House* (New York: Random House, 2018).
[2] "Remarks By President Barack Obama In Prague As Delivered, April 5," (Washington, DC: The White House, 2009), https://obamawhitehouse.archives.gov/the-press-office/remarks-president-barack-obama-prague-delivered.
[3] Steven Pifer, "Obama's Faltering Nuclear Legacy: the 3 R's," *The Washington Quarterly* 38, no. 2 (Summer 2015): 101–118.
[4] C. Raja Mohan, "Prague as the Nonproliferation Pivot," *The Washington Quarterly* 36, no. 2 (Summer 2013): 109–122.
[5] Andy Barr, "The GOP's no-compromise pledge," *Politico*, October 28, 2010, https://www.politico.com/story/2010/10/the-gops-no-compromise-pledge-044311.
[6] David Smith, "The anti-Obama: Trump's drive to destroy his predecessor's legacy," *The Guardian*, May 11, 2018.

David W. Kearn Jr., St. John's University

This chapter examines the Obama legacy on nuclear weapons.[7] The first section considers his views and experiences prior to entering the White House and explain the intellectual foundations of the "Prague Agenda." The second section will examine the administration's first major foreign policy initiative, seeking a strategic arms control agreement with Russia. The third section will examine the administration's focus on nonproliferation. The Iranian nuclear program was viewed as the primary nonproliferation challenge confronting the United States from the moment President Obama entered office and would influence virtually all aspects of US foreign policy. The fourth section revisits the Nuclear Security Summits, a novel initiative that focused on working with willing states to implement policies to eliminate or safeguard stocks of nuclear materials, thus decreasing the probability of nuclear terrorism. The fifth section examines the administration's nuclear strategy and force structure decisions, which supported both arms control and nonproliferation objectives as well as the maintenance of a strategic deterrent that was "safe, secure and effective." The chapter concludes with an assessment of President Obama's eight years in office and the impact of the Prague Agenda.

Arriving At Prague: Barack Obama's Views on Nuclear Weapons

On August 5, 2009, President Obama delivered a speech in the Czech Republic capital of Prague in which he articulated an ambitious vision for nuclear weapons in the world.

> So today, I state clearly, and with conviction America's commitment to see the peace and security of the world without nuclear weapons. I'm not naïve. This goal will not be reached quickly – perhaps not in my lifetime. It will take patience and persistence. But now we, too, must ignore the voices who tell us that the world cannot change. We have to insist, "Yes, we can."[8]

Obama's views on nuclear weapons were shaped by his experience growing up at the end of the Cold War and witnessing the peak of the nuclear arms race between the United States and the Soviet Union in the early 1980s as well as the im-

---

7 Beyond sources referenced, the discussion in this chapter is based on information from interviews with several officials that served in senior roles on nuclear issues in the Obama administration.
8 "Remarks By President Barack Obama In Prague As Delivered, April 5," (Washington, DC: The White House, 2009), https://obamawhitehouse.archives.gov/the-press-office/remarks-president-barack-obama-prague-delivered.

portant role played by arms control in ending the Superpower rivalry.[9] This interest spurred newly-elected Senator Obama to seek out Senator Richard Lugar, long-serving Republican from Indiana, who worked with former Georgia Democratic Senator Sam Nunn to create the Cooperative Threat Reduction Act, which provided financial and technical assistance to former Soviet states to remove or consolidate dangerous nuclear materials to prevent them from falling into the hands of non-state actors.[10] On one of his first congressional delegations abroad, Obama traveled with Lugar to see firsthand the extensive, beneficial progress made under the program.[11]

Beyond his general interest in nuclear issues, President-elect Obama viewed Iran's nuclear program as the central proliferation challenge of his time.[12] During the 2008 primaries, Obama responded to a journalist that he would be willing to speak with the representatives of the Iranian or North Korean regimes without preconditions. His rivals pounced on the statement for perceived "naïveté" and a signal of "weakness."[13] However, Obama strongly believed that well-formulated diplomacy could achieve important outcomes, without the exorbitant costs of military intervention employed by the outgoing Bush administration. It was critical to build a strong foundation of multilateral support for enhanced sanctions against the regime to compel Iran to the negotiating table.[14]

Upon securing the Democratic nomination, Obama assembled a talented team of advisers on nuclear issues that could broadly be divided into two camps. In the first were optimistic (typically younger) experts, focused on the opportunity to achieve significant reductions in the US nuclear arsenal with the ultimate, long-term goal of abolishing nuclear weapons. In the second, were more traditional national security experts who viewed arms control as useful and nonproliferation as important but focused on the continued need for a strong strategic deterrent in a changing world. These advisers embodied the contrasting views that President Obama sought to balance during his time in office.[15]

---

9 Obama, *A Promised Land*, 90.
10 Kennette Benedict, "Nunn-Lugar: 20 years of Cooperative threat Reduction," *Bulletin of the Atomic* Scientists, December 19, 2011.
11 Obama, *A Promised Land*, 91–92.
12 Obama, *A Promised Land*, 520.
13 Obama, *A Promised Land*, 148–149.
14 Obama, *A Promised Land*, 530–531, 691; Rhodes, *The World As It Is*, 41–42. Gary Samore, "Making a Difference: Creating and Implementing the Prague Agenda," *Carnegie Corporation of New York Magazine*, 9, no. 2 (Summer 2013): 22–31.
15 Obama, *A Promised Land*, 473–475.

The dueling impulses between the idealistic, long-term, transformative goal of a world without nuclear weapons and pragmatic assessments of what could be achieved in the short run can also be seen in the Prague speech. He committed the United States to seek a world without nuclear weapons but was clear in articulating the difficulty of achieving such a lofty goal.[16] The road would be long and would require addressing current proliferation challenges. He also explained the most pressing threat confronting the United States and the global community:

> In a strange turn of history, the threat of global nuclear war has gone down, but the risk of a nuclear attack has gone up. More nations have acquired these weapons. Testing has continued. Black market trade in nuclear secrets and nuclear materials abound. The technology to build a bomb has spread. Terrorists are determined to buy, build, or steal one. Our efforts to contain these dangers are centered on a global nonproliferation regime, but as more people and nations break the rules, we could reach the point where the center cannot hold.[17]

He proceeded to lay out an ambitious agenda, starting with measures to be taken by existing nuclear weapons states. "Concrete steps," including the negotiation of a new strategic arms control treaty with Russia, the ratification of the Comprehensive Test Ban Treaty (CTBT) by the United States, which had been observed (but not ratified) since the 1990s, and the negotiation and signing of a Fissile Material Cutoff Treaty (FMCT), which would limit the global stocks of materials necessary to produce nuclear weapons.[18]

A second major line of effort would consist of strengthening the nonproliferation regime through greater multilateral coordination and action. He highlighted North Korea's continued violations of UN sanctions, and underscored the threat of Iran's nuclear program, providing an outline of what would become the Iran nuclear deal.[19] Finally, to prevent nuclear terrorism, the United States would host a Nuclear Security Summit in Washington, DC, which would focus on removing or safeguarding materials that terrorists could use to create nuclear weapons.[20]

The Prague speech reflected Obama's idealism and sincere desire for transformative outcomes, but in practice his administration's policies would be tempered by a realistic understanding of what was possible. While a world without nuclear weapons was a long-term, transformational aspiration, the Obama ad-

---

16 Ben Rhodes, Obama's chief speech writer worried whether Obama was "setting the bar too high" in the speech. *The World As It Is*, 42.
17 "Remarks By President Barack Obama In Prague As Delivered, August 5."
18 "Remarks By President Barack Obama In Prague As Delivered, August 5."
19 "Remarks By President Barack Obama In Prague As Delivered, August 5."
20 "Remarks By President Barack Obama In Prague As Delivered, August 5."

ministration would embrace a pragmatic approach to nuclear issues, sensitive to geopolitical and domestic dynamics, to achieve tangible results.

Strategic Arms Control: A Promising (New) START

A formal strategic arms control treaty with the Russia was an early priority. The proposed agreement would replace the 1991 Strategic Arms Reduction Treaty (START I), concluded at the end of the Cold War with the Soviet Union by the George H.W. Bush administration, rather than the Strategic Offensive Reductions Treaty (SORT – also known as the "Moscow Treaty") signed by George W. Bush and Vladimir Putin in 2002.[21] The former was viewed as a model because it specifically laid out counting rules and procedures for verification and monitoring, including the sharing of critical technical information, something Moscow desired.[22]

For Obama's team, resetting relations with Moscow was an important diplomatic priority and "New START" was a useful vehicle. Relations with Russia had soured toward the end of the second Bush term, as Vladimir Putin criticized US hegemony and bemoaned the unipolar system that had emerged after the collapse of the Soviet Union.[23] Putin had stepped aside after his second term, and his hand-picked successor, Dmitry Medvedev, had authorized Russian military intervention in Georgia in 2008.[24] This did not augur well for US-Russia relations moving forward.

However, President Obama found a surprisingly constructive partner in Medvedev.[25] He proved willing to explore a broad reset of relations, and strategic arms control was viewed as an important first step. Obama persuaded Medvedev that a follow on to START I could be negotiated quickly if it focused exclusively on strategic offensive forces and avoided other contentious issues, such as NATO's deploy-

---

[21] On START I, see Daryl Kimball, "Fact Sheet: START I at a glance," Arms Control Association, accessed January 23, 2023, https://www.armscontrol.org/factsheets/start1; On the Moscow or SORT Treaty, see Daryl Kimball, "Fact Sheet: The Strategic Offensive Reduction Treaty (SORT) at a glance," Arms Control Association, accessed January 23, 2023, https://www.armscontrol.org/factsheets/sort-glance.
[22] Rose Gottemoeller, *Negotiating the New START Treaty* (Amherst: Cambria Press, 2021), 8–9.
[23] Thom Shanker, and Mark Landler, "Putin Say US Is Undermining Global Stability," *The New York Times*, February 11, 2007.
[24] Luke Harding, and Ian Traynor, "Russians march into Georgia as full-scale war looms," *The Guardian*, August 11, 2008.
[25] Obama, *A Promised Land*, 517–522; Gottemoeller, *Negotiating the New START Treaty*, 9–11.

ment of ballistic missile defenses (BMD), which could be addressed in subsequent discussions.[26]

Nevertheless, negotiations were not easy.[27] The process extended months past the initial target deadline of December 2009 (to avoid a lapse as START I expired) in large part due to Russian negotiating tactics and attempts to move the discussion into areas that had previously been agreed to be "off the table."[28] Negotiations nearly broke down in late December 2009 when then-Prime Minister Putin public weighed in on "unsatisfactory" details of the agreement.[29] Ultimately, the negotiations lasted for almost a year, with eight sessions moving between Geneva and Moscow, leading to a formal signing ceremony between Obama and Medvedev in Prague in April 2010.[30]

The final document set limits on deployed warheads at 1550 – a two thirds reduction in forces from the original START Treaty – with sub-limits on deployed launchers, or intercontinental ballistic missiles (ICBMs), submarine-launched ballistic missiles (SLBMs) and bombers (700) as well as deployed and nondeployed forces (800). The Treaty also established inspection, verification, and information-sharing protocols and would last for 10 years.[31]

Much of the remainder of 2010 involved Senate Hearings on ratification of the Treaty, a challenging process as mid-term Congressional elections approached in November. Criticism of the draft treaty focused mostly on tangential issues, but the administration's reaffirmation of its planned modernization of the US nuclear arsenal was enough to blunt Republican opposition.[32] The New START Treaty ultimately received significant bipartisan support in a vote of 71 to 26 with 13 Republicans joining all 56 Democrats and two Independents during the lame duck session in December 2010.[33] The Treaty was ratified in the Russian Duma in January and entered into force on February 5, 2011, when Secretary of State Hillary Clinton and

---

26 Obama, *A Promised Land*, 520–522; Gottemoeller, *Negotiating the New START Treaty*, 9–10.
27 Gottemoeller, *Negotiating the New START Treaty*, 47–56, 114–117, 174–176.
28 Gottemoeller, *Negotiating the New START Treaty*, 18, 23.
29 Gottemoeller, *Negotiating the New START Treaty*, 93–94; Peter Baker, and Dan Bilefsky, "Twists and Turns on Way to Arms Reduction Pact," *The New York Times*, April 8, 2010.
30 Mark Tran, "Barack Obama signs nuclear treaty with Russia," *The Guardian*, April 8, 2010.
31 See "New START Treaty," US Department of State, accessed January 23, 2023, https://www.state.gov/new-start/.
32 Obama, *A Promised Land*, 737–738; Robert M. Gates, *Duty: Memoirs of a Secretary at War* (New York: Knopf, 2014), 406–409; Gottemoeller, *Negotiating the New START Treaty*, 155–169.
33 Peter Baker, "Senate Passes Arms Control Treaty With Russia," *The New York Times*, December 22, 2010.

Foreign Minister Sergey Lavrov exchanged instruments of ratification at the Munich Security Conference.[34]

The successful negotiation and ratification of a strategic control arms treaty in less than two years was a major accomplishment by almost any objective metric. The Treaty also represented a high-water mark in US-Russia relations. It soon became apparent that Moscow had little interest in pursuing further reductions in strategic forces, and no appetite to address the issue of Russia's tactical nuclear forces.[35] An arrangement that adequately addressed Moscow's concerns over NATO BMD also proved impossible.[36]

Nonproliferation: The Long Road to an Iranian Nuclear Deal

Beyond the security benefits of a strategic arms control treaty with Russia, New START contributed to the forging of a coalition to increase economic pressure on Iran.[37] Obama engaged in personal outreach to stress to allies and important partners – including in Moscow and Beijing – the dangers of an Iranian nuclear weapon for the volatile Middle East region and beyond.[38] The administration sought to maximize leverage on Tehran to bring the regime to the negotiating table. Dismantling the Iranian nuclear program and closing off pathways to a future nuclear weapon in return for sanctions relief was the administration's primary long-term foreign policy objective.[39]

Obama's national security team devised a shrewd plan to illustrate Tehran's intransigence and build pressure on the regime. After the US rejoined the P5+1 process (the permanent five members of the United Nations Security Council, as well as Germany and the European Union), Tehran was offered a "nuclear fuel swap" in October 2009. In return for surrendering its stockpile of uranium, US partners Russia and France would transport and reprocess the material, respectively, and provide Iran with safe, low enriched uranium (LEU) for use in the Tehran Research

---

34 Mark Landler, and Steven Erlanger, "US and Russia Activate Arms Treaty," *New York Times*, February 5, 2011.
35 Interviews with former Obama administration national security officials, August 2022.
36 Interviews with former Obama administration national security officials, August 2022.
37 Obama, *A Promised Land*, 689–694.
38 Obama, *A Promised Land*, 691–692.
39 Obama, *A Promised Land*, 520.

Reactor (TRR) as part of Iran's civilian nuclear activities.[40] Effectively portraying the swap as a major benefit for the Iranians, the dubious nature of the regime's motives was made apparent when President Ahmadinejad walked away from the overture. US intelligence also discovered a secret nuclear related facility near the city of Qom.[41] The rejection of the TRR swap and the subsequent revelation of this second enrichment facility provided the administration with the opportunity to galvanize the international community behind enhanced multilateral economic sanctions (UNSC Resolution 1929, adopted in June 2010) that would cripple the Iranian economy.[42] Iran's domestic GDP contracted by approximately seven percent in 2012.[43] Still, little progress was likely with Ahmadinejad in power.

The June 2013 election of Hassan Rouhani, a moderate who campaigned on improving Iran's economy and working with the UN, offered a promising opportunity.[44] Soon after a telephone call between Obama and Rouhani (after a failed impromptu attempt to meet at the UN General Assembly in New York) the following September, secret negotiations were initiated by US and Iranian representatives in Oman, followed by senior State Department officials engaging with Iranian diplomats and other representatives of the P5+1 in Geneva.[45] This led to a breakthrough in November 2013.[46]

The first phase of the deal was scheduled to last six months, beginning in January 2014 but would ultimately take nearly 18, with the P5+1 and Iran finalizing a comprehensive agreement on July 14, 2015.[47] Iran agreed to pause ongoing development and reverse enrichment while also allowing International Atomic Energy Agency (IAEA) representatives to inspect sites and assess the state of Iran's capabilities in exchange for limited sanctions relief.[48] Upon certification of completion of this phase by the IAEA, the full agreement, the Joint Comprehensive

---

40 Obama, *A Promised Land*, 716–719; Gates, *Duty*, 390–391; Rhodes, *The World As It Is*, 174.
41 Obama, *A Promised Land*; Rhodes, *The World As It Is*, 174.
42 Obama, *A Promised Land*, 737–738.
43 "Six charts that show how hard US sanctions have hit Iran," *BBC* (online), December 9, 2019, https://www.bbc.com/news/world-middle-east-48119109.
44 Rhodes, *The World As It Is*, 247.
45 Rhodes, *The World As It Is*, 247–253; Wendy Sherman, "How We Got the Iran Deal, And Why We'll Miss It," *Foreign Affairs* (September/October 2018): 186–196, 190–191.
46 Rhodes, *The World As It Is*, 250–253; Sherman, "How We Got the Iran Deal," 193–195.
47 Kelsey Davenport, "The Joint Comprehensive Plan of Action (JCPOA) at a Glance," *Arms Control Association*, March 2020, https://www.armscontrol.org/factsheets/JCPOA-at-a-glance; Kelsey Davenport, "Timeline of Nuclear Diplomacy with Iran," *Arms Control Associations*, January 2023, https://www.armscontrol.org/factsheets/Timeline-of-Nuclear-Diplomacy-With-Iran.
48 Joby Warrick, and William Booth, "US, Iranian officials hold direct talks as diplomats press Tehran to accept 'freeze' on nuclear program," *The Washington Post*, November 8, 2013.

Plan of Action (JCPOA), would enter into effect: existing stockpiles of weapons grade material would be removed (25,000 pounds of enriched uranium, sufficient for eight to 10 weapons if fully processed), advanced centrifuges decommissioned, and plutonium processing capabilities permanently closed down.[49] As Obama noted at American University on August 5, nearly a month after the conclusion of the deal in Vienna, "[a]ll pathways to Tehran acquiring a nuclear weapon had effectively been blocked."[50] In return for compliance and intrusive IAEA inspections, Iran would be allowed to access funds frozen since the overthrow of the Shah and other sanctions relief.[51]

Despite the hard work and painstaking diplomacy that had produced an agreement, the JCPOA became the object of intense political debate in Washington, DC. Given the complex nature of the Iran Deal, the administration had concluded that a formal treaty (requiring Senate ratification) was neither feasible, nor desirable. The deterrent to Iranian noncompliance was the threat of automatic reimposition (or "snapping back") of multilateral sanctions on the regime. A formal treaty was not viewed as allowing the necessary executive freedom of action to respond quickly to reported noncompliance.[52]

Congressional Republicans, skeptical that the deal would resolve the nuclear issue and opposed to Iran receiving funds that could support its nefarious activities, vehemently opposed the deal and passed legislation – the Nuclear Deal Review Act – that would effectively allow them to veto the agreement with supermajorities in both houses.[53] Israeli Prime Minister Benjamin Netanyahu lobbied American officials, including leading Democrats, to reject it, culminating in a speech to Congress in March.[54] The Obama administration was forced to engage in a multi-front campaign to sell the virtues of the agreement to skeptical domestic political audiences,

---

[49] Juliet Elperin, "Obama announces outlines of a nuclear deal: 'If Iran cheats, the world will know,'" *The Washington Post*, April 2, 2015.
[50] "Remarks by the President on the Iran Nuclear Deal, American University, August 5," (Washington, DC: The White House, 2015), https://obamawhitehouse.archives.gov/the-press-office/2015/08/05/remarks-president-iran-nuclear-deal.
[51] "Parameters for a Joint Comprehensive Plan of Action Regarding the Islamic Republic of Iran," United States, State Department, April 2, 2015, https://2009-2017.state.gov/r/pa/prs/ps/2015/04/240170.htm.
[52] Rhodes, *The World As It Is*, 348.
[53] Paul Kane, and Mike DeBonis, "Senate approves bill on reviewing proposed nuclear deal with Iran," *The Washington Post*, May 7, 2015.
[54] David Ignatius, "Why Netanyahu broke publicly with Obama over Iran," *The Washington Post*, February 19, 2015.

as well as regional allies in the Gulf.[55] They narrowly succeeded, with the bill failing to achieve the necessary votes in the Senate in September 2015.[56]

The JCPOA was not perfect, but it erected formidable barriers to an Iranian nuclear weapon. Moreover, the prospect of intrusive inspections and the solidarity of the international community behind the plan, provided both a deterrent against cheating as well as an incentive for Tehran's compliance.[57] In short, the JCPOA represented a successful diplomatic resolution to the single most acute threat to Middle East peace and the security of US allies: an Iranian nuclear weapon.[58] At the same time, because it was not a formal treaty but an executive order that required subsequent presidential authorization, it was vulnerable to reversal by a Republican successor. This is precisely what happened when President Trump terminated US participation in the JCPOA on May 18, 2018.[59]

Nuclear Security Summits: A Cooperative Innovation

A third component of the "Prague Agenda," focused squarely on the threat of nuclear terrorism, was the Nuclear Security Summit. In his Prague speech, Obama called upon the international community to achieve the ambitious goal of "a new international effort to secure all vulnerable nuclear material around the world within four years."[60] Devised by several of the Obama campaign's expert advisors, the Nuclear Security Summit initiative focused on working with willing states to identify, remove, and/or secure potential sources of nuclear or radiological materials that could be surreptitiously acquired and used by terrorists or

---

55 Rhodes, *The World As It Is*, 326–353; Steven Mufson, and David Nakamura, "To press for Iran nuclear deal, Obama invokes Iraq war," *The Washington Post*, August 5, 2015.
56 Mike DeBonis, "Democrats have enough Senate votes to stifle Iran opposition," *The Washington Post*, September 8, 2015; Karoun Demirjian, "Obama secures votes to protect Iran nuclear deal," *The Washington Post*, September 2, 2015.
57 Carol Morello, "The mechanism behind the Iran nuclear deal goes into motion," *The Washington Post*, October 18, 2015.
58 David Ignatius, "How the Iran deal became the most strategic success of Obama's presidency," *The Washington Post*, September 15, 2015; Greg Jaffe, and Steven Mufson, "Obama: Iran nuclear deal, prisoner release show the power of diplomacy," *The Washington Post*, January 17, 2016.
59 "President Donald J. Trump Ending United States Participation in an Unacceptable Iran Deal," Office of the White House, May 18, 2018, https://trumpwhitehouse.archives.gov/briefings-statements/president-donald-j-trump-ending-united-states-participation-unacceptable-iran-deal/.
60 "Remarks By President Barack Obama In Prague As Delivered, August 5."

other non-state actors.[61] During Obama's time in office, four nuclear security summits were held. The first commenced in Washington in April of 2010, followed by Seoul, South Korea in March 2012, the Hague, Netherlands in March 2014, and returning to Washington in March to April, 2016.[62]

During these summits, high-level delegations supported by technical experts drafted and delivered consensus summit communiques that embraced various collective goals of nuclear security as well as work plans and distinct actions to be taken by states to further those shared goals.[63] Fifty-three states attended the Summits, with Russia quitting the process after its intervention in Ukraine in 2014.[64]

While issues of nuclear security may seem somewhat mundane to those outside the field, the Nuclear Security Summit process delivered numerous important, tangible results that decrease the likelihood of nuclear materials falling into the hands of terrorists. Perhaps the most impressive material accomplishment was the removal of HEU and plutonium from more than 50 facilities in 30 countries. This was estimated to be enough material to create at least 160 nuclear weapons.[65] Sixteen countries and Taiwan announced the elimination of nuclear materials from their respective territories since 2009.[66]

> Over the course of the summits, at least eight participating states followed through on commitments to eliminate stockpiles of weapons-usable materials. As a result, three entire geographic regions – South America, Southeast Asia, and Central and Eastern Europe – have entirely eliminated highly-enriched uranium from their soil, and only 22 countries possess weapons-usable nuclear material, down from more than 50.[67]

States participating in the Nuclear Security Summits also committed to and reported significant progress on enhancing security at nuclear sites, borders, and ports, building capacity to detect nuclear materials, and cooperating to prevent nuclear smuggling. The Summits provided a venue for states to develop further ave-

---

[61] Interviews with former Obama administration national security officials, August 2022.
[62] Sara Z. Kutchesfahani, Kelsey Davenport, and Erin Connoly, *An Overview of State Actions to Curb Nuclear Terrorism 2010–2016* (Washington, DC: Arms Control Association, 2018).
[63] Kelsey Davenport, "Nuclear Security Summits at a Glance," Arms Control Association, June 2018, https://www.armscontrol.org/factsheets/NuclearSecuritySummit.
[64] Karen DeYoung, "Russia to skip Nuclear Security Summit scheduled for 2016 in Washington," *The Washington Post*, November 5, 2014.
[65] *Fact Sheet: The Nuclear Security Summits*.
[66] *Fact Sheet: The Nuclear Security Summits*; Ernest Moniz, *US Department of Energy Cabinet Memo, January 5, 2017* (Washington, DC: US Department of Energy, 2017), 5.
[67] Sara Z. Kutchesfahani, and Kelsey Davenport, "Why countries still must prioritize action to curb nuclear terrorism," *Bulletin of the Atomic Scientists* (August 3, 2018), https://thebulletin.org/2018/08/why-countries-still-must-prioritize-action-to-curb-nuclear-terrorism/.

nues for cooperation, supported by technical experts and international representatives to develop and share best practices and states have gone on to establish nuclear security training centers and centers of excellence since their conclusion in 2016.[68]

By engaging national leaders, the Nuclear Security Summits raised the profile of the issue of nuclear security globally, reinforced norms and accepted standards for nuclear security at the national level, and made numerous, significant material improvements in nuclear security around the globe.

Nuclear Strategy and Force Structure: An Open but Pragmatic Approach

Given the president's optimistic message at Prague, his commitment to undertake a trillion dollar modernization of the US strategic arsenal and supporting infrastructure may seem puzzling.[69] Prior to entering the White House, then-candidate Obama announced that he would follow through on the recommendations of the Strategic Posture Commission, mandated by Congress and chaired by former Defense Secretaries Richard Perry and James Schlesinger.[70] A central recommendation of the commission's 2009 final report was to maintain the strategic triad rather than move toward alternative force structures in a future modernization program.[71] Thus, the broad outline of rebuilding the existing force, within the limitations of a new strategic arms control treaty with Russia, emerged as the objective. The United States would modernize its nuclear arsenal, including rebuilding all three legs of the "strategic triad" – land-based ICBMs, long-range strategic bombers, and SLBMs and the ballistic missile submarines (SSBNs) that carry them – as well as command and control systems, and the nuclear weapons laboratory infrastructure managed by the Department of Energy, which was in serious need of refurbishment when Obama entered office.[72]

---

68 *Fact Sheet: The Nuclear Security Summits*.
69 *Fact Sheet: An Enduring Commitment to the US Nuclear Deterrent* (Washington, DC: The White House 2010).
70 Interviews with former Obama administration national security officials, August 2022.
71 William J. Perry, James R. Schlesinger, et al., *America's Strategic Posture: The Final Report of the Congressional Commission on the Strategic Posture of the United States* (Washington, DC: United States Institute of Peace, 2009).
72 Moniz, *US Department of Energy Cabinet Exit Memo*, 3, 6; Amy L. Woolf, *US Strategic Forces: Background and Issues for Congress* (Washington, DC: Congressional Research Service, 2017).

While negotiations were underway over a New Start Treaty, the Pentagon engaged in an extensive interagency process that would result in a Nuclear Posture Review (NPR).[73] In discussions leading to the 2010 NPR, the sizing of forces and numbers of warheads to achieve US security objectives was scrutinized and the 1,550 level that would emerge from New START was deemed sufficient. Subsequent Defense Department analysis supporting the 2013 Nuclear Weapons Employment Plan concluded that the US arsenal could be safely reduced by an additional third beyond New START levels.[74] However, as noted above, Moscow was unwilling to consider further reductions in the absence of an agreement on missile defenses – if at all.[75]

Beyond issues of force structure, the 2010 Nuclear Posture Review articulated many of the important ideas and concepts that had motivated the Obama administration approach to nuclear weapons and nonproliferation. It identified nuclear terrorism as the central threat facing the United States and expressed support for nonproliferation and reducing the role of nuclear weapons in US strategy.[76] However, existing global conditions required that the US maintain a "safe secure and effective nuclear arsenal."[77] Perhaps most importantly, the NPR delineated highly restrictive conditions for nuclear use: "The fundamental role of US nuclear weapons, which will continue as long as nuclear weapons exist, is to deter nuclear attack on the United States, our allies, and partners."[78] As analysts have pointed out, a "fundamental role" does not exclude "extreme circumstances" and is as not stringent as "sole purpose" in delineating conditions of potential use. It also did not endorse a "No First Use" policy as some had hoped.[79] Still, to support the NPT, the Review articulated a series of "negative security assurances," that pledged that non-nuclear weapons states under the NPT would not be targeted with nuclear weapons by the United States.[80]

Despite his clear preference for further progress on disarmament, Obama was also well aware of the growing challenges to US interests with the increasing growth and assertiveness of China and Russia's rejection of the Western order. A

---

73 *Nuclear Posture Review Report* (Washington, DC: US Department of Defense, 2010).
74 *Report on the Nuclear Employment of Strategy of the United States* (Washington, DC: US Department of Defense, 2013).
75 Gates, *Duty*, pp. 398–404, 406–9.
76 *Nuclear Posture Review Report*, 3–4.
77 *Nuclear Posture Review Report*, 5–8.
78 *Nuclear Posture Review Report*, 15.
79 Scott Sagan, and Jane Vaynam, "Introduction: Reviewing the Nuclear Posture Review," *The Nonproliferation Review* 18, no. 1 (March 2011): 17–37.
80 *Nuclear Posture Review Report*, 15. The NPR also reaffirmed the administration's support for the ratifications of the CTBT and further negotiations toward an FMCT.

"safe, secure, and effective" strategic nuclear arsenal was a foundational component of US (and allied) security and a vitally important hedge against a deteriorating geopolitical environment.

Conclusion: Assessing the Obama Legacy

Obama's time in office can be viewed favorably in several ways. First, in considering then-candidate Obama's own objectives and expectations prior to entering office, his tenure was a clear success. The signing of the New START Treaty, the diplomatic breakthrough on the Iranian nuclear program, and the Nuclear Security Summit process were significant achievements. Certainly, the Iran deal stands out as the signature foreign policy accomplishment of his administration and considering the arduous path to an agreement, and the thousands of hours of hard work put in by members of his national security team, it should be viewed as evidence of the president's boldness, commitment, and patience in working to achieve a primary objective.

At the same time, as effective as any US president may be, his or her accomplishments will ultimately be influenced by forces outside their control. In the case of the Iran deal, Obama's successor made overturning the JCPOA one of his central campaign promises.[81] The fact that the US withdrawal from the JCPOA left a vacuum that even the Biden administration has been unable to resolve only underscores the difficulty of achieving the initial agreement with Iran.[82] As a result, Iran today is closer to manufacturing a nuclear weapon.[83]

This leads to a larger point regarding nonproliferation as a US national security objective.[84] Since President John F. Kennedy first brought attention to the dangers of the spread of nuclear weapons in the 1960s, through the construction and expansion of the Nonproliferation Treaty regime, successive US administrations have grappled with the challenge of proliferation. All the while, the US "nuclear umbrella," which has served as the foundation of America's extended deterrent commitments to allies, has also played a critical role in preventing nuclear proliferation

---

81 Anne Gearan, "Trump pulls United States out of Iran nuclear deal, calling the pact an 'embarrassment,'" *The Washington Post*, May 8, 2018.
82 Anne Gearan, "Biden team exploring how US might rejoin Iran nuclear deal," *The Washington Post*, February 5, 2021.
83 Joby Warrick, "Iran begins enriching uranium to 20 percent in new breach of nuclear deal," *The Washington Post*, January 4, 2021.
84 Francis J. Gavin, "Strategies of Inhibition: US Grand Strategy, the Nuclear Revolution and Nonproliferation," *International Security* 40, no. 1 (Summer 2015): 9–46.

as allies could confidently forego independent weapons programs in return for US security guarantees. However, as the Obama administration learned, this is a delicate balance to maintain, and the perceptions of allies can shift in response to perceived threats. One of the unfortunate geopolitical realities of Obama's time in office was the increased willingness of Russia and China to challenge US and allied interests.[85] Under these circumstances, nonproliferation concerns must be weighed against deterring adversaries and reassuring allies. This was evident in the waning days of the administration when internal consideration of a formal US declaration of "no first use" of nuclear weapons met stiff resistance from allied capitals and defense officials. The proposal was shelved.[86] In an increasingly competitive world, the needs of deterrence and reassurance will often take priority over nonproliferation concerns.

More broadly, the inability to make progress toward a FMCT and the decision not to submit the CTBT for US Senate ratification were not reflective of a lack of will or desire, but shaped by a clear appreciation of what was feasible, whether in the diplomatic or domestic policy realms.[87] Likewise, the absence of progress on North Korea's nuclear weapons program was less about administration preferences than the realities of the Kim regime's commitment to build a nuclear weapons program, despite mounting pressures on its long-isolated economy.

Obama's pragmatism and willingness to adjust to realities may have contributed to the "frustration" that emerged among global civil society actors in the aftermath of a perceived breakdown of the 2015 NPT Review Conference.[88] This spurred a campaign that culminated in the adoption of the Treaty for the Prohibi-

---

85 Mohan, "Prague as the Proliferation Pivot"; Michael J. Mazarr, "The Once and Future Order: What Comes after Hegemony," *Foreign Affairs* 96, no. 1 (January/February 2017): 25–32.
86 Josh Rogin, "Obama plans major nuclear policy changes in his final months," *The Washington Post*, July 10, 2016; Josh Rogin, "US allies unite to block to Obama's nuclear 'legacy,'" *The Washington Post*, August 14, 2016.
87 The administration's focus on successful negotiation and ratification of "New START" made CTBT ratification a lesser priority. With the results of the 2010 midterm elections, ratification was never viewed as viable. The administration continued to support the ratification of the CTBT and negotiations toward an FMCT in formal documents like the *Nuclear Posture Review*. See Steven Pifer, "What's the deal with Senate Republicans and he test ban treaty?," *Brookings Commentary*, September 26, 2016, https://www.brookings.edu/articles/whats-the-deal-with-senate-republicans-and-the-test-ban-treaty/.
88 Wilfred Wan, "Why the 2015 NPT Review Conference Fell Apart," United Nations Center for Policy Research, May 28, 2015, https://cpr.unu.edu/publications/articles/why-the-2015-npt-review-conference-fell-apart.html.

tion of Nuclear Weapons (TPNW) in the United Nations in July 2017. The "Ban Treaty" has been characterized as a reflection of disappointment over the slow pace of nuclear disarmament and the Obama administration's "failures."[89]

This criticism seems particularly off base, as it ignores geopolitical trends and the national security challenges confronted by the administration. Similarly, the claim of "reluctance" on the part of the Obama administration is also misleading.[90] Obama was indeed committed to using his time in office to work toward a world without nuclear weapons. But as he noted in the Prague speech, it was unlikely that this goal could be achieved during his lifetime. This was not equivocation. Rather, it was a prudent recognition of the inescapable realities of international politics: The most powerful country in the world is constrained in its ability to achieve its goals because of actions of other sovereign states.

In the aftermath of the George W. Bush presidency, President Obama's message resonated across much of world and set high expectations that would be difficult for anyone to fulfill under the best of circumstances. However, the international system was undergoing a significant change as China's relative power expanded and Russia embraced more belligerent foreign policies. These trends created a more challenging diplomatic environment, something the president and his national security team understood and worked to address. Thus, in revisiting his time in office, President Obama comes across as a bold "progressive pragmatist," committed to doing as much as he could to achieve the ambitious nonproliferation policy goals that he set out early in his presidency, but also cognizant of shifting geopolitical realities and the increasing salience of national security interests.[91]

References

Baker, Peter. "Senate Passes Arms Control Treaty With Russia." *The New York Times*, December 22, 2010.
Baker, Peter, and Dan Bilefsky. "Twists and Turns on Way to Arms Reduction Pact." *The New York Times*, April 8, 2010.
Barr, Andy. "The GOP's no-compromise pledge." *Politico*. October 28, 2010, https://www.politico.com/story/2010/10/the-gops-no-compromise-pledge-044311.

---

89 Rick Gladstone, "A Treaty Is Reached to Ban Nuclear Arms. Now Comes the Hard Part," *The New York Times*, July 7, 2017.
90 Steven Pifer, "Obama's Faltering Nuclear Legacy."
91 Martin S. Indyk, Kenneth G. Lieberthal, and Michael E. O'Hanlon, "Scoring Obama's Foreign Policy: A Progressive Pragmatist Tries to Bend History," *Foreign Affairs* 91, no. 3 (May/June 2012): 29–43.

BBC (online). "Six charts that show how hard US sanctions have hit Iran," December 9, 2019, https://www.bbc.com/news/world-middle-east-48119109.

Benedict, Kennette. "Nunn-Lugar: 20 years of Cooperative threat Reduction." *Bulletin of the Atomic Scientists*. December 19, 2011. https://thebulletin.org/2011/12/nunn-lugar-20-years-of-cooperative-threat-reduction/.

Davenport, Kelsey. "Nuclear Security Summits at a Glance." Arms Control Association, June 2018, https://www.armscontrol.org/factsheets/NuclearSecuritySummit.

Davenport, Kelsey. "The Joint Comprehensive Plan of Action (JCPOA) at a Glance." *Arms Control Association*. March 2020, https://www.armscontrol.org/factsheets/JCPOA-at-a-glance.

Davenport, Kelsey. "Timeline of Nuclear Diplomacy with Iran." *Arms Control Associations*, January 2023, https://www.armscontrol.org/factsheets/Timeline-of-Nuclear-Diplomacy-With-Iran.

DeBonis, Mike. "Democrats have enough Senate votes to stifle Iran opposition." *The Washington Post*, September 8, 2015.

Demirjian, Karoun. "Obama secures votes to protect Iran nuclear deal." *The Washington Post*, September 2, 2015.

DeYoung, Karen. "Russia to skip Nuclear Security Summit scheduled for 2016 in Washington." *The Washington Post*, November 5, 2014.

Elperin, Juliet. "Obama announces outlines of a nuclear deal: 'If Iran cheats, the world will know.'" *The Washington Post*, April 2, 2015.

Fact Sheet: An Enduring Commitment to the US Nuclear Deterrent. Washington, DC: The White House 2010. https://obamawhitehouse.archives.gov/the-press-office/2010/11/17/fact-sheet-enduring-commitment-us-nuclear-deterrent.

Fact Sheet: Nuclear Security Summits: Securing the World from Nuclear Terrorism. Washington, DC: The White House 2016. https://obamawhitehouse.archives.gov/the-press-office/2016/03/29/fact-sheet-nuclear-security-summits-securing-world-nuclear-terrorism.

Gates, Robert M. *Duty: Memoirs of a Secretary at War*. New York: Knopf, 2014.

Gavin, Francis J. "Strategies of Inhibition: US Grand Strategy, the Nuclear Revolution and Nonproliferation." *International Security* 40, no. 1 (Summer 2015): 9–46.

Gearan, Anne. "Biden team exploring how US might rejoin Iran nuclear deal." *The Washington Post*, February 5, 2021.

Gearan, Anne. "Trump pulls United States out of Iran nuclear deal, calling the pact an 'embarrassment.'" *The Washington Post*, May 8, 2018.

Gladstone, Rick. "A Treaty Is Reached to Ban Nuclear Arms. Now Comes the Hard Part." *The New York Times*, July 7, 2017.

Gottemoeller, Rose. *Negotiating the New START Treaty*. Amherst: Cambria Press, 2021.

Harding, Luke, and Ian Traynor. "Russians march into Georgia as full-scale war looms." *The Guardian*, August 11, 2008.

Ignatius, David. "How the Iran deal became the most strategic success of Obama's presidency." *The Washington Post*, September 15, 2015.

Ignatius, David. "Why Netanyahu broke publicly with Obama over Iran." *The Washington Post*, February 19, 2015.

Indyk, Martin S., Kenneth G. Lieberthal, and Michael E. O'Hanlon. "Scoring Obama's Foreign Policy: A Progressive Pragmatist Tries to Bend History." *Foreign Affairs* 91, no. 3 (May/June 2012): 29–43.

Jaffe, Greg, and Steven Mufson. "Obama: Iran nuclear deal, prisoner release show the power of diplomacy." *The Washington Post*, January 17, 2016.

Kane, Paul, and Mike DeBonis. "Senate approves bill on reviewing proposed nuclear deal with Iran." *The Washington Post*, May 7, 2015.

Kimball, Daryl. "Fact Sheet: START I at a glance." Arms Control Association. Accessed January 23, 2023, https://www.armscontrol.org/factsheets/start1.

Kimball, Daryl. "Fact Sheet: The Strategic Offensive Reduction Treaty (SORT) at a glance." Arms Control Association. Accessed January 23, 2023, https://www.armscontrol.org/factsheets/sort-glance.

Kutchesfahani, Sara Z., and Kelsey Davenport. "Why countries still must prioritize action to curb nuclear terrorism." *Bulletin of the Atomic Scientists* (August 3, 2018), https://thebulletin.org/2018/08/why-countries-still-must-prioritize-action-to-curb-nuclear-terrorism/.

Kutchesfahani, Sara Z., Kelsey Davenport, and Erin Connoly. *An Overview of State Actions to Curb Nuclear Terrorism 2010–2016*. Washington, DC: Arms Control Association, 2018.

Landler, Mark, and Steven Erlanger. "US and Russia Activate Arms Treaty." *New York Times*, February 5, 2011.

Mazarr, Michael J. "The Once and Future Order: What Comes after Hegemony." *Foreign Affairs* 96, no. 1 (January/February 2017): 25–32.

Mohan, C. Raja. "Prague as the Nonproliferation Pivot." *The Washington Quarterly* 36, no. 2 (Summer 2013): 109–122.

Moniz, Ernest. *US Department of Energy Cabinet Memo, January 5, 2017*. Washington, DC: US Department of Energy, 2017.

Morello, Carol. "The mechanism behind the Iran nuclear deal goes into motion." *The Washington Post*, October 18, 2015.

Mufson, Steven, and David Nakamura. "To press for Iran nuclear deal, Obama invokes Iraq war." *The Washington Post*, August 5, 2015.

"New START Treaty," US Department of State, accessed January 23, 2023, https://www.state.gov/new-start/.

Nuclear Posture Review Report. Washington, DC: US Department of Defense, 2010.

Obama, Barack. *A Promised Land*. New York: Random House, 2020.

Obama, Barack. "Remarks By President Barack Obama In Prague As Delivered, April 5." Washington, DC: The White House, 2009, https://obamawhitehouse.archives.gov/the-press-office/remarks-president-barack-obama-prague-delivered.

Obama, Barack. "Remarks by the President on the Iran Nuclear Deal, American University, August 5," Washington, DC: The White House, 2015, https://obamawhitehouse.archives.gov/the-press-office/2015/08/05/remarks-president-iran-nuclear-deal.

Office of the White House. "President Donald J. Trump Ending United States Participation in an Unacceptable Iran Deal." May 18, 2018, https://trumpwhitehouse.archives.gov/briefings-statements/president-donald-j-trump-ending-united-states-participation-unacceptable-iran-deal/.

Perry, William J., James R. Schlesinger, et al., *America's Strategic Posture: The Final Report of the Congressional Commission on the Strategic Posture of the United States*. Washington, DC: United States Institute of Peace, 2009.

Pifer, Steven. "Obama's Faltering Nuclear Legacy: the 3 R's." *The Washington Quarterly* 38, no. 2 (Summer 2015): 101–118.

Pifer, Steven. "What's the deal with Senate Republicans and he test ban treaty?" *Brookings Commentary*. September 26, 2016, https://www.brookings.edu/articles/whats-the-deal-with-senate-republicans-and-the-test-ban-treaty/.

Report on the Nuclear Employment of Strategy of the United States. Washington, DC: US Department of Defense, 2013.

Rhodes, Ben. *The World As It Is: A Memoir of the Obama White House*. New York: Random House, 2018.

Rogin, Josh. "Obama plans major nuclear policy changes in his final months." *The Washington Post*, July 10, 2016

Rogin, Josh. "US allies unite to block to Obama's nuclear 'legacy.'" *The Washington Post*, August 14, 2016.

Sagan, Scott, and Jane Vaynam. "Introduction: Reviewing the Nuclear Posture Review." *The Nonproliferation Review* 18, no. 1 (March 2011): 17–37.

Samore, Gary. "Making a Difference: Creating and Implementing the Prague Agenda." *Carnegie Corporation of New York Magazine*" 9, no. 2 (Summer 2013): 22–31.

Shanker, Thom, and Mark Landler. "Putin Say US Is Undermining Global Stability." *The New York Times*, February 11, 2007.

Sherman, Wendy. "How We Got the Iran Deal, And Why We'll Miss It." *Foreign Affairs* (September/October 2018): 186–196.

Smith, David. "The anti-Obama: Trump's drive to destroy his predecessor's legacy." *The Guardian*, May 11, 2018.

Tran, Mark. "Barack Obama signs nuclear treaty with Russia." *The Guardian*, April 8, 2010.

United States, State Department. "Parameters for a Joint Comprehensive Plan of Action Regarding the Islamic Republic of Iran." April 2, 2015, https://2009-2017.state.gov/r/pa/prs/ps/2015/04/240170.htm.

Wan, Wilfred. "Why the 2015 NPT Review Conference Fell Apart." United Nations Center for Policy Research. May 28, 2015, https://cpr.unu.edu/publications/articles/why-the-2015-npt-review-conference-fell-apart.html.

Warrick, Joby. "Iran begins enriching uranium to 20 percent in new breach of nuclear deal." *The Washington Post*, January 4, 2021.

Warrick, Joby, and William Booth. "US, Iranian officials hold direct talks as diplomats press Tehran to accept 'freeze' on nuclear program." *The Washington Post*, November 8, 2013.

Woolf, Amy L. *US Strategic Forces: Background and Issues for Congress*. Washington, DC: Congressional Research Service, 2017.

Daniel E. Ponder and Jeffrey VanDenBerg
Chapter 11
Why Ask? Presidential Leverage and Obama's Decision to Seek Congressional Authorization for the Use of Force against Syria

On August 21, 2013, the Syrian regime of Bashar al-Assad launched chemical weapons against opposition-controlled areas in the residential suburbs of Damascus. Approximately 1,400 people, including over 400 children, were killed.[1] For over a year prior to this attack, concern about the considerable stockpile of chemical and biological weapons in Syria and Assad's willingness to use them to protect his hold on power had preoccupied the Obama administration.[2] Most notably, when asked about his position at a press conference in August 2012, President Obama replied: "We have been very clear to the Assad regime but also to other players on the ground that a red line for us is, we start seeing a whole bunch of weapons moving around or being utilized. That would change my calculus. That would change my equation."[3]

The horrific sarin gas attack on population centers around Damascus one year later put Obama's red line threat to the test. All signs out of the White House pointed to an imminent military response.[4] It therefore came as a surprise when, at the Rose Garden policy announcement on August 31, the president not only declared his intention to take military action but also that he would seek congressional authorization for the use of force.

---

[1] Joby Warrick, "More than 1,400 killed in Syrian Chemical Weapons Attack, US says," *Washington Post*, August 30, 2013.

[2] The August 2013 attack was not the first use of chemical agents by Assad against his own citizens in the context of the protests-turned-civil war that emerged from the 2011 Arab uprisings. American intelligence and independent researchers documented multiple previous small-scale attacks beginning in the late fall of 2012. Arms Control Association, "Timeline of Syrian Chemical Weapons Activity, 2102–2022," May 2022.

[3] Mark Landler, "Obama Threatens Force Against Syria," *New York Times*, August 20, 2012.

[4] Thom Shanker, C.J. Chivers, and Michael R. Gordon, "Obama Weighs 'Limited' Strikes Against Syrian Forces," *New York Times*, August 27, 2013. Derek Chollet, Obama's Assistant Secretary of Defense for International Security Forces, reports that following Syria's attack, "the Pentagon made plans for round-the-clock staffing, since we thought the military operation would start over the holiday." Chollet, "Obama's Red Line, Revisited," *Politico*, July 19, 2016.

Daniel E. Ponder, Jeffrey VanDenBerg, Drury University

What explains this unusual decision? Presidents rarely seek approval from Congress prior to the use of military force, particularly in instances of limited strikes such as those that Obama committed to in the case of Syria.[5] Obama argued that he wasn't constitutionally obligated to seek authorization, and that he retained the authority to order strikes even if Congress denied his request.[6] In 2011, Obama did not seek congressional authorization for the American military intervention in Libya.[7] More recently, President Trump ordered strikes against Syria in 2017 and 2018 in response to chemical weapons attacks without seeking congressional approval.

Obama's decision is additionally puzzling because it entailed significant political and strategic security risks. Domestically, it raised the possibility that "he would be the first president in modern times to lose a vote on the use of force."[8] Within the administration and among some members of Congress and international allies, there was concern about the consequences for American credibility should the US not follow through on its pledge to hold Assad accountable. Given the unlikelihood of using force following explicit congressional rejection, and the fact that the White House counsel concluded a strike would be lawful without authorization, why ask?

This chapter employs multiple methods to investigate this puzzle. Our approach, grounded in the broader literature on the domestic politics of US foreign policy, makes use of administration accounts, public opinion data, and personal interviews with members of Congress to test competing explanations.[9] We find that while some of these analyses offer a partial explanation, incorporating the concept of "presidential leverage" provides a fuller picture of the decision, and adds an important conceptual tool to the literature on the domestic politics of US foreign policy.[10]

---

[5] The president pledged "this would not be an open-ended intervention. We would not put boots on the ground. Instead, our action would be designed to be limited in duration and scope." Peter Baker and Jonathan Weisman, "Obama Seeks Approval by Congress for Syria Strikes," *New York Times*, August 31, 2013.

[6] Charlie Savage, "Obama Tests Limits of Power in Syrian Conflict," *New York Times*, September 8, 2013.

[7] Scott Wilson, "Obama Administration: Libya Action Does Not Require Congressional Approval," *New York Times*, June 15, 2011.

[8] Baker, and Weisman, "Obama Seeks Approval."

[9] For an overview of this literature, see Helen Milner and Dustin Tingley, *Sailing the Water's Edge: The Domestic Politics of American Foreign Policy* (Princeton: Princeton University Press, 2016). Research for our chapter included personal interviews with three members of Congress (two Republicans and one Democrat) who were involved in the Syria deliberations. They requested anonymity for this project.

[10] Daniel E. Ponder, *Presidential Leverage: Presidents, Approval, and the American State* (Stanford: Stanford University Press, 2018).

Presidential leverage also helps illuminate the relationship between foreign policy goals and structural and political realities during the Obama administration. During his first presidential campaign, Obama presented a vision of American foreign policy that combined transformational objectives and a predisposition toward restraint in the projection of power.[11] This "progressive pragmatism" contained inherent contradictions and trade-offs.[12] In the case of responding to Syria's chemical weapons attacks, the president's promotion of human rights and a rules-based international order ran into an institutional/political context that significantly narrowed his options.

The chapter begins by analyzing competing explanations for the decision by administration officials, members of Congress, journalists, and scholars. We then explore presidential leverage as a means to locate the president in the context of American politics and institutions writ large. We examine the "index of presidential leverage" (IPL), using it to compare Obama's decision on Syria with his Libya policy and weighing it against alternative causal factors such as the influence of public opinion. We conclude that Obama's decision was a product of constraints on presidential decision making and that these constraints are most fully captured by including IPL in the analysis.

Competing Explanations: Constitutional Principle?

At the Rose Garden announcement on Syria on August 31, Obama signaled that his decision to seek authorization was rooted in his commitment to the shared constitutional authority of Congress and the president in the use of military force.[13] The president repeated this point in the subsequent days as his administration lobbied Congress and in a September 4 press conference in Sweden. In a later essay on the Syria decision, former Deputy National Security Advisor Ben Rhodes wrote that during the deliberations Obama recalled his response to a candidate questionnaire from 2007 in which he said that "the president does not have the power under the

---

[11] Woodrow Wilson International Center for Scholars, "Security Address on Counter-Terrorism by the Honorable Barack Obama, United States Senator from Illinois," August 1, 2007. See also, Karen DeYoung, "Fulfilled-and broken-promises for America's new role in the world," *Washington Post*, November 18, 20016, and Ivo H. Daalder, "Obama's foreign policy: Not every global problem has an American solution," *Washington Post*, November 18, 2016.

[12] Martin S. Indyk, Kenneth G. Lieberthal, and Michael E. O'Hanlon, "Obama's Foreign Policy: Progressive Pragmatist," *Brookings*, March 9, 2012.

[13] White House, Office of the Press Secretary, *Statement by the President on Syria*, August 13, 2013, https://obamawhitehouse.archives.gov/the-press-office/2013/08/31/statement-president-syria.

Constitution to unilaterally authorize a military attach in a situation that does not involve stopping an actual or imminent threat to the nation."[14]

The main problem with adherence to constitutional principle as an explanatory variable is that Obama did not seek congressional authorization for military action in Libya in 2011. The administration argued that American intervention in Libya, taken in response to dictator Muammar Qaddafi's murderous rampage against pro-democracy protestors, did not require congressional approval.[15] Further diluting the constitutional principle claims for seeking authorization against Syria were the concomitant arguments by Obama that he had the authority to act alone, and that he retained the right to do so even if Congress voted against it.

Competing Explanations: A Way Out of the "Red Line" Box?

Another possible explanation is that the president ultimately decided against the wisdom of using force, and that going to Congress was designed to delay or avoid this course of action. Later interviews and memoirs paint a picture of a president concerned about the negative consequences of military options and increasingly reticent as the days passed following the August 21 chemical attacks.[16] In this telling, Obama felt trapped by his red-line commitments and pressured to engage in another unwanted American action in the Middle East. With Congress away for the Labor Day holiday, seeking authorization would provide time for alternative options to emerge and perhaps even a credibility-saving way out of military action should Congress reject his request.[17]

This analysis is difficult to square with the administration's extraordinary efforts to convince Congress to authorize force in the days following the Rose Garden announcement. The president personally lobbied congressional leaders at a White House meeting and deployed top officials to make the case for military ac-

---

14 Ben Rhodes, "Inside the White House during the Syrian 'Red Line' Crisis," *The Atlantic*, June 3, 2018.
15 Wilson, "Obama Administration: Libyan Action Does Not Require."
16 Rhodes, "Inside the White House," and Jeffrey Goldberg, "The Obama Doctrine: The US President Talks Through his Hardest Decisions About America's Role in the World," *The Atlantic*, April 15, 2016.
17 Burns and Stravers make this argument—that Obama didn't want to use military force and sought an AUMF as a way to shift the blame to Congress and avoid the "audience costs" of inaction on his red line threat. Sarah Burns and Andrew Stravers, "Obama, Congress, and Audience Costs: Shifting the Blame on the Red Line," *Political Science Quarterly* 135, no. 1 (2020): 67–101.

tion.[18] Republican senators John McCain and Lindsay Graham helped argue for authorization, as the administration employed a "flood the zone" strategy of briefings, calls, and meetings to win support in Congress.[19] In the words of one Republican House member who was invited to a briefing on Syria with Vice-President Biden in the Situation Room, "their attempts to persuade Congress weren't just for optics. They did some heavy lifting to get Congress on board. I don't think it was a charade."[20] Furthermore, if seeking congressional authorization truly was designed as a way out of using force, the lobbying efforts ran the risk of being effective – that is, working too well. In this line of reasoning, the expressions of support for military action by Speaker John Boehner and House Majority Leader Eric Cantor following the White House meeting with Obama on September 3 would have been unwelcome.[21]

Competing Explanations: Ask Congress for Political Gain?

Another possible explanation is that Obama was confident in his ability to persuade Congress, and that bringing the legislative branch on board would garner public support, demonstrate American unity in the face of this atrocity, and mute criticism from Congress if the strikes were ineffective in deterring Assad from further chemical attacks.[22] The argument suggests that Obama was operating from a position of

---

[18] In the leadup to Obama's departure for G-20 meetings on September 4, "the White House intensified what has become the most extraordinary lobbying campaign of Mr. Obama's presidency as it deployed members of his war council and enlisted political alumni of his 2008 campaign to press the argument with the public." Mark Landler, Michael R. Gordon, and Thom Shanker, "House Leaders Express Their Support for Syria Strike," *New York Times*, September 3, 2013.
[19] Jeff Mason, and Richard Cowan, "Analysis: Obama Lobbies Personally for Syria Vote," *Reuters*, September 2, 2013.
[20] Interview with authors, January 13, 2023.
[21] Aaron Blake, and David Nakamura, "Boehner and Cantor Will Support Syria Strike," *Washington Post*, September 3, 2013.
[22] Kriner makes a version of this argument. He provides persuasive experimental evidence that seeking authorization can bolster support for a president and is effective at muting later congressional criticism of the policy. Douglas Kriner, "Obama's Authorization Paradox: Syria and Congress's Continued Relevance in Military Affairs," *Presidential Studies Quarterly* 44, no. 2 (June 2014): 309–327. See also Jonah Schulhofer-Wohl, "The Obama Administration and Civil War in Syria, 2011–2016," *Journal of Transatlantic Studies* 19, no. 4 (December 2021): 517–547. However, whether Obama based his decision to go to Congress on the anticipation of these benefits is a different matter.

strength, and that Congress and the American public would rally around the president on military and security policy. Certainly, this was the public message of the administration, including at the Rose Garden announcement when Obama said that "while I believe I have the authority to carry out this military action without specific congressional authorization, I know that the country will be stronger if we take this course, and our actions will be even more effective."[23] Obama returned many times to this argument, including at a September 4 press conference in Sweden where he stated that "I did not take this to Congress just because it's an empty exercise; I think it's important to have Congress's support on it."[24]

However, the potential political and international gains would only accrue if Congress agreed, and few signs pointed to likely success on Capitol Hill. As discussed below, public opinion was strongly against the use of military force in Syria and the prospects for bringing the Republican-controlled House of Representatives along were slim. As one House member on the Foreign Affairs Committee reported, "I was deeply engaged in this discussion, listening to briefings from the Administration and researching the Assad regime. If given the chance I probably would have voted 'no' as the reasons to not support military engagement outweighed the reasons to support it."[25] Even expressions of support by Boehner and Cantor were unlikely to move many votes among the Republican rank and file. Progressive House Democrats, wary of additional entanglement in the Middle East, were also skeptical.[26]

In sum, we find that constitutional principle, avoiding military strikes, and seeking political gain provide an incomplete picture of the decision to seek congressional authorization. More persuasive are explanations that emphasize the international and domestic political constraints faced by Obama. The certainty of Russian and Chinese vetoes took any UN Security Council resolutions authorizing force in response to the chemical attacks off the table. Further isolating Obama internationally was an August 30 vote in the House of Commons rejecting British military action in Syria. At home, over 100 members of Congress, including 21 Democrats, sent the president a letter on August 29 stating that any military strikes on Syria would violate the Constitution without first getting congressional approval.[27]

---

23 White House, *Statement by the President on Syria*.
24 White House, Office of the Press Secretary, *Remarks by President Obama and Prime Minister Reinfeldt of Sweden in Joint Press Conference*, September 4, 2013, https://obamawhitehouse.archives.gov/the-press-office/2013/09/04/remarks-president-obama-and-prime-minister-reinfeldt-sweden-joint-press.
25 Interview with authors, October 22, 2022.
26 Landler, Gordon, and Shanker, "House Leaders Express Support."
27 Rebecca Shabad, "140 House Members Say Obama Needs Approval from Congress on Syria," *The Hill*, August 29, 2013.

The analysis in the following sections explores these constraints in more detail, first by assessing the impact of public opinion and then through the lens of presidential leverage.

Competing Explanations: Public Opinion?

Public opinion can constrain or provide justification or cover for political action. But this explanation on its own does not explain the different decisions Obama made in Libya and Syria. In both cases, public opinion clearly favored the president either doing nothing or seeking a diplomatic solution. If Obama was intent on pursuing military action, public opinion was undoubtedly on the side of him seeking congressional authorization. From the earliest days of the short-lived episode, the public firmly held that Obama should be required to go to Congress and receive prior approval before acting in Syria. Nearly four in five respondents (79%) held this view with only 16 percennt saying he should be able to go it alone.[28] When asked if the president or Congress should have final authority to conduct airstrikes, only 30 percent said Obama should while 61 percent said Congress.[29] Interestingly, though, this was at the same time that a clear plurality trusted Obama to handle the situation in Syria while only 34 percent said Congress.[30]

But whereas the strong public conviction that Obama should go to Congress and/or not do anything at all in Syria provided cover in 2013, it should be noted that public opinion on US intervention in Libya in 2011 was very similarly aligned against Obama using force without congressional authorization. However, in that case, he did use force, and did so without either asking or receiving congressional endorsement. In early June, 2011, 59 percent of respondents to a Fox News Poll argued that he should seek congressional authorization. A CNN Poll a few weeks prior held that 55 percent of respondents felt Congress should have final authority for using force.

Once Obama had gone to Congress, there was little public fallout. In fact, in September, more than half of the respondents to a Marist College poll (52%) felt that asking for congressional approval made the president look strong, while only 33 percent said it made him look weak. Even afterward, in November, fully one-third (33%) of respondents in a Yale/George Mason poll felt that the conflict in Syria should receive very high (11%) or high (21%) priority from the Obama

---

28 *NBC News* Poll, August 28–29, 2013.
29 *Marist College* Poll, September 7–8, 2013.
30 *ABC/Washington Post* Poll, September 12–15, 2013.

administration, with another 46 percent rating it as medium and only 21 percent feeling it should receive low priority.[31]

Presidential Leverage: A Contextual Explanation

To supplement the explanations of why Obama went to Congress for permission to engage militarily with Syria, we draw on the concept of "presidential leverage," an approach that examines a president's standing with the public relative to government writ large.[32] Leverage captures the relationship of the president's public standing to measures of public trust in government. Traditionally, the measure of presidential approval, though ubiquitous in discussions of American politics, is imperfectly employed as a gauge of presidential power or authority. The reason for its imperfection is that, while it is probably the best single indicator of how the public views the president at a given time, presidents exist in a separation of powers system, and individual measures of presidential approval do not capture that dynamic.

To approach this, our study incorporates the president's public position relative to government as a whole by measuring the ratio of presidential approval to public trust in government. The IPL (Index of Presidential Leverage) is operationalized as the ratio of a president's approval to the public's level of trust in government as a whole, and expressed as:

$$\text{IPL} = \frac{\text{President's Approval}_t}{\text{Public Trust in Government}_t}$$

The data used to construct the IPL are extracted scores of presidential approval and trust, aggregated using James Stimson's WCALC algorithm, which he developed

---

[31] Would-be presidents often argue for one path of action before they are president, and then once in the White House tend to see things differently. For example, on August 30, 2013, citizen Donald Trump tweeted: "The President must get Congressional approval before attacking Syria—big mistake if he does not!" And after a series of tweets opposed to US involvement in Syria, on September 3 he put his view succinctly: "What I'm saying is stay out of Syria." William Cummings, "Tweets show Trump was against bombing Syria before he was for it," *USA Today*, April 7, 2017. Less than four years later, President Trump faced similar public opposition to US involvement in Syria and strong public support (69%) for seeking congressional authorization, with nearly half (49%) of respondents disapproving of his handling of Syria. That proved no obstacle, though, as Trump authorized military action in both 2017 and 2018.

[32] Ponder, *Presidential Leverage*.

to calculate his widely applied measure of public mood.[33] Here, we use the same algorithm to calculate trust scores and approval scores. To calculate the approval series, we used all measures of presidential approval between January 1961 and December 2020 as reported at the American Presidency Project,[34] and again employed the WCALC algorithm to extract the scores.[35]

The trust data are more complicated, but in the end nearly as straight forward. On the trust scale, a value greater than 50 means the public trusts government more than it distrusts it, and below 50 means greater distrust. The trust data are extracted via the WCALC program from public opinion polls designed to tap the level of public trust in government.[36] But eliminating questions with a specific reference leaves the respondent free to interpret the "federal government" however they wish. The point is that the respondent interprets the government on their own terms, without prompting from the pollster.[37] This formulation yields president-specific leverage coefficients in a given time period, such as a month, quarter, or year. Since we are examining a specific time in Obama's administration (August and September, 2013), we will use quarterly data.

Presidents do not derive leverage only when they are popular. When government leaves the public disillusioned, leading to lower trust, presidents can leverage their position in the separation of powers, regardless of approval rating, and step into the trust/confidence breach to act. For example, Ponder shows that when presidential leverage is high, most of the large, impactful policy actions

---

33 James A. Stimson, *Public Opinion in America: Moods, Cycles, and Swings*, 2nd edition (Boulder: Westview Press, 1999). WCALC uses a recursive algorithm to correct for timing irregularities and produce a smoothed time series. See the website https://stimson.web.unc.edu/software/ for details.
34 https://www.presidency.ucsb.edu/statistics/data/presidential-job-approval-all-data.
35 Extraction is actually not necessary for the approval series since Gallup takes measurements on a regular basis. However, to keep both approval and trust on a constant metric, we extracted the scores. The correlation between raw approval and extracted approval scores is .98.
36 The data from 1961 to 2000 are from Luke Keele, "In Whom Do We Trust? The Rational Nature of Trust in Government," PhD dissertation, University of North Carolina, Chapel Hill, 2003, and updated through 2020 by the authors. The data are extracted using Stimson's WCALC program.
37 Keele's methodology (and our update) tracks answers to a battery of questions, for example:
1. *How much of the time do you think you can trust the government in Washington to do what is right—just about always, most of the time, or only some of the time? How much trust and confidence do you have in our Federal government when it comes to handling domestic problems in general? Overall, how much trust and confidence do you have in the federal government to do a good job in carrying out its responsibilities*? Note that none of the questions reference specific individuals or institutions. In order to minimize endogeneity, questions specifically referencing individuals such as individual presidents by name or members of the Congress or the Supreme Court, or institutions such as "the presidency," or "the Congress" are eliminated from the data.

identified by David Mayhew emanate from within the "presidential branch" rather than in Congress or elsewhere.[38]

The IPL measures the president's "place" in the political system. Unlike approval, for which presidents invest great amounts of time and effort to acquire, leverage measures the individual president squarely within public evaluation of the political system. The higher the value of the coefficient, the more the president stands "paramount" in the American political system, and thus the more leverage he enjoys. Lower values of the coefficient mean the president has little leverage. For example, if the index of presidential leverage falls below 1.0, then the president is in a range of "negative leverage," with the public exhibiting a higher level of trust in government than it approves of the president. As the value of the coefficient approaches 1.0, the position of the president is roughly equivalent to competing institutions; he has no real leverage, nor is he particularly disadvantaged or in a state of negative leverage. Finally, if leverage climbs above 1.0, the president enjoys positive leverage wherein the public places him above and perhaps distinct from the level of trust it places in the government.

Leverage suggests that whether or not presidents can systematically affect their approval ratings in the short term, it must be balanced by a signal from the public. That is, leverage is a relative term; high approval in times of high trust gives the president no significant leverage over and above that of competing institutions. Similarly, a president may have relatively low approval ratings, but if trust is down he stands "preeminent," to borrow Skowronek's term, and may be in a better strategic situation than is the case by looking at approval ratings in isolation.[39] Presidents who are well-placed in terms of leverage (i.e., exhibit high leverage coefficients) may be emboldened, and when leverage falls, they are in a weaker position. Thus, high leverage can serve as a boon for presidents seeking major, even transformational policies. Indeed, Ponder found that transformational policies, or "legacy issues," that have their origin in the White House as opposed to Congress (or elsewhere) are more likely to come to fruition when presidents are in a position

---

[38] See John Hart, *The Presidential Branch: From Washington to Clinton*, 2nd edition (Chatham: Chatham House, 1995); David Mayhew, *Divided We Govern: Party Control, Lawmaking, and Investigations, 1946–2002*, 2nd edition (New Haven: Yale University Press, 2005), and updated at http://campuspress.yale.edu/davidmayew/datasets-divided-we-govern/. To determine whether the items on Mayhew's list were created in the White House or Executive Office of the President (EOP) were cross-referenced with a list compiled by Rudalevige and updated by Ponder. Andrew Rudalevige, *Managing the President's Program: Presidential Leadership and Legislative Policy Formulation* (Princeton: Princeton University Press, 2002). For a full description, see Ponder, *Presidential Leverage*, Chapter 5.

[39] Stephen Skowronek, *The Politics Presidents Make: Leadership from John Adams to Bill Clinton* (Cambridge, MA: Harvard University Press, 1999).

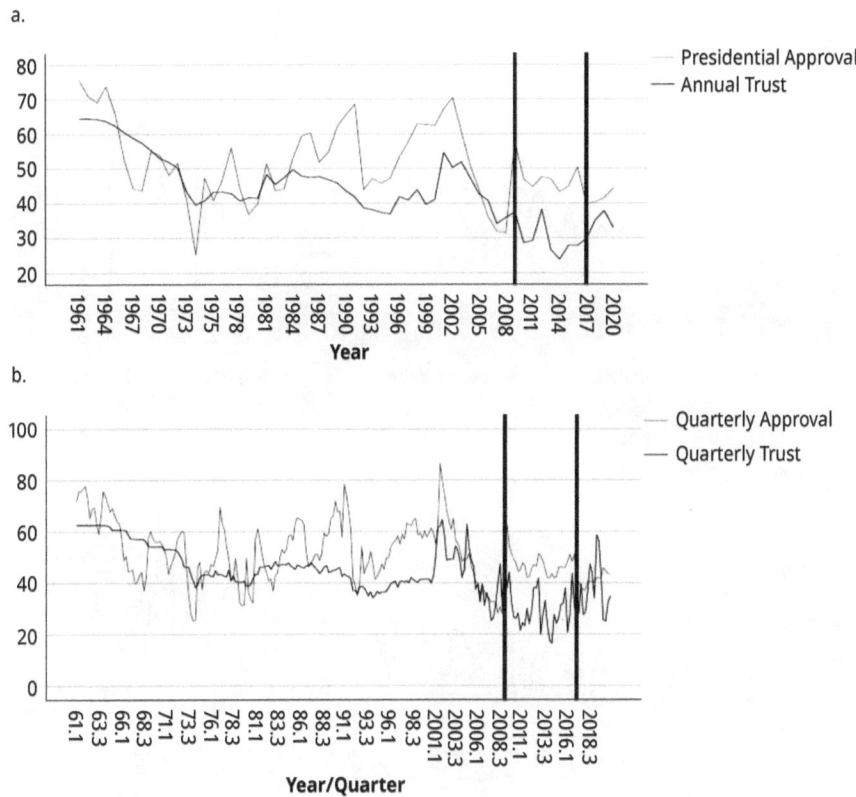

Figure 1: Quarterly Presidential Approval and Government Trust, by Year (a) and Quarter (b) 1961–2020.

of having high IPLs.[40] On the other hand, low-leveraged presidents are more likely to face significant constraints.

Consider Figure 1a, which tracks presidential approval and government trust by year, and 1b, which examines the same, but measured by quarter, from 1961 to 2020 covering Presidents Kennedy through Trump. Overall, there is little or no systematic directional trend in presidential approval, which ebbs and flows according to regular patterns, generally beginning high in an administration's early

---

40 Ponder, *Presidential Leverage*, 93–107.

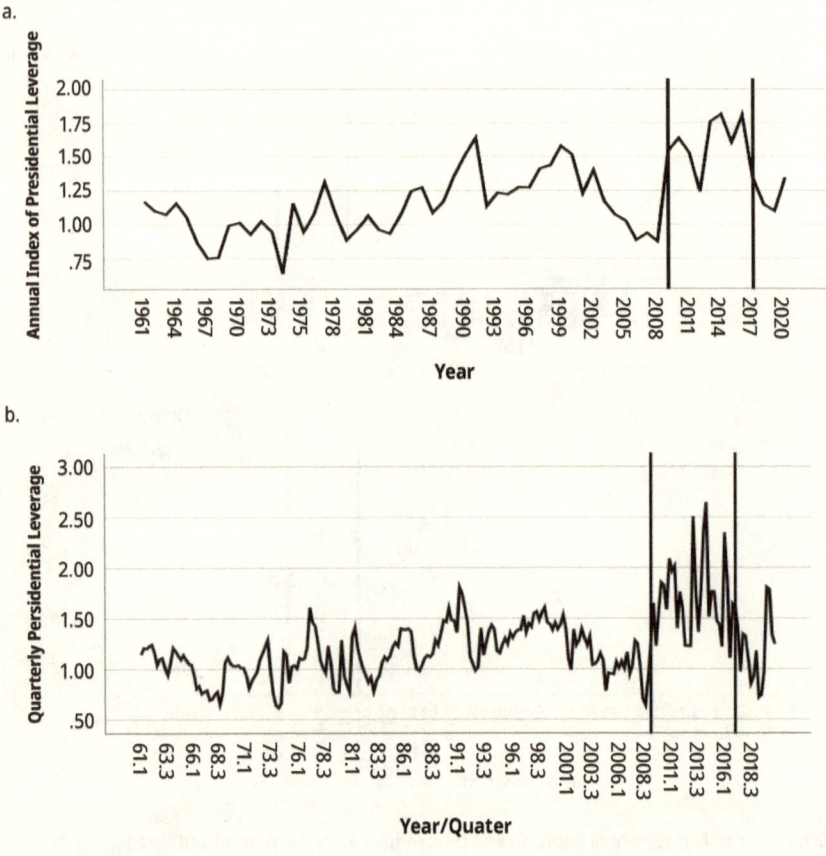

Figure 2: Index of Presidential Leverage by Year (a) and Quarter (b), 1961–2020 (Obama's administration delineated by vertical lines).

months, then decreasing, exhibiting both spikes and troughs.[41] Obama's term is highlighted between the vertical lines. Note that his approval ratings, whether measured annually or by quarter, are relatively mediocre.

Figures 2a and b track the IPL, which generally increases over time, with the major exception of the Watergate period in 1973 and 1974. The increase over time is due not simply to presidential approval, but largely to the decreasing levels of public trust in government in general, and Congress in particular. Note as well

---

41 For an overview of presidential approval and its causes, see chapter two in Robert S. Erikson, Michael MacKuen, and James Stimson, *The Macro Polity* (New York: Cambridge University Press, 2002).

that Obama, whose approval ratings as shown in Figure 1 were stubbornly mediocre, served at a time when public trust in government was extremely low, affording him a robust IPL. Thus, for the public, presidents are in some respects the only (or perhaps the best) game in town, at least as far as the elected branches are concerned. By placing approval into institutional context, we get a more nuanced picture of how presidents compare not only to other institutions at any one time in the course of history, but also how they compare to one another.

In August and September 2013, Obama's Gallup approval was consistently in the mid- to low-40s, and his third quarter extracted rating was 45.2 percent. By comparison, in 2009, just after his inauguration, his approval ratings reached as high as the mid- to upper-60s. When he engaged with Libya in April 2011, his ratings were in the mid-to low 40s, approximately the same as they were when he asked Congress for authority to use military force against Syria. What was different, however, was his IPL. Trust in government was down to just 24 and 23 percent in the first and second quarters of 2011 respectively, and his IPL registered 1.97 and 2.02. By contrast, quarterly trust was somewhat higher in the third quarter of 2013, and Obama's IPL dipped from a very strong 2.51 in the quarter of his second inaugural, and nearly 1.8 in the second quarter. His approval ratings in those first two quarters of 2013 moved above 50 and 49 percent respectively, again not particularly high, but trust in government had dipped into the low to mid 20s. While the measure of government trust considers all polls that mention trust about government generally, it is worth noting that a particularly low or high level of approval in Congress was about the same in each quarter. Congressional approval during the first quarter of 2011 was in the upper teens and even hit 24 percent in May. Similarly, Congress' approval was in the mid to upper teens during August and early September 2013. Congressional trust in the same periods was even more dismal, registering in the single digits in both quarters.

Table 1: Comparing Leverage in Libya and Syrian Situations.

Libya 2011 (Quarter 2)	Syria 2013 (Quarter 3)
Approval 46.7%	Approval 45.2%
Trust 23.20	Trust 33.04
IPL 2.01	IPL 1.37

To summarize, presidential leverage measures context, placing the president in the larger framework of public attitudes toward government. Further, high impact, transformational policies are more likely to be presidential in origin when presidents exhibit high IPLs. As we noted above, public opinion about whether Obama should commit troops in Libya and later in Syria was in each instance decidedly against him doing so. Furthermore, the public was also strongly opposed to him acting without congressional authorization and overwhelmingly supported the idea that he needed to go to Congress for permission.

However, public opinion did not prove an obstacle when Obama engaged with Libya in 2011, so it is difficult to reconcile those actions with the idea that negative opinion was the predominant constraint in Syria. Instead, presidential leverage (IPL) might offer some further insight, not as a direct cause but as a contextual framework. In terms of his IPL, Obama registered lower in only four of the 32 quarters of his presidency, and between the second and third quarters of 2013 the values of his IPL dropped nearly three standard deviations. After the immediate problem with Syria subsided, his IPL rose again to levels before the crisis. This illustrates once again the context that the IPL captures. When Obama had a much higher IPL in 2011, he did not go to Congress when considering whether to use military force in Libya, nor is there even any mention of the possibility of doing so. In the Syrian case, his approval ratings actually dropped a point or so in the ensuing quarters, but trust in the federal government dipped even further bringing Obama's IPL back to previous levels and beyond. As Table 1 shows, his IPL in the third quarter of 2013 was a much weaker 1.37, relative to 2011 when his IPL was a more robust 2.02. His approval ratings and his IPL continued to increase throughout the remainder of his presidency, even as the 2014 midterms were not kind to him or congressional Democrats.

The analysis of some members of Congress captures parts of this dynamic. When asked why they thought President Obama sought congressional authorization for striking Syria, they responded that he was "politically weak," "didn't have standing on the Hill," and that "the political deck was stacked against him."[42] While these views include those of Republicans who were unlikely to support the president, this perception of contextual institutional weakness or political constraints is consistent with our concept of leverage. When Obama used military force in Libya in early 2011, he neither asked Congress for authorization nor was in a weak position as measured by the IPL (as mentioned, both the first and second quarters of 2011 registered near 2.0). The major difference is that Obama was in a stronger public position (as measured by the IPL) in 2011 and weak in 2013. Obama enjoyed high leverage in 2011, asking no quarter from Congress and giving none in return. However, mired in a much deeper hole in 2013, Obama sought to move on a promise he had made (the red line) but found himself unable to persuade the public, and politically and institutionally constrained on unilateral action.

---

42 Interviews with authors.

Conclusion

In the end, the fact that Congress was going to reject Obama's request for authorization became moot when Russia orchestrated a deal for Assad to sign the Chemical Weapons Convention and remove chemical weapons from Syria. The military authorization bill was pulled from the congressional agenda to allow time for the diplomatic approach to play out. What this episode illustrates, we contend, is that even in the domain of military policy, where presidents typically enjoy the greatest decision-making latitude, political and institutional constraints can be determinative. Obama, who campaigned on transformational foreign policy goals, was hindered in this instance by a combination of political structure and public constraint, the latter captured by the IPL. Therefore, we argue that the concept of presidential leverage offers a useful lens to further illuminate and provide analytical context to the opportunities and constraints on presidential policy making.

References

Arms Control Association. "Timeline of Syrian Chemical Weapons Activity, 2102–2022." May 2022.
Baker, Peter, and Jonathan Weisman. "Obama Seeks Approval by Congress for Syria Strikes." *New York Times*. August 31, 2013.
Blake, Aaron, and David Nakamura. "Boehner and Cantor Will Support Syria Strike." *Washington Post*. September 3, 2013.
Burns, Sarah, and Andrew Stravers. "Obama, Congress, and Audience Costs: Shifting the Blame on the Red Line." *Political Science Quarterly* 135, no. 1 (2020): 67–101.
Chollet, Derek. "Obama's Red Line, Revisited." *Politico*. July 19, 2016.
Daalder, Ivo H. "Obama's foreign policy: Not every global problem has an American solution." *Washington Post*. November 18, 2016.
DeYoung, Karen. "Fulfilled-and broken-promises for America's new role in the world." *Washington Post*. November 18, 2016.
Erikson, Robert S., Michael MacKuen, and James Stimson. *The Macro Polity*. New York: Cambridge University Press, 2002.
Goldberg, Jeffrey. "The Obama Doctrine: The US President Talks Through his Hardest Decisions About America's Role in the World." *The Atlantic*. April 15, 2016.
Hart, John. *The Presidential Branch: From Washington to Clinton*. Second edition. Chatham: Chatham House, 1995
Indyk, Martin S., Kenneth G. Lieberthal, and Michael E. O'Hanlon. "Obama's Foreign Policy: Progressive Pragmatist." *Brookings*. March 9, 2012.
Keele, Luke. "In Whom Do We Trust? The Rational Nature of Trust in Government." PhD dissertation. University of North Carolina, Chapel Hill, 2003,
Kriner, Douglas. "Obama's Authorization Paradox: Syria and Congress's Continued Relevance in Military Affairs." *Presidential Studies Quarterly* 44, no. 2 (June 2014): 309–327.
Landler, Mark. "Obama Threatens Force Against Syria." *New York Times*. August 20, 2012.

Landler, Mark, Michael R. Gordon, and Thom Shanker. "House Leaders Express Their Support for Syria Strike." *New York Times*. September 3, 2013.

Mason, Jeff, and Richard Cowan. "Analysis: Obama Lobbies Personally for Syria Vote." *Reuters*. September 2, 2013.

Mayhew, David. *Divided We Govern: Party Control, Lawmaking, and Investigations, 1946–2002*. Second edition. New Haven: Yale University Press, 2005.

Milner, Helen, and Dustin Tingley. *Sailing the Water's Edge: The Domestic Politics of American Foreign Policy*. Princeton: Princeton University Press, 2016.

Ponder, Daniel E. *Presidential Leverage: Presidents, Approval, and the American State*. Stanford: Stanford University Press, 2018.

Rhodes, Ben. "Inside the White House during the Syrian 'Red Line' Crisis." *The Atlantic*. June 3, 2018.

Rudalevige, Andrew. *Managing the President's Program: Presidential Leadership and Legislative Policy Formulation*. Princeton: Princeton University Press, 2002.

Savage, Charlie. "Obama Tests Limits of Power in Syrian Conflict." *New York Times*. September 8, 2013.

Schulhofer-Wohl, Jonah. "The Obama Administration and Civil War in Syria, 2011–2016." *Journal of Transatlantic Studies* 19, no. 4 (December 2021): 517–547.

Shabad, Rebecca. "140 House Members Say Obama Needs Approval from Congress on Syria." *The Hill*. August 29, 2013.

Shanker, Thom, C.J. Chivers, and Michael R. Gordon. "Obama Weighs 'Limited' Strikes Against Syrian Forces." *New York Times*. August 27, 2013.

Skowronek, Stephen. *The Politics Presidents Make: Leadership from John Adams to Bill Clinton*. Cambridge, MA: Harvard University Press, 1999.

Stimson, James A. *Public Opinion in America: Moods, Cycles, and Swings*. Second edition. Boulder: Westview Press, 1999.

Warrick, Joby. "More than 1,400 killed in Syrian Chemical Weapons Attack, US says." *Washington Post*, August 30, 2013.

White House. Office of the Press Secretary. *Remarks by President Obama and Prime Minister Reinfeldt of Sweden in Joint Press Conference*. September 4, 2013, https://obamawhitehouse.archives.gov/the-press-office/2013/09/04/remarks-president-obama-and-prime-minister-reinfeldt-sweden-joint-press.

White House. Office of the Press Secretary. *Statement by the President on Syria*. August 13, 2013, https://obamawhitehouse.archives.gov/the-press-office/2013/08/31/statement-president-syria.

Wilson, Scott. "Obama Administration: Libya Action Does Not Require Congressional Approval." *New York Times*. June 15, 2011.

Woodrow Wilson International Center for Scholars. "Security Address on Counter-Terrorism by the Honorable Barack Obama, United States Senator from Illinois." August 1, 2007.

Part III: **Communication, Executive Power, and Leadership**

Donna R. Hoffman and Alison D. Howard
Chapter 12
Obama, the Pen, and the Phone: Promises to Policies

Barack Obama's campaign was based on a conception of "hope." Crowds, at his urging, often shouted "yes we can!" Campaign themes would set the stage for the presidency, and while expectations for new presidents are always high, no recent president had a higher burden. In a 2020 interview reflecting on his presidency, Obama said, "I think that the danger for someone like me, who was elected with outsized expectations and a lot of symbolism, is that sometimes your supporters feel as if you're going to wave a wand and it's all going to get done."[1] Presidents don't get wands.

The public, wanting fulfilled campaign promises and problems solved, often forgets the political system's constraints. In turn, presidents may be tempted to use the most unconstrained powers they have to fulfill expectations and accomplish goals. At one level, a policy is a policy for a president, whether made through the legislative process or unilateral presidential action. It can be advertised as an accomplishment, and credit claimed for action. For presidents today, the means may matter less in the pursuit of a promised end, which once accomplished may both help them to re-election, as well as burnish their legacy. So, while presidents don't get wands, they do get pens, and for Barack Obama, his desire to transform public policy would come to require presidential action.

Obama used the notion of the presidential pen to signal to the public how he was acting to solve problems. He used the concept of the phone to refer to rallying the public. We examine Obama's use of the pen-and-phone strategy. While we catalog his pen usage, we are especially interested in the phone, that is, the rhetoric surrounding Obama's unilateral executive actions. Presidents make choices about whether and how to rhetorically highlight their actions. While Obama's use of the "pen" isn't out of the ordinary for recent presidents, we do find he is very strategic

---

[1] Padraig Moran, "Barack Obama Reflects on 'Outsized' Expectations of his Presidency, and Convincing Michelle He Should Run," *CBC Radio*, November 23, 2020, https://www.cbc.ca/radio/thecurrent/the-current-for-nov-23-2020-1.5809458/barack-obama-reflects-on-outsized-expectations-of-his-presidency-and-convincing-michelle-he-should-run-1.5812782.

Donna R. Hoffman, University of Northern Iowa
Alison D. Howard, Dominican University of California

with his "phone." In the highest-profile remarks where Obama chose to draw public attention to executive actions, themes of fulfilling the American Dream dominated, and Obama framed his executive actions as necessary due to congressional inaction. In lower-profile remarks, economic opportunity was still a prominent theme, but a broader range of topics were also incorporated. These lower-profile remarks differed as they were more informal, personalized, and less focused on congressional intransigence. While candidate Obama had been critical of George W. Bush's exercise of executive power, by rhetorically incorporating references to the American Dream, President Obama sought to make his own exercise of executive power distinctive and transformative.

Acting Alone

The study of unilateral executive actions, or presidents acting alone, does not have a long history. Researchers have lacked consistent terminology and the instruments included have varied. One of the earliest authors on unilateral executive action was Louis Fisher, who examined executive orders and proclamations under the heading "Administrative Legislation" in *Constitutional Conflicts between Congress and the President*, first published (under a different title) in 1978.[2] Cooper's extensive work began with examining executive orders (EOs) and proclamations,[3] then EOs and memoranda.[4] His 2014 book examined "direct executive action," to which he added legislative signing statements.[5] Dodds examined what he termed "unilateral presidential directives" and included primarily EOs, memoranda, and proclamations.[6]

Other scholars have studied policy substance and choices that presidents make when using one or more types of policymaking tools. Several have concen-

---

2 Louis Fisher, *The Constitution Between Friends: Congress, the President, and the Law* (New York: St. Martin's Press, 1978).
3 Philip J. Cooper, "By Order of the President: Administration by Executive Order and Proclamation," *Administration & Society* 18, no. 2 (1986): 233–262.
4 Philip J. Cooper, "Presidential Memoranda and Executive Orders: Of Patchwork Quilts, Trump Cards, and Shell Games," *Presidential Studies Quarterly* 31, no. 1 (2001): 126–141.
5 Philip J. Cooper, *By Order of the President: The Use and Abuse of Executive Direct Action*, 2nd edition (Lawrence: University Press of Kansas, 2014).
6 Graham G. Dodds, *Take Up Your Pen: Unilateral Presidential Directives in American Politics*, (Philadelphia: University of Pennsylvania Press, 2013).

trated only on EOs.[7] While the sheer number of EOs has declined overtime,[8] Ragsdale and Theis documented the growth of EOs specifically devoted to policy (as a percentage of total EOs), illustrating that presidents have increasingly sought policy ends using that unilateral means.[9]

Others have highlighted that it is not just EOs through which presidents make unilateral policy, but also through proclamations and memoranda.[10] Unilateral executive actions (UEAs) can also be used as communication tools.[11]

There is now consensus that UEAs not only matter but are also key in the evolution of the presidency. Cooper declared, "[h]ow these devices are used matters,"[12] a simple statement necessitated because earlier scholars had not always given them much weight or import. What has received much less attention, however, is the presidential rhetoric that surrounds these instruments. We contend that how presidents choose (or not) to discuss their unilateral actions in public forums, just like the instruments themselves, also matter and are deserving of study. Whereas earlier presidents may have been reticent to flag instances of unilateral action,[13] it is worth noting the "phone" aspect of Obama's strategy was specifically about communicating unilateral actions with public audiences where he offered explanations of his actions with the "pen."

---

[7] Kenneth R. Mayer, *With the Stroke of a Pen: Executive Orders and Presidential Power*, (Princeton: Princeton University Press, 2001); William G. Howell, *Power without Persuasion: The Politics of Direct Presidential Action*, (Princeton: Princeton University Press, 2003); Adam L. Warber, *Executive Orders and the Modern Presidency: Legislating from the Oval Office*, (Boulder: Lynne Rienner Publishers, 2006); Matthew Dickinson, and Jesse Gubb, "The Limits to Power without Persuasion," *Presidential Studies Quarterly* 46, no. 1 (2016): 48–72; Brandon Rottinghaus, "Exercising Unilateral Discretion: Presidential Justifications of Unilateral Powers in a Shared System," *American Politics Research* 47, no. 1 (2019): 3–28.

[8] Mayer; Dodds, *Take Up Your Pen*.

[9] Lyn Ragsdale, and John J. Theis, "The Institutionalization of the American Presidency, 1924–92," *American Journal of Political Science* 41, no. 4 (1997): 1280–1318.

[10] Brandon Rottinghaus, and Jason Maier, "The Power of Decree: Presidential Use of Executive Proclamations, 1977–2005," *Political Research Quarterly* 60 (2007); Kenneth S. Lowande, "After the Orders: Presidential Memoranda and Unilateral Action," *Presidency Studies Quarterly* 44, no. 4 (2014): 724–724; Michelle Belco, and Brandon Rottinghaus, *The Dual Executive: Unilateral Orders in a Separated and Shared Power System* (Redwood City: Stanford University Press, 2017).

[11] Brandon Rottinghaus, and Adam L. Warber, "Unilateral Orders as Constituency Outreach: Executive Orders, Proclamations and the Public Presidency," *Presidential Studies Quarterly* 45 (2015): 289–309.

[12] Cooper, *By Order of the President: The Use and Abuse of Executive Direct Action*, 385.

[13] Howell, *Power without Persuasion*; Donna R. Hoffman, and Alison D. Howard, "Means and Ends: Advertising Executive Action from Reagan to Trump," paper presented at the Annual Meeting of the American Political Science Association Annual Meeting. Montreal, Canada, 2022.

Data and Method

To study Obama's use of the pen and the phone, we first establish terminology, which has not always been uniform. We will use the term "unilateral executive actions" (UEAs) to encompass executive orders, memoranda, and proclamations. This leaves out things such as directives, which may not be publicly available, as well as legislative signing statements, which have no force of law. We first approach our examination quantitatively, documenting UEAs and the existence of the rhetoric surrounding them. Using the *Compilation of Presidential Documents* (CPD), we searched for the terms "executive order," "proclamation," and "memorandum."[14] Searches returned both the actual instrument, as well as subsequent documents referencing these terms. This data enabled us to quantify both the instruments and rhetoric. Many referencing documents were written, such as statements, notices, and correspondence with Congress, but we only analyzed oral remarks, classified by rhetorical type. All documents were reviewed to ensure references were relevant.[15] From these oral remarks, we then determined the rate, type, and nature of Obama's UEA rhetoric.

The Pen and Phone Strategy

At the beginning of 2014, Obama consciously embarked on what was termed a pen-and-phone strategy. In remarks before the first cabinet meeting of the year, Obama referred to it;[16] these were not offhand comments. He would repeat variations of the pen-and-phone concept multiple times over the next several months. The most succinct versions he offered were "I've got a pen to take executive actions where Congress won't, and I've got a telephone to rally folks around the country on this mission."[17] Importantly, however, the 2014 pen-and-phone push was a variation of an

---

14 The *Compilation of Presidential Documents* is available through GovInfo, a service of the Government Publishing Office (GPO) at www.govingo.gov. In addition, the American Presidency Project (www.presidency.ucsb.edu) was used to supplement press interactions, as the *CPC* did not always have the full text of press interviews.

15 For example, references to other presidents' actions or to things such as the Emancipation Proclamation were excluded.

16 Barack Obama, "Remarks Prior to a Cabinet Meeting and an Exchange with Reporters," *CPD*, January 14, 2014, https://www.govinfo.gov/content/pkg/DCPD-201400019/pdf/DCPD-201400019.pdf.

17 Barack Obama, "Remarks on Expanding College Opportunity," *CPD*, January 16, 2014, https://www.govinfo.gov/content/pkg/DCPD-201400028/pdf/DCPD-201400028.pdf.

earlier strategy, the "we can't wait" initiative of 2011 to 2012.[18] In the aftermath of the 2010 midterm election, in which Republicans would control the House, Obama's administration would justify unilateral actions contrasting them with the inaction of Congress. This offered framing for the upcoming 2012 presidential election, as well. It was the pen-and-phone phrasing of the second term, however, which entered the lexicon as a reference to executive action.[19] Here we focus more on the rhetoric Obama used in relation to these actions, and ask: How often did he choose to rhetorically highlight actions? What formats did he choose to utilize? How did he go about rallying people with his "phone"?

The Pen

When Obama referenced his pen, it was framed as a way to get things done for the American people. In his first reference to the pen-and-phone strategy, he stated "we are not just going to be waiting for legislation in order to make sure that we're providing Americans the kind of help that they need."[20] Further, his view was that utilizing his pen advanced the American Dream, what he termed "making sure that this is a country where if you work hard, you can make it."[21] This would play a large role in the phone strategy through which he communicated the actions of his pen.[22]

Emphasizing unilateralism had costs. Obama, however, sought to deflect criticism of his pen strategy. In remarks in Austin, Texas, he noted, "I'm issuing Executive orders at the lowest rate in more than a hundred years."[23] During a press

---

18 The "We Can't Wait" initiative began on October 24, 2011, and continued to October 2012. According to the White House, there were 44 actions the president took in direct response to "congressional gridlock" related to economic growth; see Obama White House, "We Can't Wait," *Obama White House Archives* (2017), https://obamawhitehouse.archives.gov/economy/jobs/we-cant-wait. The "We Can't Wait" initiative put the emphasis on executive action (the pen). While the rallying aspect (the phone) wasn't included in the title, Obama did not hesitate to highlight his actions.
19 For example, see Justice Gorsuch's concurring opinion in *West Virginia v. EPA* (2022). He writes, "[b]ut the Constitution does not authorize agencies to use pen-and-phone regulations as substitutes for laws passed by the people's representatives" (19).
20 Obama, "Remarks Prior to a Cabinet Meeting."
21 Obama, "Remarks Prior to a Cabinet Meeting."
22 It should be noted that while this was the 2014 articulation of pen-and-phone, this strategy was a key feature of the Obama presidency from the beginning.
23 Obama, "Remarks on Signing a Memorandum on Helping Struggling Federal Student Loan Borrowers Manage Their Debt," *CPD*, June 9, 2014, https://www.govinfo.gov/content/pkg/DCPD-201400439/pdf/DCPD-201400439.pdf.

conference in Australia, a reporter asked Obama a wide-ranging question, a portion of which referred to his use of EOs. Obama defended his actions saying, "[w]ith respect to executive actions generally, the record will show that I have actually taken fewer executive actions than my predecessors. Nobody disputes that. What I think has changed is the reaction of some of my friends in Congress to exercising what are normal and, frankly, fairly typical exercises of Presidential authority."[24]

Obama, who put rhetorical emphasis on using his pen, was defensive about its use when questioned. Because unilateral action can carry a stigma in the US system of shared powers designed to constrain unilateralism, he noted that his actions were not out of the ordinary. Inndeed, by most measures, it wasn't. As we show in Table 1, it is true that Obama issued fewer executive orders than any of his three immediate, two-term predecessors. However, if one adds other types of UEAs, he is within five instruments of surpassing Clinton, the most active in this regard. We should caution that the distinction between types of UEAs can be vague, and that shifts in usage over time of different instruments have been observed.[25] Further, sheer counts of these documents do not tell us anything about the nature of the UEA, as they can be used for multiple purposes, and many will be for symbolic, rather than substantive, ends. In addition, there are examples of presidents remarking that they are signing one instrument, but they are, in fact, signing a different instrument. Obama was particularly prone to this error, calling both proclamations and memoranda he was signing executive orders.[26] This helps illustrate that substantive policy ends (commonly associated with EOs) can be made with all three instruments, and even the president sometimes conflates everything with an "executive order."

---

[24] Barack Obama, "The President's News Conference in Brisbane, Australia." *CPD*, November 16, 2014, https://www.govinfo.gov/content/pkg/DCPD-201400866/pdf/DCPD-201400866.pdf.
[25] Cooper, *By Order of the President: The Use and Abuse of Executive Direct Action*; Dodds, *Take Up Your Pen*; Lowande, "After the Orders."
[26] For examples, see Barack Obama, "Remarks on Energy," *CPD*, January 26, 2009, https://www.govinfo.gov/content/pkg/DCPD-200900019/pdf/DCPD-200900019.pdf; Barack Obama, "Remarks on Signing a Memorandum on Federal Benefits and Non-Discrimination," *CPD*, June 17, 2009, https://www.govinfo.gov/content/pkg/DCPD-200900475/pdf/DCPD-200900475.pdf; Barack Obama, "Remarks on Signing a Memorandum Establishing a Task Force on Childhood Obesity," *CPD*, February 9, 2010, https://www.govinfo.gov/content/pkg/DCPD-201000087/pdf/DCPD-201000087.pdf; Barack Obama, "Remarks at Univision's 'Es el Momento' Town Hall Meeting and a Question-and-Answer Session," *CPD*, March 28, 2011, https://www.govinfo.gov/content/pkg/DCPD-201100205/pdf/DCPD-201100205.pdf.

Table 1: Number of Unilateral Executive Actions by type (percent by column), Reagan to Trump.

Pres	Executive Orders	Proclamations	Memoranda	Total
Reagan	381 (22.5)	1119 (21.0)	220 (10.0)	1720 (18.7)
G.H.W. Bush	164 (9.7)	589 (11.1)	185 (8.4)	938 (10.2)
Clinton	364 (21.5)	878 (16.5)	681 (30.9)	1923 (20.9)
G.W. Bush	291 (17.2)	940 (17.7)	452 (20.5)	1683 (18.2)
Obama	276 (16.3)	1226 (23.3)	417 (18.9)	1919 (20.8)
Trump	220 (13.0)	570 (10.7)	249 (11.3)	1039 (11.3)
Total	1696	5322	2204	9222

$\chi^2 = 332.3$, $p < .001$

Table 1 indicates that recent presidents have not differed substantially in their total use of UEAs. If each is issuing at a similar rate, then two-term presidents would have 20 percent of the total and one-term presidents would have 10 percent of the total during the 40 year period under study. Our data show that individual presidents differ only slightly from those expectations. Despite an emphasis on "the pen," Obama executed UEAs at a normal rate; he has 20.8 percent, almost exactly what we would expect from a two-term president.

We do see, however, significant differences when UEAs are broken down by type in columns two through four of Table 1 (as indicated by the chi-square statistic). The use of memoranda and proclamations have substantial variability from president to president. Executive orders are the most consistently utilized across presidents, and Obama did use them less oftent than his immediate predecessors. These internal differences, however, don't affect the fact that overall, presidents are utilizing UEAs in similar numbers in their term of office, giving presidents equal opportunity to highlight those actions rhetorically if they choose to do so.

Where Obama did stand out from other presidents was having an articulated strategy for using unilateral actions linked to catch-phrases. Initially it was "we can't wait" and later he used the pen-and-phone formulation. This opened him up to criticism because he was rhetorically emphasizing a tactic of which he had been previously critical.[27] He juxtaposed his action with the intransigence of Congress, and even though UEAs are frequently limited in scope and checked (courts can review, Congress can legislate to alter, future presidents can overturn) a president can register a policy accomplishment in the short-term, and have an opportunity to advertise a policy accomplishment.

The Phone

At its core, "the phone" was a way for Obama to communicate action. It was another articulation of Teddy Roosevelt's "bully pulpit." Obama's conception of the "phone" in the pen-and-phone strategy was one he believed would allow him to unify Americans around a shared value – the American Dream. Obama's articulation of this value was a "belief that everybody has got to take responsibility, everybody has got to work hard, but if you do, that you can support a family and meet the kinds of obligations that you have to yourself and your family but also to your communities and to your Nation."[28] The concept of the American Dream played an important role in the administration's rhetorical narrative, both symbolically and substantively. It was transformative because Obama sought its realization for all Americans, creating a future that was better than the past.

When a president issues a UEA, it is public in the sense that it must satisfy the various requirements for publication and notification.[29] This does not, however, guarantee it will come to the public's attention. The president is under no requirement to make public remarks about UEAs. Thus, presidents have choices to make as to whether, how, and where they talk about their actions. When they choose to highlight actions, the forums have a range of importance and dissemination. We created five categories for the oral remarks presidents choose to make about UEAs.

---

27 In March 2008, Obama stated, "I taught constitutional law for 10 years. I take the Constitution very seriously. The biggest problems that we're facing right now have to do with George Bush trying to bring more and more power into the executive branch and not go through Congress at all. And that's what I intend to reverse when I'm president of the United States of America." Quoted in Andrew Prokop, "How Barack Obama is expanding presidential power—and what it means for the future," *Vox*, September 9, 2014, https://www.vox.com/2014/9/9/5964421/obama-lawsuit-republicans-abuse-of-power.
28 Barack Obama, "Remarks Prior to Cabinet Meeting," January 14, 2014.
29 There are exceptions to this in the case of classification, and, historically, publication requirements have varied. Memoranda are particularly problematic in that there is presidential discretion on publication; the Obama Administration, however, was generally open and transparent regarding memoranda. See Dodds, *Take Up Your Pen*, 9.

Table 2: Obama Rhetoric on Unilateral Executive Actions, 2009–2017.

Action	Instrument Count	Address[1]	Press[2]	Gen Remarks[3]	Legis Signing Remarks[4]	EA Signing Remarks[5]	Total Rhetoric
Executive Orders	276	12	23	77	1	20	133
Memoranda	417	3	2	16	0	21	42
Proclamations	1226	1	0	6	0	7	14
Total	1919	16	25	99	1	48	189

[1]Major speeches, weekly addresses, commencement speeches.
[2]Interviews, press conferences, stand-alone exchanges with reporters, townhalls moderated by media.
[3]Minor speeches, general remarks to specialized audiences, tele/videoconference remarks, general remarks with subsequent press availability.
[4]Remarks given when signing legislation.
[5]Remarks given when signing executive action.

These range from high-profile addresses and press interactions to the more intimate signing ceremonies and minor remarks. Table 2 shows the categories of rhetoric into which Obama's remarks are placed. We examine his rhetoric in terms of its potential reach. Major addresses and press interactions have higher levels of dissemination, while minor addresses/remarks and signing events will typically make less news, having lower levels of dissemination. We find Obama used slightly different strategies in these types of remarks, but the overarching theme of the American Dream is persistent.

High-Profile Remarks

Addresses

Major addresses are the most heavily prepared remarks presidents give, in part because they will garner the most attention. Thus, they are a major part of any administration's rhetorical strategy. There are, however, limited opportunities to deliver these kinds of remarks. Obama was pointed in his major addresses about why he took unilateral action; he explained that he acted because Congress did not, could not, or would not. In his January 2010 State of the Union Address, Obama noted the Senate failed to create a bipartisan fiscal commission, saying "[n]ow, yesterday the Senate blocked a bill that would have created this commission, so I'll issue an Executive order that will allow us to go forward, because I refuse to pass this problem on to another generation of Americans."[30] He reiterated this point in his weekly address a few weeks later, where he emphasized acting because "the American people are tired of politicians who talk the talk but don't walk the walk," thereby extending his rhetorical attention to this issue over the course of several weeks.[31]

In other State of the Union addresses, he continued to point out where he had taken executive action and where Congress had to act if more was to be done. In this way, he both noted his actions, but also illustrated the limits on presidential authority. In 2012, he announced an executive order to ease the red tape on federal construction projects, but noted that Congress had to act to fund those projects.[32] In the 2014 State of the Union, he announced his intention to act on the minimum wage by requiring federal contractors to pay $10.10 per hour; he then put the ball in Congress's court by noting they can do the same for "millions more."[33] He followed up by devoting his February 15, 2014, weekly address to the same issue and urged listeners to find out where their representatives stood on the issue.[34] A subsequent weekly address was also devoted to this issue drawing attention to his actions, and the lack of congressional action.[35] Similarly, in April 2014, Obama's weekly address highlighted that Congress had blocked the Paycheck Fairness Act. "That's why this week I took action to prohibit more businesses from punishing workers who discuss their salaries" and he again pointed out his action on minimum wage.[36] These ex-

---

30 Barack Obama, "Address Before a Joint Session of the Congress on the State of the Union." *CPD*, January 27, 2010, https://www.govinfo.gov/content/pkg/DCPD-201000055/pdf/DCPD-201000055.pdf.
31 Barack Obama, "The President's Weekly Address," *CPD*, February 13, 2010, https://www.govinfo.gov/content/pkg/DCPD-201000095/pdf/DCPD-201000095.pdf. Weekly addresses are included with major addresses even though there are some qualitative differences. As Han noted, they allow presidents to control their message and they generate news coverage. They also offer a way for presidents to continue to focus attention on a topic after a major address, as illustrated here. Lori Cox Han, "New Strategies for an Old Medium: The Weekly Radio Addresses of Reagan and Clinton," *Congress and the Presidency* 33 (2006): 25–45.
32 Barack Obama, "Address Before a Joint Session of Congress on the State of the Union," *CPD*, January 24, 2012, https://www.govinfo.gov/content/pkg/DCPD-201200048/pdf/DCPD-201200048.pdf.
33 Barack Obama, "Address Before a Joint Session of the Congress on the State of the Union," *CPD*, January 28, 2014, https://www.govinfo.gov/content/pkg/DCPD-201400050/pdf/DCPD-201400050.pdf.
34 Barack Obama, "The President's Weekly Address," *CPD*, February 15, 2014, https://www.govinfo.gov/content/pkg/DCPD-201400094/pdf/DCPD-201400094.pdf.
35 Barack Obama, "The President's Weekly Address," *CPD*, March 8, 2014, https://www.govinfo.gov/content/pkg/DCPD-201400153/pdf/DCPD-201400153.pdf.
36 Barack Obama, "The President's Weekly Address," *CPD*, April 12, 2014, https://www.govinfo.gov/content/pkg/DCPD-201400263/pdf/DCPD-201400263.pdf.

amples illustrate where the president presented his actions as decisive and in the public interest, whereas Congress was presented as blocking legislation in an area Obama viewed as vital. Thus, Obama's rhetorical references to Congress were not only combative, attempting to publicly pressure Congress, but they also emphasized the limits of unilateral action. By including references to the limits of presidential authority, Obama could potentially seek to tamp down the expectations gap.[37] More significantly, candidate Obama had been particularly critical of President Bush's use of executive actions. Consequently, Obama's use of UEAs, but with a rhetorical emphasis on the public interest, helped Obama and others in the administration maintain they were distinct from Bush's use of executive authority.

Emphasizing presidential action (success) and congressional inaction (failure) was especially important in 2014 before the midterm election. Obama even noted in a weekly address in March, that 2014 was a "year of action" (and this phrase was linked to an EO).[38] In the next week's address, he asked people to "call up your member of Congress" regarding the minimum wage.[39] The administration wanted to avoid the large losses the president's party had suffered in the previous midterm and one strategy for doing so was stressing the ways in which Congress was not doing its job. The issues he chose to highlight were also policies that would fulfill his conception of the American Dream, centered on various aspects of economic opportunity and well-being.

Press Interactions

Presidential press conferences and interviews are qualitatively different from addresses, as presidents are responding to questions, not presenting prepared, highly vetted remarks. In these interactions, there were several examples where Obama previewed possible executive actions; Congress was thus put on notice there would be a cost to their inaction. Examples ranged from his fiscal commission to corporate tax inversions to immigration policy. In each, Obama registered frustration with the lack of Congressional action, but he also attempted to bring pressure

---

37 Richard Waterman, Carol L. Silva, and Hank Jenkins-Smith, *The Presidential Expectations Gap: Public Attitudes Concerning the Presidency* (Ann Arbor: University of Michigan Press, 2014).
38 Barack Obama, "The President's Weekly Address," *CPD*, March 15, 2014, https://www.govinfo.gov/content/pkg/DCPD-201400170/pdf/DCPD-201400170.pdf.
39 Barack Obama, "The President's Weekly Address," *CPD*, March 22, 2014, https://www.govinfo.gov/content/pkg/DCPD-201400185/pdf/DCPD-201400185.pdf.

to bear on Congress to complete pending action. In each of these areas, the administration would eventually act, though not always with a UEA.[40]

The case of immigration reform is instructive in this regard and became prominent in Obama's press interactions. In 2011, Obama signaled a lack of authority for the president to address immigration unilaterally.[41] As Congress failed to act, he repeatedly focused on the lack of action on comprehensive immigration reform that had passed the Senate in June 2013 (after the DACA memo of 2012) but had not advanced in the House.[42] He said the following in a news conference in response to a question on potential (further) executive action.

> And I think that the best way, if folks are serious about getting immigration reform done, is going ahead and passing a bill and getting it to my desk. And then the executive actions that I take go away. They're superseded by the law that has passed. And I will engage any Member of Congress who's interested in this in how we can shape legislation that will be a significant improvement over the existing system. But what we can't do is just keep on waiting. There is a cost to waiting. There's a cost to our economy.[43]

In an interview a few days later, Obama echoed the same sentiment and noted how he stood back and tried to get the House to act.[44] Another few days passed, and in response to a question at a news conference, he stated,

---

40 The fiscal commission was created through EO 13531, February 18, 2010, https://obamawhitehouse.archives.gov/the-press-office/executive-order-national-commission-fiscal-responsibility-and-reform. However, the other areas were accomplished within the executive agencies without explicit presidential direction (as in, not with a UEA). On inversion, see US Department of the Treasury, IRS Notice 2014-52, September 23, 2014, https://www.irs.gov/irb/2014-42_IRB#NOT-2014-52. The Obama administration's notice of the exercise of prosecutorial discretion (that would become the Deferred Action for Childhood Arrivals [DACA] program), was accomplished with an administrative memorandum within the Department of Homeland Security issued by Secretary Janet Napolitano. The same is true of the subsequent administrative memorandum that announced prosecutorial discretion for parents (Deferred Action for Parents of Americans and Lawful Permanent Residents [DAPA]), issued by Secretary Jeh Johnson. See US Department of Homeland Security, Memorandum of June 15, 2012, https://www.dhs.gov/xlibrary/assets/s1-exercising-prosecutorial-discretion-individuals-who-came-to-us-as-children.pdf; US Department of Homeland Security, Memorandum of November 20, 2014, https://www.aila.org/library/dhs-exercising-prosecutorial-discretion.

41 Barack Obama, "Remarks at Univision's 'Es el Momento' Town Hall Meeting and a Question-and-Answer Session," *CPD*, March 28, 2011, https://www.govinfo.gov/content/pkg/DCPD-201100205/pdf/DCPD-201100205.pdf.

42 The DACA memo itself stemmed from the failure of Congress to pass the Development, Relief, and Education for Alien Minors (DREAM) Act.

43 Barack Obama, "The President's News Conference," *CPD*, November 5, 2014, https://www.govinfo.gov/content/pkg/DCPD-201400820/pdf/DCPD-201400820.pdf.

44 Barack Obama, "The President's News Conference," *CPD*, August 6, 2014, https://www.govinfo.gov/content/pkg/DCPD-201400597/pdf/DCPD-201400597.pdf.

> [t]here has been ample opportunity for Congress to pass a bipartisan immigration bill that would strengthen our borders, improve the legal immigration system, lift millions of people out of the shadows so they are paying taxes and getting right by the law. It passed out of the Senate. I gave the House over a year to go ahead and at least give a vote to the Senate bill; they failed to do so. And I indicated to Speaker Boehner several months ago that if in fact Congress failed to act, I would use all the lawful authority that I possess to try to make the system work better. And that's going to happen. That's going to happen before the end of the year.[45]

Deferred Action for Parents of Americans and Lawful Permanent Residents (DAPA) would be that action in late 2014.[46] With this rhetorical strategy, Obama could illustrate how Congress was urged to act and indeed should act, especially if they were displeased by earlier executive actions; by previewing he could illustrate to the public he was acting unilaterally as a last resort, but he was acting.

In addition to previewing actions, Obama took credit for executive actions in front of the press. He was often put on the defensive by questions that began with the premise he was governing by executive action. After claiming credit for multiple accomplishments at an August 2014 news conference, Obama sought to defuse criticism leveled at him:

> But the broader point . . . is that if in fact House Republicans are concerned about me acting independently of Congress – despite the fact that I've taken fewer executive actions than my [predecessors] – then the easiest way to solve it is passing legislation. Get things done.[47]

Much as we found with addresses, Obama repeatedly pointed out he was acting where Congress was gridlocked. His remarks with the press make it clear the ball was in Congress' court if they did not like his unilateral actions.

We find a consistency in messaging with Obama's pen-and-phone strategy in his most high-profile remarks. He sought to illustrate he was exercising leadership and working to solve problems that were his priorities, especially for issues that had a direct impact on people's daily economic lives. For those uncomfortable with unilateral power, he often presented his use of it as acting where Congress would not. With his pen Obama chose to illustrate his commitment to expanding the American Dream; with his phone he drew attention to these ac-

---

45 Barack Obama, "The President's News Conference With Member of Parliament and Leader of the National League for Democracy Party Aung San Suu Kyi of Burma in Rangoon, Burma," *CPD*, November 14, 2014, https://www.govinfo.gov/content/pkg/DCPD-201400857/pdf/DCPD-201400857.pdf.
46 As noted earlier, DAPA, like DACA, was accomplished with a DHS memorandum rather than a UEA from Obama.
47 Barack Obama, "The President's News Conference," *CPD*, August 1, 2014, https://www.govinfo.gov/content/pkg/DCPD-201400588/pdf/DCPD-201400588.pdf.

tions in a coordinated way. Through his UEAs on the minimum wage, overtime regulations, paycheck fairness, and immigration Obama furthered his commitment to expanding opportunity and promoting the shared values of the nation. As he stated, "the defining project of our time, of our generation, is to restore opportunity for everybody."[48]

Lower-Profile Remarks

General Remarks

It wasn't just high-profile rhetoric in which Obama referenced unilateral actions. Smaller-scale events were utilized, too. While we find Obama's pen-and-phone strategy was particularly clustered around themes surrounding the "American Dream" in high-profile remarks, lower-profile remarks allowed for a broader range of subjects. General remarks allowed Obama to be more informal, more expansive, and more personal, and to do so before more specialized audiences. The American Dream still figured prominently in these remarks. Typically given during the day, these remarks were significant, even newsworthy, but generated less attention than addresses and stand-alone press interactions. Further, the remarks were typically not solely about executive action.

For example, one of the first instances of Obama making general remarks was his appearance at the State Department two days after the inauguration. He highlighted three EOs signed earlier in the day related to detention, interrogation, and Guantanamo Bay, which were in direct response to Bush Administration actions regarding the conduct of the War on Terror. Obama said, "[m]y appearance today [at the State Department], as has been noted, underscores my commitment to the importance of diplomacy and renewing American leadership . . . ."[49] Other groups, such as the US Conference of Mayors (where he highlights the establishment of the Office of Urban Affairs), or the AFL-CIO (where he highlights reversing "antilabor Executive orders and policies") were also early audiences where Obama underscored UEAs.[50]

---

[48] Barack Obama, "Remarks at the Costco Wholesale Corporation Warehouse in Lanham, Maryland," *CPD*, January 29, 2014, https://www.govinfo.gov/content/pkg/DCPD-201400051/pdf/DCPD-201400051.pdf.

[49] Barack Obama, "Remarks at the State Department," *CPD*, January 22, 2009,.https://www.govinfo.gov/content/pkg/DCPD-200900014/pdf/DCPD-200900014.pdf.

[50] Barack Obama, "Remarks to the United States Conference of Mayors," *CPD*, February 20, 2009, https://www.govinfo.gov/content/pkg/DCPD-200900098/pdf/DCPD-200900098.pdf; Obama, "Remarks

The American Dream theme again figures prominently in Obama's lower-profile remarks. Speaking before the Export-Import Bank's Conference, Obama detailed an EO he had signed that morning, which he called the National Export Initiative, to promote American exports. He emphasizes the adventurousness and entrepreneurship of Americans and stated, "[i]t's the spirit that has advanced America's leadership in the world and held aloft the American Dream for generations."[51]

At the White House Tribal Nations Conference, Obama advertised he had signed the White House Initiative on American Indian and Alaska Native Education executive order. Addressing this audience gave him an opportunity to recognize an important constituency, highlight his actions, and connect them to fulfilling the American Dream. He notes the failures of the country's past in Indian Country and notes we will begin "building a better future together, one that honors old traditions and welcomes every Native American into the American Dream."[52]

Signing Events

Unlike general remarks where UEAs could be either a sole focus or a mention, events at which Obama signed UEAs had a focused purpose centered on the action itself. These events were often more intimate, frequently given in the White House or Eisenhower Executive Office Building. Obama tended to be more informal, and the narrative was often less structured. Obama had the opportunity to recognize key individuals, and we also found that he brought in more personal stories he believed would connect with the audience. These personal stories typically brought in American Dream elements.

As noted above, one of the first appearances Obama made was at the State Department where he highlighted executive actions he had signed earlier in the day related to US conduct in the War on Terror. Before Obama appeared at the State Department, however, he held an event in the Oval Office where those UEAs were signed, which featured retired military officers. Signing events often featured the recognition of key individuals and here Obama recognized flag officers standing behind him whom he credited with making a "passionate plea that

---

at the AFL–CIO National Convention in Pittsburgh, Pennsylvania," *CPD*, September 15, 2009, https://www.govinfo.gov/content/pkg/DCPD-200900711/pdf/DCPD-200900711.pdf.
51 Barack Obama, "Remarks at the Export-Import Bank's Annual Conference," *CPD*, March 11, 2010, https://www.govinfo.gov/content/pkg/DCPD-201000170/pdf/DCPD-201000170.pdf.
52 Barack Obama, "Remarks at the White House Tribal Nations Conference," *CPD*, December 2, 2011, https://www.govinfo.gov/content/pkg/DCPD-201100924/pdf/DCPD-201100924.pdf.

we restore the standards of due process and the core constitutional values that have made this country great, even in the midst of war, even in dealing with terrorism."[53]

When Obama renewed the White House Initiative on Historically Black Colleges and Universities by EO, he recognized key Members of Congress and HBCU personnel and students in attendance. While explaining what his EO would do, he also discussed his budget request of Congress and how he was requesting congressional action to make college more affordable. In addition, the American Dream was also referenced. HBCUs were noted as "catalysts of change where young people put their hands on the arc of history and move this Nation closer to the ideals of its founding; and the cradles of opportunity where each generation inherits the American Dream and keeps it alive for the next."[54]

In signing events, Obama utilized personal stories which drew upon the American Dream. In signing a proclamation on the 19th Anniversary of the American with Disabilities Act (ADA), he referred to Michelle Obama's father (who had multiple sclerosis), but who didn't complain, didn't miss work, "he just wanted to be given the opportunity to do right by his family."[55] Before signing, Obama recognized the ADA was part of "our obligation to ensuring [disabled Americans] every chance to pursue the American Dream."[56] The story of the president's and first lady's student debt was also something Obama mentioned on several occasions, to not only personalize his remarks, but also to signal empathy.[57]

In his lower-profile remarks, Obama incorporated plenty of references to opportunity and the American Dream, but he also included broader subject areas. His rhetoric was less confrontational than higher-profile events where it was clear one of the major purposes was to illustrate to the public what Congress needed to do (and that Obama hoped public pressure would be brought to bear). Lower-profile remarks also enabled more informality, more personalized interac-

---

53 Barack Obama, "Remarks Following a Meeting With Retired Military Officers," *CPD*, January 22, 2009, https://www.govinfo.gov/content/pkg/DCPD-200900013/pdf/DCPD-200900013.pdf.
54 Barack Obama, "Remarks on Signing an Executive Order Regarding Historically Black Colleges and Universities," *CPD*, February 26, 2010, https://www.govinfo.gov/content/pkg/DCPD-201000130/pdf/DCPD-201000130.pdf.
55 Barack Obama, "Remarks on Signing a Proclamation Honoring the 19th Anniversary of the Americans With Disabilities Act," *CPD*, July 24, 2009, https://www.govinfo.gov/content/pkg/DCPD-200900597/pdf/DCPD-200900597.pdf.
56 Obama, "Remarks on Signing a Proclamation Honoring the 19th Anniversary of the Americans With Disabilities Act."
57 Barack Obama, "Remarks on Signing a Memorandum on Helping Struggling Federal Student Loan Borrowers Manage Their Debt," *CPD*, June 9, 2014, https://www.govinfo.gov/content/pkg/DCPD-201400439/pdf/DCPD-201400439.pdf.

tions with audience members, and more narratives in which Obama brought in personal references to illustrate a connection to his actions. In this manner, unilateral power could be normalized.

Findings

Presidents are provided with opportunities to illustrate leadership and action when they choose to speak about UEAs. Through these rhetorical opportunities presidents can highlight fulfilling campaign promises, promote policy action, address specific constituencies, advance their party's goals, educate people about an issue, and attempt to push Congress into acting. Additionally, these rhetorical acts provide an opportunity to further their administration's overall governing narrative. Obama's emphasis on presidential action to help the American people, when Congress was inactive, was part of a coordinated strategy to help normalize the unilateral actions of a president who had previously been critical of his predecessor's actions but faced the reality of a divided Congress after 2010. The pen-and-phone formulation was a publicly articulated strategy whose first iteration was the "We Can't Wait" initiative in 2011. Obama's actions with the pen were not abnormal in quantity. His phone strategy, however, was particularly strategic and thematic. Being public about his unilateral actions and reasons (where there was no requirement to do so), stressing his actions' limitations, and frequently couching them in formulations of the American Dream enabled Obama to shape the public's view of unilateralism. That we see the most consistent reliance on the themes of economic opportunity and improving conditions of the American people in the most highly disseminated remarks, points to strategic rhetorical considerations. The same is true of utilizing Congress's inaction as a contrast. In addition, the policy areas most commonly focused on were often repeated. Lower-profile remarks were more expansive, and the areas highlighted were broader, but the American Dream was frequently brought into remarks, as well. The contrast with Congress that was prevalent in the high-profile remarks was also less pronounced.

Conclusion

As Obama stressed in his initial campaign for president, "in no other country on Earth is my story even possible."[58] Obama emphasized how he was, in essence, the embodiment of the American Dream to help him appeal to a broad cross-section of Americans as he campaigned to be a different, transformative kind of president who wanted to see the American Dream realized for all Americans.

From campaigning to governing Obama used the symbolism of the American Dream to explain the need for policy action. Obama's use of executive action and the choices he made about when and how to talk about these actions furthered his belief that government can and should create opportunities for people to reach their potential and for the country to continue to prosper. But there is likely another reason for this construct, as well. By being particularly critical of his predecessor's use of unilateral power, Obama needed a way to distinguish his own unilateral actions. By couching his actions as helping to fulfill the American Dream and improving economic conditions and opportunity, he could also illustrate he was merely acting in the public interest, not acting for power's sake. Obama confronted enormously high expectations and the public expected action. Soaring rhetoric from the campaign necessitated ways to highlight presidential success, wherever it could be found.

Obama's use of executive action was not exceptional compared to his predecessors. Obama publicly highlighted his actions in a variety of settings, often explaining that his use of executive action was necessary because Congress wouldn't act, hoping to avoid charges of executive overreach. Additionally, he explained that executive action was limited in scope and that legislation was the preferred mode of creating policy. Yet, given the political landscape he faced after 2010, "the pen," became one tool for Obama to use to further his administration's goals when Congress was no longer receptive to presidential leadership. "The phone" became a related tool for Obama to demonstrate leadership and establish a transformative legacy. However, by its very nature the "phone" implies that someone, on the other end, picks up. Voters, in 2014, didn't turn out to answer Obama's calls, as Senate control shifted to Republicans, thus further limiting his ability to achieve transformative policy change.

---

58 Obama, Barack. Speech at the Democratic National Convention Boston, MA. July 27, 2004.

References

Belco, Michelle, and Brandon Rottinghaus. *The Dual Executive: Unilateral Orders in a Separated and Shared Power System*. Redwood City: Stanford University Press, 2017.

Cooper, Philip J. "By Order of the President: Administration by Executive Order and Proclamation." *Administration & Society* 18, no. 2 (1986): 233–262.

Cooper, Philip J. *By Order of the President: The Use and Abuse of Executive Direct Action*. Second edition. Lawrence: University Press of Kansas, 2014.

Cooper, Philip J. "Presidential Memoranda and Executive Orders: Of Patchwork Quilts, Trump Cards, and Shell Games." *Presidential Studies Quarterly* 31, no. 1 (2001): 126–141.

Dickinson, Matthew, and Jesse Gubb. "The Limits to Power without Persuasion." *Presidential Studies Quarterly* 46, no. 1 (2016): 48–72.

Dodds, Graham G. *Take Up Your Pen: Unilateral Presidential Directives in American Politics*. Philadelphia: University of Pennsylvania Press, 2013.

Fisher, Louis. *The Constitution Between Friends: Congress, the President, and the* Law. New York: St. Martin's Press, 1978.

Han, Lori Cox. "New Strategies for an Old Medium: The Weekly Radio Addresses of Reagan and Clinton." *Congress and the Presidency* 33 (2006): 25–45.

Hoffman, Donna R., and Alison D. Howard. "Means and Ends: Advertising Executive Action from Reagan to Trump." Paper presented at the Annual Meeting of the American Political Science Association Annual Meeting. Montreal, Canada, 2022.

Howell, William G. *Power without Persuasion: The Politics of Direct Presidential Action* Princeton: Princeton University Press, 2003.

Lowande, Kenneth S. "After the Orders: Presidential Memoranda and Unilateral Action." *Presidency Studies Quarterly* 44, no. 4 (2014): 724–724.

Mayer, Kenneth R. *With the Stroke of a Pen: Executive Orders and Presidential Power*. Princeton: Princeton University Press, 2001.

Moran, Padraig. "Barack Obama Reflects on 'Outsized' Expectations of his Presidency, and Convincing Michelle He Should Run." *CBC Radio*. November 23, 2020, https://www.cbc.ca/radio/thecurrent/the-current-for-nov-23-2020-1.5809458/barack-obama-reflects-on-outsized-expectations-of-his-presidency-and-convincing-michelle-he-should-run-1.5812782.

Obama White House, "We Can't Wait," *Obama White House Archives* (2017), https://obamawhitehouse.archives.gov/economy/jobs/we-cant-wait.

Obama, Barack. "Address Before a Joint Session of Congress on the State of the Union." *CPD*. January 24, 2012, https://www.govinfo.gov/content/pkg/DCPD-201200048/pdf/DCPD-201200048.pdf.

Obama, Barack. "Address Before a Joint Session of the Congress on the State of the Union." *CPD*. January 27, 2010, https://www.govinfo.gov/content/pkg/DCPD-201000055/pdf/DCPD-201000055.pdf.

Obama, Barack. "Address Before a Joint Session of the Congress on the State of the Union." *CPD*. January 28, 2014, https://www.govinfo.gov/content/pkg/DCPD-201400050/pdf/DCPD-201400050.pdf.

Obama, Barack. "Remarks at the AFL–CIO National Convention in Pittsburgh, Pennsylvania." *CPD*. September 15, 2009, https://www.govinfo.gov/content/pkg/DCPD-200900711/pdf/DCPD-200900711.pdf.

Obama, Barack. "Remarks at the Costco Wholesale Corporation Warehouse in Lanham, Maryland." *CPD*. January 29, 2014, https://www.govinfo.gov/content/pkg/DCPD-201400051/pdf/DCPD-201400051.pdf.

Obama, Barack. "Remarks at the Export-Import Bank's Annual Conference." *CPD*. March 11, 2010, https://www.govinfo.gov/content/pkg/DCPD-201000170/pdf/DCPD-201000170.pdf.

Obama, Barack. "Remarks at the State Department." *CPD*. January 22, 2009, https://www.govinfo.gov/content/pkg/DCPD-200900014/pdf/DCPD-200900014.pdf.

Obama, Barack. "Remarks at the White House Tribal Nations Conference." *CPD*. December 2, 2011, https://www.govinfo.gov/content/pkg/DCPD-201100924/pdf/DCPD-201100924.pdf.

Obama, Barack. "Remarks at Univision's 'Es el Momento' Town Hall Meeting and a Question-and-Answer Session." *CPD*. March 28, 2011, https://www.govinfo.gov/content/pkg/DCPD-201100205/pdf/DCPD-201100205.pdf.

Obama, Barack. "Remarks Following a Meeting With Retired Military Officers." *CPD*. January 22, 2009, https://www.govinfo.gov/content/pkg/DCPD-200900013/pdf/DCPD-200900013.pdf.

Obama, Barack. "Remarks on Energy," *CPD*, January 26, 2009, https://www.govinfo.gov/content/pkg/DCPD-200900019/pdf/DCPD-200900019.pdf.

Obama, Barack. "Remarks on Expanding College Opportunity," *CPD*, January 16, 2014, https://www.govinfo.gov/content/pkg/DCPD-201400028/pdf/DCPD-201400028.pdf.

Obama, Barack. "Remarks on Signing a Memorandum Establishing a Task Force on Childhood Obesity." *CPD*. February 9, 2010, https://www.govinfo.gov/content/pkg/DCPD-201000087/pdf/DCPD-201000087.pdf.

Obama, Barack. "Remarks on Signing a Memorandum on Federal Benefits and Non-Discrimination." *CPD*. June 17, 2009, https://www.govinfo.gov/content/pkg/DCPD-200900475/pdf/DCPD-200900475.pdf.

Obama, Barack. "Remarks on Signing a Memorandum on Helping Struggling Federal Student Loan Borrowers Manage Their Debt," *CPD*, June 9, 2014, https://www.govinfo.gov/content/pkg/DCPD-201400439/pdf/DCPD-201400439.pdf.

Obama, Barack. "Remarks on Signing an Executive Order Regarding Historically Black Colleges and Universities." *CPD*. February 26, 2010, https://www.govinfo.gov/content/pkg/DCPD-201000130/pdf/DCPD-201000130.pdf.

Obama, Barack. "Remarks on Signing a Proclamation Honoring the 19th Anniversary of the Americans With Disabilities Act." *CPD*. July 24, 2009, https://www.govinfo.gov/content/pkg/DCPD-200900597/pdf/DCPD-200900597.pdf.

Obama, Barack. "Remarks Prior to a Cabinet Meeting and an Exchange with Reporters." *CPD*. January 14, 2014, https://www.govinfo.gov/content/pkg/DCPD-201400019/pdf/DCPD-201400019.pdf.

Obama, Barack. "Remarks Prior to Cabinet Meeting," January 14, 2014. https://obamawhitehouse.archives.gov/the-press-office/2014/01/14/remarks-president-cabinet-meeting.

Obama, Barack. "Remarks to the United States Conference of Mayors." *CPD*. February 20, 2009, https://www.govinfo.gov/content/pkg/DCPD-200900098/pdf/DCPD-200900098.pdf.

Obama, Barack. Speech at the Democratic National Convention Boston, MA. July 27, 2004, http://americanradioworks.publicradio.org/features/blackspeech/bobama.html.

Obama, Barack. "The President's News Conference in Brisbane, Australia." *CPD*, November 16, 2014, https://www.govinfo.gov/content/pkg/DCPD-201400866/pdf/DCPD-201400866.pdf.

Obama, Barack. "The President's News Conference With Member of Parliament and Leader of the National League for Democracy Party Aung San Suu Kyi of Burma in Rangoon, Burma." *CPD*.

November 14, 2014, https://www.govinfo.gov/content/pkg/DCPD-201400857/pdf/DCPD-201400857.pdf.

Obama, Barack. "The President's News Conference." *CPD*. August 1, 2014, https://www.govinfo.gov/content/pkg/DCPD-201400588/pdf/DCPD-201400588.pdf.

Obama, Barack. "The President's News Conference." *CPD*. August 6, 2014, https://www.govinfo.gov/content/pkg/DCPD-201400597/pdf/DCPD-201400597.pdf.

Obama, Barack. "The President's News Conference." *CPD*. November 5, 2014, https://www.govinfo.gov/content/pkg/DCPD-201400820/pdf/DCPD-201400820.pdf.

Obama, Barack. "The President's Weekly Address." *CPD*. April 12, 2014, https://www.govinfo.gov/content/pkg/DCPD-201400263/pdf/DCPD-201400263.pdf.

Obama, Barack. "The President's Weekly Address." *CPD*. February 13, 2010, https://www.govinfo.gov/content/pkg/DCPD-201000095/pdf/DCPD-201000095.pdf.

Obama, Barack. "The President's Weekly Address." *CPD*. February 15, 2014, https://www.govinfo.gov/content/pkg/DCPD-201400094/pdf/DCPD-201400094.pdf.

Obama, Barack. "The President's Weekly Address." *CPD*, March 22, 2014, https://www.govinfo.gov/content/pkg/DCPD-201400185/pdf/DCPD-201400185.pdf.

Obama, Barack. "The President's Weekly Address." *CPD*. March 15, 2014, https://www.govinfo.gov/content/pkg/DCPD-201400170/pdf/DCPD-201400170.pdf.

Obama, Barack. "The President's Weekly Address." *CPD*. March 8, 2014, https://www.govinfo.gov/content/pkg/DCPD-201400153/pdf/DCPD-201400153.pdf.

Prokop, Andrew. "How Barack Obama is expanding presidential power – and what it means for the future." *Vox*. September 9, 2014, https://www.vox.com/2014/9/9/5964421/obama-lawsuit-republicans-abuse-of-power.

Ragsdale, Lyn, and John J. Theis. "The Institutionalization of the American Presidency, 1924–92." *American Journal of Political Science* 41, no. 4 (1997): 1280–1318.

Rottinghaus, Brandon. "Exercising Unilateral Discretion: Presidential Justifications of Unilateral Powers in a Shared System." *American Politics Research* 47, no. 1 (2019): 3–28.

Rottinghaus, Brandon, and Adam L. Warber. "Unilateral Orders as Constituency Outreach: Executive Orders, Proclamations and the Public Presidency." *Presidential Studies Quarterly* 45 (2015): 289–309.

Rottinghaus, Brandon, and Jason Maier. "The Power of Decree: Presidential Use of Executive Proclamations, 1977–2005." *Political Research Quarterly* 60 (2007).

Warber, Adam L. *Executive Orders and the Modern Presidency: Legislating from the Oval Office*. Boulder: Lynne Rienner Publishers, 2006.

Waterman, Richard, Carol L. Silva, and Hank Jenkins-Smith. *The Presidential Expectations Gap: Public Attitudes Concerning the Presidency*. Ann Arbor: University of Michigan Press, 2014.

Ann E. Burnette and Wayne L. Kraemer
Chapter 13
The Genius of America and the Model Immigrant: Barack Obama's Rhetorical Characterization of DACA Recipients

Immigration has been an issue in American politics since the founding of the country. From the 1790 Naturalization Act to the present day, the US has been wrestling with the cultural ramifications of immigration and contested notions of citizenship. In 2012, President Barack Obama initiated the Deferred Action for Childhood Arrivals (DACA) program. In this chapter, we analyze Obama's explanation and defense of the DACA program and how Obama defined what it means to be an American.

Secretary of Homeland Security Janet Napolitano introduced the DACA program on June 15, 2012. DACA was an attempt to address the issue of illegal immigrants by giving those who qualified limited legal status in the US. Throughout the second term of his administration, Obama made arguments supporting DACA and the way in which the program fit into the larger debate about immigration to the US. We contend that Obama's characterization of the participants in the DACA program gives us a window into the framing of "desirable" versus "undesirable" immigrants. This framing informed and continues to inform the debate on topics relating to immigration, including comprehensive immigration reform, challenges of addressing illegal immigration, and the relationship between immigration policy and border security. This essay examines Obama's rhetorical characterization of immigrants eligible for DACA, who are often called "Dreamers." We will first examine the influence of presidential rhetoric, before, second, we provide a brief history of the DACA policy. Third, we will look at Obama's rhetoric regarding immigrants eligible for DACA and discuss two prominent themes in his rhetoric. Finally, we will discuss the implications of Obama's arguments about the Dreamers.

Impact of Presidential Rhetoric

US presidents must demonstrate political leadership, and one of the tools they use to lead is their rhetoric. Jeffrey Tulis has explained that "[a]ll presidents exer-

---

Ann E. Burnette, Wayne L. Kraemer, Texas State University

cise their office through the medium of language, written and spoken."[1] In addition to their rhetoric, presidents must also exercise their acumen with regard to policy and their skill in utilizing the political process. Sometimes there is a perceived gap between a president's rhetoric and their policies. Yet, presidential rhetoric is an important component of a president's leadership as, given the role and visibility of US presidents, the impact of their rhetoric is powerful.

Presidents' choice of language matters, especially as communication scholars argue that language affects people's perceptions. Rhetorical theorist Kenneth Burke observed that a rhetor's choice of language can never be objective; it always promotes certain values. As Kenneth Burke wrote, any language choice is "a *selection* of reality; and to this extent [it] must function also as a *deflection* of reality."[2] David Zarefsky noted that this selection and deflection also happens in presidential rhetoric. Within the sphere of politics, there are often competing definitions of events, policies, and implications,[3] and, according to Zarefsky, "characterizations of social reality are not 'given'; they are chosen from multiple possibilities and hence always could have been otherwise."[4] The way a president describes problems and policies thus defines the way audiences perceive them. Vanessa Beasley has argued that presidents' communication choices help frame the public's understanding of political issues and also perform an agenda-setting function.[5] These functions, as Beasley observed, mean that "presidential rhetoric is typically both necessary and consequential within policymaking."[6] Moreover, analyzing presidential rhetoric enables critics to better understand presidents' views on issues they address.[7] Because of the power of presidential discourse, Obama's rhetoric about the Dreamers had implications for the larger debate on immigration.

For this chapter, we examined Obama's public spoken rhetoric between 2012 and 2016, and reviewed Obama's speeches as archived in the Public Papers of the Presidents. We performed a search for all discourse that included the terms

---

[1] Jeffrey K. Tulis, "Revising the Rhetorical Presidency," in *Beyond the Rhetorical Presidency*, ed. Martin J. Medhurst (College Station: Texas A&M University Press, 1996), 3.
[2] Kenneth Burke, *Language as Symbolic Action: Essays on Life, Literature, and Method* (Berkeley: University of California Press, 1966), 45.
[3] David Zarefsky, "Presidential Rhetoric and the Power of Definition," *Presidential Studies Quarterly* 34, no. 3 (September 2004): 607–619.
[4] Zarefsky, "Presidential Rhetoric and the Power of Definition," 611.
[5] Vanessa B. Beasley, "The Rhetorical Presidency Meets the Unitary Executive: Implications for Presidential Rhetoric on Public Policy," *Rhetoric & Public Affairs* 13, no. 1 (2010): 7–36.
[6] Beasley, "The Rhetorical Presidency Meets the Unitary Executive," 10.
[7] Elizabeth A. Petre, and James T. Petre, "'There Are Certain Things Only Government Can Do': Barack Obama's Rhetoric on Food Safety and the Role of Government," *Western Journal of Communication* 86, no. 4 (2022): 443–462.

"DACA" or "Dreamers." We then identified the themes we found within Obama's rhetoric as he described who the Dreamers were and why they should be welcomed as US citizens. We analyze two of these themes: the "genius of America," and the "model immigrant." Finally, we draw conclusions about the implications of Obama's rhetorical characterizations of those who qualified for the DACA program.

Deferred Action for Childhood Arrivals (DACA)

While Obama's DACA program was controversial at the time, it was not significantly out of step with previous presidential immigration initiatives. During the 1984 presidential debate between President Ronald Reagan and former Vice President Walter Mondale, Reagan expressed the desire to give legal status to immigrants who had assimilated into American culture. Reagan argued, "I believe in the idea of amnesty for those who have put down roots and who have lived here even though some time back they may have entered illegally."[8] Following through on that promise, Reagan's 1986 Immigration Reform and Control Act "granted legalization to millions of unauthorized immigrants, mainly from Latin America, who met certain conditions."[9] The immigrants must have entered the country prior to 1982, they had to apply within a one-year window, and they had to provide extensive documentation including fingerprints, employment history, and proof of continuous residency. Former Reagan speechwriter Peter Robinson argued on NPR that Reagan's immigration policies emanated from Reagan's concept of American values, noting that "[i]t was in Ronald Reagan's bones – it was part of his understanding of America – that the country was fundamentally open to those who wanted to join us here."[10] Robinson also noted that Reagan was a Californian who continually encountered "good hard-working decent people – clearly recent arrivals from Mexico."[11]

---

8 Ronald Reagan quoted in "Debate Transcript," *Commission on Presidential Debates*, October 21, 1984, https://www.debates.org/voter-education/debate-transcripts/october-21-1984-debate-transcript/.
9 D'vera Cohn, "How US Immigration Laws and Rules Have Changed through History," *Pew Research Center*, September 30, 2015, https://www.pewresearch.org/short-reads/2015/09/30/how-u-s-immigration-laws-and-rules-have-changed-through-history/.
10 Peter Robinson quoted in "A Reagan Legacy: Amnesty for Illegal Immigrants," *NPR*, July 4, 2010, https://www.npr.org/templates/story/story.php?storyId=128303672.
11 Robinson quoted in "A Reagan Legacy."

President George H.W. Bush's Immigration Act of 1990 also considered the plight of individuals who were already in residence in the US. Bush stated that the Act provided "a complementary blending of our tradition of family reunification with increased immigration of skilled individuals to meet our economic needs."[12] According to Daniel Mann, "[t]his essentially meant that anybody who came to the United States, resided here for 15 years, and wanted to Naturalize, but did not know much English, could now Naturalize without taking this rigorous test."[13] In a provision that previewed Obama's rhetoric concerning the model immigrant, the 1990 Act also mandated the "deportation of aliens, who, by their violent criminal acts, forfeit their right to remain in this county."[14]

Immigration legislation from the Bill Clinton and George W. Bush administrations in 1996, 2002, and 2006 "were responses to concerns about terrorism and unauthorized immigration."[15] These bills highlighted issues like border control, hiring practices, and eligibility requirements. Obama's DACA program deviated from that trajectory.

The 2012 memorandum "Exercising Prosecutorial Discretion with Respect to Individuals Who Came to the United States as Children," issued by Napolitano, created a non-congressionally authorized program that permitted certain individuals who came to the United States as minors to obtain work authorization and relief from deportation for two years.[16] In order to qualify for DACA, persons had to meet several criteria. DACA-eligible individuals had to have come to the US before their 16th birthday, had to have continuously resided in the US since 2007, and could not be convicted of a felony or significant misdemeanor. They also had to be enrolled in school, or had to have graduated from high school, or had to have been honorably discharged from the military.[17] People who met these qualifications for DACA were often referred to as "Dreamers," in reference to the Development, Relief, and Education for Alien Minors (DREAM) Act, which was introduced in Congress in

---

12 George H.W. Bush, "Statement on Signing the Immigration Act of 1990," *The American Presidency Project*, November 19, 1990, https://www.presidency.ucsb.edu/documents/statement-signing-the-immigration-act-1990.
13 Daniel Mann, "George W. Bush's Legacy on Immigration," George P. Mann & Associates, December 5, 2018, https://greencard-us.com/george-h-w-bushs-legacy-on-immigration/.
14 Bush, "Statement on Signing the Immigration Act of 1990."
15 Cohn, "How US Immigration Laws."
16 "Deferred Action for Childhood Arrivals (DACA): An Overview," *American Immigration Council*, accessed January 23, 2023, https://www.americanimmigrationcouncil.org/research/deferred-action-childhood-arrivals-daca-overview.
17 "Consideration of Deferred Action for Childhood Arrivals (DACA)," *US Citizenship and Immigration Services*, accessed January 23, 2023, https://www.uscis.gov/humanitarian/consideration-of-deferred-action-for-childhood-arrivals-daca/frequently-asked-questions.

2001 but was not passed. Estimates calculated by the Immigration Policy Center showed that approximately 936,000 immigrants were eligible for DACA at the time the program was announced.[18] As of 2020, there were as many as 3.6 million potential DACA recipients residing in the United States; however, many of them either did not apply for DACA or became eligible for the program after it stopped accepting new applicants. In 2020, approximately 653,000 Dreamers were protected under DACA. Even at the height of participation, only about 800,000 Dreamers were protected.[19]

What prompted this initiative? The Obama administration met with Congressional gridlock on immigration while wanting to operate both an effective and efficient deportation system. Even after establishing deportation priorities and giving immigration enforcement field officers discretion over who to let go, low-risk undocumented immigrants continued to clog the system. Because of this impasse, the Obama administration decided to "settle on a temporary, administrative solution."[20]

In March 2011, when Immigration and Customs Enforcement Director John Morton began issuing new orders in a series of memos, immigrant advocates thought some relief was in sight. The "Morton Memos" clarified priorities; the undocumented immigrant criminal, people who had recently entered the country without permission, and those who had repeatedly done so were high-priority deportations. The "Memos" also directed agents to let people go if they met the low-priorities standards; for instance, those who had children who were under 18 or immigrants who had lived in the country for 10 years or more were directed to be let go. This worked and immigrant criminals were deported. However, some were being deported because they were driving without a license or other minor offenses and so the prosecutorial discretion for low priorities was still not creating a fair or uniform system.

In 2012, the US presidential campaign season was in full swing and immigration activists feared Republican nominee Mitt Romney more than Obama because Romney said he would not sign a DREAM Act bill. Obama had pledged during the

---

18 Nicole Prchal Svajlenka and Audrey Singer, "Immigration Facts: Deferred Action for Childhood Arrivals (DACA)," *Brookings*, August 14, 2013, https://www.brookings.edu/articles/immigration-facts-deferred-action-for-childhood-arrivals-daca/.
19 Laurence Benenson, "Fact Sheet: Deferred Action for Childhood Arrivals (DACA)," *National Immigration Forum*, October 16, 2020, https://immigrationforum.org/article/fact-sheet-on-deferred-action-for-childhood-arrivals-daca/.
20 Janell Ross, "How the Deferred Action Immigration Program Went from Dream to Reality," *Huffpost*, August 19, 2012, https://www.huffpost.com/entry/deferred-action-immigration-program_n_1786099.

2008 presidential campaign to overhaul the nation's immigration system.[21] Yet, during his first term he did not deliver on that pledge. In fact, his administration "deported more undocumented immigrants than any other in US history."[22] During 2012, there was mounting pressure on the Obama campaign to effect immigration reform. On June 5, there was a major protest by Dreamers in Colorado, followed by additional sit-ins throughout the country, including electoral swing states. Additional pressure came from a letter signed by 96 legal scholars urging administrative action. The letter argued that Obama had the authority to enact reforms and questioned why he had not used it. On June 11, 2012, *The Washington Post* ran a front-page story about a young undocumented immigrant living in the Virginia suburbs outside the nation's capital.[23] Instead of preparing for graduation, the student and her mother were getting ready for their scheduled deportation. Frank Sharry, executive director of America's Voice, an immigrant advocacy organization, said, "I think the president sees these things, I think, if no one else, Michelle [Obama] probably brings them to his attention. She gets his legacy as the black president."[24] On June 15, Obama spoke in the White House Rose Garden and announced the DACA program as a "temporary stopgap measure that lets us focus our resources wisely while giving a degree of relief and hope."[25]

Once the DACA policy was in place, the president needed to communicate a rationale for the DACA recipients to be a low priority for deportation. In analyzing President Obama's rhetoric, we found two interrelated themes that he developed that justified the DACA program. The first theme is what Obama called the "genius of America." The second theme is Obama's characterization of the Dreamers, which rendered them model immigrants who reinforced the genius of America.

The Genius of America

In a news conference with Canadian Prime Minister Justin Trudeau and Mexican President Enrique Peña Nieto, Obama observed that "America is a nation of immi-

---

21 Ross, "How the Deferred Action Immigration Program."
22 Ross, "How the Deferred Action Immigration Program."
23 Ross, "How the Deferred Action Immigration Program."
24 Frank Sharry quoted in Ross, "How the Deferred Action Immigration Program."
25 Barack Obama, "Remarks on Immigration Reform and an Exchange with Reporters," *The White House Archives*, June 15, 2012, https://obamawhitehouse.archives.gov/the-press-office/2012/06/15/remarks-president-immigration.

grants" adding that this was the strength of the US.[26] He explained that "the genius of America has been to define ourselves not by what we look like or what our last name is or what faith we practice, but our adherence to a common creed."[27]

The genius of America, in many ways, became a justification of Obama's views on immigration and a rationale for giving DACA recipients preferred status in relation to other illegal residents of the US. By examining the values and foundations of what America is and what it should strive to be, Obama makes the immigrant a significant part of the American experience. Obama observed in 2014 "'Dreamer' is more than a title, it's a pretty good description of what it means to be an American."[28] Obama's conception of Americans included immigrants as well as citizens.

The dreamer, in Obama's view, contributes to America by remaining dynamic, innovative, and ambitious. Obama explained that "at some point, there's going to be a President Rodriguez, or there's going to be a President Chin" because America "is a nation of immigrants, and ultimately, it will reflect who we are, and its politics will reflect who we are."[29]

Obama's conceptualization of the genius of America had three core concepts: citizenship, opportunity (the American dream), and diversity. We will first consider the concept of citizenship. Obama described citizenship as "a word at the very heart of our founding, a word at the very essence of our democracy, the idea that this country only works when we accept certain obligations to one another and to future generations."[30] He indicated that the concept of citizenship is constantly being tested and that it is important to debate "who we're going to be as a

---

26 Barack Obama, "News Conference with Canadian Prime Minister Justin Trudeau and Mexican President Enrique Peña Nieto," *The White House Archives*, June 29, 2016, https://obamawhitehouse.archives.gov/the-press-office/2016/06/30/remarks-president-obama-prime-minister-trudeau-canada-and-president-peña.
27 Obama, "News Conference with Canadian Prime Minister."
28 Barack Obama, "Remarks at National Hispanic Caucus Institute Annual Awards Gala," *The White House Archives*, October 2, 2014, https://obamawhitehouse.archives.gov/the-press-office/2014/10/02/remarks-president-congressional-hispanic-caucus-institute-gala.
29 Barack Obama, "Remarks and a Question-and-Answer Session at an MSNBC/Telemundo Immigration Town Hall in Miami, Florida," *The White House Archives*, February 25, 2015, https://obamawhitehouse.archives.gov/the-press-office/2015/02/25/remarks-president-immigration-town-hall-miami-fl.
30 Barack Obama, "Remarks by the President at the Democratic National Convention," *The White House Archives*, September 7, 2012, https://obamawhitehouse.archives.gov/the-press-office/2012/09/07/remarks-president-democratic-national-convention.

country."[31] This is significant because US citizens have an obligation to fight for immigrants' rights to achieve citizenship and thereby broaden the view of what it means to be an American. Through this process, Americans will decide, as Obama said, who we want to be as a country. While he realized that change would come slowly, like in any social movement, he argued that it is a constant battle. That, for Obama, was the nature of citizenship in action.

The second component of the genius of America is opportunity. In 2015, Obama made the following observation:

> And you've got to recognize that America's greatness does not come from building walls . . . . Our greatness comes from a dream that says in this country, if you work hard, you can build a better life for your family. No matter where you come from. No matter what you look like. No matter what your last name is. That's what makes America great.[32]

Indeed, it has always been the allure of American opportunity that has attracted immigrants to the US even though they faced discrimination. Obama explained in 2016 that anti-immigration sentiments are not new and that what was once said about the Irish, Polish, or Italian immigrants is "identical to what they're now saying about Mexicans, or Guatemalans, or Salvadorians or Muslims or Asians."[33] Obama posited that the contemporary anti-immigration message consisted of the same arguments and the same language as in the past. According to Obama, immigrants kept coming "because America offered possibility for their children and their grandchildren. And even if they were initially discriminated against, they understood that our system will, over time, allow them to become part of this one American family."[34]

As Obama described the genius of America, the promise of opportunity has constantly had the power to overcome rhetorical or real discrimination, and the problems America is facing now are not much different from the past. In a poignant moment from Obama's remarks at an Organizing for Action Summit in 2015, he recalled a picture that he saw in a magazine of immigrants from Ellis Island in the 1800s and 1900s. He described them as "strivers," noting that "they were escaping poverty and in search of a better life. And a lot of them didn't have

---

31 Barack Obama, "Remarks on the Supreme Court's Decisions Regarding Affirmative Action and Immigration and an Exchange with Reporters,", *The White House Archives*, June 23, 2016, https://obamawhitehouse.archives.gov/the-press-office/2016/06/23/remarks-president-supreme-court-decision-us-versus-texas.
32 Barack Obama, "Remarks by the President at Congressional Hispanic Caucus Institute Gala," *The White House Archives*, October 8, 2015, https://obamawhitehouse.archives.gov/the-press-office/2015/10/08/remarks-president-congressional-hispanic-caucus-institute-gala.
33 Obama, "News Conference with Canadian Prime Minister."
34 Obama, "News Conference with Canadian Prime Minister."

great educations, but they knew that if they were able to get here, that their kids would have a great education."[35] Obama added, "[t]he notion that somehow this generation of immigrants is different than the past is just not true. The only thing that's happened is . . . we forgot where we came from."[36]

In Obama's rhetoric, the third component of the genius of America was diversity.

The immigrants who came to Ellis Island in search of their dreams, and the immigrants who faced, and continue to face, discrimination contribute to what makes America a remarkable place. While immigrants represent different demographics, the goals and aspirations of a diverse population create shared ideals, values, and community.

Diversity truly defines America. Obama observed in 2014 that "part of what America is about is stitching together folks from different backgrounds and different faiths and different ethnicities. That's what makes us special."[37] He extended that philosophy in 2016, saying, "if one group feels that justice is being denied, that's an affront to all of us, to the values on which this Nation was founded."[38]

Because diversity is what makes us special, Obama argued that we should not isolate ourselves from those who look different or believe differently from ourselves because eventually the differences weave themselves into the fabric of American life and create community. He explained in 2016:

> And every study shows that whether it was the Irish or the Poles or the Germans or the Italians or the Chinese or the Japanese or the Mexicans or the Kenyans – [*laughter*] – whoever showed up, over time, by a second generation, third generation, those kids are Americans. They do look like us, because we don't look one way. We don't all have the same last names, but we all share a creed, and we all share a commitment to the values that founded this Nation. That's who we are. And that is what I believe most Americans recognize.[39]

Because DACA recipients embody the nature of citizenship, seek opportunity, and are diverse, they are the expression of the genius of America.

---

35 Barack Obama, "Remarks at an Organizing for Action Dinner," November 9, 2015, https://obamawhitehouse.archives.gov/the-press-office/2015/11/09/remarks-president-organizing-action-event.
36 Obama, "Remarks at an Organizing for Action Dinner."
37 Barack Obama, "Remarks in Chicago, Illinois," *The White House Archives*, November 25, 2014, https://obamawhitehouse.archives.gov/the-press-office/2014/11/25/remarks-president-immigration-chicago-il.
38 Barack Obama, "Remarks at the Asian Pacific American Institute for Congressional Studies Awards Gala Dinner," *The White House Archives*, May 5, 2016, https://obamawhitehouse.archives.gov/the-press-office/2016/05/05/remarks-president-22nd-annual-apaics-awards-gala.
39 Obama, "Remarks on the Supreme Court's Decisions."

Model Immigrants

The second major theme in Obama's rhetoric about DACA and Dreamers was his positive characterization of the undocumented immigrants who would qualify for and benefit from the program. These characterizations create a model immigrant who should not be deported. Obama developed this theme through descriptions of immigrants who were upstanding, inspirational, and desirable members of the community, and descriptions of immigrants who were negatively affected by unfair immigration policies. Obama portrayed these immigrants as people who would, under the provisions of DACA, serve their communities and contribute to the genius of America that he extolled. In many cases, he told detailed narratives to make these arguments. Narratives can be especially powerful persuasive tools, according to Alisdair MacIntyre, who has argued that humans are "essentially story-telling animals."[40] MacIntyre further claimed that "we all live our narratives in our lives and we understand our own lives in terms of narratives."[41] Obama frequently made his positive characterizations of immigrants through hypothetical or real narratives, which invited people to empathize with the immigrants in these stories.

Obama frequently talked about Dreamers as being desirable immigrants. One reason they were model immigrants is that they were already invested in American society. At a visit to Del Sol High School in Las Vegas, Obama described potential Dreamers as "young people who were brought to this country as children, young people who have grown up here, built their lives here, have futures here."[42] He pointed out that an undocumented immigrant could become a DACA-protected dreamer by demonstrating the ability to "meet some basic criteria, like pursuing an education."[43] This difference was uncomplicated and attainable. Dreamers who could meet these criteria could then assume their rightful place in American society. DACA-protected individuals could "come out of the shadows so that you can live here and work here legally, so that you can finally have the dignity of knowing you belong."[44]

The contributions that these immigrants had already made to American life was profound, according to Obama. He highlighted Dreamers who were "serving

---

[40] Alisdair MacIntyre, *After Virtue: A Study in Moral Theory* (Notre Dame: University of Notre Dame Press, 1981), 201.
[41] MacIntyre, *After Virtue*, 197.
[42] Barack Obama, "Remarks at Del Sol High School in Las Vegas, Nevada," *The White House Archives*, January 29, 2013, https://obamawhitehouse.archives.gov/the-press-office/2013/01/29/remarks-president-comprehensive-immigration-reform.
[43] Obama, "Remarks at Del Sol High School."
[44] Obama, "Remarks at Del Sol High School."

in our military, protecting us and our freedom."[45] Because their contributions were so important, Obama warned that, "[t]he notion that in some ways we would treat them as expendable makes no sense."[46] Obama underscored the value of these contributions to support the argument that there was a moral imperative for the DACA program. In one hypothetical narrative, Obama said that if there was "a young person here who has grown up here and wants to contribute to this society, wants to maybe start a business that will create jobs for other folks who are looking for work, that's the right thing to do."[47]

In defining this desirable immigrant, Obama advanced several claims. First, desirable immigrants are good for the country. They could contribute to institutions of education, or the military and they could also make contributions to the US economy. Second, the DACA policy would enable desirable immigrants to come out of the shadows and live productive, dignified lives. Finally, the need for DACA was not just practical; it was rooted in a sense of what is right.

In making the case for the DACA program, Obama often stressed that people eligible for the program were functionally Americans who were already acculturated and making contributions to American society. They just lacked citizenship status. In one extended passage, Obama told a general story of who these people were:

> Now these are young people who study in our schools, they play in our neighborhoods, they're friends with our kids, they pledge allegiance to our flag. They are Americans in their heart, in their minds, in every single way but one: on paper. They were brought to this country by their parents – sometimes even as infants – and often have no idea that they're undocumented until they apply for a job or a driver's license or a college scholarship.[48]

He again constructed a narrative to invite the audience to identify with the plight of these young immigrants:

> Put yourself in their shoes. Imagine you've done everything right your entire life – studied hard, worked hard, maybe even graduated at the top of your class – only to suddenly face the threat of deportation to a country that you know nothing about, with a language that you may not even speak.[49]

In describing potential Dreamers this way, Obama makes the following definitional claims. First, people eligible for the DACA program are innocent or blame-

---

45 Obama, "Remarks on Immigration Reform."
46 Obama, "Remarks on Immigration Reform."
47 Obama, "Remarks on Immigration Reform."
48 Obama, "Remarks on Immigration Reform."
49 Obama, "Remarks on Immigration Reform."

less; because their illegal status is not their fault, they deserve some citizenship status. Second, people eligible for the DACA program are also already acculturated to the US through their family experiences, language skills, education, and work. While they might be undocumented, they are "like us."

Obama also used real-life stories to depict Dreamers as immigrants who would suffer wrongly if not protected by DACA. These narratives had the effect of personalizing the DACA policy because the audience for these narratives could relate more directly to the people affected by the policy. On May 5, 2016, Obama told the story of a Dreamer named Regina:

> Regina came to the United States from the Philippines when she was 5 years old. But when her father, who was an engineer, fell ill, he had to give up his job, which meant he could no longer secure documentation for his family. So Regina's mom supported the family by working at a hair salon. Regina grew up as American as anybody else. She didn't even know until she was in middle school that she was undocumented. And she didn't understand until then that she'd be perpetually in danger of being deported from the only country she had ever called home. As a junior in high school, Regina requested relief under the Deferred Action for Childhood Arrivals – or DACA – policy that we put in place. And today, she's a sophomore studying economics at the University of Maryland. Her future is bright, and America is better off because she is here. That's the story of immigrants in this country.[50]

On June 11, 2013, Obama described a Dreamer named Diego Sanchez, who had come to the US with his parents from Argentina. Obama said of Sanchez, "growing up, America was his home. This is where he went to school. This is where he made friends. This is where he built a life."[51] Obama challenged: "You ask Diego, and he'll tell you, he feels American in every way except one: on paper."[52] Obama continued:

> In high school, Diego found out he was undocumented. Think about that. With all the stuff you're already dealing with in high school – [*laughter*] – and suddenly: "Oh, man. Really?" [*Laughter*] So he had done everything right – stayed out of trouble, excelled in class, contributed to his community – feeling hopeful about his future, and suddenly, he finds out he's got to live in fear of deportation: watching his friends get their licenses knowing he couldn't get one himself; seeing his classmates apply for summer jobs knowing he couldn't do that either.[53]

These narratives defined the Dreamers in specific, personal ways. They again emphasized the innocence of the Dreamers. The Dreamers' undocumented status was not a result of their choice, and they may not have even been aware of their

---

50 Obama, "Remarks at the Asian Pacific American Institute."
51 Obama, "Remarks on Immigration Reform."
52 Obama, "Remarks on Immigration Reform."
53 Obama, "Remarks on Immigration Reform."

undocumented status. These narratives also emphasized their commonality with US citizens, and invited identification with and empathy for the Dreamers.

Conclusion

In his rhetoric, Obama defined DACA recipients as embodying the genius of America and all three of its dimensions. First, with regard to citizenship, the Dreamers were good citizens who respected and loved America and embraced American values and ideals. They were American in every way except on paper. Second, the Dreamers represented opportunity; the Dreamers were good students and strivers who would make the most of the American experience. They were working, enrolled in school, or serving in the military, and they contributed to all sectors of the economy. Third, Dreamers illustrated the importance of diversity. The Dreamers were from a variety of nations and backgrounds, and they lived throughout the US.

The Dreamers, as described by Obama, also had qualities that differentiated them from other illegal immigrants and allowed Obama to give them special accommodations. In this way they constituted a model immigrant. First, the Dreamers were by definition young – they had to have come to the US before reaching their 16th birthday. Second, the Dreamers were already functionally Americans, so the difficult, lengthy work of acculturation had already been done. Finally, Dreamers were blameless for their status. Their parents brought them to the US as children, and in some cases they didn't even know that their status was illegal. These definitions of the Dreamers served as a persuasive rationale for the DACA program.

Yet, this characterization of the model immigrant also has negative implications. Yuko Kawai, in his work on the rhetorical construction of Asian Americans as a "model minority," noted, "depicting Asian Americans as the model minority simultaneously ... [downgrades] other racial minorities as 'problem' minorities."[54] If Dreamers were defined as the model immigrant, how did that define immigrants who were older, who were not already acculturated to the US, or who knowingly violated US law in order to come to the US? While the legal definition of the DACA recipients was clear, the rhetorical definition of DACA promoted specific values. In this case "desirable" immigrants were young, English-speaking, educated, goal-oriented, and non-criminal.

Mary Stuckey described the phenomenon of presidential rhetoric defining "good" and "bad" members of groups that are seeking citizenship. She noted, "[t]

---

54 Yuko Kawai, "Stereotyping Asian Americans: The Dialectic of the Model Minority and the Yellow Peril," *Howard Journal of Communications* 16 (2006): 109–130, 114.

his differentiation lays out the terms for eventual inclusion in the polity."[55] Moreover, Stuckey observed that these definitions provide an understanding of "the nature of citizenship for that president."[56] We see these dynamics in Obama's characterization of the Dreamers, as his positive portrayals of them helped advance the argument for DACA. These rhetorical depictions made a sharp distinction between "desirable" and "undesirable" immigrants, which also influenced and continues to influence the larger US debate about who is truly American.

References

American Immigration Council. "Deferred Action for Childhood Arrivals (DACA): An Overview." Accessed January 23, 2023, https://www.americanimmigrationcouncil.org/research/deferred-action-childhood-arrivals-daca-overview.

Beasley, Vanessa B. "The Rhetorical Presidency Meets the Unitary Executive: Implications for Presidential Rhetoric on Public Policy." *Rhetoric & Public Affairs* 13, no. 1 (2010): 7–36.

Benenson, Laurence. "Fact Sheet: Deferred Action for Childhood Arrivals (DACA)." *National Immigration Forum*. October 16, 2020, https://immigrationforum.org/article/fact-sheet-on-deferred-action-for-childhood-arrivals-daca/.

Burke, Kenneth. *Language as Symbolic Action: Essays on Life, Literature, and Method*. Berkeley: University of California Press, 1966.

Bush, George H.W. "Statement on Signing the Immigration Act of 1990." *The American Presidency Project*. November 19, 1990, https://www.presidency.ucsb.edu/documents/statement-signing-the-immigration-act-1990.

Cohn, D'vera. "How US Immigration Laws and Rules Have Changed through History." *Pew Research Center*. September 30, 2015, https://www.pewresearch.org/short-reads/2015/09/30/how-u-s-immigration-laws-and-rules-have-changed-through-history/.

Commission on Presidential Debates. "Debate Transcript." October 21, 1984. https://www.debates.org/voter-education/debate-transcripts/october-21-1984-debate-transcript/.

Kawai, Yuko. "Stereotyping Asian Americans: The Dialectic of the Model Minority and the Yellow Peril." *Howard Journal of Communications* 16 (2006): 109–130.

MacIntyre, Alisdair. *After Virtue: A Study in Moral Theory*. Notre Dame: University of Notre Dame Press, 1981.

Mann, Daniel. "George W. Bush's Legacy on Immigration." George P. Mann & Associates. December 5, 2018, https://greencard-us.com/george-h-w-bushs-legacy-on-immigration/.

NPR. "A Reagan Legacy: Amnesty for Illegal Immigrants." July 4, 2010. https://www.npr.org/templates/story/story.php?storyId=128303672.

---

55 Mary E. Stuckey, *Defining Americans: The Presidency and National Identity* (Lawrence: University Press of Kansas, 2004), 6.

56 Stuckey, *Defining Americans*, 6.

Obama, Barack. "News Conference with Canadian Prime Minister Justin Trudeau and Mexican President Enrique Peña Nieto." *The White House Archives*. June 29, 2016, https://obamawhitehouse.archives.gov/the-press-office/2016/06/30/remarks-president-obama-prime-minister-trudeau-canada-and-president-peña.

Obama, Barack. "Remarks and a Question-and-Answer Session at an MSNBC/Telemundo Immigration Town Hall in Miami, Florida." *The White House Archives*. February 25, 2015, https://obamawhitehouse.archives.gov/the-press-office/2015/02/25/remarks-president-immigration-town-hall-miami-fl.

Obama, Barack. "Remarks at an Organizing for Action Dinner." November 9, 2015, https://obamawhitehouse.archives.gov/the-press-office/2015/11/09/remarks-president-organizing-action-event.

Obama, Barack. "Remarks at Del Sol High School in Las Vegas, Nevada." *The White House Archives*. January 29, 2013, https://obamawhitehouse.archives.gov/the-press-office/2013/01/29/remarks-president-comprehensive-immigration-reform.

Obama, Barack. "Remarks at National Hispanic Caucus Institute Annual Awards Gala." *The White House Archives*. October 2, 2014, https://obamawhitehouse.archives.gov/the-press-office/2014/10/02/remarks-president-congressional-hispanic-caucus-institute-gala.

Obama, Barack. "Remarks at the Asian Pacific American Institute for Congressional Studies Awards Gala Dinner." *The White House Archives*. May 5, 2016, https://obamawhitehouse.archives.gov/the-press-office/2016/05/05/remarks-president-22nd-annual-apaics-awards-gala.

Obama, Barack. "Remarks by the President at Congressional Hispanic Caucus Institute Gala." *The White House Archives*. October 8, 2015, https://obamawhitehouse.archives.gov/the-press-office/2015/10/08/remarks-president-congressional-hispanic-caucus-institute-gala.

Obama, Barack. "Remarks by the President at the Democratic National Convention." *The White House Archives*. September 7, 2012, https://obamawhitehouse.archives.gov/the-press-office/2012/09/07/remarks-president-democratic-national-convention.

Obama, Barack. "Remarks in Chicago, Illinois." *The White House Archives*. November 25, 2014, https://obamawhitehouse.archives.gov/the-press-office/2014/11/25/remarks-president-immigration-chicago-il.

Obama, Barack. "Remarks on Immigration Reform and an Exchange with Reporters." *The White House Archives*. June 15, 2012, https://obamawhitehouse.archives.gov/the-press-office/2012/06/15/remarks-president-immigration.

Obama, Barack. "Remarks on the Supreme Court's Decisions Regarding Affirmative Action and Immigration and an Exchange with Reporters." *The White House Archives*. June 23, 2016, https://obamawhitehouse.archives.gov/the-press-office/2016/06/23/remarks-president-supreme-court-decision-us-versus-texas.

Petre, Elizabeth A., and James T. Petre. "'There Are Certain Things Only Government Can Do': Barack Obama's Rhetoric on Food Safety and the Role of Government." *Western Journal of Communication* 86, no. 4 (2022): 443–462.

Ross, Janell. "How the Deferred Action Immigration Program Went from Dream to Reality." *Huffpost*. August 19, 2012, https://www.huffpost.com/entry/deferred-action-immigration-program_n_1786099.

Stuckey, Mary E. *Defining Americans: The Presidency and National Identity*. Lawrence: University Press of Kansas, 2004.

Svajlenka, Nicole Prchal, and Audrey Singer. "Immigration Facts: Deferred Action for Childhood Arrivals (DACA)." *Brookings*. August 14, 2013, https://www.brookings.edu/articles/immigration-facts-deferred-action-for-childhood-arrivals-daca/.

Tulis, Jeffrey K. "Revising the Rhetorical Presidency." In *Beyond the Rhetorical Presidency*, edited by Martin J. Medhurst. College Station: Texas A&M University Press, 1996.

US Citizenship and Immigration Services. "Consideration of Deferred Action for Childhood Arrivals (DACA)." Accessed January 23, 2023, https://www.uscis.gov/humanitarian/consideration-of-deferred-action-for-childhood-arrivals-daca/frequently-asked-questions.

Zarefsky, David. "Presidential Rhetoric and the Power of Definition." *Presidential Studies Quarterly* 34, no. 3 (September 2004): 607–619.

Daryl A. Carter
Chapter 14
Race, Representation, and Reaction in the Obama Presidency

The presidency of Barack Obama was historic. He and his administration governed during a time of upheaval and unrest, as the veneer of peace between 1989 and 2001 had given way to the fervor and passion and resolve of the American people in the immediate aftermath of the attacks on September 11, 2001. The patriotic zeal was replaced by frustration over not finding Weapons of Mass Destruction (WMD) and anger over the war in Iraq. By 2006, the United States had moved away from the certitude of the Bush White House and turned Congress over to the Democratic Party for the first time in 12 years.[1] Just two years later the nation turned its attention to a talented but untested United States Senator from Illinois, Barack Obama.

This chapter examines the seeds of resistance leading up to Obama, the notion of politics as war since the 1970s, and the breaking of the dam of normalcy during the 2008 campaign and the subsequent presidential years. The actions of Bill and Hillary Clinton concerning Obama and race in Iowa, New Hampshire, and South Carolina during the primary season in 2008 are also discussed. In addition, critical flashpoints, such as Michelle Obama's remarks about being "proud of my country" are examined. Reverend Jeremiah Wright and Professor Henry Louis Gates, Jr., and the brouhahas following dissemination of Wright's inflammatory sermons earlier in the aughts, and Gates' arrest at his own home are studied. This chapter includes the tragic murder of Trayvon Martin by a vigilante, President Obama's reaction to it, and the rise of the Black Lives Movement to counter racism, inequality, inequity, and extrajudicial violence against persons of color. Finally, we examine the role of institutional resistance by elected members of Congress and others to the Obama Administration and the president's policies. By examining the aforementioned issues and incidents, we gain a much clearer and greater understanding of the Obama era and how the election of the first Black president profoundly impacted the country.

Barack Obama faced Arizona Senator John McCain in the presidential election of 2008. The economy had entered a deep recession, one which accelerated and

---

[1] John Heilemann, and Mark Halperin, *Game Change: Obama and the Clintons, McCain and Palin, and the Race of a Lifetime* (New York: HarperCollins, 2010).

Daryl A. Carter, East Tennessee State University

compounded major problems such as poverty, lack of opportunity, and economic inequality. The young leader was an unknown figure just four years earlier. Obama won due to his stellar campaign and the political weaknesses of his opponent and public fatigue of the Republican Party. The fact he won was a testament to the power of his political messaging, ideas on policy, and dynamic personal flair and style. The late Gwen Ifill noted that "Obama's unexpected breakthrough made it blazingly clear that we had reached a place we had not been before."[2] Yet the victory in the 2008 election was far removed from the growing storm, where race, representation, and reaction would limit the new administration and undermine the democratic fabric of the United States.

The Seeds of Resistance

Following the victory of the Allies in World War Two the United States focused its attention on housing, confronting the Soviet Union (USSR), a muscular version of liberalism at home and abroad which was vigorous in its opposition to communism, and economic growth and development. Politicians on the left and the right sought opportunities for personal gain, as well as to achieve policy ends. But the liberal consensus and the New Deal coalition did not exist unopposed. Many right-of-center politicians, thinkers, and activists pursued policies and goals at odds with prevailing sentiment. Even as the country turned to the left culturally and socially, individuals and groups pursued resistance, power, and control over American institutions. Right-leaning think tanks put their ideas into the public domain. Elected politicians challenged political orthodoxy. College students organized into Young Americans for Freedom (YAF) and the College Republicans. Intellectuals gathered around William F. Buckley, Russell Kirk, Ayn Rand, and others. Some people, such as Strom Thurmond, Jesse Helms, and many others, placed their bigotry on display in opposition to Civil Rights, *Brown v. Board of Education*, the Great Society, Women's Rights, and any other kind of cultural and/or social liberalism. Others still resisted New Deal economic policies and programs, while, finally, still others financed the resistance, and organized similarly-minded people with deep pockets to pursue a political agenda which continues unabated in the 2020s. During the Obama era, many of those same people would fund the Tea Party and support the Freedom Caucus. In so doing they also chal-

---

2 Gwen Ifill, *The Breakthrough: Politics and Race in the Age of Obama* (New York: DoubleDay, 2009), 16.

lenged the democratic framework undergirding the American system.³ The meddling of reactionary forces was supported by like-minded economic elites deeply troubled by the Progressive and liberal impulses of the twentieth century.⁴

Barack Obama addressed the reactionary forces of both the nation's history and its present during his landmark 2008 campaign. In March 2008, from the Constitution Center in Philadelphia, he said:

> I have brothers, sisters, nieces, nephews, uncles and cousins of every race and every hue, scattered across three continents, and for as long as I live, I will never forget that in no other country on Earth is my story even possible. . . . In the white community, the path to a more perfect union means acknowledging that what ails the African American community does not just exist in the minds of Black people; that the legacy of discrimination – and current incidents of discrimination, while less overt than in the past – are real and must be addressed, not just with words, but with deeds, by investing in our schools and our communities, by enforcing our civil rights laws and ensuring fairness in our criminal justice system by providing this generation with ladders of opportunity that were unavailable for previous generations. It requires all Americans to realize that your dreams do not have to come at the expense of my dreams; that investing in the health, welfare, and education of Black and Brown and White children will ultimately help all of America prosper.⁵

His words were meant both to cool down the Jeremiah Wright controversy, to be discussed later, as well as show understanding and optimism about America's future.

Obama was thus the catalyst for the beliefs of a certain subset of bewildered and reactionary Americans. Believing their status and power were at stake, these Americans, aided by the internet, social media, and the decline of journalism, especially at the local and regional levels, spilled out into the streets, both literally and virtually, to angrily denounce President Obama, liberals, "elites," Hollywood, immigrants, and Democrats. Further, these Americans' desire to "own the libs" were reflective of recent developments in which many conservatives, such as former House Speaker Newt Gingrich, saw politics as war, one in which the political opposition was illegitimate. The goal was to destroy the enemy, not embrace them. What had been building in the shadows was now out in the open. Since these individuals and groups saw it as their mission to protect the real America, others were easily attacked, ignored, maligned, or in some cases, assaulted and/or

---

3 Heather Cox Richardson, *Democracy Awakening: Notes on the State of America* (New York: Viking, 2023).
4 Nancy MacLean, *Democracy in Chains: The Deep History of the Radical Right's Stealth Plan for America* (New York: Viking, 2017).
5 Barack Obama, "A More Perfect Union," Speech, Constitution Center, Philadelphia, PA, March 18, 2008.

murdered. The election of the first Black president allowed for the public acceptance of hate and the legitimization of domestic extremism.

During the 2008 campaign, hate crimes and rhetoric skyrocketed. A cross was burned on a New Jersey family's front lawn. The use of the racial epithet "nigger" was used millions of times online, on social media, in chat rooms, and in public. An assessment of extremism was written by the Office of Intelligence and Analysis at the Department of Homeland Security with assistance from the Federal Bureau of Investigation (FBI). The report noted that "rightwing extremists have capitalized on the election of the first African American president, and are focusing their efforts to recruit new members, mobilize existing supporters, and broaden their scope and appeal through propaganda."[6] The FBI noted in 2010 that nearly half of the 7,699 offenses committed were motivated by racial bias.[7] In 2022, PBS' *Exploring Hate* noted that "when Obama appeared on the scene there was a massive freakout on the radical right."[8] Race, representation, and reaction were central to the Obama era and the catalyst to the present era of division and anger.

Politics by War: The GOP from the 1970s to the 2000s

By the 1970s, American politics was rapidly changing as racial progress, economic challenges, energy shortfalls, and growing anger changed the country. Since the beginning of the New Deal, the United States had in certain ways become more center-left in its political orientation. The so-called "liberal consensus" of postwar America reflected a growing acceptance of a type of politics which embraced the power of the federal government. Yet the rising waters of civil rights, women's rights, demands for reproductive freedom, and, by the end of the decade, a call for freedom from gay and lesbian Americans widened America's already sizable political and cultural fissures. As those changes came to dominate public discussions about the Cold War, freedom, traditionalism, and the future, America's political economy changed too. As Gary Gerstle has pointed out, "[t]his post-1960s

---

6 US Department of Homeland Security, *Rightwing Extremism: Current Economic and Political Climate Fueling Resurgence in Radicalization and Recruitment*, April 7, 2009.

7 Federal Bureau of Investigation, "2010 Hate Crimes Statistics," Press Release, November 14, 2011, https://archives.fbi.gov/archives/news/pressrel/press-releases/fbi-releases-2010-hate-crime-statistics.

8 "Extremism in America," *PBS*, October 25, 2022, https://www.pbs.org/wnet/exploring-hate/films/extremism-in-america/.

change in the GOP signifies that the consensus on political economy that once held sway in the United States in the 1950s and 1960s no longer exists."[9]

One of the major developments was the growth of conservatism and the far right. Political and economic elites, such as the Chamber of Commerce, National Association of Manufacturers, and the DuPont family, came after liberal cultural, domestic and economic policies and institutions. As the years went by, these individuals and groups acquired strange yet allied bedfellows. For instance, Ku Klux Klan members, John Birch Society adherents, Cold War hawks, fiscal responsibility proselytizers, religious conservatives, and anti-government zealots, increasingly took aim at the postwar consensus, thus aligning themselves with one another as the modern right grew in size. They pushed the Republican Party to the right. These groups were joined by paramilitary, separatist, and white nationalists as the country became a truly diverse multicultural and multiethnic democracy in recent decades. The Civil Rights Movement, Women's Rights, and the other various calls for freedom, as well as the withdrawal from Vietnam had created a stronger, more aggressive push led by conservatives within the Republican Party.[10] By the 2000s, the United States was increasingly divided along partisan and ideological lines. These divisions helped extremism to take center stage during the Obama era.[11]

The waters were shifting underneath the feet of the American people. Centrist calls for modernity, technological advancement, and, increasingly since Bill Clinton won the presidency in 1992, economic policy that prioritized growth, university education and graduate degrees and immigration of high-skilled workers, left many Americans feeling whipsawed by the speed with which America had changed and developed. The very ways Americans worked, lived, and played changed. Technology now allowed Americans to shop online, work online, study online, conduct business online, and self-isolate. Calls for science and technology took on almost religious overtones as many American extolled the alleged virtues of the internet. Breaking from traditional Democratic Party ideas about capital, labor, and the power of the government, Clinton seized many of the ideas articu-

---

[9] Gary Gerstle, "The Reach and Limits of the Liberal Consensus," in *The Liberal Consensus Reconsidered: American Politics and Society in the Postwar Era*, ed. Robert Mason, and Iwan Morgan (Gainesville, Florida: University Press of Florida, 2017), 64.
[10] Kim Phillips-Fein, *Invisible Hands: The Businessmen's Crusade Against the New Deal* (New York: W.W. Norton, 2009).
[11] Geoffrey Kabaservice, *Rule and Ruin: The Downfall of Moderation and the Destruction of the Republican Party, From Eisenhower to the Tea Party* (New York: Oxford University Press, 2012).

lated by Ronald Reagan and conservatives.[12] Equally important, as this author has noted, "[t]he Democratic Leadership Council's platform of devolution, 'racial deductionism,' welfare reform, values issues, and crime policy would be clearly on display during the eight years Clinton was in office."[13] The world seemed to move faster and faster as technology, deregulation, and bitter culture-war politics infected the country.

Many conservatives bemoaned a world they viewed as alien to them. Some were Christian evangelicals determined to save America from the fires of eternal damnation. But two other groups were reactionaries, and domestic extremists. These groups seized upon rapidly shifting national trends to appeal to a greater cross-section of Americans. But it would take something huge and truly monumental for many in the country to accept the mainstreaming of political extremism.[14] Obama's election was the unifying moment for reactionaries and domestic extremists to go mainstream.

2008 and Beyond: The Dam Breaks

The second term of President George W. Bush was complicated by deteriorating conditions in the wars in Iraq and Afghanistan, a slowing economy, and growing frustration over such hot button issues as immigration reform. President Bush lost much of the momentum of his first term because of his inability to find weapons of mass destruction in Iraq. The central premise for the war had been the assertion Saddam Hussein was hiding nuclear weapons and materials. Neo-conservative proponents, such as Vice President Richard Cheney, Defense Secretary Donald Rumsfeld, and Defense Deputy Secretary Paul Wolfowitz, argued America's vital national security interests were at severe risk due to the Iraqi strongman.[15] The American

---

12 Gary Gerstle, *The Rise of Fall of the Neoliberal Order: America and the World in the Free Market Era* (New York: Oxford University Press, 2022).
13 Daryl A. Carter, *Brother Bill: President Clinton and The Politics of Race and Politics* (Fayetteville, Arkansas: The University of Arkansas Press, 2016), 52.
14 Kathleen Belew, *Bring the War Home: The White Power Movement and Paramilitary America* (Cambridge, MA: Harvard University Press, 2018).
15 The term "neo-conservative" has been controversial over the last few decades. Here it is defined as politicians and others who believe in the power of the market and capitalism to improve the lives of the people. Further, neo-conservative means opposition to substantial aspects of the rights movements of the 1950s, 1960s, and 1970s. Finally, neo-conservative means the use of the power of the state to maintain global military supremacy through a large garrison state, outposts around the world, alliances with allies to strength Western hegemony, and, when necessary, the

invasion of Iraq in March 2003 quickly dispelled Saddam Hussein's regime. But it also stirred up sectarian forces intent on settling old scores and developing a brand of extremism which created headache after headache for President Bush, his administration, and the troops on the ground.[16] The headaches would later be transferred to Barack Obama.

The 2006 midterm Congressional elections delivered a stinging rebuke of President Bush. Democrats claimed a majority in both houses of Congress for the first time since the 1994 midterm elections.[17] For the final two years of his presidency, President Bush had to contend with an aggressive political foe in the Democratic majority on Capitol Hill. One of those Democrats was a first-term senator from Illinois who was elected in 2004 after delivering one of the most stirring keynote speeches in recent memory at the Democratic National Convention in Boston, Barack Obama.

Since winning his Senate election in a landslide in 2004, Barack Obama was one of the most popular and sought-after figures in the Democratic Party. Senator Obama combined youth with vigor, intelligence, and a Generation X sensibility. As a biracial man born to a white mother and African father in Hawaii in 1961, he was, in part, the product of the long civil rights movement and representative of the promises and contradictions of that generation. David Maraniss points out that "Obama often lamented that he was born too late to participate in the civil rights struggle, with its unambiguous righteousness and moral clarity."[18] A Columbia University and Harvard Law School graduate, Obama's academic pedigree and credentials were impeccable. His law practice and teaching position at the University of Chicago, as well as the legal and administrative career of his wife, Michelle Obama, put him firmly in the upper crust of American society. Yet his community organizing background and intellectual disposition set him apart from many of his contemporaries. Obama's time working as a community organizer in Chicago eventually served as a flashpoint with Republicans who accused him of harboring a far-reaching, socialist agenda. In addition, his membership of a Chicago church with a controversial pastor – Dr. Jeremiah Wright – added fuel

---

use of war. In so doing, neoconservatives have been accused of seeking to impose their political, foreign affairs, cultural, and economic ideas on the masses.
16 Harith Hasan Al-Qarawee, "Iraq's Sectarian Crisis: A Legacy of Exclusion," Carnegie Middle East Center, 2014.
17 The Democratic Party controlled the US House of Representatives from 1955 to 1995 and the US Senate for all but six years between 1955 and 1995. The Republican Revolution of 1994 devastated the Democratic Party and ushered in a new wave of political dysfunction.
18 David Maraniss, *Barack Obama: The Story* (New York: Simon & Schuster, 2012), 515.

to the fire.[19] The fears Obama's political enemies were able to stir up were not new, nor were they particularly creative. Simply put, those fears go back to the Reconstruction era when Blacks were portrayed as shiftless, corrupt, foreign, dangerous, un-American.[20] The extent to which many of his political enemies went to disparage him knew no limits. His identity was weaponized, often using well-established racial tropes.

Clinton's Campaign Comments

The victory of Barack Obama over Hillary Rodham Clinton in the Iowa caucuses was a watershed moment. It proved Obama could win an overwhelmingly white state. Moreover, it shocked the Clinton campaign which expected to do much better. After Clinton eked out a narrow victory in New Hampshire with 39 percent of the vote, all attention turned to South Carolina, where, for the first time, the campaign would face a diverse electorate. By this point both Bill and Hillary Clinton were growing frustrated with the success of Obama. President Clinton had questioned Obama's legitimacy and victory in Iowa. He called the Obama campaign a "pipe dream." Moreover, he accused the Obama campaign of playing the race card. Using language and rhetoric soon to be repeated by many conservatives, the Clintons attacked the media as sycophants of Obama and biased in their coverage of the campaign. President Clinton accused the media of "'feeding' the news media to keep issues of race alive."[21] The racially tinged comments damaged the Clinton brand. Ultimately, it led to Senator Edward Kennedy, the lion of the Senate, to endorse Obama. Many Democrats were upset with the Clintons privately. Famed journalists John Heilemann and Mark Halperin noted that President Clinton reached out to Ted Kennedy and asked for an endorsement of Hillary. "But Bill then went on, belittling Obama in a manner that deeply offended Kennedy. Recounting the conversation later to a friend, Teddy fumed that Clinton had said,

---

19 During the 2008 presidential campaign, it was discovered that Dr. Jerimiah Wright had made a number of controversial statements regarding the United States. While incendiary, to be sure, some of his remarks were deliberately hyped and misconstrued to inflame opposition to Barack Obama.
20 Ellis Cose, *Race and Reckoning: From Founding Fathers to Today's Disruptors* (New York: Amistad, 2022).
21 Katharine Q. Seelye, "Bill Clinton Accuses Obama Camp of Stirring Race Issue," *New York Times*, January 24, 2008, https://www.nytimes.com/2008/01/24/us/politics/24dems.html.

'A few years ago, his guy would have been getting us coffee.'"[22] Other moments during the campaign would also prove revealing.

Michelle's Pride in her Country

A particularly important moment took place in Milwaukee when Michelle Obama said to a campaign audience, "[f]or the first time in my adult life, I am really proud of my country." Her remarks were well understood by Black audiences. The historical lack of access to the ballot, party political organization, and the mainstream of national politics imbued a deep sense of cynicism and resentment of Black Americans. To see the Obamas breakthrough the hardest and highest of ceilings in American life gave many Americans, especially Black Americans, a sense of pride. Many white Americans, however, were angry over the remarks. The Obamas' political opponents seized on the moment to highlight the differences, racial and otherwise, between the Obamas, the Clintons, and later, the McCains.

Jeremiah Wright

The following month the Obama campaign exploded as Obama's opponents and the media discovered remarks by a Chicago pastor which proved to be incendiary and embarrassing to the campaign. For years Reverend Wright had ministered to the Obamas. He had also made comments in sermons about America, race, terrorism, and karma. These comments were used to label Barack Obama as un-American. It raised questions, pushed by many on the right, that Obama was deeply enmeshed in Black Liberation Theology, founded by the Reverend James Cone which condemns the oppression of poor and vulnerable people.[23]

---

22 Heilemann, and Halperin, *Game Change*, 218.
23 James Cone, *Black Theology & Black Power*, 50th anniversary edition (Ossining: Orbis Books, 2019). This seminal work was originally published in 1969 and was Cone's attempt to deal with the Civil Rights Movement and the increasing calls among many young Black Americans for Black Power. The book tackles oppression and repression by using a theological framework which allows for Christianity to be adopted in the struggle for freedom and liberation for peoples of color and victims of western European colonialism.

Arrest of Henry Louis Gates, Jr

Early in the Obama presidency the explosive nature of racial politics reared its ugly head when President Obama weighed in on the arrest of a Harvard University professor. Henry Louis Gates, Jr. was one of the most famous academicians in the country. He was a graduate of Yale and Cambridge. He was a university professor at Harvard, a designation awarded to a precise few at the institution because of his scholarship and tremendous influence in his areas of expertise. Gates' work on PBS and with media organizations across the country gave him both wide exposure and power. On July 16, 2009, as Gates returned to his residence in Cambridge, Massachusetts, he had difficulty getting into his home. The professor and his driver forced open the front door which had been stuck. A woman observed this and called the police department. Sergeant James Crowley and other officers came in response to the call. Crowley demanded Gates' identification. Since Gates had already been inside the home and was visibly frustrated, he took umbrage with the officers. Crowley lured Gates to step outside. When Gates did, he was arrested for disorderly conduct. Once President Obama began to comment on the arrest the story would go viral.[24]

President Obama walked into the East Room of the White House on July 23, 2009, to discuss health care with reporters and the nation. At the end, *Chicago Sun-Times* reporter Lynn Sweet asked the president about the arrest. Obama said the following:

> Now, I don't know, not having been there and not seeing all the facts, what role race played in that, but I think it's fair to say, number one, any of us would be pretty angry; number two, that the Cambridge Police acted stupidly in arresting somebody when there was already proof that they were in their own home; and three, what I think we know separate and apart from this incident is that there is a long history in this country of African Americans and Latinos being stopped by law enforcement disproportionately. That's just a fact.[25]

His response provoked a vicious response from his critics and Republicans. Out of this incident came not only the infamous "Beer Summit," where Obama had lunch with Gates and Crowley at the White House, but a disturbing narrative which pitted police against the very people they serve. In the years to come the

---

[24] Emily Guskin, Mahvish Shahid Khan, and Amy Mitchell, "The Arrest of Henry Louis Gates, Jr.," Media, Race, and Obama's First Year, Pew Research Center, July 26, 2010, https://www.pewresearch.org/journalism/2010/07/26/arrest-henry-louis-gates-jr/.

[25] Barack Obama, "The President's New Conference: Race Relations in America," *Public Papers of the Presidents, Book 2, Presidential Documents, July 1 to December 31, 2009*, July 22, 2009, https://www.govinfo.gov/content/pkg/PPP-2009-book2/pdf/PPP-2009-book2-doc-pg1141-2.pdf, 1152.

tragic killings of Black Americans in New York, Florida, Kentucky, Maryland, Philadelphia, California, Missouri, Illinois, and Minnesota, would raise grave questions about justice, fairness, and race in America. The president's reasonable response to what many at the time knew was a suspicious arrest of an older man with a limp and a cane provided an opportunity for those with political and/or racial agendas to inflame racial animus.

Response to Trayvon Martin

On the evening of February 26, 2012, in Sanford, Florida, a teenage boy was accosted by a self-appointed vigilante. Trayvon Martin was going home from a local store when George Zimmerman confronted Martin and shot him to death. The awful death of a young man for no reason by a man who had no business confronting him struck at the raw racial wounds which had been reopened since Obama's election in 2008. President Obama spoke to the nation and the press from the White House Press Briefing Room on July 19, 2013, following the verdict which exonerated Zimmerman. Obama said,

> [y]ou know, when Trayvon Martin was first shot I said that this could have been my son. Another way of saying that is Trayvon Martin could have been me 35 years ago. And when you think about why, in the African American community at least, there's a lot of pain around what happened here, I think it's important to recognize that the African American community is looking at this issue through a set of experiences and a history that doesn't go away.[26]

Evolution of Black Lives Matter

A major outgrowth of the intensifying political and racial atmosphere of the Obama era was the founding in 2013 of Black Lives Matter. After five plus years of racial antagonism and growing violence, Opal Tometi, Alicia Garza, and Patrisse founded the movement. The deaths of Trayvon Martin and Michael Brown, along with the acquittal of George Zimmerman and decision to not prosecute the officer who killed Michael Brown motivated the founders to try to eradicate po-

---

26 Barack Obama, "Remarks on the Verdict in State of Florida v. George Zimmerman," *Public Papers of the Presidents, Book 2, Presidential Documents, July 1 to December 31, 2013*, July 19, 2013, https://www.govinfo.gov/content/pkg/PPP-2013-book2/pdf/PPP-2013-book2-doc-pg824-2.pdf, 824.

lice brutality and eliminate systemic racism. #blacklivesmatters thus became a rallying cry for those Americans facing racialized violence, poverty, lack of opportunity, and hopelessness.

Almost as soon as Black Lives Matter was founded opponents, largely white Americans, starting chanting "All Lives Matters" and "Blue Lives Matters," in reference to non-Black people and law enforcement. Most Black Americans viewed the response to Black Lives Matter as problematic at the least and very racist. The Pew Research Center noted in 2022 that "[n]early four-in-ten Black adults say Black Lives Matters has done the most to help Black people in recent years."[27] This is more than respondents said about the NAACP, Black churches, the Congressional Black Caucus, and the National Urban League combined.[28] The Obama years and the ferocious reaction to those years created a need for greater advocacy aligned with the moment. The traditional Civil Rights organizations appeared to be lacking at precisely the same time as tens of millions of Americans were abandoning American institutions.

Institutional Resistance

The Republican opposition in Congress to Obama began before the election was even certified. Journalist Michael Grunwald discovered that Republican leaders, such as Senator Mitch McConnell, House Minority Whip Eric Cantor, Congressman Kevin McCarthy, and others conspired to deny the new president at every opportunity.[29] Denying the newly-minted president the traditional honeymoon period reflected both the intensity of the animosity Republicans felt toward Obama as well as the notion that politics is war. Senate Minority Leader Mitch McConnell, R-Kentucky, would loudly proclaim his number one objective was to make Obama a one-term president.

The election of Barack Obama in 2008, and reelection in 2012, allowed Donald Trump, the Tea Party, the Freedom Caucus, and many others to play on the fears and resentment of millions of Americans angered over President Obama's election(s). One of the most successful attacks on President Obama was the notion

---

[27] John Gramlich, and Khadijah Edwards, "Black Lives Matter tops list of groups that Black Americans see as helping them most in recent years," Pew Research Center, October 10, 2022, https://www.pewresearch.org/short-reads/2022/10/10/black-lives-matter-tops-list-of-groups-that-black-americans-see-as-helping-them-most-in-recent-years/.

[28] Gramlich, and Edwards, "Black Lives Matter."

[29] Michael Grunwald, *The New New Deal: The Hidden Story of Change in the Obama Era* (New York: Simon & Schuster, 2012).

that he was not an American citizen. Obama, they claimed, was not born in the United States and was, therefore, ineligible to be elected president. It was a stupid and ridiculous notion. But it had legs. As noted scholar and commentator Michael Eric Dyson points out, "[t]he birthers cut straight to the chase and argued that Obama's birth certificate was phony and that he was not born in America, a claim amplified by billionaire political huckster . . . Donald Trump."[30] Julian Zelizer, historian and commentator, put it more succinctly when he said "[t]he charge intended to discredit the legitimacy of the first African American president. The birther movement played directly into racially charged opposition to the presidency of an African American that had been barely below the surface since he ran [in 2008]."[31]

Consequently, the Tea Party, Freedom Caucus, and others were able to seize upon language previously considered outside of acceptable political discourse. Gary Gerstle has explained that despite concerns, for example, over Obama's plan to reform health care, Tea Partiers' "deeper anxiety being expressed was about a new, and nonwhite, America taking shape under Obama that would unfairly lay claim to resources and privileges that had long been rightfully reserved for true (read white) Americans."[32] Along with public displays of weapons, violent rhetoric, and near constant discussion from certain quarters about taking the country back, something profound broke during the Obama years, driven by millions of Americans who rejected a multiracial, multiethnic democracy for the United States of America. Scholar Rachel Kleinfeld has recently pointed out that better policing, greater accountability, prevention, using political rhetoric to "denounce violence," and stopping politicians from harmful speech would be helpful. She goes further in stating that "[i]n recent years, some candidates on the right have been particularly willing to use violence speech and engage with groups that spread hate."[33] Even some Democratic politicians and affiliates contributed to the deluge of conspiracy theories, hate speech, and/or gave political cover to those who whipped up extremism.

---

30 Michael Eric Dyson, *The Black Presidency: Barack Obama and the Politics of Race in America* (New York: Mariner Books, 2016), 135.
31 Julian Zelizer, "Tea Partied: President Obama's Encounters with the Conservative-Industrial Complex," in *The Presidency of Barack Obama: A First Historical Assessment*, ed. Julian E. Zelizer (Princeton: Princeton University Press, 2018), 23.
32 Gary Gerstle, "Civic Ideals, Race, and Nation in the Age of Obama," in *The Presidency of Barack Obama: A First Historical Assessment*, ed. Julian E. Zelizer (Princeton: Princeton University Press, 2018), 272.
33 Rachel Kleinfeld, "The Rise of Political Violence in the United States," *Journal of Democracy* 32, no. 4 (October 2021): 160–176.

Conclusion

The elections and presidency of Barack Obama reawakened domestic extremism in the United States. Further, domestic extremism became mainstream. Millions of rational Americans easily succumbed to the racial, cultural, and political attacks on President Obama. Often using the same language as during the Reconstruction era, these Americans cast doubt on Obama's citizenship, legitimacy, and character.[34] Ta-Nehisi Coates expertly points out, that "when it becomes clear that Good Negro Government might, in any way, empower actual Negroes over actual whites, then the fear sets in, the affirmative-action charges begin, and birtherism emerges."[35] The fears of "negro rule" were fully on display. Gary Gerstle forcefully points out that "Reconstruction's advances in the 1860s and the civil rights legislation in the 1960s had become occasions for remobilizing racial nationalist sentiment. Obama's election unleashed a similar dynamic, this time propelled by a powerful conviction forming among millions of whites: namely, that no Black man, even one who was half-white, had a right to sit in the White House."[36] In the end, the election of the first Black president created a fertile environment for the legitimization and mainstreaming of extremism. All of this took place at a time when it had become increasingly easy to hide the origins of campaign money from unsuspecting voters. The Tea Party was a perfect example of supposedly populist activism which was enriched and supported with money from select corners of America's financial elite. Consequently, the coming storm of domestic extremism and, on the one hand, the result of decades of work by various individuals and groups since the 1950s, and, on the other, the election of the first Black president was what pushed a very sizable cross section of Americans to gravitate toward extremist rhetoric, action plans, and individuals. Noted scholar Carol Anderson offers this summary:

> Somehow many have convinced themselves that the man who pulled the United States back into some semblance of financial health, reduced unemployment to its lowest level in decades, secured health insurance for millions of citizens, ended one of our recent, all-tractable wars in the Middle East, reduced the staggering deficit he inherited from George W. Bush, and masterminded the takedown of Osama bin Laden actually hates America.[37]

---

[34] Ta-Nehisi Coates, *We Were Eight Years in Power: An American Tragedy* (New York: One World Publishing, 2017).
[35] Coates, *We Were Eight Years in Power*, xv.
[36] Gary Gerstle, "Civic Ideals, Race, and Nation in the Age of Obama," 261–262.
[37] Carol Anderson, *White Rage: The Unspoken Truth of Our Racial Divide* (New York: Bloomsbury, 2016), 157.

The election of Barack Obama was like a tidal wave crashing over the American body politic. Naturally, the former president is not responsible for the chaos which ensued during and after his election. That election, nonetheless, did make it acceptable to be openly bigoted and supportive of extremist positions for the first time since the end of the Civil Rights Movement.

References

Al-Qarawee, Harith Hasan. "Iraq's Sectarian Crisis: A Legacy of Exclusion." Carnegie Middle East Center, 2014.
Anderson, Carol. *White Rage: The Unspoken Truth of Our Racial Divide*. New York: Bloomsbury, 2016.
Belew, Kathleen. *Bring the War Home: The White Power Movement and Paramilitary America*. Cambridge, MA: Harvard University Press, 2018.
Carter, Daryl A. *Brother Bill: President Clinton and The Politics of Race and Politics*. Fayetteville, Arkansas: The University of Arkansas Press, 2016.
Coates, Ta-Nehisi. *We Were Eight Years in Power: An American Tragedy*. New York: One World Publishing, 2017.
Cone, James. *Black Theology & Black Power*. 50th anniversary edition. Ossining: Orbis Books, 2019.
Cose, Ellis. *Race and Reckoning: From Founding Fathers to Today's Disruptors*. New York: Amistad, 2022.
Dyson, Michael Eric. *The Black Presidency: Barack Obama and the Politics of Race in America*. New York: Mariner Books, 2016.
Federal Bureau of Investigation. "2010 Hate Crimes Statistics." Press Release. November 14, 2011, https://archives.fbi.gov/archives/news/pressrel/press-releases/fbi-releases-2010-hate-crime-statistics.
Gerstle, Gary. "Civic Ideals, Race, and Nation in the Age of Obama." In *The Presidency of Barack Obama: A First Historical Assessment*, edited by Julian E. Zelizer. Princeton: Princeton University Press, 2018.
Gerstle, Gary. "The Reach and Limits of the Liberal Consensus." In *The Liberal Consensus Reconsidered: American Politics and Society in the Postwar Era*, edited by Robert Mason, and Iwan Morgan. Gainesville, Florida: University Press of Florida, 2017.
Gerstle, Gary. *The Rise of Fall of the Neoliberal Order: America and the World in the Free Market Era*. New York: Oxford University Press, 2022.
Gramlich, John, and Khadijah Edwards. "Black Lives Matter tops list of groups that Black Americans see as helping them most in recent years." Pew Research Center. October 10, 2022, https://www.pewresearch.org/short-reads/2022/10/10/black-lives-matter-tops-list-of-groups-that-black-americans-see-as-helping-them-most-in-recent-years/.
Grunwald, Michael. *The New New Deal: The Hidden Story of Change in the Obama Era*. New York: Simon & Schuster, 2012.
Guskin, Emily, Mahvish Shahid Khan, and Amy Mitchell. "The Arrest of Henry Louis Gates, Jr." Media, Race, and Obama's First Year. Pew Research Center. July 26, 2010, https://www.pewresearch.org/journalism/2010/07/26/arrest-henry-louis-gates-jr/.
Heilemann, John, and Mark Halperin. *Game Change: Obama and the Clintons, McCain and Palin, and the Race of a Lifetime*. New York: HarperCollins, 2010.
Ifill, Gwen. *The Breakthrough: Politics and Race in the Age of Obama*. New York: DoubleDay, 2009.

Kabaservice, Geoffrey. *Rule and Ruin: The Downfall of Moderation and the Destruction of the Republican Party, From Eisenhower to the Tea Party*. New York: Oxford University Press, 2012.

Kleinfeld, Rachel. "The Rise of Political Violence in the United States." *Journal of Democracy* 32, no. 4 (October 2021): 160–176.

MacLean, Nancy. *Democracy in Chains: The Deep History of the Radical Right's Stealth Plan for America*. New York: Viking, 2017.

Maraniss, David. *Barack Obama: The Story*. New York: Simon & Schuster, 2012.

Obama, Barack. "A More Perfect Union." Speech, Constitution Center, Philadelphia, PA, March 18, 2008. https://youtu.be/pWe7wTVbLUU.

Obama, Barack. "Remarks on the Verdict in State of Florida v. George Zimmerman." *Public Papers of the Presidents, Book 2, Presidential Documents, July 1 to December 31, 2013*. July 19, 2013, https://www.govinfo.gov/content/pkg/PPP-2013-book2/pdf/PPP-2013-book2-doc-pg824-2.pdf,824.

Obama, Barack. "The President's New Conference: Race Relations in America." *Public Papers of the Presidents, Book 2, Presidential Documents, July 1 to December 31, 2009*. July 22, 2009, https://www.govinfo.gov/content/pkg/PPP-2009-book2/pdf/PPP-2009-book2-doc-pg1141-2.pdf, 1152.

PBS. "Extremism in America." October 25, 2022, https://www.pbs.org/wnet/exploring-hate/films/extremism-in-america/.

Phillips-Fein, Kim. *Invisible Hands: The Businessmen's Crusade Against the New Deal*. New York: W.W. Norton, 2009.

Richardson, Heather Cox. *Democracy Awakening: Notes on the State of America*. New York: Viking, 2023.

Seelye, Katharine Q. "Bill Clinton Accuses Obama Camp of Stirring Race Issue." *New York Times*. January 24, 2008, https://www.nytimes.com/2008/01/24/us/politics/24dems.html.

US Department of Homeland Security. *Rightwing Extremism: Current Economic and Political Climate Fueling Resurgence in Radicalization and Recruitment*, April 7, 2009. https://irp.fas.org/eprint/rightwing.pdf.

Zelizer, Julian. "Tea Partied: President Obama's Encounters with the Conservative-Industrial Complex." In *The Presidency of Barack Obama: A First Historical Assessment*, edited by Julian E. Zelizer. Princeton: Princeton University Press, 2018.

Stanley A. Renshon
Chapter 15
Obama's Presidency: Redemption and the Misdirected Search for Presidential Greatness

In this chapter, drawing on my book,[1] and an earlier book chapter,[2] I analyze the Obama presidency from the perspective of his psychology, the political leadership he promised, the presidential leadership he provided, and the leadership the country wanted and needed.

I do so through the psychological lens of redemption for two presidents and the country they wish to redeem. I explore the mismatch between a presidential search for "greatness" and the public's desire for policies that work. I close by considering how this mismatch has also affected the current Biden presidency and led the country to the shores of a modern Rubicon.

Since my focus and that of the edited volume is on President Obama, I will of necessity analyze the developmental origins of his presidential ambitions. They owe a considerable measure to his efforts to redeem his father's own unsuccessful efforts to achieve greatness. Importantly, they also attempt to do so through the lens of an absent mother he idealized and her ideals, encapsulated in the cardinal virtue of "fairness" as a means of overcoming social injustice. There is as well Obama's personal redemption. Finally, I will also analyze the dilemmas that President Obama faced given his own substantial ambitions for greatness and the public's desire for a reliable and effective centrist presidency, not for greatness as Obama understood it.

Obama was a president with unusually strong ambitions. Most presidents want to be successful. A few, including Obama want to be "great." He is the only president who while running for office said that he wanted to be "great" president. He defined greatness as fundamentally transforming the basic nature and politics of this country by anchoring it to a much more progressive political and policy foundation, based on his views of fairness. There is a redemption element

---

[1] Stanley A. Renshon, *Barack Obama and the Politics of Redemption* (New York: Routledge Press, 2012).
[2] Stanley A. Renshon, "Unfulfilled Hopes: President Obama's Legacy," in *Looking Back on President Obama's Legacy*, ed. Wilbur C. Rich (New York: Palgrave/Macmillan, 2018), 211–248.

Stanley A. Renshon, City University of New York

to these transformational policy ambitions too. In this case, it was the country's nature and foundation that was in need of salvation.

President Obama entered office with four sets of redemption issues. One was personal, another was related to his father, the third was a legacy of his complex relationship with his mother, and the fourth was political and related to his views of this county's failure to live up to its ideals and promise.

Obama's personal redemption began with the temptations of drugs, drinking, and an underachieving work ethic as an adolescent and young adult which were symptomatic. The second was with his father's brash but failed ambition to be a transforming leader in Kenya. The third was a legacy of Obama's idealization of his mother and the resulting iconic focus on fairness. The fourth are what Obama viewed as the errors and misguided foundations of this country's foreign and domestic policies which needed to be transformed.

The Psychology of Redemption and Transformation

'Redemption' is a term more frequently heard in theology than psychology, but its basic dynamic would be familiar to any psychoanalyst. It begins with a transgression in which the person or object, or a country, violates either a personal or community norm and feels guilt or, if the transgression is public, will lead to feelings of shame. Obama has said of his past that it "left me feeling exposed, even slightly ashamed."[3] Redemption is the vehicle through which the person himself, in this case Obama, and through him his country, and his parents can reacquire standing and legitimacy in the community.

The steps through which redemption can happen are fairly clear in both personal and political life. Redemption begins with atonement. First, there must be a public acknowledgement of the error or transgression. That is ordinarily followed by a public commitment to change one's way, and some evidence you are doing so. Last, it involves some form of restitution for the transgression to make those who have been harmed whole.

---

[3] Bill Sammon, *Meet the Next President: What You Don't Know About the Candidates* (New York: Threshold, 2007), 131.

The Origins of Mr. Obama's Redemptive Ambitions

Obama's enlisting of his presidential ambition and leadership efforts in the service of redemption did not spring up spontaneously upon his election to the presidency. The motives behind his ambitions began, as they do for everyone, with his parents' psychologies and history, and the options those legacies presented to him. In Obama's case, this includes the consequences of a union between a smart and very ambitious, but emotionally flawed Kenyan, and a free-spirited woman with a somewhat romantic view of the world. Her openness to different cultures and ideas was certainly ahead of her time, but it could also tip over into reckless choices that had consequences for herself and her son.

Obama's mother presented an idealized version of his absent father to Obama. Obama's values and ideals are reflected the legacy of his mother's ideals, encapsulated in the cardinal virtue of "fairness" as a means of overcoming social injustice. The power of that legacy was enhanced by Obama's idealization of his mother after his father's iconic image suffered at the hands of reality.

Out of his parent's quickly failed biracial union, Obama was left with an absent father, a peripatetic mother who left him for long periods in the care of his Caucasian grandparents,[4] and an uncertain personal and racial identity. In a 2008 interview commenting on the absence of both his father and, for long periods his mother too, he has said of himself, "[a]t some level I had to raise myself."[5]

Like his son, Obama's father had plans to be a transformational leader and "shape the destiny of Africa."[6] Barack Obama Sr. was accepted into an economic doctoral program at Harvard and left his wife and new son to attend, but he never returned. Instead, he went back to Africa in 1965 with another American

---

[4] The first separation occurred when she sent Obama to live with his grandmother and grandfather and she stayed behind in Indonesia for a period. She did move back the following fall shortly before his one and only visit from his father, but then returned to Indonesia. In 1974, she went back to Hawaii, and she, Obama, and his younger sister lived there together for three years, after which time she returned to Indonesia for fieldwork. Obama writes that when "she suggested that I go back with her . . . I immediately said no" (Obama, Dreams from my Father, p. 75). She returned from her fieldwork in 1978 at the start of his senior year in high school, after a three-year absence, and the following fall Obama headed to Los Angeles to start his freshman year at Occidental College. See Barack Obama, *Dreams from My Father* (New York: Three Rivers Press, 2004), 60, 62, 75, 94. See also Janny Scott, *A Singular Woman: The Untold Story of Barack Obama's Mother* (New York: Riverhead, 2011).

[5] Obama quoted in Jon Meacham, "Obama on His Parent's Influence," *Newsweek*, May 25, 2008.

[6] Obama senior quoted in David Remnick, *The Bridge: The Life and Rise of Barack Obama* (New York: Knopf, 2010), 40.

woman who would become his third wife, having gained an MA in economics and large ambitions for an important government position in Kenya.

Obama said of his father that he "had returned to his native Kenya bursting with intellect and ambition, only to devolve into an embittered bureaucrat because he couldn't find a way to reconcile his ideals with political realities."[7] His dream soured as a result of a disagreement over national economic policy and his personal style. They led to a break with President Jomo Kenyatta, a rupture that helped destroy his career. He began drinking more heavily and died a bitter and defeated man.

His father's failure weighed heavily on his son. It is doubtless the source of a remark that Obama has made more than once: "Every man is either trying to live up to his father's expectations or making up for his mistakes."[8]

Obama entered his adulthood a deeply ambivalent man. He had mixed feelings about his father whom he idealized until he learned more about him later in life, and who was then knocked off his pedestal.[9] He was angry about his mother's long absences to Indonesia to live with her new husband,[10] which left Obama growing up with grandparents. However, he came to idealize her during precisely the same period when he needed an idealized replacement for his father.

Obama struggled with his racial identity. He did not more successfully resolve the gap between the grievance and post-racial elements of it until he was fully into adulthood. Then, Obama was able to express his feelings for this country even as he repeatedly detailed its failings, past and present, for which he aspired to be the instrument of its redemption and ours. In Obama's view, the country had much progressive transformational ground to cover economically and politically before it could be redeemed and live up to its true promise.

---

7 Obama quoted in Bob Secter and John McCormick, "Portrait of a Pragmatist," *Chicago Tribune*, March 30, 2007. See also Barack Obama, "Commencement Address at Knox College," June 4, 2005.
8 Obama quoted in David Mendell, *Obama: From Promise to Power* (New York: Harper Collins, 2007), 40. See also Barack Obama, *The Audacity of Hope* (New York: Three Rivers Press, 2006).
9 Obama has said, "[m]y father was a deeply troubled person. My father was an alcoholic. He was a womanizer. He did not treat his children well. I think that even my mother, who loved him and was always very generous toward him, said to me once that I probably ended up benefiting from not having grown up with him because he was very hard on those children who were in his household, and in a lot of ways he was a tortured soul." Obama quoted in Jon Meacham, "I Had to Learn to Fight," *Newsweek*, September 1, 2008.
10 Scott, *A Singular Woman*; Janny Scott, "A Free-Spirited Wanderer Who Set Obama's Path," *New York Times*, March 14, 2008.

President Obama's Redemption and Ours

Once the difficult truth of his father's failed aspirations and life became clear, it developed into both a cautionary tale and a redemptive cause. After community organizing in Chicago, successfully completing Harvard Law School, and establishing a political foundation as a fast-rising star in the Illinois legislator to pursue his national ambitions, the stage was set. He would now achieve his own redemption, but also those of his father, mother, and this country's.

Obama often talked of the importance of trying "to find something much larger than [him]self."

"In my case, it was trying to promote a fair and just society."[11] It is also the basis of Obama's egalitarian presumption that "when you spread the wealth around, it's good for everybody."[12]

In a 2001 radio interview, he lamented that the Supreme Court "never ventured into the issues of redistribution of wealth and sort of more basic issues of political and economic in this society."[13] In a campaign debate with Hillary Clinton, he said that "economic fairness" was something for which he would continue to fight. When asked why he would raise the capital gains tax when research showed that doing so actually brings in less money, he replied, "for purposes of fairness."[14]

Given the centrality of fairness and justice to Obama, it is not surprising that well before he became president, Obama named Gandhi, Lincoln, and King as the leaders he most admired. Why? Because they were able "to bring about extraordinary changes and place themselves in a difficult historical moment and be a moral center." Obama clearly intended this role for himself in his presidency as well. At a little noticed Knox College commencement speech in 2005, Obama may have well been speaking of himself as well as giving advice to his audience when he said that *"individual salvation has always depended on collective salvation."*[15]

---

11 Obama quoted in Mendell, *Obama: From Promise to Power*, 201–202, emphasis added.
12 Obama quoted in Jake Tapper, "Share the Wealth?" *ABC News*, October 14, 2008.
13 Obama quoted in Steven G. Calabresi, "Obama's 'Redistribution' Constitution," *Wall Street Journal*, October 28, 2008.
14 "Transcript: Democratic Debate in Philadelphia," *New York Times*, April 16, 2008.
15 Obama, "Commencement Address at Knox College," emphasis added.

Obama's Search for Greatness

As noted, President Obama is the only president of whom I am aware who directly and publicly said that he wanted to be a "great" president: "My attitude about something like the presidency is that you don't want to just be the president . . . You want to change the country. You want to make a unique contribution. *You want to be a great president.*"[16]

Asked what he meant in an interview on *Meet the Press*, he said:

> MR. RUSSERT: You told *Men's Vogue Magazine*, that if you wanted to be president, you shouldn't just think about being president, that you should want to be a great president. So you've clearly given this some thought.
>
> SEN. OBAMA: Yes.
>
> MR. RUSSERT: And what would, in your mind, define a great president?
>
> SEN. OBAMA: But I think, when I think about great presidents, I think about those *who transform how we think about ourselves as a country* in fundamental ways so that, that, at the end of their tenure, we have looked and said to ours – that's who we are. And, and our, our – and for me at least, that means that we have a more expansive view of our democracy, that we've included more people into the bounty of this country . . . *And they transformed the* culture and not simply promoted one or two particular issues.[17]

The exchange makes clear that Obama's progressive view of presidential greatness and transformation involves the remaking of America's basic culture. Elsewhere, he fleshed out his vision. Campaigning in Iowa for the presidency, he said directly "I want to transform this country . . ."[18] In his inaugural address, he called on his fellow citizens to help *"remake America."*[19] Not reform or change, but remake.

---

[16] Obama quoted in Jacob Weissberg, "Obama's Legacy Won't Be His Political Achievements," *Slate*, January 16, 2017, emphasis added. See also Robin Givhan, "Mussed for Success: Barack Obama's Smooth Wrinkles," *Washington Post*, August 11, 2006.
[17] "Transcript Meet the Press," *NBC*, October 22, 2006, emphasis added.
[18] Obama quoted in Richard Wolffe, *Renegade: The Making of a President* (New York: Crown, 2009), 67.
[19] Barack Obama, "Inaugural Address," Washington DC, January 21, 2009, emphasis added.

Mr. Obama's Personal Redemption

There is little evidence in Obama's early development of his trying to measure up to his father's ambitions or his mother's idealism. Obama recalled himself during his early adulthood as "Junkie, Pothead. That's where I had been headed: the final fatal role of the young would-be black man."[20] Friends from this period remember Obama as a rather straight drug dabbler, not someone teetering on the edge of a drug abyss.[21] However, the dramatic license fits in well with Obama's redemption narrative. He was someone on the brink who pulled himself back from the abyss.

When Obama first arrived in New York a friend asked him "what brings you to our fair city?" Obama's reply obviously reflected his felt need for redemption: "*I want to make amends*, make myself of some use."[22] After college Obama was drawn to political organizing. He daydreamed through "romantic images of a past I had never known. They were of the civil rights movement . . ."[23] Obama continues: "That was my idea of organizing. *It was a promise of redemption.*"[24]

However, his hoped for redemption had to first survive its brush with capitalism. Obama wrote to many civil rights organizations, received no replies, and decided to take a job at a mid-Manhattan multinational corporation. As the months passed, Obama "felt the idea of becoming an organizer slipping away from me."[25]

Obama was promoted, got his own office and secretary and had money in the bank. Yet, that brought guilt, not satisfaction. He wrote, "I would catch my reflection in the elevator doors – see myself in a suit and tie, a briefcase in my hand – and for a split second, I would imagine myself a captain of industry, barking out orders, closing the deal before I remembered who it was that I had told myself I wanted to be and *felt pangs of guilt for my lack of resolve.*"[26] During this period he wrote to his mother about his corporate job, referred to it as *"working for the enemy."*[27]

At that point, he received a reply to one of his inquiries from Marty Kaufman who was starting an organizing drive in Chicago. The temptation to which Obama almost, but didn't, succumb led him there. That was the start of his finding the

---

20 Obama, *Dreams from My Father*, 93.
21 Kristen Scharnberg, and Kim Barker, "The Not-so-simple Story of Barack Obama's Youth," *Chicago Tribune*, March 25, 2007.
22 Obama, *Dreams from My Father*, 119, emphasis added.
23 Obama, *Dreams from My Father*, 134.
24 Obama, *Dreams from My Father*, 135, emphasis added.
25 Obama, *Dreams from My Father*, 136.
26 Obama, *Dreams from My Father*, 136, emphasis added.
27 Obama's letter to his mother quoted in Remnick, *The Bridge*, 119, emphasis added.

community he had been searching for, the family that he had longed for, the work that allowed him to feel that he had redeemed the promise of his and his mother's ideals, and the vehicles of fulfilling his other personal and political redemption ambitions in the future.

Eluding Transformational Ambition: Obama's Zen Leadership Style

The words that legitimately describe Obama's emotional style is self-contained. I analyze his Zen-style persona and the psychology that anchors it in my Obama book.[28] Here I emphasize their obvious political implications, as it helped leaven the public's perceptions of Obama's strong personal and political ambitions.

During the presidential campaign, one analysis noted:

> [T]here were questions about where Obama really stood ideologically. He talked like a centrist, a pragmatist, someone who would work actively with Republicans. But his agenda – a big health care package, higher taxes on the rich, an aggressive alternative energy plan – sounded conventionally liberal.[29]

The president's calm, cool demeanor helped push questions about his transforming ambition to the sidelines. How could someone so calm be at all radical? We think of transformational presidents as mounting the barricades. However, cool calculation can be just as ambitious as clarion calls.

It was a logical step for Obama to vail his transformational ambitions with a moderate persona. From his earliest days at Harvard Law School and then in the Illinois legislature Obama developed and refined his political persona as a soft-spoken, nuanced thinker who could effectively present both his own and his opponents' points of view. In reality, he compiled one of the most liberal voting records in the Illinois legislature.[30] Obama was also voted the most liberal member of the United States Senate in 2007.[31]

In 2008, the *Washington Post* gave then candidate Obama a ringing endorsement while noting that his campaign platform, "is orthodox liberal Democratic

---

[28] Renshon, *Barack Obama and the Politics of Redemption*, Chapter 8.
[29] Dan Balz and Haynes Johnson, *The Battle for America* (New York: Viking, 2010), 304.
[30] See Peter Slevin, "Obama Forged Political Mettle in Illinois Capitol," *NBC News*, February 9, 2007; Eli Saslow, "From Outsider to Politician," *Washington Post*, October 9, 2008.
[31] Brian Friel, Richard E. Cohen, and Kirk Victor, "Obama: Most liberal senator in 2007," *National Journal*, January 31, 2008.

fare . . . ." It then raised the question, "is Obama a standard liberal clad in the soothing language of inclusiveness?"[32] I think the answer to that question is yes.

Mr. Obama's low-key style did not trump his ambitions for transformative change. In pursuing them, he demonstrated that he had both the courage of his ambitions and his ideals with regard to truly remaking America. What he didn't have was the general support of the American public for doing so, as most Americans did not support the president's transformational intentions that were the key to his presidency's greatness ambitions.

A Second Misdirection: The Presidential Policy Road Not Taken

In seeking greatness, President Obama misdirected his ambition to the wrong goal from the perspective of the presidential leadership that the country wanted and needed. Most Americans wanted a centrist president to put in place effective policies that worked. They did not support transformation policies to resolve problems they didn't believe the country had. Nor were most voters interested in elevating any particular president to the historical pantheon of greatness.

A fundamental mistake of Obama's presidency, therefore, was not to be found in any specific domestic or foreign policy. Rather, it was that Obama could have effectively provided the kind of presidential leadership that Americans wanted and thought he would provide. Obama had the skills and political support to do it. He is extremely smart, thoughtful, experienced, and entered office on a strong wave of American support and good will for his unique accomplishment in gaining the presidency.

Had he governed as a left centrist, he would have likely slowed and reduced Americans' political divisions by increasing their faith and trust in government. Reagan had done so by governing as he promised. He was, as a result, generally seen as being honest about his political intentions and, allowing his mistakes, competent.[33] President Obama's efforts at transformation in the service of his am-

---

32 "The Obama Enigma: Where Would He Lead?" *Washington Post*, February 24, 2008.
33 Reagan's presidency was accompanied by an increase in the public's faith in government which rose from 27 percent during the Carter presidency to 43 percent during his. In 1958, when Pew started to measure, this variable stood at 75 percent during the Eisenhower presidency. It began a downward slide and has not recovered those levels since. See Pew, "Public Trust in Government: 1958–2022," June 6, 2022.

bitions for greatness, partially masked by his moderate persona fueled more political division and widened the gap into which Donald Trump stepped.

Like every president, Obama faced choices. He had won. His party had control of both branches of Congress. He was aware that the country was politically divided and becoming more so. Obama could have pursued a more centrist path. How? He could have used his party's congressional majority to forge a long-sought solution to the plight of "dreamers" – young children brought to the United States by their parents bypassing immigration procedures and controls, as well as other long-standing immigration issues.

If Obama had accomplished that major legislative and political success, it would have very likely helped his party maintain unified control of government for the last two years of his first term. Instead, he chose to invest all his political capital to pass an unprecedented expansion of government regulation of America's health care system. "Obamacare" legislation passed, but at great political cost. His party lost unified control of congress after his first midterm election.

Mr. Obama's large-scale health care legislation was specifically designed to redress what he saw as major economic and health access disparities and unfairness. One commenter noted that

> [t]he bill that President Obama signed on Tuesday is the federal government's biggest attack on economic inequality since inequality began rising more than three decades ago . . . This fact helps explain why Obama was willing to spend so much political capital on the issue, *even though it did not appear to be his top priority as a presidential candidate. Beyond the health reform's effect on the medical system, it is the centerpiece of his deliberate effort to end what historians have called the age of Reagan.*[34]

President Obama made an early decision to immediately push his initiatives on health care and energy in the face of a severe recession. The decision to go full steam ahead on many fronts, including primary health care, even in the face of public opposition and election losses in New Jersey, Virginia, and Massachusetts, certainly reflected the scope and depth of the president's policy ambitions. Yet, it also reflected the fact that he was willing to take large political risks on his own behalf without the level of public understanding that could have gained them support.

In order to pass health care legislation, the president publicly and repeatedly promised that "[i]f you like your health care you can keep it," an assertion that was named "Lie of the Year."[35] The administration knew that the president's promise

---

[34] David Leonhardt, "In health care bill, Obama attacks wealth inequality," *New York Times*, March 23, 2010, emphasis added.
[35] Angie Drobnic Holan, "Lie of the Year: 'If you like your health care plan, you can keep it,'" *Politifact*, December 12, 2013.

was false when he repeatedly said it.³⁶ Obama later said he was "sorry" that "some" Americans did lose their doctors and health care that he had said they would keep.³⁷ However, he did not apologize for his knowing misrepresentation.

After losing political control of the House in the 2010 midterm election vote, President Obama faced a stark question. Was he willing to redeem his presidency by relinquishing his transformation ambitions for "greatness"? Or, would he use other means to reclaim the transformational presidency so central to what he saw as his own unique historical mission? Would he move toward the center or double down on national transformation by executive order and administrative initiatives? He chose the latter.

Thereafter, Mr. Obama pushed his versions of his transforming ambitions when, where, and to the extent that he could through administrative and legislative efforts. He did so by issuing a series of executive orders under a "We Can't Wait" rhetorical rationale.³⁸ The administration increased executive order and administrative efforts to curb greenhouse gas emissions through environmental regulations, gave states waivers from federal mandates if they agreed to education overhauls, and refocused deportation policy in a way that in effect granted relief to some illegal immigrants brought to the country as children.

Ambition's Choice: Historical Greatness or Public Trust

Personal and political ambitions are no strangers to presidents. Yet even presidents have different levels of ambition. Many want to do well; others wish to be great. The greatness of Washington, Lincoln, or FDR does not reside in their enactment of large transformative government programs. It resides in their successfully meeting the challenge of basic or dire threats to the existence of the country. Trying to pass large policy programs that transform the country when what it most arguable needs is reform, is a misreading of the real sources of greatness. The 'greats' were so because their ambitions and successful presidential leadership were preservationist and restorative not transformational.

---

36 Lisa Myers, and Hannah Rappleye, "Obama Admin. Knew Millions Could Not Keep their Health Insurance," *NBC*, October 28, 2013.
37 Chuck Todd, "Exclusive: Obama Personally Apologizes for Americans Losing Health Coverage," *NBC News*, November 7, 2013.
38 Charlie Savage, "Shift on Executive Power Lets Obama Bypass Rivals," *New York Times*, April 22, 2012.

President Obama failed in his quest for historical greatness. Elaine Kamarack writes:

> It becomes clearer every day that Barack Obama, a historic president, presided over a somewhat less than historic presidency. With only one major legislative achievement (Obamacare) – and a fragile one at that – the legacy of Obama's presidency mainly rests on its tremendous symbolic importance and the fate of a patchwork of executive actions.[39]

Obama often referenced Reagan's accomplishments telling Weissberg, "Reagan put us on a fundamentally different path because the country was ready for it." Weissberg writes of Obama's Reagan insight that "Reagan channeled disenchantment with overweening government," and that "a president needs to synthesize the moment and mood of the country."[40]

Obama had no comparable set of circumstances to support his ambitions for transformational greatness. There was no public demand for the federal government to essentially gain major control of over and manage America's health care system. Many, if not most, Americans were satisfied with their health care and certainly with their doctors. That is why the administration falsely promised they could keep them.

President Obama reached for greatness. However, he will likely be recalled as a very smart, experienced, and competent president who missed an important opportunity to reinforce the country's political center and likely somewhat reduce its political divisions. His presidency became a victim of his own transformational ambitions. He is not the only president for whom visions of achieving historical greatness distracted their focus from achieving more modest, important, and needed centrist reforms. As noted, a major Obama "dreamers" centered immigration bill was entirely achievable. It would have been a substantial legislative and political accomplishment that would have cemented Obama's reputation beyond its "inspirational" status and set the stage for further accomplishments.

Instead, relying on a "We Can't Wait" rhetorical rationale, he attempted to achieve his greatness ambitions with a variety of initiatives in diverse areas that he hoped would prove transformational. As a result, trust in government to do what is right "just about always" or "most of the time" stood at 25 percent when Obama entered office. It stood at 19 percent when he left office and Americans elected Mr. Trump.

---

[39] Elaine Kamarck, *Review of The Presidency of President Barack Obama: A First Historical Assessment*, ed. Julian E. Zelizer (Princeton, NJ: Princeton University Press, 2018), *Boston Review*, 27 March 2018.
[40] Weissberg, "Obama's Legacy Won't Be His Political Achievements."

Obama and Biden: From Liberal to Progressive Transformation

Obama was a president of enormous intelligence and considerable political skill. However, his transformational presidential ambitions faltered because of the mismatch between his redemptive and transformational ambitions, and the public's willingness and readiness to support them. That dynamic appears to be playing out again in the presidency of Joe Biden. He shares with Obama a desire for transformational presidential greatness. There is, however, one large difference between the two presidents.

Obama had the capacities to be a great president if political circumstances had aligned. He was aware of his skills and had received ample validation of them. Mr. Biden has always believed that he has never been given the credit he deserves for his superior intelligence, policy judgement, and outstanding political career. In Biden's view, achieving presidential greatness would represent a too-long delayed recognition of his career-long under-appreciation and reward for his talents. In a 1974 Senate speech on Senate pay raises, Biden said, "I don't know about the rest of you but I am worth a lot more than my salary of $42,500 a year in this body."[41]

As president Mr. Biden also had this to say about himself: "THE PRESIDENT: Well, I'll tell you what: *No one has ever done as much as President as this administration is doing. Period. Period.* (Applause.) I am committed."[42] Mr. Biden's progressive policy initiatives during the three years of his presidency make clear that transformative policies[43] in the service of achieving historical greatness is his ambition and goal.[44] Mr. Biden has also expressed agreement with the progressive assumption regarding this country and its institutions being riddled with systematic racism.[45] Obama's strong liberal transformation perspective has thus

---

41 Biden quoted in Kitty Kelly, "Death and the All-American Boy," *Washingtonian*, June 1, 1974.
42 "Remarks by President Biden at the White House Tribal Nations Summit," November 30, 2022, emphasis added.
43 Speaking on the House passage of his Build Back Better bill, Biden said, "[t]oday, the House of Representatives has taken a significant step toward making a historic investment that's going to transform America." See "Remarks by President Biden on the Ongoing Evacuation Efforts in Afghanistan and the House Vote on the Build Back Better Agenda," August 21, 2021.
44 "Executive Order on Advancing Racial Equity and Support for Underserved Communities Through the Federal Government," January 20, 2022. This is one of many progressive executive orders initiated by Biden on entering office. In addition, several of his successful initiatives like the infrastructure legislation contain many progressive features.
45 "Remarks by President Biden on the Verdict in the Derek Chauvin Trial for the Death of George Floyd," April 20, 2021.

reached its current progressive apogee in President Biden's embrace of the progressive transformist's view that the United States is fundamentally corrupted by institutionalized white supremacy and irremediable inequality. He believes these failings have been historically supported by almost all America's major cultural, economic and political institutions. A "Whole of Government" effort therefore is necessary in every area of American life to redeem it by replacing its basic foundations domestically and international with progressive alternatives.

America Approaches a Modern Rubicon

Those transformative efforts by Presidents Obama and Biden, along with President Trump's conflict-saturated efforts to slow or reverse them, have brought American politics to its modern political Rubicon. That is a phase that has come to mean a point of no return. It reflects a set of circumstances in which the return to a *status quo ante* is no longer possible because the actions of one or more parties to a deepening and irreconcilable conflict have made it ultimately impervious to compromise. That is why it is important to distinguish between transformative and preservationist ambitions. The first wants to replace what, in their view, are the unsalvageable traditional premises and foundations of the country, and the second wants to restore and modernize them. Among the examples of the first are Presidents (LB) Johnson, Obama and Biden. Among the second, one might analyze Presidents Reagan and Trump.

The country's modern Rubicon reflects a decade-long first liberal, then progressive effort to leverage major American institutions to aid in dismantling the country's existing foundations. They would be replaced with transformational progressive alternatives. In response, a nationalist preservation movement has arisen that opposes these efforts. Powerful cultural, political, and economic disputes and increasingly open conflicts now permeate almost every sector and level of American national life.

Americans have also lost confidence in the fairness and competence of a wide range of their major institutions.[46] These include government, law, civic organizations, medicine (and the helping professions), publishing, news and media organizations, and business – including major tech and social media companies. A country cannot long continue to function in such circumstances. So, the questions arise: can this impasse be resolved, and if so, how? One possibly strong remedy is for presidents that are so inclined to put aside their quests for transformational

---

46 Megan Brenan, "Americans' Confidence in Major US Institutions Dips," *Gallup*, July 14, 2021.

greatness, and concentrate on rebuilding the public's trust in the competence of their institutions, and their own centrist integrity.

References

Balz, Dan, and Haynes Johnson. *The Battle for America*. New York: Viking, 2010.
Brenan, Megan. "Americans' Confidence in Major US Institutions Dips." *Gallup*. July 14, 2021. https://news.gallup.com/poll/352316/americans-confidence-major-institutions-dips.aspx.
"Executive Order on Advancing Racial Equity and Support for Underserved Communities Through the Federal Government." January 20, 2022. https://www.whitehouse.gov/briefing-room/presidential-actions/2021/01/20/executive-order-advancing-racial-equity-and-support-for-underserved-communities-through-the-federal-government/.
Friel, Brian, Richard E. Cohen, and Kirk Victor. "Obama: Most liberal senator in 2007." *National Journal*, January 31, 2008.
Givhan, Robin. "Mussed for Success: Barack Obama's Smooth Wrinkles." *Washington Post*, August 11, 2006. https://www.washingtonpost.com/archive/lifestyle/2006/08/11/mussed-for-success-barack-obamas-smooth-wrinkles/3e12e827-0562-451c-adf3-5c29fe0ed47d/.
Holan, Angie Drobnic. "Lie of the Year: 'If you like your health care plan, you can keep it.'" *Politifact*. December 12, 2013.
Kamarck, Elaine. Review of *The Presidency of President Barack Obama: A First Historical Assessment*, ed. Julian E. Zelizer (Princeton, NJ: Princeton University Press, 2018), *Boston Review*, 27 March 2018.
Kelly, Kitty. "Death and the All-American Boy." *Washingtonian*. June 1, 1974.
Leonhardt, David. "In health care bill, Obama attacks wealth inequality." *New York Times*. March 23, 2010.
Meacham, Jon. "I Had to Learn to Fight." *Newsweek*. September 1, 2008.
Meacham, Jon. "Obama on His Parent's Influence." *Newsweek*, May 25, 2008. https://www.newsweek.com/obama-his-parents-influence-88057.
Mendell, David. *Obama: From Promise to* Power. New York: Harper Collins, 2007.
Myers, Lisa, and Hannah Rappleye. "Obama Admin. Knew Millions Could Not Keep their Health Insurance." *NBC*. October 28, 2013.
NBC. "Transcript Meet the Press." October 22, 2006.
New York Times. "Transcript: Democratic Debate in Philadelphia." April 16, 2008.
Obama, Barack. "Commencement Address at Knox College." June 4, 2005.
Obama, Barack. *Dreams from My Father*. New York: Three Rivers Press, 2004.
Obama, Barack. "Inaugural Address." Washington DC, January 21, 2009.
Obama, Barack. *The Audacity of* Hope. New York: Three Rivers Press, 2006.
"Remarks by President Biden at the White House Tribal Nations Summit." November 30, 2022.
"Remarks by President Biden on the Ongoing Evacuation Efforts in Afghanistan and the House Vote on the Build Back Better Agenda." August 21, 2021.
"Remarks by President Biden on the Verdict in the Derek Chauvin Trial for the Death of George Floyd." April 20, 2021. https://www.whitehouse.gov/briefing-room/speeches-remarks/2021/04/20/remarks-by-president-biden-on-the-verdict-in-the-derek-chauvin-trial-for-the-death-of-george-floyd/.
Remnick, David. *The Bridge: The Life and Rise of Barack Obama*. New York: Knopf, 2010.
Renshon, Stanley A. *Barack Obama and the Politics of Redemption*. New York: Routledge Press, 2012.

Renshon, Stanley A. "Unfulfilled Hopes: President Obama's Legacy." In *Looking Back on President Obama's Legacy*, edited by Wilbur C. Rich, 211–248. New York: Palgrave/Macmillan, 2018.

Sammon, Bill. *Meet the Next President: What You Don't Know About the Candidates*. New York: Threshold, 2007.

Saslow, Eli. "From Outsider to Politician." *Washington Post*. October 9, 2008.

Savage, Charlie. "Shift on Executive Power Lets Obama Bypass Rivals." *New York Times*. April 22, 2012.

Scharnberg, Kristen, and Kim Barker. "The Not-so-simple Story of Barack Obama's Youth." *Chicago Tribune*. March 25, 2007.

Scott, Janny. "A Free-Spirited Wanderer Who Set Obama's Path." *New York Times*. March 14, 2008.

Scott, Janny. *A Singular Woman: The Untold Story of Barack Obama's Mother*. New York: Riverhead, 2011.

Secter, Bob, and John McCormick. "Portrait of a Pragmatist." *Chicago Tribune*. March 30, 2007.

Slevin, Peter. "Obama Forged Political Mettle in Illinois Capitol." *NBC News*. February 9, 2007.

Todd, Chuck. "Exclusive: Obama Personally Apologizes for Americans Losing Health Coverage." *NBC News*. November 7, 2013.

Washington Post. "The Obama Enigma: Where Would He Lead?" February 24, 2008.

Weissberg, Jacob. "Obama's Legacy Won't Be His Political Achievements." *Slate*. January 16, 2017. https://slate.com/news-and-politics/2017/01/obamas-legacy-will-be-inspirational-rather-than-transformational.html.

Wolffe, Richard. *Renegade: The Making of a President*. New York: Crown, 2009.

Contributors

Sheila M. Blackford is the Scripps Librarian and Managing Editor of *American President* at the University of Virginia's Miller Center. She is the co-producer of the documentary film, *Statecraft: The Bush 41 Team*, and served as co-director of the Hillary Rodham Clinton Oral History Project from 2020 to 2024.

Jeff Bloodworth is Professor of Political History in the School of Public Service and Global Affairs at Gannon University (Erie, PA). He is currently writing a biography on Speaker Carl Albert. He is the author of *Losing the Center: A History of American Liberalism, 1968–1992* (University Press of Kentucky, 2013). His work has also appeared in *The Historian*, *Political Science & Politics*, *The Wisconsin Magazine of History*, *The Free Press*, and *Philadelphia Inquirer*.

Meena Bose is Executive Dean for Public Policy and Public Service Programs, Peter S. Kalikow School of Government, Public Policy and International Affairs, and Director of the Peter S. Kalikow Center for the Study of the American Presidency at Hofstra University. She is the author or editor of several books in presidency studies, co-author of the *American Government: Institutions and Policies* textbook (18th edition, Cengage, forthcoming 2025), and co-author of *The Paradoxes of the American Presidency* textbook (6th edition, Oxford University Press, 2022). Dr. Bose taught for six years at the United States Military Academy at West Point. She serves on the editorial board of *Political Science Quarterly* and is a member of the Council on Foreign Relations.

Ann E. Burnette is Minnie Stevens Piper Professor and Regents' Teacher in the Department of Communication Studies at Texas State University. She publishes scholarship on presidential rhetoric, political campaign rhetoric, and freedom of expression issues. She teaches graduate and undergraduate courses in political communication, persuasion, American public address, and rhetorical criticism.

Daryl A. Carter is Professor of History and Associate Dean at East Tennessee State University. He specializes in American political history and examines the intersections of race, class, politics, and power. His first book, *Brother Bill: President Clinton & The Politics of Race and Class* (University of Arkansas Press) was published in 2016.

Brendan J. Doherty is Professor of Political Science at the United States Naval Academy. His research has focused on the intersection of campaigning and governing, and he is the author of *Fundraiser in Chief: Presidents and the Politics of Campaign Cash* (University Press of Kansas, 2023) and *The Rise of the President's Permanent Campaign* (University Press of Kansas, 2012). His other published work has included studies of presidential travel and fundraising, the Electoral College, Senate leadership, proportional representation in legislatures, speech restrictions in judicial campaigns, and the Marshall Court and federalism.

Paul Fritz is Associate Professor of Political Science at Hofstra University. He specializes in international politics, security studies, international organization, and US foreign and defense policy. He has published in the *Journal of Politics*, *International Interactions*, *Foreign Policy Analysis* and other venues on alliance formation, democratic imposition, and UN Security Council reform, among other issues. He is also co-editor (with Meena Bose) of a volume on the foreign policy of the George W. Bush administration.

Jack B. Greenberg is a PhD candidate in political science at Yale University. His research focuses on presidential leadership and interbranch relations from the mid-twentieth century to the present. At Yale, he is affiliated with the Institution for Social and Policy Studies, where he runs the Dahl Research Scholars program. He earned his BA in political science, history, and leadership studies from Williams College.

Donna R. Hoffman is Chuck and Barbara Grassley Professor of Political Science at the University of Northern Iowa. She is the author (with Alison D. Howard) of *Addressing the State of the Union: The Evolution and Impact of the President's Big Speech* (Lynne Rienner, 2006), as well as numerous articles and chapters on presidential rhetoric, congressional-presidential relations, and Iowa politics.

Alison Howard is Associate Professor of Political Science, Co-Chair, Division of Public Affairs, and Director of Core Curriculum at Dominican University of California. Her research focuses on presidential rhetoric, specifically the state of the union address, political communication, pedagogy, as well as art, politics, and culture. She has published articles in *PS: Political Science and Politics*, *American Behavioral Science*, *Journal of Political Science Education*, *Social Science Quarterly*, and *Perspectives on Political Science*. She is co-author (with Donna R. Hoffman, University of Northern Iowa) of *Addressing the State of the Union: The Evolution and Impact of the President's Big Speech* (Lynne Rienner Publishers, 2006).

Nicholas Howard is an Assistant Professor of Political Science at Concordia College in Moorhead, MN. At Concordia he serves as director of the pre-law program and minor. In 2015 to 2016 he was an APSA Congressional Fellow in the office of a senior senator on the Senate Judiciary Committee. His research and teaching centers on American political institutions, policymaking, and separation of powers.

David W. Kearn, Jr. is Associate Professor of Government and Politics at St. John's University. His research and teaching interests include international relations theory, military innovation, nuclear weapons and deterrence, and arms control. He served as Strategic Advisor for Countering Weapons of Mass Destruction in the Office of the Secretary of Defense in 2016 and 2017.

Mark Kelso is Professor of Political Science at Queens University of Charlotte, where he was the 2017 winner of the Hunter-Hamilton Love of Teaching Award. His publications include "A Lasting Legacy? Presidents, National Monuments and the Antiquities Act" (*Presidential Studies Quarterly*, December 2017), "Environmental Justice and Equity" in *Handbook of Global Environmental Policy and Administration*, edited by Dennis L. Soden, and Brent S. Steel (Marcel Dekker, 1999), and "Environmental Priorities and the President as Legislative Leader," co-authored with Glen Sussman, in *The Environmental Presidency*, edited by Dennis L. Soden (SUNY Press, 1999). His current research examinees how partisanship affects presidential decisions on environmental policy.

Wayne L. Kraemer is Senior Lecturer and Director of the Lyndon Baines Johnson Debate Society at Texas State University. He publishes scholarship on political rhetoric and teaches classes in argumentation and debate, persuasion, public advocacy, and civic engagement.

Mark Owens is Assistant Professor of Political Science at The Citadel, Military College of South Carolina. He leads The Citadel Poll and is a Co-Director of The Citadel Symposium on Southern Politics. In 2015 to 2016 he was an APSA Congressional Fellow in the office of a senior senator on the Senate Judiciary Committee. His research focuses on elections, public opinion, and the separation of powers in American politics.

Barbara A. Perry is the Gerald L. Baliles Professor in Presidential Studies at the University of Virginia's Miller Center, where she co-directs the Presidential Oral History Program. She has authored or edited 17 books on presidents, First Ladies, the Kennedy family, the Supreme Court, and civil rights and civil liberties. Perry has conducted more than 140 interviews for the George H.W. Bush, George W. Bush, and Barack Obama Presidential Oral History Projects; participated in the Bill Clinton interviews; directs the Edward Kennedy Oral History Project; and co-directs the Hillary Rodham Clinton Oral History Project. She served as a US Supreme Court fellow and has worked for both Republican and Democratic members of the Senate.

Daniel E. Ponder is the L.E. Meador Professor of Political Science and Director of the Meador Center for Politics and Citizenship at Drury University. He teaches and writes about American politics, with emphasis on American national institutions. In 2019 to 2020, he served as President of the Presidency and Executive Politics Section of the American Political Science Association. Among his publications are *Good Advice: Information and Policy Making in the White House* (Texas A&M University Press, 2000) and *Presidential Leverage: Presidents, Approval, and the American State* (Stanford University Press, 2017).

Stanley A. Renshon is Professor of Political Science at the City University of New York, and a certified psychoanalyst. He is the author of over 100 articles in the fields of presidential psychology, American national identity, and American foreign policy. He has published 19 books including psychoanalytically framed analyses of presidents Bill Clinton, G.W. Bush, Barack Obama, and Donald Trump. His most recent book is *Presidential Leadership and Foreign Policy: Comparing the Trump and Biden Doctrines*, edited with Peter Suedfeld (Springer, 2024).

Andrew Rudalevige is Thomas Brackett Reed Professor of Government at Bowdoin College and past president of the Presidents and Executive Politics section of the American Political Science Association. His books include *By Executive Order: Bureaucratic Management and the Limits of Presidential Power* (Princeton University Press, 2021), which won the Neustadt and Brownlow Prizes in 2022, *The New Imperial Presidency: Renewing Presidential Power Since Watergate* (University of Michigan Press, 2006), and, as co-editor, *Executive Policymaking* (with Meena Bose, Brookings Institution Press, 2020) and *The Obama Legacy* (with Bert Rockman University Press of Kansas, 2019).

Jeffrey VanDenBerg is Professor and Chair in the Department of Political Science and International Affairs, and Director of Middle East Studies, at Drury University. He teaches courses on international relations, comparative politics, and the Middle East. VanDenBerg's research focuses on international relations in the Middle East (particularly conflict and conflict resolution) and Arab domestic politics. He is a founding member of the Middle East Studies Association's Committee for Undergraduate Education.

Acknowledgments

This edited volume was developed from Hofstra University's Thirteenth Presidential Conference: The Barack Obama Presidency – Hope and Change in April 2023. Building upon Hofstra's distinguished tradition since the early 1980s of hosting presidential conferences, the three-day event presented a multidisciplinary appraisal of Barack Obama's presidential leadership, policy making, and legacy with instructive commentary and analyses from scholars, journalist, and public officials.

We thank all conference participants for sharing their insights to expand the scholarly record of the Obama presidency. Public officials who generously shared their time, expertise, and experiences include Kara Alaimo, Nancy-Ann DeParle, Honorable Steven J. Israel, Valerie Jarrett, Kate Leone, Honorable Jacob J. Lew, Wendell Primus, Benjamin J. Rhodes, Philip M. Schiliro, Tina Tchen, and Shawn Turner. Plenary speakers who generously shared their scholarly, political, or news reporting expertise include Peter Baker, Douglas Brinkley, Laurie Buonanno, Ann Compton, George C. Edwards III, Michelle Egan, Karen Finney, John Harwood, Jennifer Mercieca, Michael Nelson, Barbara A. Perry, Elizabeth Saunders, and Chris Whipple.

We especially appreciate the wisdom and guidance of Hofstra Kalikow Senior Presidential Fellow Philip M. Schiliro (Hofstra Class of 1978, Political Science), who served as Director of Legislative Affairs in the Obama White House during negotiations and passage of the ACA. Mr. Schiliro encouraged many public officials to participate in the conference and share their recollections of the Obama presidency, particularly in reference to passage of the ACA. Scholars have a much deeper and richer understanding of the Obama presidency thanks to Mr. Schiliro's painstaking efforts and dedication to public service, presidency studies, and Hofstra.

Hofstra University's commitment to interdisciplinary study of the American presidency that bridges academic analysis with practitioner perspectives creates a welcoming community for scholarship. Hofstra Class of 1965 alumnus Peter S. Kalikow has generously supported this work through creating an endowed chair in presidential studies, an academic center that studies the American presidency, and an interdisciplinary school of government, public policy, and international affairs that examines how institutions and individuals develop public policies. His absolute dedication to democratic leadership and good governance, and his genuine enjoyment in learning about presidents and the presidency, is much appreciated and greatly admired.

Hofstra President Dr. Susan Poser, Provost and Senior Vice President for Academic Affairs Dr. Charles Riordan, and Hofstra College of Liberal Arts and Sciences Dean Dr. Eva Badowska strongly support faculty scholarship and the mission of the Peter S. Kalikow School of Government, Public Policy and International Affairs, and the Peter S. Kalikow Center for the Study of the American Presidency. Their continuing engagement in research on the presidency and public policy motivates the Hofstra community to maintain an active scholarly agenda.

The Department of Political Science at Hofstra provides a collegial community that nurtures excellence in teaching and scholarship. Department Chair Dr. Carolyn Dudek strongly supports faculty research, and is a model of academic excellence in teaching, research, and leadership. Dr. (and former Dean) Bernard J. Firestone, Dr. Leslie Feldman, and Dr. Rosanna Perotti have been active participants, leaders, and invaluable sources of counsel in many of Hofstra's presidential conferences as well as other programming on the presidency. Dr. Craig Burnett directed Hofstra's Kalikow School Poll for the 2020 presidential election cycle, which provided important insights for the Obama Conference, and generously shares his expertise in American politics for presidency and policy events. Special thanks to Dr. Richard Himelfarb, who served as Associate Director for the Obama Conference and has dedicated time and energy to presidency studies at Hofstra for many years. Dr. David Green, Dr. Takashi Kanatsu, Dr. Stefanie Nanes, and Professor William Schaefer participated in the Obama conference, and have generously shared their expertise in other programs about the presidency.

Many of our Hofstra colleagues expanded our thinking about the Obama presidency through their work on the conference committee, and we thank them for their guidance and their dedication to presidency studies. We are especially grateful to the Hofstra Cultural Center for their adroit management of the Obama Conference and assiduous attention to detail for event planning as well as post-conference projects.

Three students in Hofstra University's Rabinowitz Honors College Undergraduate Research Assistant Program advanced this study significantly in multiple stages of the project. Alexa Paturzo conducted extensive research on the Obama presidency that was instructive for conceptual development. Peri Allen completed several annotated bibliographies and biographical summaries for the Obama Conference that contributed to the research and writing in this volume. We extend special thanks to Danny DeCrescenzo for his careful reading of chapters in the fall of 2023, thoughtful recommendations, and keen attention to detail, which was instrumental in identifying several important revisions.

De Gruyter Acquisitions Editor Ze'ev Sudry provided critical guidance and support for developing this edited volume. His dedication to presidency studies, meticulous suggestions for a cohesive analysis, and unending good cheer are much appreciated, as is the fine work of the De Gruyter production team. Six scholarly reviewers provided important feedback in early stages of the project, and we thank them for their instructive recommendations. Most of all, we thank the contributors for sharing their expertise and original scholarship in this volume, patiently responding to multiple requests from us throughout the editorial process, and fundamentally advancing the study of the Obama presidency.

Meena Bose
Executive Dean, Public Policy and Public Service Programs
Director, Peter S. Kalikow Center for the Study of the American Presidency
Peter S. Kalikow Endowed Chair in Presidential Studies
Professor of Political Science
Peter S. Kalikow School of Government, Public Policy and International Affairs
Hofstra University

Paul Fritz
Associate Professor of Political Science
Peter S. Kalikow School of Government, Public Policy and International Affairs
Hofstra University

Index

Note: Page numbers in *italics* indicate figures, **bold** indicate tables in the text, and references following "n" refer notes.

Ackerman, B. 95
Adler, J. 102
Affordable Care Act (ACA) 2, 65, 94–98, 106, 132, 137
agency-centered approach 56
al-Assad, B. 160, 187–188, 191
American Dream concept 205–206, 209, 212–213, 215, 217–222, 233
American liberalism 59, 64, 66
American with Disabilities Act (ADA) 220
Anderson, C. 256
arms control 167–173, 169, 178
– New START Treaty 152, 159, 161, 171–173, 179–181
– US-Russian cooperation on 152, 155, 168, 170–173, 178
Austin-Boston alliance 45
Axelrod, D. 95

Barnes, M. 57
Barrett, C. 128
Baucus, M. 57
Beasley, V. 228
Beer Summit 252
Biden, J. 20, 22, 39, 56, 79, 83–86, **84**, 103, 128, 180, 191, 259, 271–272
bin Laden, O. 2, 256
Black, D. 96–97
Black Lives Matter 253–254
blue-collar laborers 43
Boehner, J. 191
Bolten, J. 66n60
Boxer, B. 58
Brands, H. 153
Breyer, S. 25, 137
Browner, C. 133
Brown, M. 253
Burke, K. 228
Burton, B. 22
Burwell, S. M. 133, 134

Bush, George H.W. 21, *21*, 72, 78, 80, **81**, 95, 111, *116*, 117, *118*, 119, *120–122*, *125–127*, 134–135, 171, **211**, 230
Bush, George W. 19–22, *21*, 37, 48, 55, 59, 61, 66n60, 71–72, 77, **77**, 80, **81**, 82–85, 94–95, 109–111, *116*, 117, *118*, 119, 120, *120–123*, 124, *125–127*, 134–135, 152, 156, 169, 171, 182, 206, **211**, 215, 218, 230, 248–249, 256
Butts, C. 133

Cantor, E. 105
cap-and-trade legislation 58
capitalism 28, 248n15
– crony 45
– moral 42–45
Carter, A. 138–139
Carter, J. 17, 20, *21*, 74, 77, **81**, 109, 110, 134, 135, 136
Cheney, D. 17, 248
citizenship 233–235, 237–240, 256
Civil Rights Movement 247, 249, 251n23, 257, 265
Clean Air Act 78, 82, 101–102
Clinton, B. 20–21, 23, 34, 38, 48, 56, 84, 91, 111, 230, 243, 247, 250
Clinton, H. 26, 47, 59, 132, 134, 139–140, 172, 243, 250–251, 263
Coates, Ta-Nehisi 256
College Republicans 244
Comprehensive Test Ban Treaty (CTBT) 170, 181
Cone, J. 251
congressional authorization 187–188, 190–194, 200
constitutional principle 189–190, 192
Cooper, P. J. 206, 207
Crowley, J. 252
cultural liberalism 244
Cutter, S. 133

Daschle, T. 65
Daynes, B. 72

284 — Index

Deferred Action for Childhood Arrivals (DACA) 103–105, 216, 227, 229–237
  see also immigration
  – defined 239
  – policy 238
  – qualifications for 230–231, 238
Deferred Action for Parents of Americans and Lawful Permanent Residents (DAPA) 104, 105, 217
Derthick, M. 92
Development, Relief, and Education for Alien Minors (DREAM) Act 230–231
diversity 109, 233, 235, 239
  – absence of 111
  – demographic 129
  – in judicial appointments 112, 114, 136
  – racial 116–117, *116*, *118*, *120*, *122*
Dodds, Graham G. 206
Dreamers 106, 227–232, 236–240
Dueck, C. 153
Duncan, A. 137
Dunn, A. 133
Dyson, M. E. 255

electoral politics 13, 18, 22
Emanuel, R. 56–57
empathy 220, 239
  – through diversity 117–118
  – for judicial selection 111, 112–113, 119–122
  – toward minority groups 116
  – standard 113, 119, 124, 128–129
entitlement liberalism 46–47
environment 56, 58, 79–80, **81**, 83n64, 85, 86, 96, 111, 145, 154, 180, 182, 256, 269
environmental groups 74–76
environmental initiatives 82–83
environmentalism, death of 73
environmental policy 70, 73–74, 79–80, 82–83, **84**, 85–86
environmental protection 71, 72, 82, 92, 100–103
Environmental Protection Agency (EPA) 102–103
  – administrator **75**, 76, **77**
  – appointments to 74
  – budget 80–81
  – interpretation of CAA 101
  – workforce 81
environmental spending 81–82

environmental treaty ratification 78
ethnicity 36, 38, 43, 125, 128, 136, 235, 247, 255
extremism 247, 249, 255
  – domestic 246, 256
  – political 248

fairness 245, 253, 259–261, 272
  – economic 263
  – unfairness 268
  – women's equality 140
  – workplace 136
Federal Bureau of Investigation (FBI) 246
Federal Election Commission (FEC) 18–19, 24
fiscal commission 213, 215, 216n40
Fisher, L. 206
Fisher, R. 60
Fissile Material Cutoff Treaty (FMCT) 170, 181
Forgotten Man populism 45
fundraising 13–28

Garland, M. 137
Gates, H. L., Jr. 243, 252
gender 111, 113, 132 see also women
  – based violence 144–145
  – domestic policy 133–139
  – dynamics in communities 143
  – equality 140–142, 146
  – equity 146
  – health care 132
  – inequality 145
  – integration 142, 145
  – international policy 139–146
  – judicial nominees and 117, *118*, 120, *121*, 122, *123*, 128
  – wage discrimination and 131
genius of America 229, 232–236, 239
  see also citizenship; diversity; opportunity
Gerstle, G. 246–247, 255, 256
Gingrich, N. 73, 245
Ginsburg, R. B. 131, 135
Goldberg, J. 158
Goldstein, J. 115
Gore, A. 38
Graham, J. 95
Graham, L. 58, 191
grand strategy 151–154, 156–158, 161–164
greatness 234

- ambitions for 268–270
- defined 259
- historical 270–271
- presidential 259, 264, 267, 271
- transformational 270, 272–273
Grunwald, M. 254

Halperin, M. 250
Hamilton, D. 113–114
health care 60–62, 68, 92, 96–98, 132, 140, 252, 266, 269–270 *see also* Obamacare
- costs 57, 63
- forum 59
- gender policies and 132
- legislation 63, 136, 268
- marketplace 98
- quality 65
- reform 2, 56–59, 63–66, 71, 82, 255
Heilemann, J. 250
Hennock, F. 111n10
high-profile remarks 221
- addresses 213–215
- pen-and-phone strategy in 217, 218
- press interactions 215–218
Hillary Victory Fund 27
Holmes, O. W. 112–113, 129
Hudson, Valerie M. 140
Humphrey, H. 34, 35

Ifill, G. 244
immigration 92, 96, 103–105, 217–218, 228, 233, 268
- anti-immigration 234
- congressional action on 103, 231
- desirable vs. undesirable immigrants 227, 240
- Dreamers 227–232, 236–240, 270
- enforcement 231
- policy 215, 227, 229, 236
- reform 216, 227, 232, 248
- of skilled individuals 230, 247
index of presidential leverage (IPL) 189, 194, 196–201, *198*
institutional resistance 254–255
International Atomic Energy Agency (IAEA) 174, 175
international policy, gender 139–146
Iran 155
- Nuclear Deal 152, 159–162, 173–176, 180

- nuclear program 160, 167–170, 173, 176, 180
- US-Russian relations and 152, 155, 159–162

Jacksonian populism 35, 43–45
Jackson, K. B. 128
Jackson, L. 76
Jacobs, Lawrence R. 73
Jarrett, V. 133–134, 138
Jewell, S. 76, 134
Joint Comprehensive Plan of Action (JCPOA) 47, 174–176, 180
judicial appointment 109–110, 137
- administration's legacy of 128–129
- Ivy League 127, *127*
- nomination philosophy 112–114
- nominee selection 115–128
- presidential strategy in 111
- of women 109, 113, 117, *118*, 119–121, 128, 131, 135–136
judicial nominee 109–114, 128–129
- divided government and 119–122, *122–123*
- duration in committee 124–126, *125–126*
- education of 126–128, *127*
- gender and 117, *118*, 120, *121*, 122, *123*, 128
- race and 113, 115–122, *116*, *118*, *120*, *122*, 124–125, *126*, 128
- senatorial partisanship and selection 119, *120–121*

Kagan, E. 91, 101–102, 113, 117–118, 135, 137
Kamarack, E. 270
Kaufman, M. 265
Kaufman, R. 153
Kawai, Y. 239
Kennedy, A. 105
Kennedy, E. 133, 250
Kennedy, John F. 55, 66, 99, 180, 197
Kennedy, T. 64–66, 109, 250
Kenyatta, J. 262
Kerry, J. 15, 16, 37, 38, 57
Kleinfeld, R. 255
Klein, J. 142
Klyza, C. M. 73, 85
Kyl, J. 113, 118n24

labor 96, 98–100, 143, 247
- blue-collar laborers 43

- loses 44
- manual jobs 34
- organized 35–36, 41
- unions 18
- white ethnic laborers 43
laissez faire liberalism 44
Landy, Marc K. 74
Larson, D. W. 156
Leidl, P. 140
liberal consensus 244, 246
liberal international order 154, 155, 162
liberalism 46, 65
- American 59, 64, 66
- cultural and social 244
- entitlement 46–47
- *laissez faire* 44
- New Deal 46
- opportunity 45, 46
Libya
- American military intervention in 47, 154, 188, 190, 193, 199–200
- leverage in **199**
- public opinion on 193, 199–200
- US-Russian relations and 154–155, 162
Lieberman, J. 57
Lilly Ledbetter Fair Pay Restoration Act 62, 131, 136
lower-profile remarks 206, 220–221
- general remarks 218–219
- pen-and-phone strategy in 218
Lugar, R. 113, 169
Lynch, L. 134

MacIntyre, A. 236
MacIntyre, D. 238
Mann, D. 230
Maraniss, D. 249
Martin, T. 243, 253
Mazur, M. 96
McCain, J. 15–16, 36, 37, 41, 55, 58, 191, 243
McCarthy, G. 76
McConnell, M. 91
McCutcheon, S. 25
Mead, W. R. 45
Medvedev, D. 151, 155, 157n18, 159n25, 162n34, 171–172
Messina, J. 22

Mondale, W. 229
moral capitalism 42–45
moral economy 45–46
Morton, J. 231
Moscow Treaty 171
Muñoz, C. 133

Napolitano, J. 134, 227
Nathan, R. 91
National Action Plan on Women, Peace, and Security 132, 143
National Security Strategy 140, 153, 159
negro rule 256
Netanyahu, B. 175
Neustadt, R. 86
New Deal 34, 35, 39, 45–46, 244, 246
New Foundation program 61, 62, 63
New Politics liberals 46
New START Treaty 152, 159, 161, 171–173, 179–180, 181n87
Nieto, E. P. 232
Nixon, R. 34, 35, 56, 72, 74, **75, 77**, 80, **81**, 93
nonproliferation 167–170, 173, 179–182
Nuclear Posture Review (NPR) 179
Nuclear Security Summit 167, 168, 170, 176–178, 180
nuclear weapons 167–168, 173, 176, 177, 182, 248
- goal of abolishing 169–170
- laboratory infrastructure 178–180
- No First Use policy 179, 181
- US-Russian cooperation on 157, 159–160
Nunn, S. 169

Obama, M. 131–133, 137, 220, 232, 243, 249, 251
Obamacare 47, 96, 98, 268, 270
Obama Victory Fund (OVF) 13, 20, 26
Office of Global Women's Issues (GWI) 132, 141, 142
opportunity 92–93, 219–220, 233–235, 239
- economic 206, 215, 221
- equality of 45, 46
opportunity liberalism 45, 46

Paris Climate Agreement 47, 74, 78, 79, 86
pen-and-phone strategy 205, 208–209, 222
- findings of 221
- in high-profile remarks 217, 218
- in lower-profile remarks 218

– pen in 209–212
– phone in 212–213
– in signing events 219–221
Perry, R. 178
Podesta, J. 61
Power, S. 134
Prague Agenda 167–168, 176
presidential leverage 187–188, 193–201
presidential rhetoric, influence of 207, 227–228, 239
press interactions 215–218
Pritzker, P. 134
prosecutorial discretion 104, 216, 231
Psaki, J. 133
public funding 19, 27–28
– for general election 13, 15–16
– for nominating contest 13, 15
– obsolescence of 14, 23
– phases of 15
– post-convention 16
public opinion 57, 72, 83–85, 195
– on environmental issues 82
– on use of military force in Syria 192, 199–200
– on US intervention in Libya 193, 199–200
public trust 194–195, 198–199, 269–270
Putin, V. 157–158, 161–164, 171–172

Qaddafi, M. 190
Quadrennial Diplomacy and Development Review (QDDR) 132, 142

race/racism 33, 38, 47, 67, 99, 111, 136, 139, 243, 248–256, 274
– bias 246
– diversity 116–117, *116*, *118*, *120*, *122*
– identity 261–262
– judicial nominees and 113, 115–122, *116*, *118*, *120*, *122*, 124–125, *126*, 128
– wage discrimination and 131
Ragsdale, L. 207
Reagan, R. 21, *21*, 34, 42, 48, 60, 72–74, **77**, **81**, 110, 134, 135, **211**, 229, 248, 267–268, 270, 272
redemption 263
– ambitions, origins of 261–262, 271
– personal 265–266
– psychology of 260–261
Reid, H. 56, 114

Rhodes, B. 189
Rice, S. 133, 134
Roberts, J. 25, 98
Roberts, Marc J. 74
Robinson, P. 229
Romer, C. 134
Romney, M. 16, 40–42
Roosevelt, F. D. 2, 34, 43–45, 56, 72, 77, 93, 269
– moral economy 45–46
Roosevelt, Theodore 76–77, 212
Rorschach test 41, 56
Rouhani, H. 174
Rove, K. 16
Ruemmler, K. 133, 136
Rumsfeld, D. 248
rural populists 33, 35–40, 42–46
Russo-American relations *see* US-Russian relations

Salazar, K. 76
Sanders, B. 57
Scalia, A. 101–102, 105, 137, 198
Schambra, W. 60
Schlesinger, J. 178
Sebelius, S. 134
Sessions, J. 105
Sharry, F. 232
Sheppard, K. 82
Sher, S. 133
Shevchenko, A. 156
signing events, pen-and-phone strategy in 219–221
Skocpol, T. 73
Skowronek, S. 196
social injustice 259, 261
social liberalism 244
Soden, Dennis L. 72, 74
Solis, H. 134
Sotomayor, S. 113, 114, 128, 135, 137
Sousa, D. 73, 85
Springsteen, B. *see* working-class whites in North
Stanley, R. *see* rural populists
Steele, Brent S. 74
Stimson, J. 194–195
Stuckey, M. 239–240
Super PACs 20, 22–23, 26–27
– emergence of 13, 17–19, 23
– fundraising 13, 17, 22–24

Suskind, R. 63
Sussman, G. 72s
Sutphen, M. 62, 63, 133
Sweet, L. 252
Syria 162, 187–200, 232
– American military intervention in 190, 192–194, 199
– chemical weapons 160–161, 189, 201
– leverage in **199**
– public opinion on 192, 199–200
– US-Russian relations and 162, 164

Tchen, T. 133, 138
Tea Party, The 244, 254, 255, 256
Theis, John J. 207
Thomas, Stephen R. 74
Treaty for the Prohibition of Nuclear Weapons (TPNW) 181–182
Trudeau, J. 232
Trump, D. 20–22, 26, 40, 42, 61, 79, 83, **84**, 85–86, 93, 98–99, 103n43, 105–106, 111, *116*, 117, *118*, 119, *120–123*, 124, *125–127*, 146, 176, 188, 194n31, 197, **211**, 254–255, 268, 270, 272
Tulis, J. 227

unilateral executive actions (UEAs) 207–208, 210–212, **211**, 215–219, 221
United States Agency for International Development (USAID) 141–146
US-Russian relations 151
– arms control and 152, 155, 168, 170–173, 178
– Iran and 152, 155, 159–162
– Libya and 154–155, 162
– limited transactional cooperation 159–163
– limits of cooperation with status-seeking 156–158
– Syria and 162, 164
– weapons of mass destruction and 151–152, 157, 159–161, 163

Verveer, M. 141, 143

Waxman, H. 58, 63
WCALC algorithm 194–195
weapons of mass destruction (WMD) 151–152, 157, 159–161, 163, 243, 248
Webb, J. 57
"We Can't Wait" initiative 95, 209, 221, 269, 270
Weissberg, J. 270
White House Council for Women and Girls 132, 133, 138
Winfrey, O. 139
Wolfowitz, P. 248
women 140–141 *see also* gender
– in agriculture 142–143
– disparity in pay between men and 131
– domestic policy and 133–139
– insurance coverage for 137
– international policy 139–146
– judicial appointment of 109, 113, 117, *118*, 119–121, 128, 131, 135–136
– labor time 143
– leadership 143
– rights 132, 140, 146–147, 246
– sexual assault on 138
– violence against 132, 140, 143–144
Women, Peace, and Security Act 144, 146
Women's Empowerment in Agriculture Index (WEAI) 142
Women's Rights 244, 247
Wood, D. 135
working-class whites in North 33–35, 38–42, 43–47
Wright, J. 243, 245, 249–251

Young Americans for Freedom (YAF) 244

Zarefsky, D. 228
Zelizer, J. 255
Zen leadership 266–267
Zimmerman, G. 253

www.ingramcontent.com/pod-product-compliance
Lightning Source LLC
Chambersburg PA
CBHW030119240426
43673CB00041B/1334